Mirror on America

Short Essays and Images
from Popular Culture

Mirror on America

Short Essays and Images
from Popular Culture

THIRD EDITION

JOAN T. MIMS

ELIZABETH M. NOLLEN
West Chester University

BEDFORD/ST. MARTIN'S   Boston ◆ New York

FOR BEDFORD/ST. MARTIN'S

Senior Developmental Editor: John Sullivan
Production Editor: Jessica Skrocki
Senior Production Supervisor: Joe Ford
Senior Marketing Manager: Rachel Falk
Art Director: Lucy Krikorian
Text Design: Claire Seng-Niemoeller
Copy Editor: Rosemary Winfield
Cover Design: Hannus Design Associates
Cover Art: "Americana" by Ugo Nespolo
Composition: Macmillan India
Printing and Binding: R.R. Donnelley & Sons Company

President: Joan E. Feinberg
Editorial Director: Denise B. Wydra
Editor in Chief: Karen S. Henry
Director of Marketing: Karen Melton Soeltz
Director of Editing, Design, and Production: Marcia Cohen
Managing Editor: Erica T. Appel

For information, write: Bedford/St. Martin's, 75 Arlington Street, Boston, MA 02116   (617-399-4000)

ISBN: 0-312-43658-0
EAN: 978-0-312-43658-2

ACKNOWLEDGMENTS

Lorraine Ali. "Do I Look Like Public Enemy Number One?" From *Mademoiselle* (1999). Copyright © 1999. Reprinted by permission of the author. "Same Old Song: Controversy over pop music is as old as Elvis, but now we're in a cultural arms race." From *Newsweek*, October 9, 2000, p. 68. Copyright 2000 Newsweek, Inc. All rights reserved.

Acknowledgments and copyrights are continued at the back of the book on pages 391–393, which constitute an extension of the copyright page. It is a violation of the law to reproduce these selections by any means whatsoever without the written permission of the copyright holder.

For Paul, with anticipation—The ring and I are ready for another 35.

For Derek and Jason, with pride and thanks—Because you and others serve,

Americans are free to enjoy our popular culture.

For Laurie, with appreciation—It's great to have another girl in the family!

J. T. M.

To my father, who, at the age of ninety, dedicated his final book to me.
I now return the favor:

"A man tells his stories so many times that he becomes the stories.

They live on after him. . . . And in that way, he becomes immortal."
—*Tim Burton's* Big Fish

To my mother and brother and to Julia, Laura, and Dennis,
who have inspired me to tell my own stories.

To the rest of my family and those friends and colleagues
who have nurtured my mind, body, and soul.

And to all those students who have made my teaching
a pleasure and have taught me so much.

E. M. N.

Preface for Instructors

If popular culture is a kind of mirror that reflects society and its values and preferences, it also forms one of the largest arenas for communication among all members of that society, irrespective of age, gender, ethnicity, or social standing. *Mirror on America: Short Essays and Images from Popular Culture*, Third Edition, gives students the context they need to understand this public dialogue and the critical thinking and writing skills necessary to participate intelligently. Composed primarily of short, high-interest essays and striking, thought-provoking images, the text's seven thematic chapters present material that may already be familiar to students in new and thoughtful ways. The text guides their responses and helps them think and write critically about the popular culture surrounding them.

We turned to the subject of popular culture because, after teaching for many years, we became frustrated in our search for a reader that would at once interest and challenge students. Many writing texts underestimate students' social awareness and critical thinking capabilities. *Mirror on America* attempts to address this misconception by coupling thought-provoking editorial guidance with highly readable yet challenging selections of various types and difficulty levels including articles from popular periodicals, essays, cartoons, photographs, paintings, and advertisements.

Beginning with a student-friendly introduction, *Mirror on America* defines popular culture as "that collection of objects, people, events, and places that serves to mirror society and its members and to reflect their values and preferences." Also discussing the importance of reading and writing about popular culture, the introduction stresses that although all components of pop culture may not be of equal quality, they play a crucial role in our daily lives, as well as in our shared social history.

Nine Chapters on Popular Culture

The first chapter, "Active, Involved Reading and the Writing Process: Establishing the Connection," demonstrates the essential link between the reading and writing processes by teaching students to read thoughtfully and to recognize such fundamental concerns as audience, tone, and purpose. We think that students who are able to recognize these essentials are more likely to consider them in their own writing. In this chapter we outline for students the various types of questions accompanying each selection and guide them through two sample readings. The second half of Chapter 1 guides the student step by step from active reading to self-generated writing and concludes with a new student essay written in response to two new professional essays. Chapter 2, "Deconstructing Media: Analyzing an Image," provides guidance on looking critically at visual images. Several sample images, as well as a new student essay analyzing an advertisement, help students to see how they can decode visual media.

Following the initial chapters are seven chapters on specific areas of popular culture. Chapters 3, 4, and 5, titled "Define 'American': Reflections on Cultural Identity," " 'Tell Me What You Don't Like About Yourself': Cultural Reflections on Body Image," and "The Fabric of Our Lives: Fashion Trends and the Signals They Send," deal with the ways popular culture affects us personally. These are followed by four chapters that deal with areas of culture that affect us in a more global sense: Chapter 6, "Fantasies for Sale: Marketing American Culture," Chapter 7, "Flickering Illusions: Television and Movie Messages," Chapter 8, "Stop! Listen. What's That Sound? How Music and Culture Mix It Up," and Chapter 9, "This Blog's 4 U: Pop Culture Powers Up."

Readable, High-Interest Selections

Like the chapter topics, selections were chosen for their currency, high interest, challenging ideas, and readability. They were also chosen with an eye to their ability to generate engaging discussion and writing activities. Selected from sources such as newspapers, magazines, webzines, and essay collections, most readings range from three to five pages—about the same length as the papers that students will be asked to write. Also included are some longer readings that expose students to more elaborate, fully developed arguments, thus enriching their composition experience. Well-known authors, including Julia Alvarez, Stephen King, and John Leo, write on topics such as American standards of beauty, the appeal of horror movies, and the strategies of advertising. In each chapter a pair of readings shows different perspectives on the same issue.

Striking Visuals

More accurately than other, more traditional texts, *Mirror on America*, Third Edition, reflects the students' world by including a wealth of images such as movie stills, paintings, drawings, advertisements, photographs, and cartoons. Every chapter opens with a striking image. These opening visuals are accompanied by questions and prompts for thinking that encourage students to approach the chapter with a critical eye. The "Focusing on Yesterday, Focusing on Today" visuals and apparatus at the end of each chapter ask students to examine their current culture by comparing and contrasting it with the culture of the past.

Helpful Guidance for Students

Abundant editorial apparatus in *Mirror on America*, Third Edition, guides students through the discovery process by asking them carefully wrought questions and by offering them context before and after every chapter and every selection.

At the beginning of each chapter, focused activities guide students to the chapter's topic:

- A caption and questions accompany the chapter-opening visual to stimulate discussion or writing.
- A "Gearing Up" journal and discussion prompt asks students to reflect briefly in writing about the topic for that chapter. This feature may also be used as a homework assignment.
- A brief, attention-grabbing introduction provides valuable context for the chapter's selections and focuses students' attention more fully on the chapter's topic.
- "Collaborating" activities introduce students to major concerns of the chapter and give them a chance to exchange ideas with their classmates.

Each reading selection is preceded by relevant information and two activities:

- An informative headnote to the selection provides students with cultural context, as well as a brief biographical sketch about the selection's author.
- "Thinking Ahead" questions ask students to reflect briefly on the topic of the selection.
- "Increasing Vocabulary" words give students a prereading list of unfamiliar words to look up and incorporate into their personal vocabularies.

In addition to the glosses for each reading, there are ESL glosses throughout to explain contexts and terminology that might be unfamiliar to the growing population of students whose first language is not English.

Each reading selection is followed by four sets of questions:

- "Exercising Vocabulary" questions ask students to derive the meaning of especially interesting words from their context and to apply and compare that meaning to usage in other contexts.
- "Probing Content" questions call for students to engage in thoughtful discussion of the selection's subject.
- "Considering Craft" questions require students to focus on particular techniques used by the writers to accomplish their goals.
- "Responding to the Writer" questions ask students to reflect on some aspect of the reading and to question and comment on the writer's message while connecting it to their own experiences.

Each chapter concludes with several student activities, including the "Focusing on Yesterday, Focusing on Today" activities discussed earlier.

- "Drawing Connections" questions, which appear before the end of each chapter, ask students to compare and contrast how the authors of explicitly paired readings explain their points of view.
- "Reflecting on the Writing" questions ask students to connect ideas from the essays within or across chapters and to draw their own conclusions.
- "Connecting to the Culture" questions ask students to reflect on personal experiences similar to those represented in the readings and to consider how their own life experiences are connected to popular culture in general.

The section "Evaluating and Documenting Sources" at the end of the book offers essential coverage of MLA documentation style. This section features MLA citation models, as well as an annotation of a Web page and an exercise asking students to examine a Web source.

What's New in the Third Edition

TEXT SELECTIONS

To keep pace with the ever-changing rhythm of American popular culture, we have included fifty-three provocative readings, more than half of which are new. These updated readings offer wide-ranging perspectives on popular culture. The selections encourage students to explore the impact multicultural groups can have on American popular culture, and *Mirror on America* now features more diverse topics and writers. For instance, a profile by Andrew Nelson of Wilma Mankiller, the first female chief of the Cherokee Nation, explores the hurdles she has overcome as a female Native American. Christopher Stahl, in "I Ruck, Therefore I Am: Rugby and the Gay Male Body," discusses gay athletes' self-image.

A new chapter on technology, Chapter 9, "This Blog's 4 U," includes readings on text messaging, online role-playing games, and high-tech gadgets, turning a critical eye on how the latest technology trends affect culture.

Paired selections at the end of every chapter better model effective arguments. These essays present different—often opposing—stances on a topic, offering an effective way for students to understand the issues at stake and formulate arguments about them. We think you'll find these readings will generate lively discussion in your classroom.

IMAGE SELECTIONS

Because our students are highly tuned to visual information and their lives are media saturated, we have expanded our coverage of analyzing visuals and offered students a variety of vivid images—twenty-one new to this edition—and more help understanding and responding to them. A new Chapter 2, "Deconstructing Media: Analyzing an Image," provides students with a framework for reading and writing about visuals. A sample student paper, "Monumental Taste: Using Patriotism to Market Diet Coke," models the kind of critical analysis students are expected to write. The opening visuals for each chapter, "Looking Ahead," and the pair of images, "Focusing on Yesterday, Focusing on Today," at the end of each chapter have been carefully updated to focus on such contemporary cultural phenomena as the iPod and the soaring popularity of plastic surgery.

Companion Web Site at bedfordstmartins.com/mirror

Web links throughout the text direct students to the companion Web site, where you and your students will find useful online resources, including *TopLinks*—a dynamic database of annotated links that relate to each topic in the book and that provide opportunities for further exploration and possible essay ideas. Students may use the online Reading Quizzes to test themselves on the content of each reading. Each quiz offers automatic feedback and immediate scoring, and instructors can track their students' progress. Instructors can also use Testing Tool Kit: A Writing and Grammar Test Bank to create secure, customized tests and quizzes for their students. The Testing Tool Kit CD-ROM includes nearly 2,000 items at two levels of difficulty.

Student Resources

- *Re:Writing* (bedfordstmartins.com/rewriting): This portal collects the most popular and widely used free online resources from Bedford/St. Martin's in a convenient and easy-to-navigate Web site. Offerings include research and documentation advice, visual analysis exercises, and access to Exercise Central, as well as instructor resources such as bibliographies and online journals.

- *Exercise Central* (bedfordstmartins.com/exercisecentral): The largest collection of editing exercises available online, Exercise Central offers more than 8,000 items, with instant scoring and feedback and an online gradebook for instructors.

- *Exercise Central to Go* CD-ROM: This freestanding package includes practice items (drawn from Exercise Central) for basic writers. No Internet connection is necessary.

- *The Bedford/St. Martin's ESL Workbook*: This ancillary covers grammar issues for multilingual students with varying English-language skills and cultural backgrounds. To reinforce each lesson, instructional introductions are followed by illustrative examples and exercises.

Resources for Instructors

The instructor's manual, *Resources for Teaching* MIRROR ON AMERICA: SHORT ESSAYS AND IMAGES FROM POPULAR CULTURE, Third Edition, is designed as a practical ancillary offering additional ways to present the material effectively and exercises originating from imaginative alternatives that work well in the classroom. We do not claim to provide all the alternative teaching strategies and resources here. Instead we hope that those we do offer lead to stimulating classroom experiences.

After suggestions on strategies for teaching Chapters 1 and 2, the instructor's manual offers the following material for each additional chapter:

- A brief chapter introduction from the instructor's point of view
- A short discussion of the chapter's opening image
- Comments on "Focusing on Yesterday, Focusing on Today"
- Additional resources

For each selection, the instructor's manual offers additional apparatus:

- A brief introduction to the selection
- "Questions for Discussion"
- "Group Activities"
- "Out of Class Projects"
- "Additional Writing Assignments"

Through class-testing many of the selections, writing suggestions, and activities in the text, we have found reading and writing about contemporary popular culture to be a highly effective means of teaching students to connect to larger cultural and discourse communities through their own reading and writing. We sincerely hope that you have equally successful classroom experiences as you use *Mirror on America: Short Essays and Images from Popular Culture*, Third Edition, with your own students.

Acknowledgments

We would like to thank Barbara Heinssen for signing this book, thus making our affiliation with Bedford/St. Martin's possible. We have found it a privilege to work with a team of highly competent people at Bedford/St. Martin's, one of the last publishing houses to truly take the time to develop its writers. We especially wish to thank Bedford's past president, Chuck Christensen; its president, Joan Feinberg; its editorial director, Denise Wydra; and its editor in chief in Boston, Karen Henry, for sharing our vision and allowing us to share it with others. Special thanks go to developmental editor Aron Keesbury and his editorial assistant (now editor), Ellen Thibault, for their work on the first edition. Their insight, inventiveness, and general good humor made our collaboration productive and enjoyable. Amanda Bristow, who edited the second edition, and her assistants Karin Halbert (now editor) and Christina Gerogiannis, helped transform that edition into an even more relevant and usable textbook by lending their fresh, vibrant perspectives.

For this edition, we had the honor and privilege of working with editor John Sullivan, whose vast experience proved invaluable. His professionalism, clear vision, and understanding made him a pleasure to work with. We appreciate the efforts of editorial assistant Kaitlin Hannon, who helped out with the innumerable details that go into producing a textbook. Our thanks also go to the production team, including Erica Appel and Jessica Skrocki, who skillfully engineered and guided the manuscript into book form. Copyeditor Rosemary Winfield's suggestions were invaluable. We also wish to recognize the hard work of Martha Shethar, who cleared permissions for all of the images, and Patty Wise, who updated the online reading quizzes and wrote new headnotes and updated existing ones. We are very grateful to Sandy Schechter and Warren Drabek, who cleared text permissions for the book. We would also like to thank Anabel F. Hart and Robert E. Arthur, two extremely talented young writers who provided the student essays for Chapters 1 and 2.

We also owe a debt of gratitude to a group of people who were instrumental in the revision of this book. We thank our reviewers for their many helpful suggestions: Marielle Ainsworth, Eastern New Mexico University–Roswell; Martin Arida, Valencia Community College East; Nicole Banks, Black Hawk Community College; Lynette Beers, Saddleback College; Crystal Bickford, Nichols College; Michele Boldt, Mt. Hood Community College; Virginia Brackett, Triton College; Heather Byland, University of Alabama–Huntsville; Trevor Calvert, Cabot College; Nancy Canavera and her students, Charleston Southern University; Cheryl Cardoza, Truckee Meadows Community College; Edward Casper, Edmonds Community College; Joel Dailey, Delgado Community College; Tracy Duckart, Humboldt State University; Patricia Ellis, Bentley College; Andrea Feldman, University of Colorado at Boulder; Robert Forman, St. John's University; Robin Griffin, Truckee Meadows Community College; Jeremiah Hall, California State University–Fullerton; Julie Hawk, University of Alabama–Huntsville; Lauren Ingraham, University of Tennessee–Chattanooga; Rita Hamada-Kahn, California Polytech State University–Pomona; Roopa Madhvapathy, Cogswell Polytech College; Heather Powers, Indiana University of Pennsylvania; Lynn Searfoss, Appalachian State University; and Patricia Tyrer, West Texas A&M. Finally, this book never would have been written had it not been for the many students we have taught over the years in our composition classrooms. With them, we have tested many of the topics, strategies, and activities that comprise this text, and from them we have learned much of what we know about teaching writing and about popular culture today.

Introduction for Students

This is not your usual English textbook. The material focuses on reading and writing about things in your world, like television, movies, music, and technology, often called *popular culture*. Why read and write about popular culture? In order to answer this question, we first need to understand what popular culture is and why it is important.

To arrive at a working definition, we can break the term down into its two components: *popular* and *culture*. In the most general sense, *popular* means "of the people"—the common people or the population at large, not the elite or chosen few. But more often, *popular* suggests choice, or preference. We usually use this term when we mean something or someone that many ordinary people prefer or value. When you think of popular culture, then, think of the People's Choice Awards as opposed to the Academy Awards.

That brings us to the second term, *culture*. Broadly defined, *culture* refers to the body of beliefs, behaviors, values, and thoughts that influence us every day. It contains not only the good, but also the bad—the high and the low. We normally associate the word *culture*, however, not with the masses—the ordinary man and woman on the street—but with the educated and financially privileged. We think of *Masterpiece Theatre*, not *The Osbournes*. If a person is cultured, we generally think she possesses good taste, is refined and educated, and is also probably upper-class. If *popular* usually means "chosen by the common people," and *culture* is often associated with the chosen few, then what do these two seemingly contradictory terms mean when they are used together?

We may borrow the Cotton Institute slogan from television commercials to help us arrive at a working definition of popular culture: it is "the fabric of our lives." Pop culture is made up of all the objects, people, events, and places to which most of us readily relate and which comprise a society at any given time, past or present. The objects and people that are widely recognized as symbols of our culture are often referred to as cultural icons. The four components of pop culture—objects, people, events, and places—can be real or imagined. Let's look at some examples:

1. Objects as cultural icons include Barbie dolls, rap songs, television shows, clothing, iPods, advertisements, and even Cinderella's glass slipper.

2. People or characters as cultural icons include Paris Hilton, Johnny Depp, Batman, Lance Armstrong, the Energizer Bunny, Homer Simpson, and the Aflack Duck.

3. Events, activities, or rituals in popular culture are those that large groups of people participate in or can relate to, including 9/11, the Olympics, the Super Bowl, Thanksgiving dinner, high school proms, Fourth of July fireworks, and the MTV Movie Awards.

4. Places in pop culture are settings that hold special shared meaning for many people and include shopping malls, megaplexes, amusement parks, Mount Rushmore, Las Vegas, Hollywood, the White House, and the Statue of Liberty.

These four elements of popular culture form a mirror in which each of us, as members of a common society, can see ourselves reflected as part of an interconnected, greater whole. At the same time, pop culture not only reflects our tastes and preferences at any given time, past or present, but also plays a role in determining future fads and trends. From the time we get up in the morning until the time we go to bed, and from the time we enter this world until the time we leave it, we are immersed in popular culture. We may agree that not all of its components are of the highest quality or in the best taste, but we would all have to concede that they play an integral part in our daily lives, as well as in our shared social history. Popular culture is part of what makes us all Americans.

It is important to remember that pop culture is not fixed in time. The popular or mass culture of the past may become the high or elite culture of the present, and that same elite culture may simultaneously be repopularized as it is once again embraced by the masses. Consider the case of William Shakespeare. If you read *Macbeth* or *Hamlet* in high school, you probably did not associate those difficult-to-read plays with pop culture. Remember, however, that Shakespeare's plays, much like blockbuster movies today, were extremely popular during the time they were written and enjoyed wide attendance by large, enthusiastic audiences. Shakespeare was tuned in to those audiences, which were made up of all segments of society, from the educated nobility to the illiterate "groundlings," so named because they sat or stood on the ground near the stage. Thus, during his time, Shakespeare's plays were seen as popular entertainment. It was only in later years that his plays were appropriated by learned scholars in universities who sought to analyze them word by word as they continue to do today.

Interestingly enough, as evidence of Shakespeare's popular appeal in the second half of the twentieth century and into the new millennium, entertainment moguls have sought to revitalize his plays by taking them out of the hands of university professors and giving them back to the masses. Not only serious students of Shakespeare but also people who have never read a word of his plays have been able to enjoy his works through both cinematic and live theater productions. Let's examine several of these revisionings of Shakespeare's works from the second half of the twentieth century through the present day.

You may be familiar with *West Side Story*, which recasts *Romeo and Juliet* as the story of a couple struggling to maintain a relationship against a backdrop of gang warfare in a New York City Puerto Rican neighborhood. First the story was a Broadway hit; then a film version was made which drew a much larger audience. Similarly, famed director Baz Luhrmann's 1996 cinematic version of *Romeo and Juliet*, starring Leonardo DiCaprio and Claire Danes, features tough modern gangs, a cross-dressing Mercutio, and a powerful musical score performed by contemporary artists such as Radiohead and Garbage. The 1999 Academy Awards were dominated by the Hollywood blockbuster *Shakespeare in Love*, a rollicking spoof featuring a young Shakespeare with writer's block, played by Joseph Fiennes, who is lovestruck by a beautiful woman, played by Gwyneth Paltrow. Since then, there have been several other popular reincarnations of Shakespeare classics set in contemporary America, featuring young stars like Julia Stiles, Heath Ledger, Jet Li, and Aaliyah. These films, which target the teenage market, include *O*, a modern-day retelling of Othello; *10 Things I Hate about You*, based on *The Taming of the Shrew*; and *Romeo Must Die*, yet another retelling of the classic love story *Romeo and Juliet*.

Perhaps the most exciting example of Shakespeare's reaching the masses in much the same way he did in his own day is New York City's Shakespeare in the Park series. The aptly named Public Theater, which celebrated its fiftieth anniversary in 2005, sponsors this series and provides equal accessibility to people of all ages, ethnicities, and educational and income levels. Anyone can see the Bard's plays for free in beautiful Central Park, and tickets or reservations are not required. The public is encouraged to attend rehearsals and even meet the actors, some of whom are Hollywood's brightest stars, such as Kevin Kline and Denzel Washington. Shakespeare in the Park has become not only a national, but also an international phenomenon.

Thus Shakespeare is once again finding his way back to the masses. According to The Public Theater's website, "The Public is an American theater that embraces the complexities of contemporary society and nurtures both artists and audiences through its commitment to the idea that The Public should be a place of inclusion and a forum for ideas." This sounds a lot like the mission of popular culture studies. Since academics are already studying and writing scholarly articles on the impact of rap music, soap operas, the Internet, films, and video games, which contemporary composers and screenwriters do you think will someday take their place alongside Shakespeare?

Popular culture, then, is that collection of objects, people, events, and places that serves to mirror society and its members and to reflect their values and preferences. By studying pop culture, you gain valuable new insights about yourself and make richer connections to all aspects of the society in which you live. Finally, we hope that you find it not only fulfilling but also fun to read and write about popular culture, a subject with which you are intimately connected every day of your life.

Contents

7. Flickering Illusions: Television and Movie Messages   238

8. Stop! Listen. What's That Sound? How Music and Culture Mix It Up   286

Rhetorical Table of Contents

The rhetorical strategies—analysis, argument, cause and effect, comparison and contrast, definition, description, evaluation, illustration and example, narration, and process analysis—are listed alphabetically for quick reference.

Cause and Effect

Comparison and Contrast

Definition

Description

Evaluation

Illustration and Example

Narration

Process Analysis

CHAPTER 1

Active, Involved Reading
and the Writing Process
Establishing the Connection

If this is a writing course, why is there so much to read in this text? Why is reading the first thing we want to discuss with you?

It's simple, really. People who write well read often. They read to find ideas, both for what to write about and for how to write. Reading makes us think, and good writing requires thought beforehand, during, and afterward. Reading helps us identify things we'd like to model in our own work and things we'll never do, no matter what. Reading opens windows and doors to the world we share and offers mirrors in which we can look at our culture and ourselves.

Reading with a Difference

The kind of reading this discussion involves may not be the kind of reading you are used to. If you think of reading as a sit-still, passive, try-to-stay-awake-until-the-end-of-the-chapter event, you'll need to rethink. Real reading means really getting involved with the text, whether the text is song lyrics, a magazine or newspaper item, a poem, a chapter in a chemistry book, or an essay in this text. The more of your five senses you involve, the better.

Getting into Reading

This text includes some things that should make the reading and writing experience more manageable for you and more interesting, too. Each unit begins with an image like a photograph or an advertisement. This opening visual gives you a first glimpse of the chapter's topic and helps you begin to think about that topic. Next is the "Gearing Up" section—a journal and discussion prompt to help you reflect on your previous involvement with that chapter's topic and to get you started writing. Next is introductory text that provides some background thoughts about the chapter and raises some questions to help you relate your own experiences to the topic for reading and discussion. Each chapter also includes a

1

"Collaborating" opening activity that suggests questions for you and your classmates to brainstorm about together before you begin to read and discuss the individual selections in each chapter.

Now you are ready to move on to the reading selections in the chapter. Each essay is introduced by a brief headnote about the selection's writer, subject matter, and the time and place of first publication. Next are "Thinking Ahead," a journal prompt that deals with the topic addressed by that particular reading selection, and an "Increasing Vocabulary" word list, which contains some words from the reading that you may find unfamiliar. Looking up definitions for these words and writing those definitions in your own words in a vocabulary notebook will help you to expand the number of words at your command when you write or read. The reading selection is next. This may be an essay, an article, or a column from a newspaper, magazine, or Webzine.

Five sets of questions follow the reading selection. "Exercising Vocabulary" gives you a chance to explore the use and meaning of some especially interesting words. "Probing Content" asks questions about the writer's subject matter. "Considering Craft" questions are about why and how the writer has put together the selection as he or she has chosen to do. "Responding to the Writer" allows you to examine your own reactions and respond to issues the writer has raised. "Drawing Connections" questions ask you to compare how writers in the paired essays make their points about similar topics.

To understand how all these parts work together, let's look at a sample essay. First, read the brief introduction to the essay's subject and author. Many readers may be tempted to skip right over this information because it isn't part of the essay, but that's a mistake. To see why, let's work with the headnote to a sample essay.

Schlock Waves Felt across U.S. Campuses

Eric L. Wee

The debate about the value of popular culture has been raging for centuries. But whether or not it is valuable, each one of us interacts with and is influenced by popular culture every day. What it may lack in historical validity and academic esteem, it certainly makes up for in immediacy and relevance. In the *Washington Post* in June 1998, Eric L. Wee first published this snapshot from the mecca of popular culture studies, the annual conference of the Popular Culture Association and the American Culture Association. By introducing us to some of the presenters and their topics, Wee raises numerous questions about pop culture as an academic discipline. Can important lessons about the human condition be derived from watching soap operas? Is the impetus to include popular studies courses on campus just a way to fill seats and shore up sagging enrollment figures? Wee frames the argument but leaves it up to the reader to draw conclusions. Wee, a former *Washington Post* reporter, is a frequent contributor to the *Washington Post Magazine*. He was a finalist for the Pulitzer Prize in feature writing in 1999 and won a prestigious award for education reporting in 2004.

This headnote offers several important pieces of information. It introduces the occasion that prompted Wee to write—the 1998 Popular Culture Conference—and explains how this author chooses to approach his topic. The headnote also introduces us to some of the questions that are raised by the commentary. Finally, it tells us when and where the article first appeared and a little background information about the author so that we can think accurately about his perspective on the topic and the original intended audience. How does the information in the headnote influence your reading?

Thinking Ahead

Following our sample essay's headnote are a few sentences under the heading "Thinking Ahead." This journal and discussion prompt helps you focus your initial thoughts about the essay's subject. If you have never kept a journal before, you'll find that it's a good way to learn to transfer your thoughts and ideas to paper. Don't worry too much about grammar and spelling as you write in your journal; the important thing here is just to get started writing. These journal notes may be seeds for your more formal essays later. Let's look at a sample journal prompt and one possible response for "Schlock Waves Felt across U.S. Campuses."

THINKING AHEAD

To what extent should we examine popular culture? If popular culture is constantly changing, what value is there in studying it? Are there any life lessons to be learned from studying television shows, movies, music lyrics and videos, advertisements, and other components of everyday life?

Now here is a journal entry written in response to this prompt:

> *It just seems too easy. If I can learn the same lessons from studying episodes of SpongeBob that I can from reading Leo Tolstoy's novels, why would I wade through all those eight-syllable names? I get it that the same themes from those hundred-year-old novels are being replayed over and over in movies and TV shows — love, death, crime, jealousy. So humanity just keeps repeating the same mistakes. If studying violent movies would help us learn to reduce the violence, then that would be valuable. But what if studying violent movies encourages some people to commit violence and even teaches them new ways to be violent? I can't see a lot of parents wanting to spend money for their kids to take classes where they study Jennifer Lopez and Brad Pitt. It just doesn't seem academic enough.*

Remember that everyone's journal response will be different. The task of the journal prompt is to get you to think about a subject in a way that you might not have before, so the writing in your journal won't be a finished product. Your response will just be your initial ideas transferred from your head onto the paper.

Increasing Vocabulary

The next thing included for our sample essay is a list of vocabulary words. Following each word in parentheses is an abbreviation for the part of speech that tells how the word is used in context—*n.* for noun, *v.* for verb, *adj.* for adjective, or *adv.* for adverb—so you'll know where you might use this word in a sentence. Next is a number in parentheses; this is the paragraph number in the essay where the word appears. This allows you to see where and how the writer has used this word. The words aren't defined; keep a vocabulary list in your notebook with definitions that you put into your own words after reading the dictionary definition. Don't be tempted to simply copy words from the dictionary onto your notebook page, however. That may give you penmanship practice, but it won't help your personal vocabulary grow. Think about building blocks. Someone with more building blocks can build a more complete castle than someone else with fewer blocks. Words are the building blocks of essays and conversations. Read what the dictionary has to say, and write down a definition that makes sense to you. Then go back and reread the word in context to make sure your definition fits the author's intent. The objective is for you to be able to use this new word in your own conversations and writing.

Our "Increasing Vocabulary" list may not cover all the words in the selection that you find unfamiliar. We explain some unusual words or names, which you probably would not use in your own writing or conversation, at the bottom of the page where they are used to help you understand what the author is trying to say. Always feel free to add words you'd like to master from each essay to a list in your notebook.

Here is our vocabulary list for "Schlock Waves Felt across U.S. Campuses" with some working definitions that a student might supply:

INCREASING VOCABULARY

paradigms (n.) (3)   *Examples that serve as models.*
angst (n.) (7)   *Anxiety.*
avant-garde (adj.) (11)   *Ahead of its time.*
archetypes (n.) (22)   *Models from which other like things are copied.*
mundane (adj.) (25)   *Ordinary.*
smut (n.) (32)   *Something indecent.*
plumb (v.) (36)   *To examine carefully.*
turgid (adj.) (36)   *Swollen, overblown.*

Reading a Sample Essay

Once you have read the introduction to the reading selection, responded to the "Thinking Ahead" journal prompt, and defined the words on the "Increasing Vocabulary" list, you are ready to read the selection itself. But reading doesn't mean you become a spectator. You don't learn about playing a sport just by watching, and you don't learn everything a text has to offer just by letting your eyes wander over the lines. That's why annotating is essential for really involved reading. Annotating means to read and to mark the text with a highlighter, pencil, or pen. When you annotate, you open up a dialogue between yourself and the text. You communicate.

Here's how annotating works. Circle any unfamiliar vocabulary words so you can look them up later. Some may be in our vocabulary list, but some may not. Some of the words or phrases that are explained at the bottom of the page may be marked *ESL*, which means that students for whom English is a second language may not have heard that term before. Underline or highlight important sentences, especially the *thesis*, or main idea, and the *topic sentences* for each paragraph. Mark sentences or phrases that appeal to you or seem especially well worded. Jot down questions in the margin. Draw connections between the author's experiences and your own. Put question marks by whatever you don't accept as true or just don't understand. React to what you're reading!

Here is a copy of our sample essay, "Schlock Waves Felt across U.S. Campuses," with annotations. Don't worry if you would have marked different words and phrases and recorded different comments; that's fine. This is just to show you how one reader has actively read and annotated this essay.

Schlock Waves Felt across U.S. Campuses

Eric L. Wee

directions based on pop culture — awesome opener!

Go past the 24-screen cineplex playing two shows of *Titanic.* Go past Planet Hollywood. Past the Virgin Megastore. Past McDonald's.

Who's they?
creates suspense

And then you'll see where they gather. At the Buena Vista Hotel in the heart of Disney World, you'll find the people who are studying everything you can't get away from. The professors

Like what?

look up

of popular culture. They see revelations in Calvin Klein underwear ads; they construct new literary paradigms from R.E.M.[1] lyrics; they analyze porno flicks as if they were fine art. On many campuses, they're scorned by colleagues. But here, they're among friends. Here, for four days in early April, 1,500 members of the Popular Culture Association and the American Culture Association presented papers on such topics as "Godlike Knowledge and

Milton's poem

Human Understanding in *Paradise Lost* and *Star Trek*"—and they were taken seriously.

Isn't pop culture all about the present?

The study of popular culture, they'll tell you, is the future. As incredible as it seems, they may be right.

Drop in on a lecture by Lynnea Chapman King, an English doctoral candidate from Texas Tech University. Her specialty and dissertation topic: "The Films of Generation X." The canon comprises youth-oriented movies made from 1982 to 1997. First she shows a clip from *Fast Times at Ridgemont High*, then one from

Who fits in this group?

great film!

The Breakfast Club—all the way up to *Romy and Michele's High School Reunion*. She's grouped the 18 films of the Gen X canon into subgenres, including high school films (*Ferris Bueller's Day Off*), post–high school (*Less Than Zero*) and post-college (*St. Elmo's Fire*). She talks about how these movies reflect the angst

I can relate!

people in their late 20s and early 30s feel about family, their futures and death—and it all seems to be making sense.

Then it hits you:

How nice for her! What are her career options?

Ms. Chapman King, age 30, is earning a Ph.D. in *Pretty in Pink.* She's made herself an expert on movies she happens to like. She explains that these are all very significant films, worthy of her scholarship.

Is this worth a degree?

"I think that in 10 years we'll look back and say, 'Yes, I can see that *The Breakfast Club* and, yes, *Reality Bites* and, yes, *Before Sunrise* are a beautiful and valuable reflection of society, and

Plato radical?

standing alone are examples of good filmmaking.'" There was a time when teaching Plato at Oxford was considered radical. Eng-

French for??

Why? Because it was British?

lish literature as a field of study was considered avant-garde on American campuses in the 19th century.

Credibility

Still, the old canon provided certain constants. For decades, college students mostly studied the big thinkers and writers who had withstood the test of time. Aristotle, Shakespeare, Wordsworth.

true!

But inevitably the people being studied were dead, white, male—and hard to relate to.

The '60s turned everything upside down. Students—and professors—began occupying buildings and issuing demands.

Feminist movement

Why weren't we studying the histories of nonwhite people? Why was everything from a male perspective?

civil rights

Riding this crest of change have been the pop-culture profs. Once the kooky idea of a few people at Bowling Green State University in Ohio, the concept has spread and become institutionalized

[1] **R.E.M.:** An alternative rock band.

Okay, but what's the career path? Where are the jobs?

good word choice

in colleges nationwide during the past three decades. Traditionalists may still sneer at popular culture studies, but as an academic discipline, it's not about to disappear.

Students like it. Baby boom-era professors, themselves reared on television, like teaching these classes, too. They're popular—they bring in bodies. And they bring in tuition dollars. "We're no longer in the closet," says Ray Browne, the silver-haired academic who is acknowledged as the godfather of the movement. They used to call him a nut. Now they call him professor emeritus. In 1970, Dr. Browne set up the nation's first popular culture studies program at Bowling Green and also started the Popular Culture Association. Now, just look around. Hundreds of scholars have flocked to Disney World from schools such as Michigan State, Carnegie-Mellon and Virginia Tech. They may not be Ivy League, but pop-culture studies have pervaded those hallowed halls as well. By Dr. Browne's estimate, at least 2 million students are taking pop-culture courses in some form (up from 1 million in 1983).

11   *always about money — student consumers*

prestigious campuses

This was written in 1998. What's the number for this year? Up or down?

Nice phrase— "ivory tower" thinking

powerful image

Of course, not everybody is studying Capt. Kirk. There are some panels here on Depression-era workers and World War II veterans. For too long, scholars ignored everyday people and their everyday lives, Dr. Browne says; academia has been been guilty of arrogant intellectual snobbery.

The explosion of mass media has helped fuel popular culture's growth since World War II, creating a nurturing environment for such studies.

12

makes pop culture's growth sound like a wildfire

13

check mythology textbook

Today popular culture invades all of our lives in an unprecedented way: Television, movies and the Internet bombard us with images, archetypes and knowledge. City after city has become almost indistinguishable with look-alike shopping malls.

14   *remember Mall Rats and Dawn of the Dead*

or just fast food?

This mass culture provides brain food for hungry scholars. How much more can be said about Shakespeare after 400 years? But much can be learned from Homer Simpson.

15   *really!*

Name came up in philosophy class — who is he?

definitely applies!

And can we apply Descartes'[2] concept of evil genius to a *Star Trek: The Next Generation* episode? Well, a philosophy professor from Susquehanna University in Pennsylvania is doing just that down the hall.

16   *comic books use this theme*

Is there any limit to what's legitimate to study here? No, says Dr. Browne. After arguing so long for the study of the mundane, he is not about to start setting limits. Joseph Slade, Ph.D., looks like a distinguished professor. As he stands at the lectern in front of about a dozen fellow academics, he sounds as if he could be giving a discourse on economic theory. But this evening he's lecturing on fetishes. He's just handed out a reading/watching list with titles including *Hidden Obsessions*, *Les Femmes Érotiques* and *Latex*. He switches on the TV. Two women on the screen are appreciating each other.

17

weird topic!

that's being tactful!

What's audience reaction?

Above the pulsating music, he starts talking about the director's style. "Mostly he's interested in female desire," says Dr. Slade. "The notion is that women are so voracious in their sexual appetite that they will mate with anything."

18   *certainly not flattering*

don't seem to go together

Dr. Slade is director of graduate studies at the University of Ohio's school of telecommunications. He began his porn studies about 27 years ago while a doctoral student at New York University. One night he got sick of working on his dissertation and decided to go walking in Times Square.

19   *Scholars and porn?*

[2] **Descartes:** Seventeenth-century French philosopher and mathematician.

like a résumé?

good question!

But does popular = worthy of study?

money again

makes sense — soaps are all over social issues

Why? Is this a bad thing?

Is this a title you'd want?

odd comparison

dig up?

What does this last sentence mean? What does Eric Wee really think about value of pop culture?

There he saw the light — specifically the garish neon lights of   20
a triple-X movie house. He watched one hard-core film. Then he
watched another. After a third trip, he wrote a paper about the
experience. Today his curriculum vitae describes him as one of
America's leading experts on adult film, having analyzed more
than 7,000 movies (that's about a dozen a month).

Why study smut?   21

Because, according to Dr. Slade, adult movies portray basic   22
human nature. And, it's popular. Erotic or hard-core video titles
account for $4.2 billion in business, he says. Did you know that
we spend as much on adult movies as we do on hot dogs?

In another conference room, "Hormones and Heartache: 23
Coming of Age in Pine Valley" is the topic. It's a discussion of
the characters in soap operas, specifically *All My Children*.

Kathy Lyday-Lee, an English professor at Elon College in   24
North Carolina, is there. She's going to teach a course called
"Soap Operas and Social Issues" this summer. Not that such a
class will stick out in a schedule that also includes "The World of
NASCAR"[3] and "The Culture and Business of Nashville."

She sees the study of soap operas as a way to teach her stu-   25
dents about social changes as well as broadcasting history. Yet
for all the rational-sounding statements you hear from the con-
ferees, you begin to sense the real reason they study pop culture is
much more simple: They can't help themselves. After endless
years in higher education, constantly trying to plumb meaning
from turgid texts, they can't shut off when they hit the streets or
turn on the tube.

Thinking about the Reading

After reading and annotating the piece of writing, you are ready to
continue the conversation with the text, guided by several sets of
questions. The first set is called "Exercising Vocabulary." These
questions are different from the "Increasing Vocabulary" list you
looked at before the reading selection. There you were locating definitions and thinking about adding those words to your own speaking and writing vocabulary. Here you examine just a few words
from the reading selection in closer detail. You are asked to draw
some conclusions and occasionally to do some detective work to arrive at a meaning for an unfamiliar word.

Here is the "Exercising Vocabulary" section for "Schlock Waves
Felt across U.S. Campuses." We have supplied possible answers so
you can see how this section works.

EXERCISING VOCABULARY

1. Wee changes a word in a common phrase to create an unusual title for
this piece. What is the common phrase? What does it normally describe? What does *schlock* mean? Why has Wee substituted it here?

---

[3] **NASCAR:** National Association for Stock Car Auto Racing.

The phrase you usually hear is "shock waves," and it is usually used to describe the aftermath of an earthquake. Schlock is a slang word that means something cheap, something not as good as another. Wee uses this word because some people think that popular culture is inferior to classics like Shakespeare's plays, Van Gogh's paintings, or Bach's music.

2. In paragraph 4, Wee uses the word *canon* to talk about a group of "youth-oriented movies." When traditional professors of literature talk about the canon, what do they mean? What usually is included in this canon? What effect does Wee achieve by using the word here?

The canon usually refers to an officially recognized list of the best of a group. The canon in literature usually refers to famous, accepted works, like novels by Jane Austen or F. Scott Fitzgerald. Wee uses the really formal word canon here to indicate a group of movies because he's saying that the people who study popular culture feel that this group of movies is just as worthy of serious study as those novels.

The next set of questions is called "Probing Content," and these questions are designed to get you to examine closely what the writer is saying. Often a second part of the question asks you to think more deeply or to draw a conclusion. Be sure to answer all the parts of each question. You'll remember answers to some of these questions from your first reading, but for others you'll need to reread carefully. Here are "Probing Content" questions for "Schlock Waves Felt across U.S. Campuses" with some suggested answers. Of course, you might think of equally good but different answers.

PROBING CONTENT

1. In paragraph 3, Wee notes that attendees at the Popular Culture Conference will tell you that "the study of popular culture . . . is the future." Why is this statement ironic? Does Wee believe this?

This statement is ironic because popular culture is all about what's hot right now, not in the future. Wee does seem to think that the study of popular culture, whatever that is at the time, is not going away because of the constant influence of popular culture on our lives (para. 14).

2. What's the problem with studying people who are all "dead, white, male" (para. 8)? What period of time marked a rebellion against such a limited scope to education? How does popular culture relate to opening up the canon?

We can't relate to dead, white males. In the 1960s, people began to demand a study of people and things that were more representative of themselves and their lives. Pop culture insists that we recognize other artists who might be nonwhite and female.

3. Who is considered the father of the popular culture studies movement? What did he do to establish the scholastic nature of popular culture? Why did he want to study popular culture?

> *Dr. Ray Browne is "the godfather of the movement" (para. 11). He established the first popular culture studies program at a university in Bowling Green, Ohio. Dr. Browne thought that academics needed to get over their "intellectual snobbery" to study what was really important to the common people.*

4. What attracts scholars to the study of popular culture? How can this kind of study benefit us all?

> *Many people think that everything has already been said about Shakespeare, but applying his themes to new movies is a new area of academic thought. Applying the concepts of old masters to new material makes the old masters relevant to the twenty-first century. Maybe we can learn from their lessons if those lessons fit our generation and our everyday lives.*

While the "Probing Content" questions examine what the writer has to say about the subject, the next set of questions, "Considering Craft," encourages you to find out how the writer has packaged that information. You are asked to consider the writer's purpose, audience, language and tone, sentence structure, title, introduction and conclusion, and organization—the very things you must consider when you write your own papers. Here are some sample "Considering Craft" questions for "Schlock Waves Felt across U.S. Campuses" with some possible answers.

CONSIDERING CRAFT

1. Wee begins this commentary by offering directions. Reread paragraph 1. Why does he choose this introduction? Why does he phrase his directions in these terms? How does this introduction set a framework for the essay?

> *Wee wants to direct us to the Popular Culture Conference. The directions he uses are all related to popular culture — a multiscreen theater, a restaurant everyone thinks is cool, a music store, and that old standby of pop culture, McDonald's. This introduction sets a framework for the whole essay about the value of popular culture; popular culture guides the direction of our lives.*

2. In paragraph 21, Wee remarks that Dr. Joseph Slade "saw the light" while walking in Times Square. In what context is this expression most familiar? What is ironic about this use of language?

> *The expression "to see the light" is often used in a religious sense. Here, however, Dr. Slade sees the light while looking at a triple-X movie house, which seems to point to sin, not redemption. And the light that he found led him to view and study pornographic movies.*

3. Describe the author's tone in this piece. What does he hope to generate in the reader?

> *Wee's tone in this commentary is matter-of-fact. He presents the material and lets the reader draw his or her own conclusions about the merits of studying popular culture. Because he doesn't judge the merits himself, his writing makes the reader weigh the value of studying popular culture and draw his or her own conclusions.*

The final section concluding each reading selection is called "Responding to the Writer." Here you are asked to react to something particular the writer has suggested. This helps you to clarify and sum up your thoughts on the topic you've been reading and thinking about. Here's a sample "Responding to the Writer" for our sample essay, with one possible response.

RESPONDING TO THE WRITER

According to Eric Wee, the study of popular culture as an academic discipline is "not about to disappear" (para. 10). Explain why you agree or disagree with this statement.

> *I don't think that the study of popular culture is going to disappear because it has been firmly established in some academic circles, like at Bowling Green University. Students like the classes, so they sign up for them, which makes money for the universities. And life lessons can really be learned from studying Homer Simpson, as well as from studying Shakespeare.*

Within each chapter, you'll find paired selections that express two different viewpoints about an issue approached in that chapter. These paired selections encourage you to examine two sides of an issue and to weigh the strength of each author's position. Let's read a second essay about studying popular culture.

Pop Culture Studies Turns 25

DAVID JACOBSON

In this essay, David Jacobson ferrets out the roots of the popular culture movement. He quotes a number of people involved with the movement and examines their motives and their experiences. Why are scholars attracted to the study of popular culture? How concrete is the foundation on which they build their research? Pop culture saturates modern society, but does saturation alone make it important? Are television sitcoms, comic books, and lawn ornaments worthy of serious academic study at the university level? Who decides what we should study, anyway, and how does that change over time? Jacobson traces the relatively short history of a controversial — critics would say dubious — new field of academic study, popular culture studies, started by Ray Browne at Ohio's Bowling Green State University. In "Pop Culture Studies Turns 25," which was published in the online magazine *Salon.com* in 1999, the writer credits Browne's popular culture movement with wide influence but notes that no other university has established a full academic department devoted to the subject. David Jacobson is a San Francisco–based humorist and journalist whose work appears in such popular publications as *Salon.com, Esquire, Maxim, Details,* and *Life.*

THINKING AHEAD

Who first thought about studying popular culture? What was the motivation? How academic can such study really be?

INCREASING VOCABULARY

punted (v.) (1)	barraged (v.) (14)
pandering (n.) (3)	garnered (v.) (15)
tongs (n.) (6)	nonplused (adj.) (16)
aesthetics (n.) (7)	demurs (v.) (17)
esoteric (adj.) (7)	turgid (adj.) (26)
unarticulated (adj.) (8)	regurgitates (v.) (30)
commodified (adj.) (9)	indelible (adj.) (32)
catalyst (n.) (11)	arcane (adj.) (34)

Somehow you expect Ray Browne to look a little bit more, you know, 1
radical. Maybe an earring as big as a migration tag or one of those Einstein quantum 'fros. After all, he's the godfather of popular culture studies; the founder and still editor in his emeritus[1] years of the *Journal of Popular Culture,* filled with dense analyses of slam-dancing, country music

---

[1] **emeritus:** Retired honorably.

and computer games; the co-founder of the Popular Culture Association, whose 1,000-plus scholars annually present papers on everything from R.E.M. lyrics to porno flicks; the professor who was punted from the English department at Bowling Green State 25 years ago because he was "disgracing the university," but who promptly established the only graduate program and undergraduate major in popular culture in our galaxy; the guy whose career, by his own account, constituted "a kind of class-action suit against conventional points of view and fields of study in the humanities."

But there he is, in all his photos, stolid and blandly groomed, looking like the office manager of some midsized widget[2] company. Yet his embodiment of the average Joe is utterly appropriate. After all, Browne's fundamental notion is that academia should pay the same kind of serious attention to the "common, everyday culture" of the masses—from sitcoms to bestsellers, from rap to lawn ornaments—as it traditionally has to elite stuff.   2

In the quarter century since Browne founded the popular culture movement, it has had wide influence. But no other school has followed Bowling Green State and established a full department, not to mention a library bursting at the seams with romance novels and *Star Trek* memorabilia, and a busy press publishing the history of American skinheads and collections of soap opera criticism. And even when it's studied under English or mass media, popular culture remains plenty controversial, mocked by the same media that feeds off it, derided by traditionalists hurling jeremiads[3] about pandering and raising important questions about what is worthy of academic attention.   3

When he boldly confronted tradition, Browne wasn't dabbling in the era's academic anarchy so much as honoring his own roots and character. He was raised by a free-thinking agnostic father in the heart of the Bible Belt—a poor kid in rural Depression-era Alabama who never stopped questioning privilege. In the Army, he saw plenty of the stockade, because "I did not have enough 'Sirs' in my vocabulary," he writes in *Against Academia*, his brief memoir and history of popular culture studies. So it's not surprising that, while Browne cut his academic teeth on more traditional literature and folklore, he ultimately rebelled.   4

Browne was among the unwashed masses who poured through the college gates sprung open by the G.I. Bill.[4] Like later generations of women, minorities and gays, some of those newcomers noticed that their own culture, in this case that of the vast lower- and middle-class majority, was largely ignored by academics.   5

To the extent that popular culture was being examined back then, it was through the telescopic lens of history or with the long, cold tongs of the social sciences. But Browne insisted on also looking at contemporary   6

---

[2] **ESL** **widget:** A small mechanical device, a gadget.
[3] jeremiads: Expressions of mourning or sorrow (from the book of Jeremiah in the Bible).
[4] **ESL** **G.I. Bill:** Congressional legislation that provides money for education and home loans to military veterans.

material and applying to it the kind of close, comparative analysis that had previously been reserved for highbrow culture.

Browne and his cohorts insisted that there were alternative and significant aesthetics afoot below the esoteric radar of traditional scholars.   7

"People make choices as to what book to read or movie to see, and just as regularly evaluate the experience: This was a good thriller, this is a great party song," writes BGSU pop culture professor Jack Santino in summarizing the program's "socio-aesthetic approach." "These aesthetic criteria are generally unarticulated; it is the task of the researcher to identify them."   8

Of course, the same folks in and out of academia who criticize postmodern theorists for trivializing the object of study, reducing Shakespeare to a commodified text, also rip pop culture scholars for studying trivial objects, approaching video games as if they held the depths of Shakespeare.   9

In fact, Browne's most radical argument may be that you can teach critical thinking and gain as good a liberal arts education using pop materials as with the old highbrow ones. "There's just as much glory and virtue in being a Madonna person as in being a Hemingway person," he says. "If you want to study culture through Madonna, it seems to me that's a marvelous opportunity."   10

While a department of popular culture plopped down amid the cornfields south of Toledo might seem like an intellectual Christo project, it made political sense. If Browne was the catalyst, the administration at relatively unknown Bowling Green State was also open to an unorthodox department that might put them on the academic map.   11

Popular culture studies rapidly grew in size and notoriety. And BGSU's eight-member faculty now teaches at least 2,000 students a year. Eventually, it set up shop in an uncannily appropriate house built from a 1930s Montgomery Ward[5] kit. The department was also distinguished by its high profile in national and even international media attention.   12

"Some people were delighted by that and some people were embarrassed by that," says Michael Marsden, who worked with Browne at the outset and is now dean of liberal arts at Northern Michigan University.   13

Marsden suffered his share of knocks as a popular culture scholar. After being barraged with faculty criticism when he became a certified Miss Ohio judge, in order to get "privileged information" for his research on beauty pageants, he fought back. "I'll file a grievance if you're suggesting there's some aspect of culture that's forbidden to be studied," he said.   14

A conference on "the history of roller coasters" at Ohio's famed Cedar Point amusement park garnered accusations that scholars were "squandering taxpayer money and doing foolish things," recalls Marsden. Two decades later, "that roller coaster course" is still cited by critics knocking the Bowling Green program.   15

Yet such criticism still leaves pop culture scholars nonplused. Why should the study of a leisure activity necessarily be a leisurely activity   16

---

[5] **Montgomery Ward:** A department store chain no longer operating.

itself? Department veterans like Professor Christopher Geist say popular culture's more outrageous, perhaps publicity-seeking past has cast an undeservedly anti-intellectual image.

While the ever-rebellious Browne still asserts, "I have never come across something that I find worthless," Geist demurs: "I'm not at all afraid to say some TV rots the brain, but I want to understand why people are drawn to it."   17

Given crisscrossing paths of intellectual discovery, given the rise first of American studies, then mass media studies and, more recently, "cultural studies," it's tough to know how much of pop culture in academia was spurred by BGSU's program. But sometimes the effect is obvious. In the 1980s, Robert Thompson, a graduate student at Northwestern University, wrote a paper analyzing the appeal of top TV programs that is a model of pop culture scholarship. Drawing from studies that concluded that television viewing is characterized by inattention (up to two-thirds of viewers are engaged in other activities while watching), Thompson analyzed then-top-rated shows like *The Love Boat* and found that they appealed to their distracted viewers with lots of short scenes and reiterated exposition: "A moment's viewing at any time—is enough to get a summary and an update."   18

As he concluded: "All the things that make these shows appear inartistic—superficial themes, limited character development, low intellectual demand—are really their strong points."   19

Thompson's paper "*The Love Boat*: High Art on the High Seas" not only predicted the mega-popularity of multi-plot micro-scene shows like *ER* and *Seinfeld*, it launched his career as a pop culture scholar when it was published in Browne's *Journal of American Culture* in 1983.   20

Looking back over 15 annual conferences of the Popular Culture Association he's attended, Thompson says: "There was room for fans, aficionados[6] and lunatics. To put it bluntly—it was more open and exciting intellectually than most of the established, traditional fields."   21

Earning his doctorate in TV studies, Thompson founded the Center for the Study of Popular Television at Syracuse University. "I really want to do to TV what English professors did to novels," he says. "I want to engage our culture of choice, popular culture, television, with the same sincerity and seriousness."   22

At BGSU, there's a bulletin board near the pop culture mailboxes where secretaries tack up media requests for commentary. The department can't afford to return all the long-distance calls. Still, they pour in, highlighting the media's strange relationship with pop culture studies.   23

Journalists love having a bona fide professor lend guru-esque legitimacy to stories. Last year alone, Browne was quoted in the *Wall Street Journal* about shortening cycles of nostalgia and in the *Buffalo News* on criminality and pro athletes. In the *Los Angeles Times*, he discussed super-tiny   24

---

[6] **aficionados:** Enthusiastic fans.

cellular phones, and in the *Arizona Republic*, he dissected oversized restaurant servings.

But when pop culture studies is itself the subject, then the media invariably stress the supposedly oxymoronic clang of the professorial and the popular.

"Schlock Waves Felt across U.S. Campuses" went a typical *Dallas Morning News* headline (atop a *Washington Post* feature originally labeled "Pop Goes the Culture") about this year's meeting of the Popular Culture Association. The piece concludes: "They can't help themselves. After endless years in higher education, constantly trying to plumb meaning from turgid texts, they can't shut off when they hit the streets or turn on the tube."

In other words: Academics should stick to old, high-falutin'[7] stuff or the mostly incomprehensible warrens of advanced science. Leave the popular and contemporary to non-egghead journalists who presumably won't over-plumb.

Competitiveness aside, the media's knee-jerk knock on pop studies reflects a disconcerting reality. When the subjects are as opaque to the untutored as Milton or Dante, the average citizen has to assume that the academics are scoring fresh, brilliant points in their ivory tower[8] toils. But if the starting point is familiar, then folks can choose to see all the humanities as just a nutty game of intellectual free association.

Some articles in the *Journal of Popular Culture* are rich with insight. A recent piece on slam-dancing truly mines the subject, employing everything from Turner's social drama theory to field observation at nightclubs. It even traces the mosh pit's cultural appropriation by, of all places, Disney World. By contrast a piece in an earlier issue that asks, "If Aristotle were alive today, what books would he read, what television shows would he watch?" (Answers: Tony Hillerman and the defunct *Strange Luck*) just seems like cheesy dorm-room riffing.[9]

But whether or not pop culture scholarship is always profound and unique, the media's mockery merely regurgitates conventional wisdom. The *New York Times'* Russell Baker called Thompson's TV studies center at Syracuse "a vision of hell," insisting that TV is trash and that only time can reveal the useful material. Essentially, he implied that this is a supernatural, not an intellectual process: "Until the ages have spoken, [these shows] remain junk."

Despite such criticism from the popular press, these days it's tough to find purity in the opposing academic camps. Rebels like Browne and Marsden insist pop culture taught well must be historically and culturally comparative. And a traditionalist like Sanford Pinsker, Shadek Professor of Humanities at Franklin and Marshall College and journal editor of the *National Association of Scholars* ("dedicated to the restoration of intellectual substance"), teaches a course in American humor, drawing on magazine

[7] **high-falutin':** Thinking too highly of oneself; pretentious.
[8] **ivory tower:** Removed from practical things.
[9] **riffing:** Composing without preparation.

essays from Calvin Trillin and Garrison Keillor. Some might consider that pop studies.

Still, there are indelible differences. "You can find the heroic character- 32 istics of *Beowulf* in Batman comics," concedes Pinsker. "But the differences are what's important. The literary texture. The depth of vision."

Pop culture scholars would counter that the similarities really are 33 important in helping students make sense of daily life. As Marsden puts it, "Culture changes but it doesn't disappear. It's like energy that just seeks another form."

Both sides wheel out the big guns of economic loathing. Browne ar- 34 gues that academics have long traded in arcane knowledge that they have marketed as valuable. Pinsker sees pop culture as dumbing down curricula for mass markets: "Sheer economic facts have a lot more to do with this than Ray Browne ever did. What we need now in colleges are customers and what you do with customers is you make them happy: Here's a product you can sell."

Back at Bowling Green State, the Popular Culture Library reflects the 35 discipline's continued boom and maturation. "We're still taming the frontier here," says head librarian Alison Scott, riding herd on a half-million items that include "a comprehensive collection of not only Harlequin romances, but Silhouettes, Heart Songs, Zebras, Intrigues and Candle Lights."

But the library's hubcap collection has been dispatched to a car mu- 36 seum. The miniature liquor bottles? Also gone. "We didn't have the cars, or the liquor—or any useful information as to how to place them in a larger cultural context," says Scott.

And even as Scott gets invited to "speak on the question of comic 37 books in academic libraries, pulp magazines[10] in research libraries," by traditional librarians taking pop culture more seriously, she seeks to increase BGSU's 19th-century materials.

Scott sounds positively Pinsker-esque when she notes, "We have 38 young students who are just shocked when you infer that there was popular culture before they were born. And these kids were born in 1980."

EXERCISING VOCABULARY

1. Jacobson notes that Ray Browne might look more radical if he had "one of those Einstein quantum 'fros" (para. 1). What is a " 'fro"? Why would this indicate a radical person? Who is Albert Einstein?

2. The author uses the word *aesthetics* several times in this piece. What are aesthetics? What does Jack Santino mean when he says that Browne's popular culture program has a "socio-aesthetic approach" (para. 8)?

3. In paragraph 25, Jacobson refers to the "oxymoronic clang of the professorial and the popular." What is an oxymoron? How well does the term apply here? Why?

---

[10] **pulp magazines:** Magazines printed on poor quality paper.

PROBING CONTENT

1. What has been ironic about the career of Ray Browne? What is ironic about the man himself? How was his frequent incarceration in a U.S. Army stockade a foreshadowing of his life in academia?

2. Explain the odd relationship between the media and popular culture. In what way does this odd relationship benefit both?

3. What did critics cite as their objections to a conference on the history of roller coasters? Why might these same objections be leveled at all popular culture studies?

4. According to Robert Thompson, what's the attraction of studying popular culture? How did Thompson become involved?

CONSIDERING CRAFT

1. Jacobson includes a number of paradoxes in this essay. What is a paradox? Reread paragraphs 3, 9, and 19. How does illuminating these paradoxes further the author's point of view?

2. In paragraph 11, Jacobson refers to the popular culture studies program at Bowling Green as being "like an intellectual Christo project." Who is Christo? What kinds of projects does he do? Why does the author choose this simile? How effective is this word choice?

RESPONDING TO THE WRITER

Michael Marsden notes that "Culture changes but it doesn't disappear. It's like energy that just seeks another form" (para. 33). Do you agree? In what ways does popular culture simply change forms to adapt to a new time and generation? Give an example from your own lifetime of a cultural force that has changed form.

After the paired selections in each chapter, you will find "Drawing Connections" questions that ask you to compare and contrast how the authors of the paired selections explain their points of view on similar topics.

DRAWING CONNECTIONS

In "Pop Culture Studies Turns 25," David Jacobson quotes Sanford Pinsker who argues that the study of pop culture is "dumbing down curricula for mass markets" (para. 34). In "Schlock Waves Felt across U.S. Campuses," Eric L. Wee reveals that one attraction of pop culture studies is that such classes bring in students and thus bring in tuition money. Do you think economics is a driving factor behind the study of popular culture? If this is true, why is it significant?

You'll move through the process of prereading, reading, and postreading described above for each reading selection that your instructor assigns.

At the end of all the reading selections in a chapter are several additional features about that chapter's subject called "Wrapping Up." The first is called "Focusing on Yesterday, Focusing on Today." This feature shows you two images, such as a poster and a photograph. One image is an example of popular culture from the past; the other image is an example of contemporary popular culture. Both reflect some aspect of the chapter's subject. The accompanying questions will ask you to think and write about how these two images relate to one another.

Finally, at the end of each chapter are two types of writing suggestions for developing your own essays. Some of these writing prompts are called "Reflecting on the Writing." They ask you to link selections within the chapter just completed and also selections from various chapters within the text as you develop your essay response. The final set of writing suggestions is called "Connecting to the Culture." These writing prompts encourage you to use your own experiences and observations to express your ideas about some aspect of the chapter's topic.

Now it's time to apply the ideas you have been developing while you were reading and answering questions. It's time to write about all the things you have to say.

Writing with a Difference

Getting into Writing

Writing is often not easy. There are probably a few hundred people for whom writing is as easy as bicycling is for Lance Armstrong. For most of us, though, writing is hard work. Like accurate golf shots, good writing takes practice.

For some of us, the hardest part is just getting started. There is something about blank sheets of paper or computer screens that is downright intimidating. So the first and most important thing is to put something on that paper or screen. If it loosens up your writing hand to doodle in the margins first, then doodle. But eventually (and sometime before 3 a.m. the day the paper is due), it's a good idea to get moving in the right direction.

If your creative juices are a little slow to flow, try *brainstorming*. This simply means that you commit to paper whatever ideas related to your topic pop into your head. You don't evaluate them. You just get them down on paper. You don't organize them, reflect on them, or worry about spelling them correctly. You just write them down. There are several popular ways to brainstorm. Lots of people like to do *outlines*, with or without the proper Roman numerals. This method lets you list ideas vertically. Writers who think less in straight lines may want to try *clustering*, also called *webbing*. This is a lot like doodling with intent. Write your subject in the center of your blank page, and circle it. Draw lines radiating out from the center, and at the end of each line write some other words related to your subject. Each of these spokes can have words radiating from

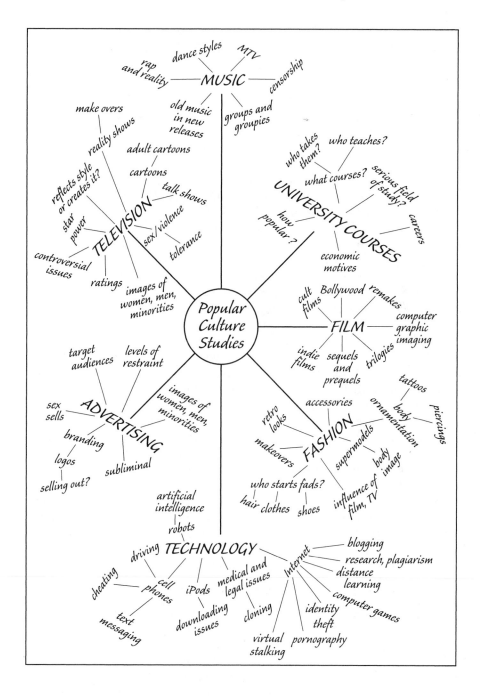

it, too. Let's return to our sample paired essays. If a student were brainstorming to write an essay about studying popular culture, one web might look like the one found on page 21.

Planning Purpose, Audience, and Attitude

Before trying to impose any kind of structure or judgment on her random bursts of thought, a good writer has to consider several important things: (1) Why am I writing this paper? (2) For whom am I writing this paper? (3) What is my own attitude about this subject, and how much do I want this attitude reflected in the tone of my paper?

Let's think about your purpose for writing a paper. You think, "I am writing this because I am in this composition class, and the professor said to write a paper." Okay, true, but there's more to purpose than that. Are you hoping to entertain your readers? Inform them? Persuade them to take some action or change an opinion? Your answers to these questions determine how you approach your subject and develop your paper.

Something else that determines how you approach your writing is the intended audience. Who are your readers? How old are they? What are their interests? What do they already know about your topic, and what will you need to explain? Why should this group of people care about your topic? What attitudes do they already hold about this issue? The language you choose is affected by the audience that you expect to reach. An essay about rap music that you are writing for your peers won't need all the explanations that the same essay would need if you were writing it for forty-year-olds.

Once you have determined your purpose and your audience, you are ready to determine the tone of your essay. What is your own attitude toward your subject? To what extent should your writing reflect this attitude to best achieve your purpose for the audience you have identified? Do you want to be completely serious about your subject? Will injecting some humor make your audience more receptive to your writing? How formal or informal should the language of the essay be?

Hooking the Reader

Once you have some ideas about why you are writing, who your audience is, and what your attitude about your subject is, the next step is to write a draft. How do you start? Some order has to be made of this potentially useful chaos. Good essays begin with good introductions, so we'll talk about that first. But remember: The introduction doesn't have to be written at this point. Some very good authors write the whole essay and then write the introduction last. That's fine. The introduction has to be at the beginning eventually, but no law says it has to be there in the draft. Too many good essays remain locked in the creators' heads because their writers can't think up an introduction and so never start at all.

At whatever point you are ready to write your introduction, keep in mind one essential thing: If you don't get your audience's attention right away, you lose them. Even though the students who are assigned to read your paper for peer editing will keep reading, and the professor who is paid to read it will do so, other readers need to be involved, or hooked, before they will be receptive to your viewpoint and your ideas. Advertisers figure they have only a precious few seconds to hook you as a potential customer, so they pull out all the stops to grab your attention before you flip that page in the magazine or punch that remote control. As a writer, you have to pull out all the stops to hook your readers. What really nails a reader's attention? This depends on the reader, but some tried and true methods work on many readers:

1. First, you might start with a very brief story, also called an *anecdote*. We all love human interest and personal narrative. Make your readers want more information, want answers, and feel curious about what else you'll say.

2. Interesting quotations make good openings, especially if they are startling or are attributed to someone famous. As quotations, though, dictionary definitions are rarely effective as introductions. Statistics can be useful if they are really amazing.

3. A thought-provoking or controversial question can be a good way to get a reader's attention.

Identifying a Thesis

Besides catching your reader's attention, your introduction may perform another important task: The introduction may house your *thesis statement*. This quick but thorough statement of the main point of the paper may be the first or last sentence of the first paragraph, but it could also be the last sentence of the essay. Where the thesis is located depends on your purpose for writing, your audience, and the effect you wish to create. If you begin with one of the three attention-getters we've mentioned, you'll want to follow up your brief narrative, quotation, or question with a few general statements about your topic, gradually narrowing the focus until you reach your specific thesis, possibly at the end of the first or second paragraph. If you have identified your audience as receptive to your attitude about your subject, then you may choose to state the thesis early in your paper and follow with supporting points that will have your readers nodding in agreement. However, if your purpose is to persuade an audience that is not so likeminded, then you will want to offer convincing proof first and present your thesis later in the paper when readers have already begun to agree with your opinion.

Wherever it occurs, a good thesis can go a long way toward making your essay effective. How do you recognize or create a good thesis statement? First, a good thesis is not simply a fact. Facts don't allow for a lot of fascinating development; they just are. A good thesis expresses the writer's point of view on a topic about which more than one valid opinion exists. Your thesis must be focused. Remember that there's a difference between a subject and a thesis. A subject or topic is what the essay is about—for example, Barbie dolls. A thesis statement expresses the author's attitude about that subject: "Barbie dolls are an expression of society's misguided and demoralizing view of ideal womanhood," or "Barbie dolls are a positive influence on young girls because they indicate the wide variety of career choices available to women today." Everything in your essay must clearly relate to the development of this thesis or main idea.

Supporting the Thesis

The development of your thesis forms the body of your paper. The major points you wish to make about your thesis become the *topic sentences,* or one-sentence summaries, for various paragraphs. What information do you use for support? Where do you find this information? How much support is enough, and how much is too much?

All the support that anyone can apply to any idea fits into one of two categories: The information is gathered either from personal experience or from a source outside the self. Personal experience knowledge is whatever the writer has gathered through eyewitness encounters in which he has participated directly and personally. Outside source knowledge explains how we know everything else we know. Such outside source knowledge is often informal. We know that it would be painful to fall down a flight of stairs even though we might never have had such an experience and never looked in a medical book to see which body parts would likely be damaged.

However, such outside source knowledge may also be formal and deliberately sought, as when we look up the salaries of professional athletes in *Sports Illustrated* or schedule an interview with the football coach to talk about whether college athletes should be paid. In your writing, you may find it helpful to refer to ideas expressed in the essays in this text. In any case, you must avoid intellectual theft, called plagiarism. Carefully cite the source of the material you are using and put quotation marks around any words taken directly from someone else, whether they are in written or oral form and whether they are expressed in a few words or a few sentences. You can acknowledge sources by using any one of several styles of documentation. Your instructor will let you know which system to use. In the appendix of this book, you'll find a section called "Evaluating Sources" that can help you determine the validity of sources and one way to document them correctly.

Organizing the Content

The best way to arrange supporting details for your thesis is the one that is best for your purpose and your audience. Some essays begin with a forceful point of support on the first page, and other essays start softly and work up to a big crescendo of convincing examples or argument near the end. You might try sketching out your pieces of support in various arrangements on a sheet of paper to see which order feels most comfortable. Rarely will only one arrangement work. You are looking for whatever organization best moves along your thesis and seems most natural to you.

Connecting the Pieces

The best supporting information in the world won't move your thesis forward if the parts of the paper aren't unified so that your reader can follow your train of thought. Think of the paragraphs of your essay as links in a chain: Each link must be equally strong, no link can be open-ended, and each one must be connected to the link above and the link below. Strong transitional words or phrases can smoothly carry the thesis idea and the reader from one topic sentence and one paragraph to the next one. One way to facilitate this transition process is to use words like *however, nevertheless, furthermore, consequently,* and *in addition.* Another effective transition is to identify a key word or brief phrase in the last sentence of a paragraph and then repeat that word or phrase in the first sentence of the next paragraph. Try to avoid overusing simple and obvious transitions like *first, next,* and *finally* because too many simple transitions may make your ideas seem simplistic.

Arriving at a Conclusion

Before you know it, you're ready to arrive at your conclusion. The most important rule about conclusions is to make sure there is one. Do not simply repeat something you have already said, which may lead your readers to believe that you don't respect their intelligence. But do remember that your reader best retains whatever she reads last. The conclusion is your chance to make sure the points you've raised really stick. Therefore, make sure that your main idea—your thesis—is central to your concluding paragraph. Look at how you stated the thesis earlier, and word it a little differently in your conclusion. Some of the same advice that we discussed about introductions applies here: End on a memorable note. Make your essay the one the instructor is still pondering on the ride home.

Titling the Paper and Other Final Steps

If you haven't titled your paper already, you'll want to add a title now. A good title is not just a statement of the subject. It sheds light on which aspects of the subject are covered and how the subject is approached. Like an introduction, a good title also catches a reader's interest. Titles usually are not complete sentences.

Take time to present your paper well. You've worked hard on the ideas. Don't minimize the effect with sloppy margins, inaccurate page numbers, and other unusual printer misdeeds. Remember that your peers and your instructor are evaluating what you have produced, not your intentions.

Revising the Paper

After all this work, surely the paper is ready for the instructor. Not yet. What you have now is a first draft—a fairly complete first draft, admittedly, but still a first draft. You may think it's only the not-so-good writers who go through numerous drafts, but you'd be wrong: Good writers write and rewrite and revise and rewrite. Grammar and spelling errors that seem unimportant by themselves may distract your reader from your carefully prepared chain of ideas. Thankfully, there is a logical pattern to the revising part of the writing process, too.

Start revising with the big things. It's tempting to spell check first because it's easy and concrete, but that's a mistake for two reasons: (1) Spell checking is editing, not revising, and (2) You may decide to delete two of the paragraphs you just spent time spell checking. Ask yourself some hard questions. Does each paragraph contribute to the development of your thesis? If you find a paragraph that doesn't fit under that thesis umbrella, you have only two options: Delete the paragraph, or rewrite the thesis statement to make it broad enough to accommodate the additional material. Are the degree of explanation and the level of language appropriate for your audience? Does each support paragraph carry its own weight, or do some of them seem skimpy and underdeveloped? Does your essay accomplish the purpose you established?

Read the last sentence of each paragraph and the first sentence of the next paragraph. Are your transitions smooth enough? Your reader should get a sense of moving up an escalator, not a sense of being bounced down a staircase, landing with a thud on each topic sentence.

Editing the Paper

Now you are ready to do some editing. Look at the sentences within each paragraph. Are fragments masquerading as sentences? This is a good time to find a quiet spot and read your essay aloud. Once two senses— sight and sound—are involved, you have twice as much opportunity to find something that's not right yet. It's fine to run the spell checker at this stage, but if your problem is with usage— like using *to* when you mean *too*—then the spell checker cannot help you. It's best to keep a dictionary ready and be your own spell checker. Keep a grammar handbook handy to consult when you are unsure about matters like usage, punctuation, and sentence structure. Remember that your instructor has office hours and that your college or university probably has a tutoring or writing center where you can get help with revising and editing.

Peer Editing

Once you have completed your own initial revising and editing, your instructor may suggest that your class practice peer editing. No matter how good a writer you are, having someone else take a fresh look at your writing can be beneficial. Here are some general suggestions for specific things to evaluate when you edit a classmate's paper:

1. Read the first paragraph and stop reading. How interested are you in continuing to read? What about the introduction grabs your attention? If you wouldn't be the least bit disappointed if someone took this paper away from you right now, your classmate needs a better introduction. What can you suggest?

2. Continue reading through the first page of the paper. First write down the essay's subject, and then write down the main idea. If you can't find the thesis, make a note of that. If you are unsure of the thesis, write down what you think it might be. Take a minute now to check with the author. If you have identified the thesis correctly, that's fine. If you have identified the wrong message as the thesis, help the author clarify the main idea before you continue reading.

3. Continue reading. Is support for the thesis adequate? Are the examples specific enough? Detailed enough? Frequent enough? If not, make some suggestions. Is the thesis supported to your satisfaction? Why or why not?

4. What is the writer's attitude toward his subject? To what extent is the tone appropriate for the audience? How does the tone advance the writer's purpose or detract from it? When are changes in tone used appropriately or inappropriately?

5. Are there adequate transitions between sentences and paragraphs? Remember, this should feel like a smooth escalator ride. What does the writer do to make sure ideas flow smoothly throughout the paper? Can you easily follow the forward progression of the author's train of thought? If not, suggest some possible revisions.

6. Complete your reading of the essay. What about the final paragraph makes you feel a sense of completion? Is the essay finished, or does it just stop? How effective is the conclusion? What is memorable about it? What would make it stronger?

7. Review the paper now for mistakes in spelling or usage. Make a note of repetitive mistakes and comment on any awkward points of grammar. Don't attempt to note each error. Be especially alert for the kinds of errors that disrupt the flow of a paper, like fragments, run-ons, comma splices, or sentences that don't make sense.

8. Return the paper to its author and discuss your notes. Leave your notes with the author so that he or she can use them in the final stages of revising and editing. Evaluate the input you have received

about your own paper. Resist the urge to be defensive. You are not obligated to make every change suggested, but you should honestly evaluate the comments and use those that seem justified to improve your work.

Gaining from the Effort

Writing is like almost anything else: The more you practice, the better you get. We've said the same thing about reading earlier: People who read often and actively read well. The same is true of writing. For some people, writing is fun. For other people, writing is anything but fun. In either case, good writing is hard work. But perhaps no other skill except speech says so much about you to others and has so much to do with how far and how fast you advance in your career. Writing is not just a college skill; writing is a life skill. Your willingness to better your writing ability is directly related to the impression you create, the salary you can expect to earn, and the level of advancement in life you can expect to attain.

Forget the five-paragraph boxes your writing may have been restricted to before now. Remember that formulas work well in math but cramp your style in writing. Swear off procrastination and karate chop writer's block. There are no topics in this text that you don't already know something about. You have significant things to say. Start writing them down.

A Sample Student Essay

Here is a draft of a student essay written in response to a writing prompt associated with the two sample essays in this chapter. Keep in mind that all the writing prompts can be approached from a number of different perspectives. This example reflects one student's decisions about purpose, audience, tone, and writing style.

CONNECTING TO THE CULTURE

Ray Browne asserts in "Pop Culture Studies Turns 25," "There's just as much glory and virtue in being a Madonna person as in being a Hemingway person." And Eric L. Wee comments that attendees at the Popular Culture Conference believe that "the study of popular culture . . . is the future." Write an essay in which you either support or argue against the study of popular culture as an academic pursuit. Be sure to include the reasons that popular culture study does or does not merit the time and effort of professors and students and how such study, whether undertaken or avoided, might impact a university education.

The Importance of Reflecting on Popular Culture

ANABEL F. HART

With millions of students enrolled in related classes, popular culture studies are just that--_popular_. Despite their success among members of my generation, such studies are still often thought of as unworthy of critical analysis in the classroom. In other words, many scholars would not see any value in comparing the public outrage that Janet Jackson's "wardrobe malfunction" triggered to the outrage that Michelangelo sparked by leaving his statue of David totally nude. Who knew in the 1950s that Elvis's controversial gyrating hips would start a movement that continues to this day, fifty years later? That is why popular culture studies are important. They allow students and professors to gain new perspective and to reflect on the society in which they live.

In "Schlock Waves Felt across U.S. Campuses," Eric L. Wee states, "There was a time when teaching Plato at Oxford was considered radical. English literature as a field of study was considered avant-garde on American campuses in the 19th century" (para. 7). Such a statement reveals how substantially times have changed and simultaneously demonstrates how every culture experiences its own shock waves of scandal and controversy. Plato stirred up his own controversy with his unorthodox teachings, yet his ideas and ethics withstood the test of time.

Here's a more popular example: When professors ponder cultural genius, the poetry and plays of William Shakespeare often surface. Like Plato, Shakespeare's works have been studied and interpreted worldwide for centuries, and Shakespeare's understanding of human character and his insight into the culture of his time have led to his wide-ranging appeal around the world. In addition, Shakespeare was knowledgeable about other areas of study. His allusions to the Bible, art, law, politics, sports, and history made him popular in his day among a wide cross-section of society. Despite Shakespeare's ability to perceive and explain such things, scholars believe that he was never professionally schooled in these subjects. Such talent makes this author an opportune historical figure to study. He is considered by many to be the greatest poet and dramatist in the history of the English language, and his astonishing popularity is reflected in classrooms around the world. Today, further testimony to Shakespeare's popularity, not only among students but also the general public, is reflected in the many modern dramatic and film adaptations of his works.

However, that does not mean that there aren't prodigious thinkers living today that students may find even more compelling and relevant to their own life experiences. Authors, directors, musicians, and even advertisers have something important to say. Take the novelist J. K. Rowling, for instance. She, like Shakespeare, has won the respect of the masses from Brazil to Japan with her best-selling series of books following the life of a troubled teenaged wizard, Harry Potter. In Rowling's early descriptions, Harry is an awkward boy, plagued by the memory of his troubled past. Throughout the texts, he faces difficulties that many readers, especially young ones, can relate to. In a way, this gives Rowling the advantage over Shakespeare. We students can more easily relate to this contemporary artist who is familiar with the society in which we live. I know I'm more comfortable discussing the virtue of humility in The Sorcerer's Stone than I am talking about either Platonic ideals or notions of familial love and justice in Shakespeare's King Lear.

In "Pop Culture Studies Turns 25," author David Jacobson questions those critics who "rip" popular culture scholars for daring to deemphasize "highbrow" works of art like Shakespeare's plays in favor of close analysis of "unworthy," lowbrow topics like video gaming. Even though such careful study might have once been reserved for authors like Plato and Shakespeare, Jacobson seems to agree with Dr. Ray Browne, the "godfather" of the pop culture studies movement, that "you can teach critical thinking and gain as good a liberal arts education using pop materials as with the old highbrow ones" (para. 10). The same people who disparage the study of "lowbrow subjects" like video games may be uncomfortable with professors who endorse the Harry Potter novels as meaningful literature. However, students today find Rowling's exploration of moral and ethical issues, rather than Shakespeare's, more relevant to their own lives.

Despite Eric L. Wee's concerns, popular culture studies do much more than "bring in bodies" and "tuition dollars" (para. 11). Analysis of the society in which we live will help students gain a better perspective and understanding of the world, resulting in a richer and more relevant educational experience. Is that not the human ideal? Scientists created the scientific method, a means of thinking that orbits around human discovery, in order to apply scientific thinking to everyday situations. Dr. Ray Browne insists that popular culture not be studied in a vacuum. Such an educational philosophy helps professors and students alike reach the goal of all successful teaching: to understand the world around us.

Popular culture studies do merit the time of both the teacher and the learner. By reflecting upon the ever-changing society around us, we not only gain a better understanding of cultural changes and of people's reactions to them, but ultimately a deeper understanding of ourselves. As Ray Browne says in "Pop Culture Studies Turns 25," "There is just as much glory and virtue in being a Madonna person as in being a Hemingway person. . . . If you want to study culture through Madonna, it seems to me that's a marvelous opportunity" (para. 10). It seems that way to me and to millions of other college students, as well.

CHAPTER 2

Deconstructing Media
Analyzing an Image

We are a visual culture. We see thousands of visual images every day, yet we pay attention to only a few of them. Vision is our primary way of receiving information from the world around us. There is so much to see that we filter out what we don't need or what doesn't grab our immediate attention. Movie posters try to convince us to see a summertime blockbuster, magazine ads try to lure us into buying a particular product, artists and photographers try to get us to feel a certain emotion, while billboards demand our attention no matter where we turn. All visual media compete to send us their messages. The choices we make and the things we buy, even how we perceive and value ourselves, are all affected by the images that are presented to us. You'll discover as you work through this book that American popular culture relies heavily on visual representation; even music is represented visually through the use of music videos. In this text you will see a number of the kinds of visual images you encounter every-day—advertisements, photographs, movie stills, comic strips, and cartoons. Learning to "read" these images and discovering what responses they are intended to provoke in us is an important part of understanding our culture.

The Message of Media

Let's picture an imaginary advertisement. The woman is beautiful and graceful. The man appears wealthy and sophisticated. The white sand beach is wide and private; the sparkling blue water is cool and clear; tropical sunshine bathes the scene. The car in the foreground is a gold-colored luxury convertible. But why aren't the car's tires getting mired in the sand? Why aren't the woman's white shoulders sunburning? In reality, these might be issues you or I would have to think about, but this ad has nothing to do with reality. This is advertising—that shadow world that separates us from our money by luring us into popular mythology.

What mythology? Here's how it goes: Unpopular? Popularity is as easy as changing the brand of jeans you wear. Unsuccessful? You must drive the wrong kind of car. Unattractive? Just wear a new shade of lipstick. Misunderstood? It's not your personality; it's your poor cellular service.

We are in general a well-educated society. Why, then, are we so easily misled? Why do we buy the myths that advertising sells? We buy—and buy and buy and buy—because we desperately want the myths of advertising to be true.

For some time now, our culture has been as visual as we are verbal. We absorb images faster than our brains can process data, but the images remain imprinted in our minds. All those images influence our thoughts and the decisions we make in ways we may never have considered. From the time that we begin to learn to read, we are encouraged to recognize the power of words—to interact with a text, to weigh it for prejudice, to appreciate it with discernment. But images are as powerful as words, and they communicate ideas and impressions that we, as thinking individuals, should *question*, just as we question what we are told or what we read. How can the same skills we use to read be applied to "reading" visual images like billboards, photographs, political cartoons, drawings, paintings, and images on television, movie, and computer screens?

Asking the Right Questions

Effectively deconstructing media images depends on taking those images apart and asking the right questions.

1. What do I see when I look at the image?

    How is color used?

    What is the significance of the layout?

    What are the relative sizes of the objects that compose the image?

2. What is the role of text (any language that accompanies the image)?
3. Where did I first see this image?
4. Who is the target audience?
5. What is the purpose of this image?
6. What is its message?

The easiest questions help solve the mystery of the more difficult ones, so let's think about the obvious. What is really there to be seen when you look at the photo, the ad, or the cartoon strip?

Taking the Image Apart

COLOR

Although the images you see in this textbook are reproduced in black and white, most of the media representations around you make careful use of color. When you encounter an image, is your eye drawn to a certain spot on a page by the strength of a color, by the contrast of colors, or by the absence of color? How is color being used to catch your eye and hold your focus on a certain part of the visual?

LAYOUT

Closely related to the use of color is the layout of objects on a page. What relationships are established by how close or how far apart objects or people are placed? What is your eye drawn to first because of its position? Sometimes the focal point will be right in the center of the ad or photo and therefore obvious to the viewer. At other times, the object the composer of the image most wants you to appreciate, the one that is central to the image's message, may be easily overlooked. Because English is read from top to bottom and left to right, we tend to look first to the upper left-hand corner of a page. That spot is often used to locate the composer's focal point. At other times the eye may come to rest at the bottom right-hand corner of a page. Look at the "Declaration of Independence" advertisement that opens Chapter 6 to see how this visual strategy works. Where is your eye drawn on the page?

SIZE

The relative size of the people and objects in an image may also help the designer communicate his or her message. A viewer's eye may be drawn to the largest object first, but that may not be where the message lies. To help you see how relative size of objects can communicate a strong message, look at the photograph titled "To Have and To Hold" in this chapter (p. 36).

TEXT

Deciding whether a visual image should be accompanied by text or written language is another significant consideration for the photographer, artist, or ad designer. Sometimes the image may be so powerful on its own that text would be an irritating distraction. Think about the photograph of the Marines raising the flag on Iwo Jima during World War II or the shot of the three firefighters raising the flag at Ground Zero in New York City after 9/11. These images speak for themselves. When text is included, other factors have to be examined. How much text is there? Where is it located? How big is the type size? Is more than one font used? Does the text actually deliver the message? Does it enhance the message? Is part of the text a familiar slogan associated with the product like Burger King's "Have it your way"? Is a well-known and easily recognized logo or symbol like the Nike Swoosh part of the text? All of these considerations hinge on the importance of the text to the overall message of the visual image.

LOCATION

To properly evaluate a visual image, the discerning viewer must know where the image appeared. Did you see this image on a billboard? On the side of a bus? In the pages of a magazine? Images in *Smithsonian* magazine will have a different purpose than those in *Maxim*. The location of a visual will help you determine the intended target audience.

TARGET AUDIENCE

For whom is this image intended? What are the characteristics of this target audience of viewers? What is the age range? What is their socioeconomic status? What work do they do? Where and how do they live? All this information must be taken into account by the photographer, artist, or designer if the image is to convey its intended message. For example, an ad for baby formula would most likely not hit its target audience if it were placed in *Rolling Stone*, and an ad for a jeweled navel ring in *House Beautiful* probably would not find a receptive audience.

PURPOSE

Every image has a purpose. If the image is an advertisement on a billboard, on a Web site, or in a magazine, the most obvious question to ask is "What is this ad for?" In today's ads, the answer isn't always readily apparent. The actual object being sold may be a tiny speck on the page or even completely absent. In the imaginary ad described earlier, the product might be the woman's alluring sundress, the man's starched khakis and sports shirt, or the convertible. Or maybe it's an ad for an exotic vacation spot. If the image is a photograph, its purpose may be to commemorate a special moment, object, or person or to illustrate an event or feeling. If the image is a cartoon, its purpose may be to entertain or to make a political or social statement through humor.

MESSAGE

"What is the purpose of this image?" may be the most obvious question to ask, but it isn't the most important one. The most important question is "What is the message of this image?" That's a very different question. This question challenges the viewer to probe beyond the obvious visual effects—color, shading, size of objects, text or lack thereof, relative placement of objects—to ferret out the message. This message always seeks to evoke a response from the viewer: Wear this, drink this, click here, think this way, feel this emotion, affirm this value. Using all the information you have assembled by answering the earlier questions, answer this one.

Now you are prepared to deconstruct or "read" the visual images that form such a large part of our popular culture.

Reading Visual Images

Let's practice with two different types of images: a photograph and a cartoon strip.

Look at the following image and consider some questions. What do you see in this photograph by Jean-Christian Bourcart? What event is being captured? What do the sizes and positions of the two figures indicate about their relationship? How many modern couples would find this pose an appealing one to place in their wedding albums?

How is color used?   You are seeing this photograph in black and white, but it's easy for your mind to fill in the color here—green grass and greener trees. Even in color, however, the two principal figures would be largely black and white. The white dress of the bride and the black formal wear on the groom let us know right away what event we are viewing. Here the lack of bright color works to emphasize the serious moment being captured on film.

To Have and To Hold

What is the significance of the layout?   Think about the layout and composition of this photograph. Why did Bourcart place the couple outdoors? Perhaps he used a natural setting to reinforce the notion that a wedding is a "natural" cultural ritual. Practically speaking, this shot would have been difficult to frame indoors; the relative depth perception of the two figures is what makes the composition unique.

What is the relative size of the objects that compose the image?   In this particular photo, relative size is the most important feature. Things are not equal. The groom is front and center, dominant, in control. The tiny, fragile doll bride held in his hand resembles the decorative figurine often found atop a wedding cake.

What is the role of text?   No text accompanied the original photograph. The original title in French was "Le Plus Beau Jour De La Vie," which means "the most beautiful day of one's life."

What was the original location of the image?   This photograph appeared in *Doubletake* magazine. Certainly the source is appropriate, since, after the first casual glance, the viewer's eye locks onto the two figures in their unusual pose.

Who is the target audience?   The target audience might include future brides and bridegrooms, anyone interested in photography, or an even wider group of people who are intrigued by the unusual ways that the eye conveys messages about the world and the culture around us.

What is the purpose of this image?   At first glance, this photograph may have been taken to capture an unusual image. Perhaps its intent is to preserve, in a whimsical way, one significant day in the life of a couple. Many families have albums full of wedding photos. But perhaps this photographer had something more serious in mind.

What is the message?   What is the photographer really trying to accomplish? Certainly he has chosen an off-balance approach to arrest our attention. But more is being said. Perhaps Bourcart wishes to tell us what he believes marriage offers young couples. Does he wish to make a statement about male-female relationships? On a day that seems perfect, is there an indication that life won't be "happily ever after" for this bride and groom?

Next let's work on deconstructing a very different type of visual representation, a comic strip (p. 38).

What do you see when you look at this image?   With a comic strip, the viewer's eyes must travel left to right across the panels, focusing on a number of frames, each of which may offer a visual, text, or both. Often

the strip's creator relies on a steady group of repeat readers who over time have learned to appreciate the personalities of the strip's characters and the subtle messages they deliver from the writer.

How is color used?   Although most strips appear in black and white in daily newspapers, many appear in color on Sundays, giving readers a chance to learn more about the characters and the strip's designer. This *Mallard Fillmore* strip appeared in a Sunday newspaper with minimal but effective colorization. Against a light blue background, the duck is green with a yellow bill, and the soda can is a lighter shade of green. We know it's a Sprite can because Mallard says so. The human finger is peach-colored.

What is the significance of the layout?   To some extent, the layout of a cartoon strip is prescribed: It is a series of panels. But the artist still has a great deal of flexibility with layout within the various panels. The most interesting feature in this layout is the shifting view we have of Mallard the duck. At first we see his face, but he turns to the side when addressed by the finger, and by the middle of the strip he has his back to us. We viewers are made to feel outside the conversation, as though we are merely eavesdropping. By the last two panels, Mallard has turned his face to the readers, making us a part of the scam he's pulling.

What is the relative size of objects that compose the image?   It's certainly no accident that the clearly recognizable "invisible finger of marketing" is as large as Mallard's head in every panel except the final one, when Mallard takes control of the situation. From time to time, as consumers we may feel "under the thumb" of advertising; this comic strip offers a graphic rendering of that concept.

What is the role of text?   As in many comic strips, the text here is crucial to the message. Generally, comic strips rely much more on text than ads or photographs do. The first significant language issue arises in the title of this strip. Mallard Fillmore's name is a play on the name of an American president, Millard Fillmore, whose term of office reflected his own rather lackluster personality. A mallard is actually one type of duck. We'll pursue the rest of the text when we examine the message of the strip.

What was the original location of this image?   This comic strip is syndicated and appears regularly in many newspapers across the country.

Who is the target audience?   The target audience of this comic strip is not children. Although the duck might catch their eye, the level of sophistication of the humor clearly places this strip beyond their understanding. And certainly a degree of sophistication is required to grasp the irony here. The reader needs to know something about popular culture: What's a Sprite? Nikes? Lugz? What's hip-hop? What's an icon? Knowing that the U.S. government at times pays farmers not to grow certain crops such as soybeans in order not to flood the market and drive prices down explains the fifth panel. Bruce Tinsley, the strip's writer, is not expecting everyone to agree with his opinion, but his target audience is every consumer who is subject to advertising's wiles.

What is the purpose of this image?   Because this is a cartoon strip, we expect it to be entertaining or humorous. To determine if that is its only purpose, let's think about the message.

What is the message?   So what is Tinsley trying to say? Here is an ordinary duck, who might as well be you the reader, attempting to drink a popular beverage with a powerful marketing firm behind it. According to the finger of advertising, the entire ad campaign designed to elevate Sprite to a new level of "cool" or popularity could be devastated if Sprite were to be associated with this quite ordinary duck. The duck, however, represents the consumer, and he's not as dumb as he looks. He asks to be paid not to harm Sprite's fledgling coolness: He wants to be paid not to drink it. But he plans to take the cash, succumb to the lure of advertising—and buy Nikes or Lugz. What a cycle! What a message! Manufacturers pay advertisers to manufacture an image for a product, and that image alone—not the product—often fuels our wants and loosens our wallets.

Writing about an Image

Using these same questions we have been asking, let's see what one student has to say about decoding a third kind of media, an advertisement.

Monumental Taste: Using Patriotism to Market Diet Coke

ROBERT E. ARTHUR

What do I see as I flip through a magazine and come across this advertisement? Mount Tastemore, South Dacola, a revamped version of Mount Rushmore, where the fathers of our nation's history--Washington, Jefferson, Roosevelt, and Lincoln--are all smiling back at me, seeming to be very pleased with the beverage they are holding. There are people lined up at the bottom, many dressed in our nation's colors of red, white, and blue, staring up and pointing excitedly at the iconic landmark. One man, dressed in a blue sweatshirt, is holding a can of the ever-wonderful diet Coke in one hand and pointing eagerly skyward with the other. I focus on the four presidents smiling out at me, all of whom seem to be offering me their diet Cokes. I see the advertisers' way of promoting the cola by revising one of our nation's most recognizable and sacred landmarks. My eyes then drift upward towards the title, "Monumental Taste," which provides a further explanation of the advertisement by its play on words. After being subconsciously persuaded by the ad's graphics, my attention shifts to the text underneath the visual, which reinforces the ad's message, "Mt. Tastemore, South Dacola--the most refreshing tourist attraction in America," and the play on words of the diet Coke logo, "Just for the monumental taste of it!" Finally, my eyes move to the order form for the Special Offer mentioned at the bottom of the page and the legalese that accompanies it. I've been hooked, and this is exactly what the advertisers want.

The advertisement's color scheme not only attracts the eye of the consumer, but also furthers the patriotic theme in the ad. The red in the soda cans, the clear blue sky above the presidents' heads, and the large white letters spelling out "Monumental Taste" above the landmark add to this red, white, and blue theme. Also, the adoring spectators lined up at the bottom, many sporting our nation's colors, seem entranced by the remarkable landmark. These colors were wisely chosen by the advertisement's designers. In the U.S. flag, white stands for purity while red signifies valor and hardiness (and coincidentally is used in many restaurants because it is an appetite stimulant). Finally, blue represents justice, perseverance, and vigilance. Why not showcase these meaningful patriotic colors when trying to sell "all-American" products like diet Coke? After all, few consumers who see this ad will remember that the U.S. government took possession of Mount Rushmore and the surrounding Black Hills region from the Sioux Indians in 1877, only three years after gold was discovered there. However, that isn't what the advertisers want the potential buyer to reflect on here.

While the colors of an advertisement are often responsible for its initial impact on the reader, the text provided with the visual plays a key role in the message to the consumer. The text, especially the title, "Monumental Taste," provides a better explanation of the ad, using an adjective with both literal and figurative meanings to get the point across in a humorous way. Viewers of all ages can easily recognize the double meaning of the phrase and also pick up on the opinion that not only is this soda's taste remarkable, it's good enough for Honest Abe and his peers, too. Of all of the inhabitants of Mount Tastemore, Lincoln is the only one holding a caffeine-<u>free</u> diet Coke, which is most likely a play on his monumental role in the freeing of thousands of African slaves. The can he is holding is also the only one boasting red, white, and blue lettering, thus furthering the patriotic theme throughout the advertisement. The ad's slogan, "Mt. Tastemore, South Dacola--the most refreshing tourist attraction in America," is another way humor is injected into the text of the advertisement, making it more appealing to those of us who enjoy tastefully humorous things.

In reality, the head of Washington stands as high as a five-story building (about 60 feet). This head would thus be fitting for a person about 465 feet tall. In the advertisement, both the title and the soda cans are much larger in scale than Mt. Tastemore itself. This sizing persuades the reader to focus her attention on these areas first. The twelve people staring up at the presidents are dwarfed by them but are still clearly visible. The text at the bottom of the visual is smaller than that in the title or on the diet Coke cans, but important parts of it are much bigger than that and thus more significant. For example, "Mt. Tastemore, South Dacola--the most refreshing tourist attraction in America," "diet Coke duffel," and "Just for the <u>monumental</u> taste of it!" are significantly larger than the surrounding text.

The purpose of creating such an advertisement is obvious--to persuade people to drink diet Coke. But by offering the duffel bag as an added incentive, the people who see the ad will not only buy diet Coke but will become living billboards for the product as they carry their diet Coke duffels around with them on their "tasteful" travels. These duffel bags, emblazoned with the huge red letters spelling out the product's name, are an excellent example of effective co-branding.

Advertisements don't need to say, "Buy this product, or you won't be cool." We do that for them. What if the paparazzi catch a celebrity strolling down Rodeo Drive with one of these "haute couture" duffel bags casually thrown over her shoulder? Presto! Fans will rush to order their own duffels, thus becoming walking billboards for the product just as the advertisers intended. For good measure, these consumers will be further influenced by the subliminal message delivered by the small "d" in the brand's name. They will believe that whoever drinks diet Coke will not only be cool, but thinner, too. So these proud duffel bag-toting Americans are not only patriotic but cool and thin as well. Soon, as more and more people proudly sport their diet Coke duffels while sipping their diet Cokes, advertisers will enlarge the promotional campaign to extol the soda's fabulous taste to consumers around the globe. Isn't it cool to look and buy "American" even if you don't live here? After all, if this "refreshing" and "monumental" drink is good enough for America's most beloved leaders, it should be good enough for those millions of global consumers who wish to "get a taste of" our popular culture.

You'll have a chance to practice your media-deconstructing skills throughout this text, from the images at the beginning of each chapter to paired images from the past and the present that bring each chapter to a close. Remember to ask yourself the questions we've identified. Look closely—and then look beyond what's on the page to see what's really being communicated.

Gearing Up to Read Images

Locate an ad, a photograph, or a cartoon strip that appeals to you. Write a brief paragraph stating your initial reaction to the image. Then decode the image by applying the questions identified throughout this chapter. How did your initial impressions change after a careful study of the image?

Collaborating

1. Locate a visual image that you think communicates a significant message, and bring it to class. Working with three or four other students, discuss the images you've each chosen, and determine which one is the most effective and why. Then plan and deliver a presentation to your classmates in which your group deconstructs the image you have selected.

2. Working in a small group, assemble a collection of various types of magazines such as music, home and garden, news, sports, and fashion.

Analyze the types of ads, photos, and other visuals you find to determine the target audiences. How do the target audiences differ? Evaluate the match between readers of each type of magazine and the products being advertised. Discuss why the advertisers you see chose to invest their marketing dollars in that particular type of magazine. Report your conclusions in a short paper, or present them orally to the rest of the class.

CHAPTER 3

Define "American"
Reflections on Cultural Identity

The stresses of a "melting pot" culture are clearly revealed in the cover photograph from this 1999 *National Geographic*. While the mother's traditional sari reflects her heritage, the daughter's sleek jumpsuit makes a bold statement about her own cultural affiliation. "Like Mother—Not Likely!"

• What does the women's clothing say about them and their cultural beliefs?

• How would you interpret the facial expressions in this photo?

• What does the mother's and daughter's body language reveal about them?

Research this topic with TopLinks at bedfordstmartins.com/toplinks.

GEARING UP

How would you define "American"? Think about the forces that have helped shape your sense of who you are as a person living in America today. Consider your gender, your sexual preference, your personal appearance, and your ethnicity. How have these forces influenced you? How has your definition of what it means to be an American changed since you were a child?

How do I look to other people? Do I fit in? Do I want to fit in? Will I find my own place in the culture I live in? What should I call myself? Just who am I?

These are questions that all people ask themselves at some time in their lives. Many factors affect people's self-image. One is biological: our gender, our sexual preference, and our physical appearance. The other is cultural and is composed of two segments: the culture of our ancestors and the larger contemporary culture that we participate in, better known as popular culture.

Cultural diversity has become a hot—and sometimes heated—topic in the United States. Should we learn about and celebrate the differences among people of different ethnicities and cultural heritages? Or should we deemphasize those differences and concentrate on the similarities among people? Many people reject the notion that the United States is a melting pot where everyone is simply an "American." Instead, they see America as a salad bowl containing a mix of ethnicities that complement one another and that deserve to maintain their cultural identities within the larger U.S. popular culture. But can too much attention be paid to cultural diversity? Does an appreciation of other ethnic groups unite or further divide us as a people? How do a person's gender and sexual preference enter into the cultural mix?

What happens to members of minority groups when the ideals of their own culture collide with those of the dominant American popular culture? The media are gradually presenting a more accurate reflection of the actual U.S. population, as witnessed by the increasing numbers of models and actors of varying ethnicities and sexual preferences. However, many Americans still feel separated from society's mainstream because they find it difficult to relate to the majority of people that stare out at them from the pages of glossy fashion magazines or from television or movie screens. Those Americans who do not resemble society's supposed role models or live the lifestyle that the media seem to privilege can feel rejected by the mainstream.

The writers in this chapter come from diverse cultural backgrounds and reflect a wide variety of lifestyles. As these authors detail their individual struggles with cultural self-image and awareness, they encourage you to examine the richness of our country's diversity. Reading these essays will help you to reflect on what goes into the continual reevaluation and reshaping of your own cultural identity as a man or woman living in the United States today.

COLLABORATING

In groups of four to six students, spend fifteen to twenty minutes discussing the major cultural influences on an individual's self-image as a child and as an adolescent. Consider such influences as ethnicity, gender, sexual preference, home life, peers, teachers, and the media. Make a list of the major influences, and then discuss them as a class.

They've Got to Be Carefully Taught

SUSAN BRADY KONIG

This essay is a mother's humorous account of Cultural Diversity Month at her daughter's preschool. Through humor, Susan Brady Konig ponders some very serious questions: Can too much emphasis on cultural diversity actually do more harm than good? Does it serve to confuse rather than to clarify, to separate rather than to unify?

Konig was born in Paris, France, in 1962, but was educated in the United States. An experienced journalist, Konig has been an editor for *Seventeen* magazine, has worked as a columnist for the *New York Post*, and has written articles for such wide ranging publications as the *Washington Post, Us, Travel & Leisure, Ladies' Home Journal*, and the *National Review*. She is currently a regular contributor to *National Review Online*. Her first book, *Why Animals Sleep So Close to the Road (and Other Lies I Tell My Children)*, was published in May 2005. "They've Got to Be Carefully Taught" originally appeared in the September 15, 1997, issue of the *National Review*.

THINKING AHEAD

Think back to your early school days. How was the issue of cultural diversity handled? What special occasions were celebrated to highlight diversity issues? How did these events affect your own cultural awareness?

INCREASING VOCABULARY

badgered (v.) (6)	culmination (n.) (21)
decidedly (adv.) (14)	disparity (n.) (21)
opted (v.) (20)	concerted (adj.) (24)

1   At my daughter's preschool it's time for all the children to learn that they are different from one another. Even though these kids are at that remarkable age when they are thoroughly color blind, their teachers are spending a month emphasizing race, color, and background. The little tots are being taught in no uncertain terms that their hair is different, their skin is different, and their parents come from different places. It's Cultural Diversity Month.

2   I hadn't really given much thought to the ethnic and national backgrounds of Sarah's classmates. I can guarantee that Sarah, being two and a half, gave the subject absolutely no thought. Her teachers, however, had apparently given it quite a lot of thought. They sent a letter asking each parent to contribute to the cultural-awareness effort by "providing any information and/or material regarding your family's cultural background.

For example: favorite recipe or song." All well and good, unless your culture isn't diverse enough.

The next day I take Sarah to school and her teacher, Miss Laura, anxious to get this Cultural Diversity show on the road, begins the interrogation. 3

"Where are you and your husband from?" she cheerily demands. 4

"We're Americans," I reply—less, I must confess, out of patriotism than from sheer lack of coffee. It was barely 9:00 a.m. 5

"Yes, of course, but where are you from?" I'm beginning to feel like a nightclub patron being badgered by a no-talent stand-up comic.[1] 6

"We're native New Yorkers." 7

"But where are your people from?" 8

"Well," I dive in with a sigh, "my family is originally Irish on both sides. My husband's father was from Czechoslovakia and his mother is from the Bronx, but her grandparents were from the Ukraine." 9

"Can you cook Irish?" 10

"I could bring in potatoes and beer for the whole class." 11

Miss Laura doesn't get it. 12

"Look," I say, "we're Americans. Our kids are Americans. We tell them about American history and George Washington and apple pie and all that stuff. If you want me to do something American, I can do that." 13

She is decidedly unexcited. 14

A few days later, she tells me that she was trying to explain to Sarah that her dad is from Ireland. 15

"Wrong," I say, "but go on." 16

"He's not from Ireland?" 17

"No," I sigh. "He's from Queens. I'm from Ireland. I mean I'm Irish—that is, my great-grandparents were. Don't get me wrong, I'm proud of my heritage—but that's entirely beside the point. I told you we tell Sarah she's American." 18

"Well, anyway," she smiles, "Sarah thinks her Daddy's from *Iceland!* Isn't that cute?" 19

Later in the month, Miss Laura admits that her class is not quite getting the whole skin-color thing. "I tried to show them how we all have different skin," she chuckled. Apparently, little Henry is the only one who successfully grasped the concept. He now runs around the classroom announcing to anyone who'll listen, "I'm white!" Miss Laura asked the children what color her own skin was. (She is a light-skinned Hispanic, which would make her skin color . . . what? Caramel? Mochaccino?[2]) The kids opted for purple or orange. "They looked at me like I was crazy!" Miss Laura said. I just smile. 20

The culmination of Cultural Diversity Month, the day when the parents come into class and join their children in a glorious celebration of multicultural disparity, has arrived. As I arrive I see a large collage on the wall 21

---

[1] **ESL** **stand-up comic:** A comedian who performs while standing on a stage.
[2] **mochaccino:** A frothy coffee beverage made from espresso, steamed milk, and chocolate syrup.

depicting the earth, with all the children's names placed next to the country they are from. Next to my daughter's name it says "Ireland." I politely remind Miss Laura that Sarah is, in fact, from America and suggest that, by insisting otherwise, she is confusing my daughter. She reluctantly changes Sarah's affiliation to USA. It will be the only one of its kind on the wall.

The mom from Brazil brings in a bunch of great music, and the whole class is doing the samba[3] and running around in a conga line.[4] It's very cute. Then I get up to teach the children an indigenous folk tune from the culture of Sarah's people, passed down through the generations from her grandparents to her parents and now to Sarah—a song called "Take Me Out to the Ballgame." First I explain to the kids that Sarah was born right here in New York—and that's in what country, Sarah? Sarah looks at me and says, "France." I look at Miss Laura, who just shrugs.   22

I stand there in my baseball cap and sing my song. The teacher tries to rush me off. I say, "Don't you want them to learn it?" They took long enough learning to samba! I am granted permission to sing it one more time. The kids join in on the "root, root, root" and the "1, 2, 3 strikes you're out," but they can see their teacher isn't enthusiastic.   23

So now these sweet, innocent babies who thought they were all the same are becoming culturally aware. Two little girls are touching each other's hair and saying, "Your hair is blonde, just like mine." Off to one side a little dark-haired girl stands alone, excluded. She looks confused as to what to do next. She knows she's not blonde. Sure, all children notice these things eventually, but, thanks to the concerted efforts of their teachers, these two- and three-year-olds are talking about things that separate rather than connect.   24

And Sarah only knows what she has been taught: Little Henry is white, her daddy's from Iceland, and New York's in France.   25

EXERCISING VOCABULARY

1. What does Konig mean when she describes the children in her daughter's class as "color blind" (para. 1)? How does this expression acquire additional meaning when used in the context of this essay?

2. What does Konig's description of Miss Laura's questions as an "interrogation" (para. 3) suggest about the writer's attitude toward the teacher? What kinds of situations or settings do you think of when you hear the word *interrogation*?

3. Why does the writer call "Take Me Out to the Ballgame" an "indigenous folk tune" (para. 22)? What does *indigenous* mean? What kinds of songs are usually referred to as indigenous folk tunes?

---

[3] **samba:** A Brazilian dance of African origin; also, the music for this dance.
[4] **conga line:** A Cuban dance of African origin performed by a group, usually in single file, involving three steps followed by a kick.

PROBING CONTENT

1. For what reasons does the writer disagree with Miss Laura's strategy? What does she think the students are learning as a result of their classroom activities on diversity?

2. The words *American* or *Americans* are repeated four times in paragraph 13. What does the writer mean when she says that her family is American? To what else besides the geographical location of their home is she referring?

3. Describe the effect of Cultural Diversity Month on the preschool students. From Konig's description, what do the children appear to learn? What positive lessons do they fail to learn?

CONSIDERING CRAFT

1. Find several examples of the writer's use of dialogue in this essay. How does the dialogue affect your attitude about the characters?

2. Describe the writer's tone in this essay. Why does she choose this tone? What kind of response is she hoping to get from the reader as a result?

3. In paragraph 21, the author refers to events at the preschool as "a glorious celebration of multicultural disparity." What word usually appears in place of *disparity*? Why does Konig change the word?

RESPONDING TO THE WRITER

Explain why you agree or disagree with Konig's idea that too much emphasis on cultural diversity may actually separate people of different ethnicities and cultures rather than bring them together.

For a quiz on this reading, go to bedfordstmartins.com/mirror.

I Want to Be Miss America

JULIA ALVAREZ

In "I Want to Be Miss America," Julia Alvarez examines an American tradition from an outsider's point of view. After moving to the United States from the Dominican Republic at the age of ten, Alvarez desperately wanted to belong. Watching the Miss America pageant for clues about how to look more "American," she and her sisters learned more than just how to "translate [their] looks into English." Coming from a culture where girls were expected only to grow up and become housewives, Alvarez learned that girls could excel in other areas: Miss America could be beautiful and succeed as a doctor, for example. Nevertheless, the pageant presented a limited vision of what was considered beautiful and made Alvarez feel insecure, as if she could never be a "Made-in-the-U.S.A. beauty" like the women on television.

A prolific writer, Alvarez has published sixteen books, including *How the Garcia Girls Lost Their Accents* (1991), winner of the PEN/Oakland Award, and *In the Time of the Butterflies* (1994), a National Book Critics Circle Finalist. *In the Time of the Butterflies* was made into a 2001 feature film produced by and starring Salma Hayek, with Marc Anthony and Edward James Olmos. Alvarez's *Before We Were Free* (2002) won the 2004 Pura Belpré Medal for narrative from the American Library Association. Other recent works, *In the Name of Salomé* (2000), *A Cafecito Story* (2001), and *How Tía Lola Came to Visit Stay* (2001), also won top book and media awards. Alvarez currently teaches creative writing at Middlebury College in Vermont. "I Want to Be Miss America" was first published in her collection of essays *Something to Declare* (1999).

THINKING AHEAD

Within every culture, there are some firmly held beliefs about what constitutes "beauty." How are these ideals a reflection of the values of the culture? When have you questioned any of the beauty ideals in your own culture? What caused you to begin to question them?

INCREASING VOCABULARY

acute (adj.) (5)	aspirations (n.) (18)
sallow (adj.) (9)	prodigies (n.) (19)
gawk (v.) (11)	sappy (adj.) (20)
sashayed (v.) (14)	diaphanous (adj.) (21)
inane (adj.) (18)	gratifying (adj.) (22)

As young teenagers in our new country, my three sisters and I searched for clues on how to look as if we belonged here. We collected magazines, studied our classmates and our new TV, which was where we discovered the Miss America contest.

Watching the pageant became an annual event in our family. Once a year, we all plopped down in our parents' bedroom, with Mami and Papi presiding from their bed. In our nightgowns, we watched the fifty young women who had the American look we longed for.

The beginning was always the best part—all fifty contestants came on for one and only one appearance. In alphabetical order, they stepped forward and enthusiastically introduced themselves by name and state. "Hi! I'm! Susie! Martin! Miss! Alaska!" Their voices rang with false cheer. You could hear, not far off, years of high-school cheerleading, pom-poms, bleachers full of moon-eyed boys, and moms on phones, signing them up for all manner of lessons and making dentist appointments.

There they stood, fifty puzzle pieces forming the pretty face of America, so we thought, though most of the color had been left out, except for one, or possibly two, light-skinned black girls. If there was a "Hispanic," she usually looked all-American, and only the last name, López or Rodríguez, often mispronounced, showed a trace of a great-great-grandfather with a dark, curled mustache and a sombrero charging the Alamo.[1] During the initial roll-call, what most amazed us was that some contestants were ever picked in the first place. There were homely girls with cross-eyed smiles or chipmunk cheeks. My mother would inevitably shake her head and say, "The truth is, these Americans believe in democracy—even in looks."

We were beginning to feel at home. Our acute homesickness had passed, and now we were like people recovered from a shipwreck, looking around at our new country, glad to be here. "I want to be in America," my mother hummed after we'd gone to see *West Side Story*,[2] and her four daughters chorused, "OK by me in America." We bought a house in Queens, New York, in a neighborhood that was mostly German and Irish, where we were the only "Hispanics." Actually, no one ever called us that. Our teachers and classmates at the local Catholic schools referred to us as "Porto Ricans" or "Spanish." No one knew where the Dominican Republic was on the map. "South of Florida," I explained, "in the same general vicinity as Bermuda and Jamaica." I could just as well have said west of Puerto Rico or east of Cuba or right next to Haiti, but I wanted us to sound like a vacation spot, not a Third World country, a place they would look down on.

Although we wanted to look like we belonged here, the four sisters, our looks didn't seem to fit in. We complained about how short we were,

---

[1] **ESL the Alamo:** Former Franciscan mission in San Antonio, Texas, where Texans lost a heroic battle in the Texas war of independence against Mexico.

[2] **ESL** *West Side Story*: Broadway musical (1957) and film (1961) that featured clashes between rival gangs in a modern-day Romeo and Juliet story.

about how our hair frizzed, how our figures didn't curve like those of the bathing beauties we'd seen on TV.

"The grass always grows on the other side of the fence," my mother   7
scolded. Her daughters looked fine just the way they were.

But how could we trust her opinion about what looked good when   8
she couldn't even get the sayings of our new country right? No, we knew better. We would have to translate our looks into English, iron and tweeze them out, straighten them, mold them into Made-in-the-U.S.A. beauty.

So we painstakingly rolled our long, curly hair round and round,   9
using our heads as giant rollers, ironing it until we had long, shining shanks, like our classmates and the contestants, only darker. Our skin was diagnosed by beauty consultants in department stores as sallow; we definitely needed a strong foundation to tone down that olive. We wore tights even in the summer to hide the legs Mami would not let us shave. We begged for permission, dreaming of the contestants' long, silky limbs. We were ten, fourteen, fifteen, and sixteen—merely children, Mami explained. We had long lives ahead of us in which to shave.

We defied her. Giggly and red-faced, we all pitched in to buy a big   10
tube of Nair[3] at the local drugstore. We acted as if we were purchasing contraceptives. That night we crowded into the bathroom, and I, the most courageous along these lines, offered one of my legs as a guinea pig. When it didn't become gangrenous or fall off as Mami had predicted, we creamed the other seven legs. We beamed at each other; we were one step closer to that runway, those flashing cameras, those oohs and ahhs from the audience.

Mami didn't even notice our Naired legs; she was too busy disapprov-   11
ing of the other changes. Our clothes, for one. "You're going to wear that in public!" She'd gawk, as if to say, What will the Americans think of us?

"This is what the Americans wear," we would argue back.   12

But the dresses we had picked out made us look cheap, she said, like   13
bad, fast girls—gringas without vergüenza, without shame. She preferred her choices: fuchsia skirts with matching vests, flowered dresses with bows at the neck or gathers where you wanted to look slim, everything bright and busy, like something someone might wear in a foreign country.

Our father didn't really notice our new look at all but, if called upon   14
to comment, would say absently that we looked beautiful. "Like Marilina Monroe." Still, during the pageant, he would offer insights into what he thought made a winner. "Personality, Mami," my father would say from his post at the head of the bed, "Personality is the key," though his favorite contestants, whom he always championed in the name of personality, tended to be the fuller girls with big breasts who gushed shamelessly at Bert Parks.[4] "Ay, Papi," we would groan, rolling our eyes at each other. Sometimes, as the girl sashayed back down the aisle, Papi would break out

---

[3] **ESL** **Nair:** A brand of hair-removal lotion.
[4] **ESL** **Bert Parks:** Long-time host of the Miss America Pageant.

in a little Dominican song that he sang whenever a girl had a lot of swing in her walk:

> Yo no tumbo caña,
> Que la tumba el viento,
> Que la tumba Dora
> Con su movimiento!

> ("I don't have to cut the cane,
> The wind knocks it down,
> The wind of Dora's movement
> As she walks downtown.")

My father would stop on a New York City street when a young woman swung by and sing this song out loud to the great embarrassment of his daughters. We were sure that one day when we weren't around to make him look like the respectable father of four girls, he would be arrested.   15

My mother never seemed to have a favorite contestant. She was an ex-beauty herself, and no one seemed to measure up to her high standards. She liked the good girls who had common sense and talked about their education and about how they owed everything to their mothers. "Tell that to my daughters," my mother would address the screen, as if none of us were there to hear her. If we challenged her — how exactly did we not appreciate her? — she'd maintain a wounded silence for the rest of the evening. Until the very end of the show, that is, when all our disagreements were forgotten and we waited anxiously to see which of the two finalists holding hands on that near-empty stage would be the next reigning queen of beauty. How can they hold hands? I always wondered. Don't they secretly wish the other person would, well, die?   16

My sisters and I always had plenty of commentary on all the contestants. We were hardly strangers to this ritual of picking the beauty. In our own family, we had a running competition as to who was the prettiest of the four girls. We coveted one another's best feature: the oldest's dark, almond-shaped eyes, the youngest's great mane of hair, the third oldest's height and figure. I didn't have a preferred feature, but I was often voted the cutest, though my oldest sister liked to remind me that I had the kind of looks that wouldn't age well. Although she was only eleven months older than I was, she seemed years older, ages wiser. She bragged about the new kind of math she was learning in high school, called algebra, which she said I would never be able to figure out. I believed her. Dumb and ex-cute, that's what I would grow up to be.   17

As for the prettiest Miss America, we sisters kept our choices secret until the very end. The range was limited — pretty white women who all really wanted to be wives and mothers. But even the small and inane set of options these girls represented seemed boundless compared with what we were used to. We were being groomed to go from being dutiful daughters to being dutiful wives with hymens intact. No stops along the way that   18 might endanger the latter; no careers, no colleges, no shared apartments with girlfriends, no boyfriends, no social lives. But the young women on-screen, who were being held up as models in this new country, were in college, or at least headed there. They wanted to do this, they were going to do that with their lives. Everything in our native culture had instructed us otherwise: girls were to have no aspirations beyond being good wives and mothers.

Sometimes there would even be a contestant headed for law school or   19 medical school. "I wouldn't mind having an office visit with her," my father would say, smirking. The women who caught my attention were the prodigies who bounded onstage and danced to tapes of themselves playing original compositions on the piano, always dressed in costumes they had sewn, with a backdrop of easels holding paintings they'd painted. "Overkill," my older sister insisted. But if one good thing came out of our watching this yearly parade of American beauties, it was that subtle permission we all felt as a family: a girl could excel outside the home and still be a winner.

Every year, the queen came down the runway in her long gown with a   20 sash like an old-world general's belt of ammunition. Down the walkway she paraded, smiling and waving while Bert sang his sappy song that made our eyes fill with tears. When she stopped at the very end of the stage and the camera zoomed in on her misty-eyed beauty and the credits began to appear on the screen, I always felt let down. I knew I would never be one of those girls, ever. It wasn't just the blond, blue-eyed looks or the beautiful, leggy figure. It was who she was—an American—and we were not. We were foreigners, dark-haired and dark-eyed with olive skin that could never, no matter the sun blocks or foundation makeup, be made into peaches and cream.[5]

Had we been able to see into the future, beyond our noses, which   21 we thought weren't the right shape; beyond our curly hair, which we wanted to be straight; and beyond the screen, which inspired us with a limited vision of what was considered beautiful in America, we would have been able to see the late sixties coming. Soon, ethnic looks would be in. Even Barbie, that quintessential white girl, would suddenly be available in different shades of skin color with bright, colorful outfits that looked like the ones Mami had picked out for us. Our classmates in college wore long braids like Native Americans and embroidered shawls and peasant blouses from South America, and long, diaphanous skirts and dangly earrings from India. They wanted to look exotic—they wanted to look like us.

We felt then a gratifying sense of inclusion, but it had unfortunately   22 come too late. We had already acquired the habit of doubting ourselves as well as the place we came from. To this day, after three decades of living in America, I feel like a stranger in what I now consider my own country.

---

[5] **ESL peaches and cream:** A complimentary description of Caucasian skin.

I am still that young teenager sitting in front of the black-and-white TV in my parents' bedroom, knowing in my bones I will never be the beauty queen. There she is, Miss America, but even in my up-to-date, enlightened dreams, she never wears my face.

EXERCISING VOCABULARY

1. Define *quintessential* and then explain why Alvarez calls Barbie "that quintessential white girl" (para. 21).

2. In her final sentence, why does Alvarez refer to her adult dreams as "enlightened"? How have her dreams changed since her childhood? How truly enlightened are her dreams?

PROBING CONTENT

1. How does the Miss America pageant that Alvarez watches support or deny her mother's assertion that "Americans believe in democracy — even in looks" (para. 4)?

2. When Alvarez explains where her family came from, what geographic reference points does she use to help friends locate the Dominican Republic? Why does she choose these landmarks instead of others?

3. Why don't the Alvarez girls trust the opinion of their mother about what looks good? Why is their father's opinion also suspect?

4. What hopes for the future were Julia Alvarez and her sisters expected to have? How were these expectations at odds with the plans of some of the Miss America contestants? How did this difference make the girls feel?

5. How did a change in the appearance of Barbie dolls mirror what Alvarez saw at college? How does Alvarez feel about this development?

CONSIDERING CRAFT

1. Why does Alvarez put an exclamation point after every word of the contestant's introduction in paragraph 3? What does this unusual punctuation achieve?

2. In paragraph 4, Alvarez writes, "There they stood, fifty puzzle pieces forming the pretty face of America...though most of the color had been left out." How does this figurative language reinforce the main idea of her essay?

3. Reread paragraph 13. Explain the irony in the last sentence. Why does Alvarez use irony here?

4. How does Alvarez's concluding paragraph differ in tone from the first paragraph of her essay? What message does this difference in tone convey to the reader?

RESPONDING TO THE WRITER

Do you identify with the strong need of Alvarez and her sisters "to look as if we belonged" (para. 1)? Why are some people so motivated not to express and celebrate their differences but to simply "fit in"?

For a quiz on these readings, go to bedfordstmartins.com/mirror.

There She Was

EXAMINING THE IMAGE

This photograph shows the contestants in the 1924 Miss America pageant. At that time, women represented their cities, not their states. Compare these contestants with those you have seen on television.

1. Are these early Miss America contestants representative of the American population as a whole? Why or why not?

2. How do the women in the photograph compare to today's contestants? How are they similar? How are they different?

3. What effect have women's changing roles in society had on these differences?

4. Would the Alvarez sisters find a role model among these young women? Why or why not?

Do I Look Like Public Enemy Number One?

LORRAINE ALI

"Do I Look Like Public Enemy Number One?" is Lorraine Ali's personal account of growing up Arabic in the United States and the prejudices she has faced while living an almost double life—as both an American and an Arab. In her teenage years, Ali realized that "an entire race of people was judged by its ~~terrorist~~ most violent individuals" and that she would be "identified as part of a culture that America loved to hate." As she recalls her struggle to appreciate her _background_ ethnic heritage, Ali raises some important questions: How can an American of a different ethnic background forge an identity between two cultures? How does prejudice caused by racial stereotypes affect a person's self-image?

Ali is a general editor and music critic at _Newsweek_, covering everything from Christian alternative rock to Latino Lone Star rap. She occasionally writes about Arab American culture and Middle Eastern affairs, including a unique experience she recently shared with her sister. Because she is the daughter of an Iraqi-born father, Ali voted in the Iraq elections of January 2005 from a southern California polling place. Named 1997's Music Journalist of the Year, Ali has been a senior critic for _Rolling Stone_ and a contributor to the _New York Times_, _GQ_, and VH-1's 2002 to 2003 series _One Hit Wonders_. Her music criticism appears in several books, including _Da Capo Best Music Writing 2001: The Year's Finest Writing on Rock, Pop, Jazz, Country, and More_ (2001), edited by Nick Hornby and Ben Schafer, and _Kill Your Idols: A New Generation of Rock Writers Reconsiders the Classics_ (2004), edited by Jim Derogatis and Carmél Carrillo. "Do I Look Like Public Enemy Number One?" was first published in _Mademoiselle_ in 1999. _(editors talk about everything with different cultures)_

THINKING AHEAD

Since the attack on America on September 11, 2001, Arab Americans have been under uncomfortable scrutiny and often unwarranted suspicion. Have terrorist actions by a radical few forever affected our ability to treat all people as the individuals they are? What repercussions will such a shift in thought have on the American way of life?

INCREASING VOCABULARY

stock (adj.) (1)
retort (n.) (2)
composite (n.) (2)
outmoded (adj.) (3)
pundit (n.) (3)

shoddy (adj.) (6)
mesmerized (v.) (7)
subversive (adj.) (7)
exacerbated (v.) (10)
pseudonyms (n.) (12)
forge (v.) (15)

"**Y**ou're not a terrorist, are you?" That was pretty much a stock   1
question I faced growing up. Classmates usually asked it after they
heard my last name: "Ali" sounded Arabic; therefore, I must be
some kind of bomb-lobbing religious fanatic with a grudge against Western society. It didn't matter that just before my Middle Eastern heritage
was revealed, my friend and I might have been discussing the merits of
rock versus disco, or the newest flavor of Bonne Bell Lip Smacker.[1]

I could never find the right retort; I either played along ("Yeah, and   2
I'm going to blow up the math building first") or laughed and shrugged it
off. How was I going to explain that my background meant far more than
buzz words like *fanatic* and *terrorist* could say? Back in the '70s and '80s,
all Americans knew of the Middle East came from television and newspapers. "Arab" meant a contemptible composite of images: angry Palestinian refugees, irate Iranian hostage-takers, extremist leaders like Libya's
Muammar al-Qaddafi or Iran's Ayatollah Khomeini, and long gas lines at
home. What my limited teenage vernacular couldn't express was that an
entire race of people was being judged by its most violent individuals.

Twenty years later, I'm still trying to explain. Not much has changed   3
in the '90s. In fact, now that Russia has been outmoded as Public Enemy
Number One, Arabs have been promoted into that position. Whenever a
disaster strikes without a clear cause, fingers point toward Islam. When an
explosion downed TWA Flight 800, pundits prematurely blamed "Arab
terrorists." Early coverage following the Oklahoma City bombing featured experts saying it "showed Middle Eastern traits." Over the next six
days there were 150 documented hate crimes against Arab Americans;
phone calls to radio talk shows demanded detainment and deportation of
Middle Easterners. Last fall, *The Siege* depicted Moslems terrorizing Manhattan, and TV's *Days of Our Lives* showed a female character being kid-
napped by an Arabian sultan, held hostage in a harem, and threatened
with death if she didn't learn how to belly dance properly. Whatever!

My Childhood Had Nothing to Do with Belly Dancing

Defending my ethnicity has always seemed ironic to me because I consider   4
myself a fake Arab. I am half of European ancestry and half Arab, and I
grew up in the suburban sprawl of Los Angeles' San Fernando Valley. My
skin is pale olive rather than smooth brown like my dad's, and my eyes
are green, not black like my sisters' (they got all the Arab genes). Even my
name, Lorraine Mahia Ali, saves all the Arab parts for last.

I also didn't grow up Moslem, like my dad, who emigrated from   5
Baghdad, Iraq's capital, in 1956. In the old country he wore a galabiya (or
robe), didn't eat pork, and prayed toward Mecca five times a day. To me,
an American girl who wore short-shorts, ate Pop Rocks,[2] and listened to

---

[1] **ESL** **Bonne Bell Lip Smacker:** A brand of flavored lip gloss.
[2] **Pop Rocks:** A type of fizzy candy popular in the 1970s.

Van Halen,[3] his former life sounded like a fairy tale. The Baghdad of his childhood was an ancient city where he and his brothers swam in the Tigris River, where he did accounting on an abacus[4] in his father's tea shop, where his mother blamed his sister's polio on a neighbor's evil eye, where his entire neighborhood watched Flash Gordon[5] movies projected on the side of a bakery wall.

a way for making calculations

My father's world only started to seem real to me when I visited Iraq the summer after fifth grade and stayed in his family's small stucco house. I remember feeling both completely at home and totally foreign. My sister Lela and I spoke to amused neighbors in shoddy sign language, sat cross-legged on the floor in our Mickey Mouse T-shirts, rolling cigarettes to sell at market for my arthritic Bedouin[6] grandma, and sang silly songs in pidgin[7] Arabic with my Uncle Brahim. Afterward, I wrote a back-to-school essay in which I referred to my grandparents as Hajia and Haja Hassan, thinking their names were the Arab equivalent of Mary Ellen and Billy Bob. "You're such a dumb-ass," said Lela. "It just means grandma and grandpa." But she was wrong too. It actually meant they had completed their Haj duty—a religious journey to Mecca in Saudi Arabia that millions of Muslims embark on each year.

poor quality

At home, my American side continued to be shamefully ignorant of all things Arab, but my Arab side began to notice some pretty hideous stereotypes. Saturday-morning cartoons depicted Arabs as ruthless, bumbling, and hygienically challenged. I'd glimpse grotesque illustrations of Arab leaders in my dad's paper. At the mall with my mom, we'd pass such joke items as an Arab face on a bull's-eye. She tried to explain to me that things weren't always this way, that there was a time when Americans were mesmerized by Arabia and Omar Sharif[8] made women swoon. A time when a WASP[9] girl like my mom, raised in a conservative, middle-class family, could be considered romantic and daring, not subversive, for dating my dad. In effect, my mom belonged to the last generation to think sheiks were chic.

keeping traditional values

tribe

Not so in my generation. My mother tells me that when my oldest sister was five, she said to a playmate that her dad "was an Arab, but not a bad one." In elementary school, we forced smiles through taunts like, "Hey, Ali, where's your oilcan?" Teachers were even more hurtful: During roll call on her first day of junior high, Lela was made to sit through a twenty-minute lecture about the bloodshed and barbarism of Arabs toward Israel and the world. As far as I knew, Lela had never shed anyone's

---

[3] **ESL** **Van Halen:** A rock musical group first popular in the 1980s.
[4] **abacus:** An ancient device for calculating numbers.
[5] **ESL** **Flash Gordon:** The hero of a comic book series that originated in 1934 about a space traveler battling evildoers.
[6] **Bedouin:** A tent dweller of the desert; a wanderer.
[7] **pidgin:** A simplified form of a language.
[8] **ESL** **Omar Sharif:** An Egyptian actor best known for his charismatic performances in the films *Lawrence of Arabia* and *Doctor Zhivago*.
[9] **ESL** **WASP:** Slang term for white Anglo-Saxon Protestant.

blood except for mine, when she punched me in the nose over a pack of Pixie Sticks.[10] But that didn't matter. As Arabs, we were guilty by association, even at the age of twelve.

By High School, I Was Beginning to Believe the Hype

It's awful to admit, but I was sometimes embarrassed by my dad.   9

I know it's every teen's job to think her parents are the most shameful   10
creatures to walk the planet, but this basic need to reject him was exacerbated by the horrible images of Arabs around me. When he drove me to school, my dad would pop in a cassette of Quran suras (recorded prayers) and recite the lines in a language I didn't understand, yet somehow the twisting, weaving words sounded as natural as the whoosh of the Santa Ana winds through the dusty hills where we lived. His brown hands would rise off the steering wheel at high points of the prayer, the sun illuminating the big white moons of his fingernails. The mass of voices on tape would swell up and answer the Mezzuin[11] like a gospel congregation responding to a preacher. It was beautiful, but I still made my dad turn it down as we approached my school. I knew I'd be identified as part of a culture that America loved to hate.

My dad must have felt this, too. He spoke his native tongue only in   11
the company of Arabic friends and never taught my sisters or me the language, something he would regret until the day he died. His background was a mystery to me. I'd pester him for answers: "Do you dream in English or Arabic?" I'd ask, while he was busy doing dad work like fixing someone's busted Schwinn[12] or putting up Christmas lights. "Oh, I don't know," he'd answer playfully. "In dreams, I can't tell the difference."

Outside the safety of our home, he could. He wanted respect; there-   12
fore, he felt he must act American. Though he truly loved listening to Roberta Flack[13] and wearing Adidas sweatsuits, I can't imagine he enjoyed making dinner reservations under pseudonyms like Mr. Allen. He knew that as Mr. Ali, he might never get a table.

Desert Storm Warning

Fifteen years later, "Ali" was still not a well-received name. We were at   13
war with the Middle East. It was January 16, 1991, and Iraq's Saddam Hussein had just invaded Kuwait. I will never forget the night CNN's Bernard Shaw lay terrified on the floor of his Baghdad hotel as a cameraman shot footage of the brand-new war outside his window. I was twenty-six and working for a glossy music magazine called *Creem*. When the news broke that we were bombing Baghdad in an operation called Desert Storm, I went home early and sat helpless in my Hollywood apartment,

[10] **Pixie Sticks:** A type of powdered candy that comes in a paper straw.
[11] **Mezzuin:** An Islamic cantor who sings to lead worshipers in prayer.
[12] **ESL Schwinn:** A popular bicycle manufacturer.
[13] **ESL Roberta Flack:** A jazz and pop singer who first gained popularity in the early 1970s.

crying. Before me on the TV was a man dressed in a galabiya, just like the kind my dad used to wear around the house, aiming an ancient-looking gun turret toward our space-age planes in the sky. He looked terrified, too. With every missile we fired, I watched the Baghdad I knew slip away and wondered just who was being hit. Was it Aunt Niama? My cousin Afrah?

Back at work, I had to put up with "funny" faxes of camels, SCUD missiles, and dead Arabs. To my colleagues, the Arabs I loved and respected were now simply targets. Outside the office, there was a virtual free-for-all of racist slogans. Arab-hating sentiment came out on bumper stickers like "Kick Their Ass and Take Their Gas." Military footage even documented our pilots joking as they bombed around fleeing civilians. They called it a turkey shoot. A turkey shoot? Those were people. 14

Arabs bleed and perish just like Americans. I know, because two years before we started dropping bombs on Baghdad, I watched my father die. He did not dissolve like a cartoon character, nor defy death like a Hollywood villain. Instead, chemotherapy shrunk his 180-pound body down to 120, turned his beautiful skin from brown to ashen beige, and rendered his opalescent[14] white fingernails a dull shade of gray. When he finally let go, I thought he took all the secrets of my Arabness with him, all the good things America didn't want me to know. But I look in the mirror and see my father's wide nose on my face and Hajia's think lines forming between my brows. I also see my mom's fair skin, and her mother's high cheekbones. I realize it's my responsibility to somehow forge an identity between dueling cultures, to focus on the humanity, not the terror, that bridges both worlds. 15

> Thesis

EXERCISING VOCABULARY

1. In paragraph 2, the author regrets "what my limited teenage vernacular couldn't express." What does *vernacular* mean? What is the purpose of a group having its own vernacular?

2. What does it mean to possess and to give the "evil eye"? How does Ali's inclusion of this phrase in paragraph 5 contribute to your understanding of the gap between her life and the early life of her father?

3. Ali states that "now that Russia has been outmoded as Public Enemy Number One, Arabs have been promoted into that position" (para. 3). What is ironic about her use of the word *promoted* in this context?

PROBING CONTENT

1. In Ali's opinion, how did television enhance the image of the "bad Arab"?

2. What elementary school experience stimulated Ali's awareness of her family's cultural heritage? How did that experience color her everyday thinking?

---

[14] **opalescent:** Reflecting an iridescent light.

3. What examples does the author provide to show how carefully she and her family tried to keep their two cultures from clashing?

CONSIDERING CRAFT

1. In paragraph 5, what strong images does Ali choose to represent her American childhood? What images represent her father's childhood? How does her inclusion of these images convey the gap between her father's culture and the one in which she was raised?

2. How does Ali use her personal experience to make a broad statement about how people of one culture relate to those from a different background? How effective is this writing strategy?

RESPONDING TO THE WRITER

Explain how Ali's phrase "dueling cultures" (para. 15) has taken on a very different meaning since this essay was first published in 1999. In light of recent events, what would you say to Ali about her effort "to focus on the humanity, not the terror" (para. 15) that bridges Middle Eastern and American culture?

For a quiz on this reading, go to bedfordstmartins.com/mirror.

Wilma Mankiller

ANDREW NELSON

Where do leaders come from? Why do hardship and oppression silence some but awaken others? Is the name Mankiller an asset or hindrance for a feminist leader? In "Wilma Mankiller," published in *Salon.com* on November 20, 2001, Andrew Nelson traces the inspiring journey of Wilma Mankiller from her hard-scrabble childhood in rural Oklahoma, to a bourgeois existence as a San Francisco housewife and mother, to her ultimate role as the first female chief of the Cherokee Nation. Mankiller didn't feel the stirrings of social empowerment until her mid-twenties, when in November 1969, Native Americans — later joined by TV news crews, politicians, and movie stars like Jane Fonda and Candice Bergen — "occupied" Alcatraz Island in the San Francisco Bay. For nineteen months, they protested its sale to a commercial developer. Decades later, as chief of her nation, she championed education and health care, even while battling gender chauvinism among her own tribe.

Andrew Nelson is a writer and award-winning multimedia producer who lives in San Francisco. His writing has appeared in *Salon.com*, *National Geographic*, *VIA*, and *San Francisco Magazine*, and he won a 1987 Young Journalists Award from *Rolling Stone*. A former senior producer at *Britannica.com*, Nelson's multimedia work has won many awards, including Macintosh Game of the Year for his best-selling 1998 computer game *Titanic: Adventure Out of Time*.

THINKING AHEAD

How much do you know about Native American culture in America today? Where have you gained this knowledge? How much of it is accurate? What stereotypes remain concerning Native Americans?

INCREASING VOCABULARY

infrastructure (n.) (3)	buffetted (v.) (8)
tenure (n.) (3)	refuge (n.) (9)
patronizing (adj.) (4)	tedious (adj.) (13)
misguided (adj.) (7)	replete (adj.) (13)
diffuse (v.) (7)	formidable (adj.) (23)

S an Francisco transformed many people living there during the 1960s. Its shabby, lunch-pail-toting neighborhoods became crucibles for a society recasting its values. The fire eventually caught a shy housewife and mother in her 20s named Mrs. Hugo Olaya and alchemized her into Wilma Pearl Mankiller, a symbol of both feminism and Native American self-determination.

In 1985 Mankiller, now 57, became the first female chief of the Chero- 2
kee Nation, the 220,000-member Native American tribe based in Tahlequah,
Okla., to which she belongs. She did it not only by overcoming the usual bar-
riers set against Native Americans, but also by vaulting the chauvinistic hurdles imposed by her fellow Cherokees, who had never been led by a woman.

Once chief, Mankiller took the traditional "women's issues" of educa- 3
tion and health care and made them tribal priorities. She raised $20 mil-
lion to build a much-needed infrastructure for schools and other projects,
including an $8 million job-training center. The largest Cherokee health
clinic was started under her tenure in Stilwell, Okla., and is now named in
her honor. Mankiller also sought to reunite the Eastern Cherokee, a group
based in North Carolina, with the larger Western division.

She ruled with grace and humor—she often teased patronizing Anglos 4
by telling them her surname was due to her reputation; in fact, "Mankiller"
is a Cherokee military term for a village protector—and with organizational
smarts learned in the blue-collar neighborhoods of clapboard and "ethnic
politics" that circled San Francisco Bay.

Her journey—from complacency to activism to political power— 5
followed a familiar boomer[1] flight path, but hers was a working woman's
ascendancy. It was born in the rural grit[2] of Adair County, Okla., and the
tough industrial neighborhood of San Francisco's Hunters Point. Elite,
tree-shaded suburbs like Pasadena or Grosse Pointe that shaped so many
'60s radicals couldn't have been more remote to Mankiller.

Mankiller grew up on her father Charley's ancestral Oklahoma lands. 6
"Dirt poor" was how she described her early life. The Mankillers frequently ate suppers of squirrel and other game. The house had no electric-
ity. Her parents used coal oil for illumination.

In 1956 Charley Mankiller, eager to provide a better life for his grow- 7
ing family, moved them from Oklahoma to California as part of a Bureau
of Indian Affairs (BIA) program, initiated by the same bureaucrats who
had "relocated" Japanese-Americans during World War II. The program,
a misguided experiment in social engineering, transplanted rural Native
Americans to jobs in industrial cities, thus serving to weaken reservation
ties and diffuse the little political clout the tribes held. It was another insult in a history of them stretching back two centuries.

In 1838 the Cherokee Nation was ripped from its ancestral homelands 8
in the Carolinas, Tennessee and Georgia by U.S. Army troops acting under
orders from the federal government. The forced march to the Oklahoma
reservations, the famous "Trail of Tears," killed thousands of men, women
and children. Buffeted by white assaults—both physical and legal—the
Cherokees would spend more than 100 years as wards of the state. It wasn't
until 1970 that Washington allowed the tribe to elect its leaders directly.

---

[1] **ESL boomer:** Shortened form of *baby boomer*, referring to a person born during an increase in population, especially the one following World War II.
[2] **ESL grit:** Toughness; determination.

Wilma was 11 when the Mankillers arrived in San Francisco. Charley   9
found work as a rope maker and the family settled down. Wilma had a difficult transition. She and her siblings were the proverbial hicks[3] in the big
city. A kindly Mexican family showed them how to work a telephone and
taught Wilma to roller skate. Charley Mankiller had instilled in his children a pride in their heritage, and San Francisco's Indian Center, located in
the Mission District, fostered it. The center became Wilma's after-school
refuge. The city's diversity exposed her to other things. In high school,
African-American girlfriends influenced Mankiller's taste in popular culture. While white girls swooned over Fabian[4] and Elvis, Mankiller absorbed Etta James[5] and B. B. King.[6] Life in a poor black neighborhood,
Mankiller told a Sweet Briar College audience in 1993, taught her other
valuable lessons.

"What I learned from my experience in living in a community of al-   10
most all African-American people," she said, "is that poor people have a
much, much greater capacity for solving their own problems than most
people give them credit for."

Mankiller exhibited no appetite for intellectual ambition as a   11
teenager. In her 1993 autobiography, *Mankiller: A Chief and Her People*,
co-written with Michael Wallis, she recalled hating the classroom. When
she graduated from high school in June 1963, she expected that to be the
end of formal schooling.

"There were never plans for me to go to college," she said. "That   12
thought never even entered my head."

Instead, a tedious pink-collar job followed graduation, as did a fast   13
courtship and marriage to a handsome Ecuadorean college student, Hugo
Olaya, with whom Mankiller had two children. Olaya's family was middle-
class; his prospects were good. At 17 the pretty girl, whose dark, flashing
eyes gave her a resemblance to actress Natalie Wood, settled down to live
the life of a California hausfrau[7] — replete with psychedelic pantsuits, baby
strollers and European vacations.

The social protests of the '60s didn't touch Mankiller directly until the   14
decade's last days. On Nov. 9, 1969, 19 Native Americans made their way
out to Alcatraz Island, the abandoned federal prison in the middle of San
Francisco Bay. The hunk of sandstone, in full view of San Francisco's corporate skyline, was supposed to be handed over to Texas oil tycoon Lamar
Hunt and turned into a futuristic shopping mall and revolving restaurant.
Instead, the 19 Native Americans claimed the island "in the name of Indians
of All Tribes," transforming it into a symbol of Native American liberation.

Led by Mohawk tribesman Richard Oakes and Adam Nordwell, a   15
Minnesota Chippewa, the protesters carried what they considered a fair

[3] **ESL hicks:** Derogatory term for unsophisticated and uncultured rural or small-town people.
[4] **Fabian:** Fabian Forte, popular late 1950s and early 1960s American singer.
[5] **Etta James:** Blues singer popular from the 1960s through today.
[6] **ESL B. B. King:** Contemporary blues guitarist.
[7] **hausfrau:** German for Housewife.

price for the island: $24 worth of glass beads and red cloth. The beads and cloth were comparable to the ones the Europeans had used to buy Manhattan, but the federal government declined their offer. Coast Guard patrols escorted the protesters back to the mainland.

On Nov. 20 the protesters, now numbering 89, returned for another oc-   16
cupation of the island. This time they stayed 19 months. The rebellion soon bore all the trappings of a media circus. TV news crews hired speedboats to get close to the action, while tourists snapped photos from tour liners. Politicians dropped by. Jane Fonda and Anthony Quinn vowed solidarity. Candice Bergen showed up with a sleeping bag and crashed on the floor.

Mankiller didn't come to Alcatraz in those first two waves, and her   17
siblings Richard, James and Vanessa got there ahead of her. She had stayed in the background, but when she finally arrived, Alcatraz became a pivotal point in her life. While she had been conscious of Native American issues before that time, these protests "flashed like bright comets."

"Every day that passed seemed to give me more self-respect and sense   18
of pride," she wrote.

Pop culture discovered Native American issues around then, too, and   19
glommed onto Red Pride. Dustin Hoffman played the Cheyenne-raised hero in Arthur Penn's film *Little Big Man*, released in 1970. Soon after, Cherokee injustices made the Top 40 with the Paul Revere and the Raiders' hit "Indian Reservation." Meanwhile, Mankiller found herself spending time at the Indian Center helping with fundraising and organizational efforts. She became acting director of East Oakland's Native American Youth Center.

Soon Mankiller's expanding idea of herself (she was now taking college   20
classes in social work) clashed with the more traditional family her husband envisioned. He forbade her to buy a car; she got a little red Mazda with a stick shift and drove to tribal meetings all over the West Coast. Mankiller's favorite song now, and the one she liked to dance to with her daughters, was Aretha Franklin's "Respect."

She and Olaya divorced in 1974. Mankiller found a job as an Oak-   21
land social worker. When she decided to return to Oklahoma with her daughters, she left California in a U-Haul with $20 in her pocket.

"I came home in 1976," she says. "I had no job, very little money, no   22
car, had no idea what I was going to do, but knew it was time to go home."

Mankiller soon found a position as a community coordinator in the   23
Cherokee tribal headquarters. The tribe was beginning to operate with less dependence on the BIA. Reforming the BIA, observed one Creek chief, was like rotating four bald tires on a car: Nothing changed. There were others ways to wrest money from the government. Mankiller, now finishing her degree at the University of Arkansas, became adept in the art of organizing as well as grant and proposal writing. She was proving to be a formidable leader.

In 1979 a head-on car crash seriously injured Mankiller and killed the   24
other driver. By awful coincidence that driver was Sherry Morris, one of

Mankiller's best friends. Mankiller spent the next year in rehab wracked with physical pain and guilt. Then, in November 1980, she was diagnosed with the neuromuscular disease myasthenia gravis. An operation to remove her thymus[8] cured her of the illness and she returned to her job in January 1981 to supervise the rejuvenation of the Cherokee town of Bell, Okla. The job involved urban planning and constructing a 16-mile water pipeline, and Mankiller excelled at it. She also met her second husband, Charlie Soap. They married in 1986.

Just three years before, ruling Cherokee Chief Ross Swimmer had asked Mankiller to run as his deputy in the next tribal election. After much debate she accepted and was promptly criticized—not for her liberal Democratic politics but for her gender. Mankiller described herself as "stunned" by the hostility. Charley Mankiller's daughter toughened her hide. 25

"I expected my politics to be the issue," she said later. "They weren't. The issue was my being a woman, and I wouldn't have it. I simply told myself that it was a foolish issue, and I wouldn't argue with a fool." 26

Swimmer and Mankiller won the election. Ironically, it was Ronald Reagan, whose policies Mankiller opposed, who gave her the opportunity to become Cherokee chief when he appointed Swimmer head of the BIA in September 1985. Succeeding him, Mankiller served as chief for the next 10 years—winning her second term with 82 percent of the vote. 27

As chief, Mankiller oversaw a historic self-determination agreement, making the Cherokee Nation one of six tribes to assume responsibility for BIA funds formerly spent by the bureau. She oversaw an annual budget of more than $75 million and more than 1,200 employees. Much of her focus was on developing adequate health care for her tribe. *Ms.* magazine named her 1987's "Woman of the Year." She was becoming a national figure, hobnobbing[9] with Bill Clinton and other leaders. 28

"People are always enormously disappointed when they meet me," she said, "because I'm not handing out crystals or am not laden with Native American jewelry." 29

In 1995 Mankiller was diagnosed with lymphoma—it's now in remission—and did not seek another term. Joe Byrd was elected chief. His administration soon derailed over bitter tribal constitutional controversies. In 1999 Chad Smith, a legal scholar Mankiller endorsed, became chief and the political infighting abated. 30

Mankiller has remained in the public eye. In 1995 she received a Chubb Fellowship from Yale University, and in 1998 President Clinton presented her with the Presidential Medal of Freedom. 31

Illness continues to plague her. In 1990 and 1998 Mankiller underwent two kidney transplants, and in 1999 she was diagnosed with breast 32

---

[8] **thymus:** Gland involved with the body's immune system.
[9] **hobnobbing:** Associating with.

cancer. But she still lectures and stays active in the issues that have shaped so much of her life.

"If we're ever going to collectively begin to grapple with the prob-   33
lems that we have collectively," Mankiller has said, "we're going to have to move back the veil and deal with each other on a more human level."

With the courage to sweep old restrictions aside, Mankiller continues   34
to be a warrior not just for the Cherokee but for humanity itself.

EXERCISING VOCABULARY

1. Examine the second and third sentences of the essay. In these sentences, Nelson describes the transformation of Mrs. Hugo Olaya into Wilma Pearl Mankiller. Why does the author use words like *crucibles, recasting, fire,* and *alchemized*? What is alchemy? Why does the author use this metaphor to describe Mankiller?

2. In paragraph 13 of the essay, the author writes about the "tedious pink-collar job" that Mankiller held after graduation. What are some characteristics of a pink-collar job? Give some examples. How does this kind of job compare with the jobs held by people who lived in the "blue-collar neighborhoods" that the author mentions in paragraph 4?

3. When Mankiller became involved in politics, the hostility she faced "toughened her hide" (para. 25). What does this expression mean? How did toughening her hide benefit Mankiller?

PROBING CONTENT

1. What does "Mankiller" mean in Cherokee (para. 4)? How might Wilma Mankiller's name be misunderstood by non-Cherokee people? What does their misunderstanding say about these people?

2. Describe Wilma Mankiller's early years. How did her upbringing help shape her character?

3. How did the siege of Alcatraz Island influence Mankiller? Name some of the others who became involved.

4. What kind of a leader was Wilma Mankiller? How exactly did she help her people? How did the courage Mankiller displayed in public struggles factor into her private life?

CONSIDERING CRAFT

1. How does the subject matter of paragraph 8 compare with that of the rest of the essay? Why does the author choose to include this information?

2. In paragraph 2, the author uses a sports metaphor to describe Mankiller's rise to power. Examine this metaphor. What does "vaulting the chauvinistic hurdles

imposed by her fellow Cherokees" mean? How does this comparison affect your reading?

3. In paragraph 19, Nelson states that in the early 1970s, popular culture "glommed onto Red Pride." What does he mean by this? How does his word choice here convey his attitude?

RESPONDING TO THE WRITER

After reading this essay, how has your thinking changed about the Native American culture and the Cherokee in particular? How did you respond to the idea of a female chief? How does Wilma Mankiller's story challenge stereotypes about both women and Native Americans?

For a quiz on this reading, go to bedfordstmartins.com/mirror.

I Ruck, Therefore I Am:
Rugby and the Gay Male Body

CHRISTOPHER STAHL

Are certain sports inherently more masculine than others? Does an athlete's sexual orientation have any effect on athletic ability? How does physical violence fit into the masculine ideal? Is this different for gay men and straight men? Is it difficult to see gay men as heroes in American culture? On September 11, 2001, an openly gay collegiate rugby champion named Mark Bingham helped fight the terrorists who hijacked Flight 93 and lost his life along with everyone else on the plane. Christopher Stahl connects all these points by writing about one of the lesser known consequences of that terrorist attack: the rise of gay rugby. Stahl details the physical pain and emotional joy of his first experience on a gay rugby team, gains a new experience of what it means to be "gay and tough," and even observes straight "ruggers" reassessing what they consider "manly." Stahl is a writing consultant for New York University. "I Ruck, Therefore I Am," was published June 22, 2004, in *The Village Voice*, in its 25th Annual Queer Issue.

THINKING AHEAD

How much do you know about gay athletes or athletic events? To what extent does knowing an athlete's sexual preference affect your experience of a sporting event?

INCREASING VOCABULARY

channel (v.) (3)	vibe (n.) (9)
emulate (v.) (5)	mayhem (n.) (9)
hybrid (n.) (6)	faux (adj.) (11)
enshrines (v.) (6)	tersely (adv.) (13)
bawdy (adj.) (9)	

This last half-hour is agony. My coach calls them zigzags: a crosscut combination of jogs and sprints up the length of a 100-by-70 meter playing field. "I can't make up for your lack of experience," he says, "but I can make you fitter. Faster. More focused." I do four zigzags per practice, if my knee holds out.

In rugby, this field is called a pitch. On Randall's Island, where my team practices, it's a rectangle of dirt, rocks, and broken glass. After a tackle, my arms and legs are covered with scrapes. It's all part of learning to take a hit. My team, the Gotham Knights, is training for the 2004

Bingham Cup, the world championship for gay rugby. I joined the team nearly a year ago. Within a few weeks, I had cleats, shorts, socks, a mouth guard, a jersey. (Protective cups are not allowed.) Within another month, I was in physical therapy for a ligament torn by a bad tackle. By February, I was relearning how to run, doing zigzags, getting tackled again.

To put yourself repeatedly in harm's way is to risk being labeled self-destructive. Some might even call it macho. Yet I'm drawn to this grueling, often bloody contact sport because its raw physicality allows me to channel a kind of masculinity that, while it may seem similar to straight-male jockitude, actually transforms it in subtle ways. Recovering from my injury, I rack up small victories in practice: first time jumping on one leg, first successful tackle, first zigzag. Second. Third. It takes almost the entire spring season before I can do all four. Call it masculinity by trial. My body is changing. Who I am has changed.

Among gay men, rugby has seen a surge in popularity. The number of teams worldwide has more than tripled in the past two years, mostly in the United States. After Mark Bingham, an openly gay businessman and collegiate rugby champion from San Francisco, helped overpower the terrorists who hijacked Flight 93 on 9–11, more than a dozen new gay teams formed, many in Texas and on the West Coast.

Part of this popularity is a tribute to Bingham and a chance for gay men to emulate someone whose heroism was acknowledged on a national stage that's usually hostile to rough queer bodies. With 590 athletes from nine countries, the 2004 Bingham Cup, which took place in London in May, was the largest amateur rugby tournament in the world. This diversity suggests that more than hero worship is in play.

The rugger is an unlikely sex symbol — a hybrid of jock, bear, and the guy who might have beaten you up in high school. Porn sites like ScrumDown and ruggerbugger trade on the eroticism of the sport by posting naked shots from professional games and straight amateur clubs. Members of London's Kings Cross Steelers, the first gay rugby team (founded in 1995), recently posed shirtless in a gay rag,[1] and this month several members of my team appeared in *Out* as part of a fall fashion spread.[2] Turning the rugby player into a lust object enshrines the sexy violence in the sport — members of my team are always showing each other their bruises — but I think gay men find ruggers desirable for other reasons.

Gay men have a strained relationship with their bodies. We are taught so often that our desires are wrong, that we never will be butch[3] enough, and that we never were. Team sports raise the threat of exposure and incompetence before other boys. We train ourselves to look too critically at

[1] **ESL rag:** Slang term for a newspaper or magazine.
[2] **ESL spread:** An advertisement or story that occupies two or more pages in a magazine or book.
[3] **ESL butch:** Slang term for masculine.

ourselves lest we fail to perform the correct rituals of manliness. You can't be self-conscious in rugby. To hesitate is to lose the ball or to miss the tackle. You have to act even if the action is wrong.

When I was growing up in suburban Ohio, football was second only   8
to Protestantism as an organized religion. In high school, football players were treated as divine beings, but I never wanted to be like them. Rugby is a blank slate for me: Similar to football in its outlines, it lacks the cultural baggage that comes with being the American sport. I can be tough without feeling like I'm part of a predetermined narrative about American manhood.

Rugby first exploded on American college campuses in the 1960s,   9
and one reason why, argues Timothy Chandler of Kent State University, is that its free-form rugged playing style offered an alternative to football. The intense bonding among players, the public nudity on the pitch, and the bawdy, blasphemous, sometimes sexist drinking songs made rugby disliked by college administrators but popular among young men attracted to its anti-authoritarian vibe. Even today, football doesn't seem to offer gay men the same opportunities for unconventional fellowship and mayhem. For gay bodies, rugby rituals seem both ironic and real. It's small wonder that Oscar Wilde called it "a good game for rough girls, but not for delicate boys."

Football is too traditional, relying on individual players assigned spe-   10
cialized tasks. Rugby is communal. Tackled, I go down and a ruck—a sudden mass of shoving bodies—forms over me. Several of my teammates try to push several of their teammates back and win possession of the ball. Cleated boots strike the ground around me like hard leather rain. It's a thrilling place to be.

London. To my right, a dozen burly Irishmen clap their arms around   11
each other's shoulders. Kicking their legs as self-proclaimed "international drag[4] terrorist" Rose Garden belts show tunes from the stage, the members of the Emerald Warriors—Ireland's first gay rugby team—personify the high spirits of the room. The carnival tone had already been set by a Queen Elizabeth II look-alike. "I thought I would be meeting with heads of state," Her Faux Majesty had twittered as she looked at the throng of ruggers, "since my advisers told me that a load of queens[5] were visiting London. All I see is a jolly good bunch of boys." Welcome to the 2004 Bingham Cup.

Facing other gay teams, our playing feels different. We engage in the   12
game's smashmouth[6] violence without feeling the usual pressure to dominate or to judge. What we begin to realize is that, for this weekend, we can take the hyper-masculine elements of the sport and live them differently.

---

[4] ESL **drag:** Dressed as a member of the opposite sex.
[5] ESL **queens:** Slang term for homosexual men.
[6] ESL **smashmouth:** Slang term for extremely physical.

In the end, the San Francisco Fog won the tournament, but we made the quarter-finals—and that was fine. It's not that we are athletically gifted, but rugby allows us to be gay and tough. And it allows us to forge a brotherhood based on mutual risk and sacrifice.

Since most gay teams are geographically scattered, we join straight   13
leagues (or unions) where we are met initially with curiosity or hostility. On the eve of our first match last fall, someone on the opposing team sent a warning to his club's message board that we would hit on them during the game. One of his teammates tersely replied that perhaps he ought to just worry about being hit, period.

Such toughness causes straight ruggers to reassess what they consider   14
manly. Initial perceptions of the Knights as weak shifted after the first few league games. "Other captains would tell us their teams would lose it when they were down a few tries. To see us come back and lay it on the line with the crazy scores we had was inspiring," notes our club's president, Adam Josephs. "We got their respect as ruggers and men." We learn how to get hit and to fall. We learn to hit back, to live in those moments of intense play, and we all go out drinking and singing afterward.

In our last game of the fall season, I witness rugby-playing gay men   15
create a world where these rough practices are transformed into something wonderful and unexpected. Sidelined by my injury, I feel out of place watching my teammates hurl themselves again and again at their opponents, a straight team from Long Island. Suddenly, a Knight sees an opening and charges through. He's tackled, but another is there to take the ball from him. Then we are all in the pack of men rucking near the goal line. The referee's flag goes up. A whistle splits the air. After a stunned silence, we erupt in shouts. One teammate has tears streaming down his face. We have scored our first goal (or try) against a straight team, and now the world is different.

"Who did it? Who did it?" we whisper to one another. But it doesn't   16
matter, because in that moment we all have done it. We are divine. It is who I want to be.

EXERCISING VOCABULARY

1. In paragragh 3, the author coins the word *jockitude*. What is a jock? What characteristics constitute jockitude?

2. Stahl writes that rugby is a "blank slate" for him (para. 8). What is a slate? What does the term "blank slate" mean? In what ways is rugby a blank slate for the author?

3. The author says that "Similar to football in its outlines, [rugby] lacks the cultural baggage that comes with being the American sport" (para. 8). What does Stahl mean by "cultural baggage"? What cultural baggage does football carry with it?

PROBING CONTENT

1. What event caused a surge in the popularity of rugby among gay men? Why did more gay men start playing rugby after this event?

2. What kind of relationship do gay men have with their bodies? What about gay ruggers?

3. In what ways has playing rugby changed the author? What possibilities has playing rugby introduced for Stahl?

4. How does rugby differ from American football? Why does the author include this information in his essay?

CONSIDERING CRAFT

1. Which famous quotation does the title of the essay recall? Why did the author choose this title? How effective is his choice?

2. The essay includes a lot of rugby jargon. Find several examples and examine their use in the essay. Why does Stahl use these terms that may be unfamiliar to many readers?

3. This essay was first published in *The Village Voice*, a publication whose readership includes a large gay audience. How does this knowledge about the original audience of the essay affect your reading of it?

4. The author ends the essay with an anecdote or short story. How effective is this strategy? Why?

RESPONDING TO THE WRITER

Think of a time when watching or participating in an athletic event caused you to reevaluate your self-image. Compare your experience with Stahl's.

For a quiz on this reading, go to bedfordstmartins.com/mirror.

How Boys Become Men

JON KATZ

Are boys taught to endure pain rather than show fear? Do men receive little mercy as boys, making it difficult for them to show any themselves? Jon Katz explores these questions in "How Boys Become Men," first published in the January 1993 issue of *Glamour*. Drawing on an experience from his childhood, Katz shows how the lessons boys learn affect their behavior as men. According to Katz, the boyhood "Code of Conduct"—with its unspoken but unyielding rules about expressing emotion—explains why some men may seem insensitive. "Boys are rewarded for throwing hard. Most other activities—reading, befriending girls, or just thinking—are considered weird. And if there's one thing boys don't want to be, it's weird," Katz writes. Do you think that this statement still applies to boys growing up in America today?

Katz has worked as an editor and reporter at the *Washington Post*, the *Boston Globe*, and the *Philadelphia Inquirer* and as a media critic for *New York* magazine and *Rolling Stone*. He has written eleven books, most of which are mystery novels. His most recent work, *A Dog Year: Twelve Months, Four Dogs, and Me* (2002), is a memoir. He is also a frequent contributor to the Web site slashdot.org, where he is known for exploring connections among bullying, teen ostracism, computer games, and violent incidents like the Columbine High School shootings.

THINKING AHEAD

Think back to your childhood. Describe the ways in which little boys treated one another. In what ways were they kind or cruel to their playmates? Why do you think they behaved the way they did?

INCREASING VOCABULARY

whooshing (v.) (1)

audible (adj.) (2)

ethics (n.) (3)

remote (adj.) (4)

ruthless (adj.) (5)

empathy (n.) (5)

resignedly (adv.) (7)

wary (adj.) (18)

intervening (v.) (18)

balk (v.) (18)

stigmatized (v.) (18)

evolves (v.) (20)

rumpled (adj.) (20)

Two nine-year-old boys, neighbors and friends, were walking home from school. The one in the bright blue windbreaker was laughing and swinging a heavy-looking book bag toward the head of his friend, who kept ducking and stepping back. "What's the matter?" asked the kid with the bag, whooshing it over his head. "You chicken?"[1]

His friend stopped, stood still and braced himself. The bag slammed into the side of his face, the thump audible all the way across the street where I stood watching. The impact knocked him to the ground, where he lay mildly stunned for a second. Then he struggled up, rubbing the side of his head. "See?" he said proudly. "I'm no chicken."

No. A chicken would probably have had the sense to get out of the way. This boy was already well on the road to becoming a man, having learned one of the central ethics of his gender: Experience pain rather than show fear.

Women tend to see men as a giant problem in need of solution. They tell us that we're remote and uncommunicative, that we need to demonstrate less machismo and more commitment, more humanity. But if you don't understand something about boys, you can't understand why men are the way we are, why we find it so difficult to make friends or to acknowledge our fears and problems.

Boys live in a world with its own Code of Conduct, a set of ruthless, unspoken, and unyielding rules:

Don't be a goody-goody.[2]

Never rat.[3] If your parents ask about bruises, shrug.

Never admit fear. Ride the roller coaster, join the fistfight, do what you have to do. Asking for help is for sissies.

Empathy is for nerds.[4] You can help your best buddy, under certain circumstances. Everyone else is on his own.

Never discuss anything of substance with anybody. Grunt, shrug, dump on teachers, laugh at wimps,[5] talk about comic books. Anything else is risky.

Boys are rewarded for throwing hard. Most other activities—reading, befriending girls, or just thinking—are considered weird. And if there's one thing boys don't want to be, it's weird.

More than anything else, boys are supposed to learn how to handle themselves. I remember the bitter fifth-grade conflict I touched off by elbowing aside a bigger boy named Barry and seizing the cafeteria's last carton of chocolate milk. Teased for getting aced out by a wimp, he had to reclaim his place in the pack. Our fistfight, at recess, ended with my knees

---

[1] **ESL chicken:** A slang mocking term for someone who is afraid of something.
[2] **ESL goody-goody:** A slang mocking term for someone who is eager to please.
[3] **ESL rat:** A slang mocking term for someone who gives away information.
[4] **ESL nerds:** A slang mocking term for unpopular people.
[5] **ESL wimps:** A slang mocking term for people who are afraid of doing something.

buckling and my lip bleeding while my friends, sympathetic but out of range, watched resignedly.

When I got home, my mother took one look at my swollen face and screamed. I wouldn't tell her anything, but when my father got home I cracked and confessed, pleading with them to do nothing. Instead, they called Barry's parents, who restricted his television for a week.   8

The following morning, Barry and six of his pals stepped out from behind a stand of trees. "It's the rat," said Barry.   9

I bled a little more. Rat was scrawled in crayon across my desk.   10

They were waiting for me after school for a number of afternoons to follow. I tried varying my routes and avoiding bushes and hedges. It usually didn't work.   11

I was as ashamed for telling as I was frightened. "You did ask for it," said my best friend. Frontier Justice has nothing on Boy Justice.   12

In panic, I appealed to a cousin who was several years older. He followed me home from school, and when Barry's gang surrounded me, he came barreling toward us. "Stay away from my cousin," he shouted, "or I'll kill you."   13

After they were gone, however, my cousin could barely stop laughing. "You were afraid of them?" he howled. "They barely came up to my waist."   14

Men remember receiving little mercy as boys; maybe that's why it's sometimes difficult for them to show any.   15

"I know lots of men who had happy childhoods, but none who have happy memories of the way other boys treated them," says a friend. "It's a macho marathon from third grade up, when you start butting each other in the stomach."   16

"The thing is," adds another friend, "you learn early on to hide what you feel. It's never safe to say, 'I'm scared.' My girlfriend asks me why I don't talk more about what I'm feeling. I've gotten better at it, but it will never come naturally."   17

You don't need to be a shrink[6] to see how the lessons boys learn affect their behavior as men. Men are being asked, more and more, to show sensitivity, but they dread the very word. They struggle to build their increasingly uncertain work lives but will deny they're in trouble. They want love, affection, and support but don't know how to ask for them. They hide their weaknesses and fears from all, even those they care for. They've learned to be wary of intervening when they see others in trouble. They often still balk at being stigmatized as weird.   18

Some men get shocked into sensitivity — when they lose their jobs, their wives, or their lovers. Others learn it through a strong marriage, or through their own children.   19

It may be a long while, however, before male culture evolves to the point that boys can learn more from one another than how to hit curve balls. Last month, walking my dog past the playground near my house,   20

---

[6] **ESL shrink:** A slang term for psychiatrist.

I saw three boys encircling a fourth, laughing and pushing him. He was skinny and rumpled, and he looked frightened. One boy knelt behind him while another pushed him from the front, a trick familiar to any former boy. He fell backward.

When the others ran off, he brushed the dirt off his elbows and walked toward the swings. His eyes were moist and he was struggling for control. 　21

"Hi," I said through the chain-link fence. "How ya doing?" 　22

"Fine," he said quickly, kicking his legs out and beginning his swing. 　23

EXERCISING VOCABULARY

1. In paragraph 5, Katz writes that boys live by a set of "unyielding rules." What does it mean to yield? In what context do you normally see this word used? Examine the rules Katz lists. In what sense are these rules unyielding?

2. In paragraph 12, Katz compares the justice boys practice on each other to "Frontier Justice." Where was the American frontier? What kind of justice ruled there? Who made the laws and enforced them? In what ways are "Frontier Justice" and "Boy Justice" alike?

3. In paragraph 16, the author quotes a friend who says that for boys, "It's a macho marathon from third grade up." What does the word *macho* mean? What is the noun form of this adjective? What is a marathon? What then does Katz mean by the phrase "macho marathon"? How effective is this image?

PROBING CONTENT

1. Describe the "Code of Conduct" by which the author believes boys live (para. 5). How do these rules affect boys' behavior?

2. What happened between the author and Barry? How did Katz's parents respond? What saved the situation?

3. How do "the lessons boys learn affect their behavior as men" (para. 18)? How do some men change their behavior when they become adults? What helps them to do so?

4. What happens to the little boy Katz saw on the playground? What does the boy's reaction imply about the future of male behavior?

CONSIDERING CRAFT

1. This essay was originally published in *Glamour*, a magazine for young women. Why do you think the author would choose a women's publication for his article? What message is he trying to relay to these readers?

2. The author opens and closes this essay with anecdotes, or short personal narratives. What message does Katz want the reader to take away from each of these anecdotes? How effective is this strategy for opening and closing his essay?

RESPONDING TO THE WRITER

How accurate do you find Katz's representation of boys' behavior? Do you agree that "Men are being asked, more and more, to show sensitivity, but they dread the very word" (para. 18)? Cite examples from personal experience to defend your position.

For a quiz on this reading, go to bedfordstmartins.com/mirror.

Men Peek Out from the Cave

J. PEDER ZANE

Does equality for one group mean "less quality" for another group? As American society redefines its expectations for women, aren't expectations for men automatically redefined as well? If so, what if men don't want to change? In "Men Peek Out from the Cave," J. Peder Zane describes an emerging male ethos in the form of an exaggerated creature he calls "Neanderman." Zane's Neanderman scorns sensitivity training and proudly wallows in beer-soaked *Girls Gone Wild* videos. He says the character proliferates in masculine pop culture, from men's magazines like *Maxim* and *Gear*, films like *Old School*, television's *The Man Show*, and certain all-sports radio stations that promote "balls and babes." While admitting to a little Neanderman-ism within himself, Zane calls the movement "pathetic," writing that the "male desire to regress is a direct response to female progress."

J. Peder Zane is currently the book review editor and books columnist for the *News & Observer* in Raleigh, North Carolina, where "Men Peek Out from the Cave" appeared on July 6, 2003. In 1999 he won the Distinguished Writing Award for Commentary from the American Society of Newspaper Editors. In 2004 he published *Remarkable Reads: 34 Writers and Their Adventures in Reading*, a collection of essays in which he and other writers from the *News & Observer* discuss their favorite authors.

THINKING AHEAD

How would you describe the modern American man? What cultural forces influence his actions? Why?

INCREASING VOCABULARY

fixated (v.) (1)	median (adj.) (5)
populist (adj.) (1)	ruinous (adj.) (6)
icon (n.) (2)	glimmers (n.) (7)
primal (adj.) (2)	pun (n.) (7)
swaggering (adj.) (2)	mogul (n.) (8)
pithily (adv.) (3)	gush (v.) (9)
pathetic (adj.) (5)	diverge (v.) (11)
regress (v.) (5)	ubiquitous (adj.) (11)

Men are working overtime to give masculinity a bad name. In the   1
1980s and '90s, male fantasies fixated on cigar-chomping gazillionaires[1] in shiny Armani[2] suits and colorful Ferragamo[3] ties. In
the new millennium, masters of the universe have been replaced by a
coarser, more populist ideal: the beer swilling,[4] tail-chasing[5] Neanderman.

Evidence of this new icon are as plentiful as mosquitoes. Hip-hop   2
music has few women but plenty of hos.[6] Lad mags[7] such as *Maxim* and
Gear draw millions of readers with a primal mix of submissive women
and swaggering men. Films like *Old School*, in which a group of men address their midlife crisis by starting an *Animal House*-type fraternity, have
given guys something to watch while they wait for their *Girls Gone Wild*
videos to rewind. All-sports radio stations including Raleigh's 850 the
Buzz have tapped the male psyche by mixing balls and babes.

But network television, the hearth of modern culture, is ground zero   3
for the Neanderman sensibility. Beer commercials are built around male
fantasies of catfights[8] between scantily clad bimbos.[9] "Reality" programs
like *Joe Millionaire* and *The Bachelor* imagine a world where every chick
digs you. The Neanderman ethos[10] is pithily grunted in the theme song to
Comedy Central's popular program *The Man Show*: "Grab a beer and
drop your pants / Send the wife and kid to France / It's *The Man Show*!!!"

Because there's a little Neanderman in me—on more than one occasion   4
my remote has stopped working after taking my TV to *The Man Show*—
my guess is that he galumphs[11] around in most men. The mind may say no,
but other parts of the body say yes, yes, YES to a dreamy world that is just
as we'd hoped it would be when we were 13.

The rise of the Neanderman would be funny if it weren't so pathetic.   5
The male desire to regress is a direct response to female progress; men are
clinging to the fantasy of power precisely because it is slipping from their
grasp in the real world. Yes, most CEOs[12] and high ranking government
officials are men, but most men aren't CEOs or senators. In median America women are on the ascent. In a nation where education is the gateway
to success, roughly six out of every 10 recipients of bachelor's or master's
degrees are women, and the gap is widening.

---

[1] **ESL gazillionaires:** Slang term for extremely rich people.
[2] **Armani:** Giorgio Armani, a famous Italian fashion designer.
[3] **Ferragamo:** Salvatore Ferragamo, a famous Italian fashion designer.
[4] **ESL swilling:** Slang for drinking.
[5] **ESL tail-chasing:** Slang for pursuing women.
[6] **ESL hos:** Slang for whores or prostitutes.
[7] **ESL lad mags:** Slang for men's magazines.
[8] **ESL catfights:** Slang for physical fights between two women.
[9] **ESL bimbos:** Derogatory term for young women who are thought to lack intelligence or
    to have an exaggerated idea of their sexual appeal.
[10] **ethos:** The fundamental and distinctive character of a group, social context, or time pe-
    riod, expressed in attitudes, habits, and beliefs.
[11] **galumphs:** Walks or runs in a boisterous or clumsy way.
[12] **CEOs:** Chief Executive Officers.

Men today are looking back at 40 years of feminist sensitivity training and asking, "What has it got me?" Ever more confident women no longer feel the need to keep men in line, so they don't raise much of a peep when men act like boys. They recognize that male sexism is, in some ways, good for them, because it limits men's ability to compete in the real world. In the big picture, it is, of course, ruinous for all.

The broad societal forces that encourage men to behave badly will not be overcome easily. But glimmers of hope for Neanderman backlash are appearing on bookstore shelves. They are the male version of the confessional novels women have been devouring since Bridget Jones[13] hit the scene. Imagine any priapic[14] pun you want to describe this male version of chick lit[15]—being a family newspaper, we'll call it Richard lit. But a raft[16] of novels featuring male narrators obsessing over their love lives suggests a willingness among some members of the hirsute[17] set to admit they have . . . feelings.

These works include *Love and Other Recreational Sports* by John Dearie, which describes a 35-year-old New York banker's efforts to find true love after being dumped at the altar; *Man and Wife* by Tony Parsons, whose protagonist is a recently remarried father juggling his new family and his old; and *Flabbergasted* by Ray Blackstone, a light comic novel about a single man's plan to find love at his local Presbyterian church in Greenville, S.C. In August we'll see *Love Me* by Garrison Keillor, which tells of a man who renews his life by writing a lonely hearts column, and September will bring *Swagbelly: A Novel for Today's Gentleman* by D.J. Levian, whose protagonist is a divorced pornography mogul who learns that rafts of money and centerfold[18] sex do not always bring happiness.

No one will confuse these early examples of Richard lit with chick lit. Their narrators do not gush emotion but work to dam the floodgates of feeling. Keillor's narrator tells us, "Communication is an injurious thing in marriage," a point that is echoed by Levian's hero: "What I want, always wanted, and always will, is to become rich enough not to have complicated feelings."

These books have not come to praise Neanderman, though, but to bury him. They tend to cast traditional male traits as a problem, and use them as a source of ridicule. After one incredibly brief exchange, the hero of *Flabbergasted* deadpans,[19] "I suppose, for two single males, we'd just had what amounts to a deep conversation."

---

[13] **Bridget Jones:** Heroine of two comic novels by Helen Fielding titled *Bridget Jones's Diary* and *Bridget Jones: The Edge of Reason.*
[14] **priapic:** Showing a preoccupation with male sexual activity.
[15] **ESL chick lit:** Slang for fiction, often romance, that appeals to a primarily female audience.
[16] **raft:** Abundance.
[17] **hirsute:** Hairy.
[18] **ESL centerfold:** The center two pages of a men's or women's magazine that features a sexy, often nude, person.
[19] **deadpans:** Speaks without expression.

Of course, these Richard lit authors are playing off the same stereo-   11
types as *The Man Show*—if you ever have the occasion to talk to a
walking/talking man, you'll find he can do more than grunt. But as
much as the images of popular culture may diverge from reality, they
also have the power to shape it. Today the ubiquitous Neanderman
rules the male imagination, but the emergence of Richard lit suggests
men might still be evolving.

EXERCISING VOCABULARY

1. What is a neologism? What root word does the author use to create the neologism *Neanderman*? Why does he use that root word? What connotations
does that word carry with it?

2. In paragraph 9, Zane writes about narrators who "work to dam the floodgates of feeling." What does "dam the floodgates" mean literally? Then what
does it mean to "dam the floodgates of feeling"?

PROBING CONTENT

1. According to the author, what is the new masculine icon? Which male image
has it replaced?

2. How has television fostered this new icon? Discuss specific examples.

3. What is responsible for "the rise of the Neanderman" (para. 5)? What role do
women play in this rise?

4. What is "Neanderman backlash" (para. 7)? What evidence is there of
this backlash? What is the difference between "Richard lit" and "chick lit"
(para. 7)?

CONSIDERING CRAFT

1. What is the significance of the title? What does the author hope to convey
by the image the title creates?

2. Zane describes network television as "the hearth of modern culture" and
"ground zero for the Neanderman sensibility" (para. 3). Analyze these metaphors. Why does the author compare TV to a hearth and to ground zero?
What does this comparison suggest about his view of the importance of television in popular culture?

3. What is a rhetorical question? Examine the rhetorical question in paragraph 6.
Why does Zane include it?

4. The author alludes to several films, televison shows, and books in his essay.
Choose two or three examples, and explain how these references affect your
reading.

RESPONDING TO THE WRITER

Do you believe that most men you know are Neandermen? Defend your response using specific examples from your own experience.

DRAWING CONNECTIONS

1. How would Jon Katz ("How Boys Become Men") respond to J. Peder Zane's Neanderman ("Men Peek Out from the Cave")? Would he be surprised? Why or why not?

2. How would Zane ("Men Peek Out from the Cave") respond to Katz's assertion in "How Boys Become Men" that boys' "Code of Conduct" has lifelong repercussions? How could this Code and what he calls "Frontier Justice" contribute to American boys' becoming Neandermen?

3. Compare the endings of Zane's "Men Peek Out from the Cave" and Katz's "How Boys Become Men." Does Katz hold out any hope that American boys, as adults, will be able to overcome their macho upbringing to become caring individuals? Why or why not? How does Zane feel about the future of Neandermen?

4. How would Jon Katz react to Zane's statement that "male sexism . . . limits men's ability to compete in the real world" (para. 6)? Support your answer with textual evidence from Katz's essay.

Wrapping Up Chapter 3

REFLECTING ON THE WRITING

1. Several of the selections in this chapter are written by members of minority communities. Drawing on two or more of those selections, write an essay in which you compare the writers' problematic experiences developing their self-images in a culture that they believe extends more privileges to people who look like members of the majority group.

2. Like Alvarez and Ali, you may feel self-conscious about your physical appearance. Why do you feel this way? How much of your dissatisfaction is related to the ethnic group to which you belong? How much is related to other cultural factors? Would you consider changing your appearance to "fit in" with the standard American ideal of beauty? What would you change? How do you think your life would improve as a result of such changes?

3. Pick the selection or selections from this chapter with which you most closely identify to use as a starting point. Write an essay in which you describe your experience with cultural identity or that of someone you know well. You might want to use one or more selections to get ideas for the approach, structure, or tone of your paper.

4. Like several of the authors in this chapter, you may have experienced a time when your gender or sexual preference clashed with the culture around you. Describe an occasion when you were forced to reassess what it means to be a male or female in America today and the ways in which your gender or sexual orientation affects your standing in society.

CONNECTING TO THE CULTURE

1. Think about celebrities who have helped to shape your cultural self-image. They might be models, sports figures, musicians, or television personalities. They might have had positive, negative, or mixed influences on you. Write an essay in which you trace the influence these people have had on your cultural self-image.

2. Since you have been attending college, what new cultural influences have you experienced? Have they been positive, negative, or mixed? To what extent have you been influenced? In what ways have these influences changed you?

3. What influence has your particular cultural group had on the formation of your self-image? Give specific examples.

4. Imagine yourself as a current or future parent and identify some negative cultural influences on the formation of self-image in children. Detail how you would attempt to curb those influences.

5. What role do you think television plays in shaping and reinforcing our ideas about people of cultures or races different from our own? Cite specific examples of television shows to support your points.

FOCUSING ON YESTERDAY, FOCUSING ON TODAY

Norman Rockwell's art for *The Saturday Evening Post* has long been considered a staple of American popular culture. This New England artist rendered the everyday moments that have defined our society, catching our humanity and our frailty in a way that everyone can relate to and few other artists can match. In this iconic 1943 painting, *Freedom from Want*, Rockwell captures a moment familiar to many Americans, the extended family gathered around the table celebrating Thanksgiving. The song lyrics "Over the river and through the woods to Grandmother's house we go" may come to mind as we seem to be invited into this happy gathering by the smiling figures around the table.

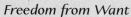

Freedom from Want

This contemporary drawing by Charlie Powell titled *One Big Happy Family* accompanied a November 19, 2004, article in *Salon.com* that commented on the recent, divisive presidential elections. It captures a "family" moment that is similar to Rockwell's but that has a different artistic style and cast of characters. *One Big Happy Family* lacks the trademark photographic quality of Norman Rockwell's "Kodak moment" on canvas, but it is eye-catching in its own way. As we examine these modern figures gathered around the table for their own turkey feast, we find ourselves composing our own story about the scene depicted in the drawing as we imagine the table conversation and the connections among the guests. The faces have certainly changed, but many similarities remain between these two images.

Both of these images celebrate what many call the most "American" of holidays, Thanksgiving. What is ironic about this? Who is missing from each of these pictures? What important cultural group is not represented?

As you examine these images, consider these questions: What images of America do these two visuals represent? How do they reflect the changes in American culture during the more than sixty years that separate them? What has stayed the same? What has changed? How accurate are the titles of both images, considering when each was created? To what extent do these two visuals reflect Thanksgiving celebrations that you have experienced? How do your family's cultural traditions compare with those depicted in the two images?

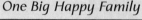

One Big Happy Family

CHAPTER 4

"Tell Me What You Don't Like about Yourself"

Cultural Reflections on Body Image

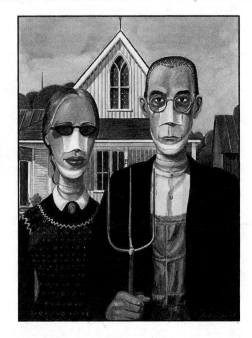

This illustration accompanied the May 31, 2004, *U.S. News & World Report* cover story titled "Makeover Nation." Its inspiration is Grant Wood's iconic oil painting *American Gothic*, which features a serious-looking farm couple, with the farmer holding a pitchfork. Recently, Wood's painting has appeared in the opening credits of the popular television show *Desperate Housewives*. It has also inspired a poster for the reality television show *The Simple Life*.

- Why did the artist choose the painting *American Gothic* for his inspiration?
- What modern touches did the artist add to Wood's painting?
- Why did the artist make the changes he did?
- What message about current American culture does this visual convey?

Research this topic with TopLinks at bedfordstmartins.com/toplinks.

GEARING UP

Think about the forces that have shaped your impressions of what your body should look like. Make a list of the major influences. These might include people you know, television and movie actors, fashion models, makeover shows, advertisements, magazines, Web sites, or even music videos. Then think about specific times during your teen years when you were satisfied or dissatisfied with the way you looked. Why did you feel the way you did? How did these feelings affect you? To what extent do you still feel the effects today?

We are aware of body image from the time we are toddlers. "What a pretty little girl" or "What a big strong boy" echoes in our ears and in our minds. At an early age, we begin to realize that there are very specific feminine and masculine ideals of beauty. Although these can be somewhat culture-specific, all Americans, regardless of ethnicity, quickly discover that the dominant ideal is represented by a young, attractive man or woman who has a fit body, good hair and skin, and a winning smile. Think about the Abercrombie & Fitch models frolicking on the beach, the famous faces selling Revlon cosmetics, or the curvaceous Victoria's Secret models lounging in sexy lingerie. Think, too, of the movie stars, television actors, and sports stars you watch and have possibly come to idolize. Do you feel that their good looks often contribute substantially to their success? Hasn't research shown that attractive people have an edge over those judged less attractive when all other attributes are equal? Is it an accident that the great majority of American presidents have been more than six feet tall and that tall men are more successful than short men in the world of business?

Most of us never have and never will look like these "beautiful" people. Luckily, for many of us, our appearance does not become a major lifelong obsession as it does for some patients of the suave plastic surgeons on the TV show *Nip/Tuck*, who croon at the beginning of each consultation: "Tell me what you don't like about yourself." Though we may have grown up playing with Barbie or Ken (in their WASP or ethnic versions), we didn't grow up thinking we had to look like them or like Paris or Ashton. Even though most people find the teenage years difficult because that is when we begin to discover who we are, we generally grow into fairly confident adults who are comfortable with our self-image, including our looks. Most of us have decided to make the most of our good features and to downplay or simply live with the less than perfect ones.

For some people, however, the search for the perfect body becomes a distracting, even life-threatening, obsession. In an effort to improve what they were born with or to reverse the march of time, men and women alike have succumbed to some form of makeover madness like fad diets and exercise programs, diet pills and steroids, antiaging concoctions, liposuction, botox and collagen injections, and cosmetic surgery to resculpt their bodies. Some even fall victim to eating disorders or abuse drugs. In this chapter, you will read selections by a variety of authors about their own struggles with or reflections on body image. Some of the essays are humorous, and some are serious. All, however, should make you think about your own self-image and the cultural influences that have helped to form it.

COLLABORATING

In groups of four to six students, discuss the question "What makes people attractive?" Brainstorm a list of ten attributes for men and ten for women. Then study your lists to determine how many of these qualities relate to body image. Share your observations with the rest of the class.

My Inner Shrimp

GARRY TRUDEAU

Garry Trudeau's humorous essay "My Inner Shrimp" examines the impact of body image on the fragile self-esteem of a teenager. As a short high school student, Trudeau tried to overcome this dilemma by hanging from door frames, sleeping on his back, and doing floor exercises. His sense of self became so wrapped up in his appearance that he attributed all his normal teenage problems to his height. Even though Trudeau had a delayed growth spurt and is now over six feet tall, he admits that he still has the "soul of a shrimp." Do you, like Trudeau, believe that adolescent insecurities follow us into adulthood? Do you still see yourself as others saw you during your high school years?

Trudeau is well known for his comic strip *Doonesbury*, for which he won a Pulitzer Prize in 1975. He has contributed articles to *The New Yorker, The New Republic, Harper's,* the *Washington Post, Time,* and the *New York Times.* "My Inner Shrimp" first appeared in the *New York Times Magazine* on March 31, 1997.

THINKING AHEAD

Describe a time when you were dissatisfied with the way you look, when your "inner" and "outer" body image were at odds. How did this affect you?

INCREASING VOCABULARY

diminutive (adj.) (1)	compelling (adj.) (9)
harrowing (adj.) (1)	contingent (n.) (10)
ascended (v.) (3)	ignominiously (adv.) (10)
excruciatingly (adv.) (3)	taunt (v.) (10)
resolutely (adv.) (4)	ancillary (adj.) (11)
perverse (adj.) (9)	calamities (n.) (12)

For the rest of my days, I shall be a recovering short person. Even from my lofty perch of something over six feet (as if I don't know within a micron), I have the soul of a shrimp. I feel the pain of the diminutive, irrespective of whether they feel it themselves, because my visit to the planet of the teenage midgets was harrowing, humiliating, and extended. I even perceive my last-minute escape to have been flukish,[1] somehow unearned — as if the Commissioner of Growth Spurts had been an old classmate of my father.

My most recent reminder of all this came the afternoon I went hunting for a new office. I had noticed a building under construction in my

---

[1] **flukish:** Relating to good or bad luck.

neighborhood—a brick warren[2] of duplexes, with wide, westerly-facing windows, promising ideal light for a working studio. When I was ushered into the model unit, my pulse quickened: The soaring, twenty-two-foot living room walls were gloriously aglow with the remains of the day. I bonded immediately.

Almost as an afterthought, I ascended the staircase to inspect the loft, ducking as I entered the bedroom. To my great surprise, I stayed ducked: The room was a little more than six feet in height. While my head technically cleared the ceiling, the effect was excruciatingly oppressive. This certainly wasn't a space I wanted to spend any time in, much less take out a mortgage on.

Puzzled, I wandered down to the sales office and asked if there were any other units to look at. No, replied a resolutely unpleasant receptionist, it was the last one. Besides, they were all exactly alike.

"Are you aware of how low the bedroom ceilings are?" I asked.

She shot me an evil look. "Of course we are," she snapped. "There were some problems with the building codes. The architect knows all about the ceilings.

"He's not an idiot, you know," she added, perfectly anticipating my next question.

She abruptly turned away, but it was too late. She'd just confirmed that a major New York developer, working with a fully licensed architect, had knowingly created an entire twelve-story apartment building virtually uninhabitable by anyone of even average height. It was an exclusive high-rise for shorties.

Once I knew that, of course, I couldn't stay away. For days thereafter, as I walked to work, some perverse, unreasoning force would draw me back to the building. But it wasn't just the absurdity, the stone silliness of its design that had me in its grip; it was something far more compelling. Like some haunted veteran come again to an ancient battlefield, I was revisiting my perilous past.

When I was fourteen, I was the third-smallest in a high school class of one hundred boys, routinely mistaken for a sixth grader. My first week of school, I was drafted into a contingent of students ignominiously dubbed the "Midgets," so grouped by taller boys presumably so they could taunt us with more perfect efficiency. Inexplicably, some of my fellow Midgets refused to be diminished by the experience, but I retreated into self-pity. I sent away for a book on how to grow tall, and committed to memory its tips on overcoming one's genetic destiny—or at least making the most of a regrettable situation. The book cited historical figures who had gone the latter route—Alexander the Great, Caesar, Napoleon (the mind involuntarily added Hitler). Strategies for stretching the limbs were suggested—hanging from door frames, sleeping on your back, doing assorted floor exercises—all

---

[2] **warren:** A mazelike place where one could easily become lost.

of which I incorporated into my daily routine (get up, brush teeth, hang from door frame). I also learned the importance of meeting girls early in the day, when, the book assured me, my rested spine rendered me perceptibly taller.

For six years, my condition persisted; I grew, but at nowhere near the   11
rate of my peers. I perceived other problems as ancillary, and loaded up the stature issue with freight shipped in daily from every corner of my life. Lack of athletic success, all absence of a social life, the inevitable run-ins with bullies—all could be attributed to the missing inches. The night I found myself sobbing in my father's arms was the low point; we both knew it was one problem he couldn't fix.

Of course what we couldn't have known was that he and my mother   12
already had. They had given me a delayed developmental timetable. In my seventeenth year, I miraculously shot up six inches, just in time for graduation and a fresh start. I was, in the space of a few months, reborn—and I made the most of it. Which is to say that thereafter, all of life's disappointments, reversals, and calamities still arrived on schedule—but blissfully free of subtext.

Once you stop being the butt, of course, any problem recedes, if only   13
to give way to a new one. And yet the impact of being literally looked down on, of being *made* to feel small, is forever. It teaches you how to stretch, how to survive the scorn of others for things that are beyond your control. Not growing forces you to grow up fast.

Sometimes I think I'd like to return to a high-school reunion to sur-   14
prise my classmates. Not that they didn't know me when I finally started catching up. They did, but I doubt they'd remember. Adolescent hierarchies have a way of enduring; I'm sure I am still recalled as the Midget I myself have never really left behind.

Of course, if I'm going to show up, it'll have to be soon. I'm starting   15
to shrink.

EXERCISING VOCABULARY

1. Trudeau refers to himself in the opening sentence as a "recovering short person." What type of person do you usually think of when you hear the word *recovering*? How does the author's word choice prepare you for the subject of this essay?

2. In paragraph 12, Trudeau explains that when he was seventeen, "all of life's disappointments, reversals, and calamities still arrived on schedule—but blissfully free of subtext." What is a subtext? What is the subtext to which the author is referring in this sentence?

3. Trudeau states that "Adolescent hierarchies have a way of enduring" (para. 14). What is a hierarchy? Give an example. What does he mean when he refers to adolescent hierarchies? Give some examples from your own experience to explain your response.

PROBING CONTENT

1. What effect did the author's visit to the new apartment building have on him? Why did it affect him this way?

2. What problem did Trudeau have in high school? How did he react to the nickname he was given? How did his reaction differ from that of others with the same problem? How did he attempt to overcome this problem?

3. What happened when Trudeau was seventeen? How did this affect Trudeau's outlook on life?

4. Has Trudeau completely overcome his high school anxiety? Support your response with material from his essay.

CONSIDERING CRAFT

1. Trudeau is a well-known cartoonist. Describe his tone in this essay. How does he use humor to drive home his argument? Refer to several specific examples, including the title.

2. In paragraph 9, Trudeau describes himself as a "haunted veteran come again to an ancient battlefield, . . . revisiting my perilous past." Examine this comparison. What kind of figure of speech is it? How effective is its use here?

3. Trudeau's use of irony often enhances his writing. In paragraph 10, he writes, "some of my fellow Midgets refused to be diminished by the experience." How is this statement ironic? What effect does he achieve by using irony here?

RESPONDING TO THE WRITER

How do you respond to Trudeau's obsession with his "inner shrimp"? Do you empathize with him? If so, why? Or do you think he makes too much of his problem, especially since many will say he should have grown out of it? Explain your response.

For a quiz on this reading, go to bedfordstmartins.com/mirror.

Dying to Be Bigger

H. D.

The potentially devastating effects of anabolic steroids and other performance-enhancing drugs continue to receive media attention and have even been the subject of U.S. Senate hearings. From Olympic medalists to high school football players, some athletes seem drawn to these so-called wonder drugs. The baseball steroids scandal may forever tarnish the accomplishments of homerun sluggers like Mark McGwire, who in 1998 shattered a thirty-seven-year-old record for most homeruns hit in a single season, and Barry Bonds, who overtook McGwire's record three years later. Why do athletes, who perhaps value their bodies more than the rest of us value ours, place an irreplaceable asset at such potentially disastrous risk? Is the quest to be the biggest, the fastest, the buffest, the best really worth the possible negative consequences?

In "Dying to Be Bigger," a young man recounts his own frightening experiences with steroids. While steroids are not abused solely by males, many young men have been seduced by this supposedly fast track to physical prowess and optimal performance. H. D., who was born in 1970, wrote this personal account while he was a university undergraduate. He graduated in August 1993 with plans to pursue a doctorate in clinical psychology. His essay was first published in *Seventeen* magazine in December 1991.

THINKING AHEAD

Have you ever been tempted to take radical steps to enhance your physical attractiveness? Have you known others who have sought to change their bodies through the use of steroids, diet pills, plastic surgery, rigid dieting, or excessive exercise? What do people who take such steps expect to achieve? How significant are the risks? Why are some people willing to accept the potentially negative and even dangerous consequences of these behaviors?

INCREASING VOCABULARY

maiming (v.) (1)

cocky (adj.) (2)

perversion (n.) (7)

equine (adj.) (13)

plummeted (v.) (16)

celibacy (n.) (17)

ramification (n.) (21)

depleted (v.) (21)

fluctuated (v.) (22)

I was only fifteen years old when I first started maiming my body with the abuse of anabolic steroids.[1] I was always trying to fit in with the "cool" crowd in junior high and high school. Willingly smoking or buying pot when offered, socially drinking in excess, displaying a macho image — and, of course, the infamous "kiss and tell" were essentials in completing my insecure mentality.

Being an immature, cocky kid from a somewhat wealthy family, I wasn't very well liked in general. In light of this, I got beat up a lot, especially in my first year of public high school.

I was one of only three sophomores to get a varsity letter in football. At five-foot-nine and 174 pounds, I was muscularly inferior to the guys on the same athletic level and quite conscious of the fact. So when I heard about this wonderful drug called steroids from a teammate, I didn't think twice about asking to buy some. I could hardly wait to take them and start getting bigger.

I bought three months' worth of Dianobol (an oral form of steroids and one of the most harmful). I paid fifty-five dollars. I was told to take maybe two or three per day. I totally ignored the directions and warnings and immediately started taking five per day. This is how eager I was to be bigger and possibly "cooler."

Within only a week, everything about me started to change. I was transforming mentally and physically. My attention span became almost nonexistent. Along with becoming extremely aggressive, I began to abandon nearly all academic and family responsibilities. In almost no time, I became flustered and agitated with simple everyday activities. My narcissistic ways brought me to engage in verbal as well as physical fights with family, friends, teachers, but mostly strangers.

My bodily transformations were clearly visible. In less than a month, I took the entire three-month supply. I gained nearly thirty pounds. Most of my weight was from water retention, although at the time I believed it to be muscle. Instead of having pimples like the average teenager, my acne took the form of grotesque, cystlike blood clots that would occasionally burst while I was lifting weights. My nipples became the size of grapes and hurt severely, which is common among male steroid users. My hormonal level was completely out of whack.[2]

At first I had such an overload of testosterone that I would have to masturbate daily, at minimum, in order to prevent having "wet dreams." Obviously these factors enhanced my lust, which eventually led to acute perversion. My then almost-horrifying physique prevented me from having any sexual encounters.

All of these factors led to my classification as a wretched menace. My parents grew sick and tired of all the trouble I began to get in. They were

[1] **anabolic steroids:** Hormones used by athletes to temporarily increase muscle size and metabolism.
[2] **ESL out of whack:** Not normal.

scared of me, it seemed. They cared so much about my welfare, education, and state of mind that they sent me to a boarding school that summer.

I could not obtain any more steroids there, and for a couple of months 9 it seemed I had subtle withdrawal symptoms and severe side effects. Most of the time that summer I was either depressed or filled with intense anger, both of which were uncontrollable unless I was in a state of intoxication from any mind-altering drug.

After a year of being steroid-free, things started to look promising for 10 me, and I eventually gained control over myself. Just when I started getting letters from big-name colleges to play football for them, I suffered a herniated disc. I was unable to participate in any form of physical activity the entire school year.

In the fall, I attended a university in the Northeast, where I was on the 11 football team but did not play due to my injury. I lifted weights with the team every day. I wasn't very big at the time, even after many weeks of working out. Once again I found myself to be physically inferior and insecure about my physique. And again I came into contact with many teammates using steroids.

My roommate was a six-foot-three, 250-pound linebacker who played 12 on the varsity squad as a freshman. As the weeks passed, I learned of my roommate's heavy steroid use. I was exposed to dozens of different steroids I had never even heard of. Living in the same room with him, I watched his almost daily injections. After months of enduring his drug offerings, I gave in.

By the spring of my freshman year, I had become drastically far from 13 normal in every way. My body had stopped producing hormones due to the amount of synthetic testosterone I injected into my system. At five-foot-eleven, 225 pounds, disproportionately huge, acne-infested, outrageously aggressive, and nearing complete sterility, I was in a terrible state of body and mind. Normal thoughts of my future (not pertaining to football), friends, family, reputation, moral status, etc., were entirely beyond me. My whole entire essence had become one of a primitive barbarian. This was when I was taking something called Sustunon (prepackaged in a syringe labeled "For equine use only") containing four types of testosterone. I was "stacking" (a term used by steroid users which means mixing different types) to get well-cut definition along with mass.

It was around this time when I was arrested for threatening a secu- 14 rity guard. When the campus police came to arrest me, they saw how aggressive and large my roommate and I were. So they searched our room and found dozens of bottles and hundreds of dollars' worth of steroids and syringes. We had a trial, and the outcome was that I could only return the next year if I got drug-tested on a monthly basis. I certainly had no will-power or desire to quit my steroid abuse, so I transferred schools.

After a summer of even more heavy-duty abuse, I decided to attend 15 a school that would cater to my instinctively backward ways. That fall

I entered a large university in the South. Once again I simply lifted weights without being involved in competition or football. It was there that I finally realized how out of hand I'd become with my steroid problem.

Gradually I started to taper down my dosages. Accompanying my reduction, I began to drink more and more. My grades plummeted again. I began going to bars and keg parties on a nightly basis.   16

My celibacy, mental state, aggressiveness, lack of athletic competition, and alcohol problem brought me to enjoy passing my pain onto others by means of physical aggression. I got into a fight almost every time I drank. In the midst of my insane state, I was arrested for assault. I was in really deep this time. Finally I realized how different from everybody else I'd become, and I decided not to taper off but to quit completely.   17

The average person seems to think that steroids just make you bigger. But they are a drug, and an addictive one at that. This drug does not put you in a stupor or in a hallucinogenic state but rather gives you an up, all-around "bad-ass" mentality that far exceeds that of either normal life or any other narcotic I've tried with not taking steroids. Only lately are scientists and researchers discovering how addictive steroids are—only now, after hundreds of thousands may have done such extreme damage to their lives, bodies, and minds.   18

One of the main components of steroid addiction is how unsatisfied the user is with his overall appearance. Although I was massive and had dramatic muscular definition, I was never content with my body, despite frequent compliments. I was always changing types of steroids, places of injection, workouts, diet, etc. I always found myself saying, "This one oughta do it" or "I'll quit when I hit 230 pounds."   19

When someone is using steroids, he has psychological disorders that increase when usage stops. One disorder is anxiety from the loss of the superior feeling you get from the drug. Losing the muscle mass, high energy level, and superhuman sensation that you're so accustomed to is terrifying.   20

Another ramification of taking artificial testosterone over time is the effect on the natural testosterone level (thus the male sex drive). As a result of my steroid use, my natural testosterone level was ultimately depleted to the point where my sex drive was drastically reduced in comparison to the average twenty-one-year-old male. My testicles shriveled up, causing physical pain as well as extreme mental anguish. Thus I desired girls less. This however did lead me to treat them as people, not as objects of my desires. It was a beginning step on the way to a more sane and civil mentality.   21

The worst symptoms of my withdrawal after many months of drug abuse were emotional. My emotions fluctuated dramatically, and I rapidly became more sensitive. My hope is that this feeling of being trailed by isolation and aloneness will diminish and leave me free of its constant haunting.   22

EXERCISING VOCABULARY

1. How does H. D.'s use of such words as *maiming, grotesque, perversion, wretched,* and *depleted* help the reader form a clear impression of the author's self-image?

2. In Greek mythology, who is Narcissus? What happened to him? Why is the adjective derived from his name, *narcissistic* (para. 5), particularly suitable for this narrative?

PROBING CONTENT

1. When did the writer begin taking anabolic steroids? Why did he believe that doing so was necessary?

2. What physical changes did H. D.'s body undergo? How were these physical changes related to what happened to him mentally?

3. Why did H. D. resume steroid use after his drug-free summer at boarding school? Why did he keep changing his dosage, the type of steroids he used, and the place in which he injected himself? How much steroid use would the writer have considered enough?

4. What triggered the writer's decision to stop using steroids? What withdrawal symptoms did he experience? Compare H. D.'s self-image at the beginning of this essay with his self-image at its conclusion.

CONSIDERING CRAFT

1. What does *dying* mean in the essay's title? How could H. D.'s use of this word mean more than one thing? How does this title reflect the main idea of the essay?

2. The writer includes many graphic and painful details about his condition. What purpose do these details serve? Why are they necessary in this essay?

3. What is H. D.'s purpose in telling his own story? Why does he not use his full name? What reaction might H. D. hope his readers will have?

4. How would you characterize the writer's attitude toward his use of steroids? How does this tone change throughout the narrative? By the end, how do you feel toward H. D.?

5. This essay was originally published in *Seventeen* magazine. Who is the usual target audience for this magazine? How does knowing this affect your understanding of the essay?

RESPONDING TO THE WRITER

How would you respond if H. D.'s story were shared with you by a friend as his or her personal experience? Would you feel sympathetic? Judgmental? What opinion or advice would you give your friend?

For a quiz on this reading, go to bedfordstmartins.com/mirror.

The Eye of the Beholder

GRACE SUH

Have you ever been tempted to completely remake yourself? Did you want to look especially good for a special event or person, or were you just tired of the same old you? When Grace Suh, a Korean American, treats herself to a makeover at the cosmetics counter at Neiman Marcus, a luxury department store, she gets much more than she bargains for. As a result of her experience, Suh makes a crucial discovery about what it means to be an Asian American woman in a society that values Western ideals of beauty. By reading Suh's candid and funny description of her disastrous makeover, which first appeared in *A. Magazine* in 1992, we become passengers on her journey to selfhood.

Grace Suh is a native of Seoul, Korea, but she was raised in Wisconsin and Chicago. She now lives in New York City, where she works in academic publishing and is a poetry editor for the *Asian Pacific American Journal*. This essay appears in *Echoes: New Korean American Writings* (2003), edited by Elaine H. Kim and Laura Hyun Yi Kang.

THINKING AHEAD

Reflect on a time when you did something solely to fit in with a certain group. What was the outcome? To what extent did your efforts achieve the desired effect?

INCREASING VOCABULARY

stark (adj.) (2)	wafted (v.) (9)
renounced (v.) (3)	impeccably (adv.) (10)
bourgeois (adj.) (3)	reverie (n.) (11)
icons (n.) (5)	mannequin (n.) (11)
imperious (adj.) (6)	distorted (v.) (20)
aloof (adj.) (6)	recessed (v.) (25)
scrutiny (n.) (9)	

Several summers ago, on one of those endless August evenings when the sun hangs suspended just above the horizon, I made up my mind to become beautiful.

It happened as I walked by one of those mirrored glass-clad office towers, and caught a glimpse of my reflection out of the corner of my eye. The glass on this particular building was green, which might have accounted for the sickly tone of my complexion, but there was no explaining away the limp, ragged hair, the dark circles under my eyes, the

facial blemishes, the shapeless, wrinkled clothes. The overall effect—
the whole being greater than the sum of its parts—was one of stark
ugliness.

I'd come home from college having renounced bourgeois suburban   3
values, like hygiene and grooming. Now, home for the summer, I washed
my hair and changed clothes only when I felt like it, and spent most of my
time sitting on the lawn eating mini rice cakes and Snickers[1] and reading
dogeared[2] back issues of *National Geographic.*

But that painfully epiphanous day, standing there on the hot side-   4
walk, I suddenly understood what my mother had been gently hinting
these past months: I was no longer just plain, no longer merely unattractive. No, I had broken the Unsightliness Barrier. I was now UGLY, and
aggressively so.

And so, in an unusual exertion of will, I resolved to fight back against   5
the forces of entropy.[3] I envisioned it as reclamation work, like scything
down a lawn that has grown into meadow, or restoring a damaged fresco.[4]
For the first time in ages, I felt elated and hopeful. I nearly sprinted into the
nearby Neiman Marcus. As I entered the cool, hushed, dimly lit first floor
and saw the gleaming counters lined with vials of magical balm, the priestesses of beauty in their sacred smocks, and the glossy photographic icons
of the goddesses themselves—Paulina, Linda, Cindy, Vendella—in a wild,
reckless burst of inspiration I thought to myself, Heck, why just okay?
Why not BEAUTIFUL?

At the Estée Lauder[5] counter, I spied a polished, middle-aged woman   6
whom I hoped might be less imperious than the aloof amazons at the
Chanel counter.

"Could I help you?" the woman (I thought of her as "Estée") asked.   7

"Yes," I blurted. "I look terrible. I need a complete makeover—skin,   8
face, everything."

After a wordless scrutiny of my face, she motioned me to sit down   9
and began. She cleansed my skin with a bright blue mud masque and
clear, tingling astringent and then applied a film of moisturizer, working
extra amounts into the rough patches. Under the soft pressure of her fingers, I began to relax. From my perch, I happily took in the dizzying, colorful swirl of beautiful women and products all around me. I breathed in
the billows of perfume that wafted through the air. I whispered the names
of products under my breath like a healing mantra:[6] cooling eye gel, gentle
exfoliant,[7] night time neck area reenergizer, moisture recharging intensifier,

---

[1] **ESL Snickers:** A candy bar.
[2] **ESL dogeared:** With page corners turned down.
[3] **entropy:** In physics, the tendency of things to move toward disorder.
[4] **fresco:** A painting that is created on wet plaster.
[5] **ESL Estée Lauder:** A manufacturer of expensive cosmetics.
[6] **mantra:** A sacred formula chanted repeatedly in prayer or incantation.
[7] **exfoliant:** A mixture that causes peeling off in layers.

ultra-hydrating complex, emulsifying[8] immunage. I felt immersed in femininity, intoxicated by beauty.

I was flooded with gratitude at the patience and determination with   10
which Estée toiled away at my face, painting on swaths of lip gloss, blush, and foundation. She was not working in vain, I vowed, as I sucked in my cheeks on her command. I would buy all these products. I would use them every day. I studied her gleaming, polished features—her lacquered nails, the glittering mosaic of her eyeshadow, the complex red shimmer of her mouth, her flawless, dewy skin—and tried to imagine myself as impeccably groomed as she.

Estée's voice interrupted my reverie, telling me to blot my lips. I stuck   11
the tissue into my mouth and clamped down, watching myself in the mirror. My skin was a blankly even shade of pale, my cheeks and lips glaringly bright in contrast. My face had a strange plastic sheen, like a mannequin's. I grimaced as Estée applied the second lipstick coat: Was this right? Didn't I look kind of—fake? But she smiled back at me, clearly pleased with her work. I was ashamed of myself: Well, what did I expect? It wasn't like she had anything great to start with.

"Now," she announced, "Time for the biggie—Eyes."   12

"Oh. Well, actually, I want to look good and everything, but, I mean,   13
I'm sure you could tell, I'm not really into a complicated beauty routine." My voice faded into a faint giggle.

"So?" Estée snapped.   14

"Sooo." I tried again, "I've never really used eye makeup, except, you   15
know, for a little mascara sometimes, and I don't really feel comfortable—"

Estée was firm. "Well, the fact is that the eyes are the windows of the   16
face. They're the focal point. An eye routine doesn't have to be complicated, but it's important to emphasize the eyes with some color, or they'll look washed out."

I certainly didn't want that. I leaned back again in my chair and closed   17
my eyes.

Estée explained as she went: "I'm covering your lids with this cham-   18
pagne color. It's a real versatile base, 'cause it goes with almost any other color you put on top of it." I felt the velvety pad of the applicator sweep over my lids in a soothing rhythm.

"Now, being an Oriental, you don't have a lid fold, so I'm going to   19
draw one with this charcoal shadow. Then, I fill in below the line with a lighter charcoal color with a bit of blue in it—frosted midnight—and then above it, on the outsides of your lids, I'm going to apply this plum color. There. Hold on a minute. Okay. Open up."

I stared at the face in the mirror, at my eyes. The drawn-on fold and   20
dark, heavy shadows distorted and reproportioned my whole face. Not one of the features in the mirror was recognizable, not the waxy white skin or

[8] **emulsifying:** Making a suspension of two liquids that do not mix, such as oil and water.

the redrawn crimson lips or the sharp, deep cheekbones, and especially, not the eyes. I felt negated; I had been blotted out and another face drawn in my place. I looked up at Estée, and in that moment I hated her. "I look terrible," I said.

Her back stiffened. "What do you mean?" she demanded.   21

"Hideous. I don't even look human. Look at my eyes. You can't even   22
see me!" My voice was hoarse.

She looked. After a moment, she straightened up again, "Well, I'll   23
admit, the eyeshadow doesn't look great." She began to put away the pencils and brushes. "But at least now you have an eyelid."

I told myself that she was a pathetic, middle-aged woman with a boring   24
ing job and a meaningless life. I had my whole life before me. All she had
was the newest Richard Chamberlain[9] miniseries.

But it didn't matter. The fact of the matter was that she was pretty,   25
and I was not. Her blue eyes were recessed in an intricate pattern of folds
and hollows. Mine bulged out.

I bought the skincare system and the foundation and the blush and the   26
lip liner pencil and the lipstick and the primer and the eyeliner and the
eyeshadows—all four colors. The stuff filled a bag the size of a shoebox.
It cost a lot. Estée handed me my receipt with a flourish, and I told her,
"Thank you."

In the mezzanine[10] level washroom, I set my bag down on the counter   27
and scrubbed my face with water and slimy pink soap from the dispenser.
I splashed my face with cold water until it felt tight, and dried my raw
skin with brown paper towels that scratched.

As the sun sank into the Chicago skyline, I boarded the Burlington   28
Northern Commuter[11] for home and found a seat in the corner. I set the
shopping bag down beside me, and heaped its gilt boxes and frosted glass
bottles into my lap. Looking out the window, I saw that night had fallen.
Instead of trees and backyard fences I saw my profile—the same reflection, I realized, that I'd seen hours ago in the side of the green glass office
building. I did have eyelids, of course. Just not a fold. I wasn't pretty. But
I was familiar and comforting. I was myself.

The next stop was mine. I arranged the things carefully back in the rectangular bag, large bottles of toner and moisturizer first, then the short cylinders of masque and scrub and powder, small bottles of foundation and   29
primer, the little logs of pencils and lipstick, then the flat boxed compacts of
blush and eyeshadow. The packages fit around each other cleverly, like
pieces in a puzzle. The conductor called out, "Fairview Avenue," and I stood
up. Hurrying down the aisle, I looked back once at the neatly packed bag on
the seat behind me, and jumped out just as the doors were closing shut.

[9] Richard Chamberlain: An actor who starred in the television program Dr. Kildare in the
      1960s and in the television miniseries Shogun and The Thorn Birds in the 1980s.
[10] mezzanine: A low-ceilinged story between two main stories of a building.
[11] Burlington Northern Commuter: A commuter train that ran from Chicago to the city's
      northern suburbs.

EXERCISING VOCABULARY

1. What is an epiphany? How is Suh's day of beauty "painfully epiphanous" (para. 4)? What lessons does she learn?

2. Suh says in paragraph 4 that she "had broken the Unsightliness Barrier." What other barrier do scientists and engineers usually refer to breaking? Why does Suh choose this image?

3. Suh refers to famous models in paragraph 5 as "goddesses" and to their pictures as "icons." How are these two words used in a religious sense? How does that affect your reading of Suh's paragraph?

PROBING CONTENT

1. What causes Suh to get a makeover? What feelings lead her to make this decision?

2. On which facial feature does Estée focus? What is the significance of this? What does it say about Estée's ideas about beauty?

3. What is the writer's reaction to the makeover? According to Suh, whom does she look like now?

4. What causes the writer to leave the makeup behind her on the commuter train? What does she feel like after she does this?

5. What lesson do you think Suh learns from her experience at Neiman Marcus?

CONSIDERING CRAFT

1. Of what common phrase does the title of the essay remind you? How does this phrase relate to the general message of the essay?

2. How does Suh's tone or attitude change as she begins to describe the cosmetic counters at Neiman Marcus? Why does it change? Why does Suh call the saleswomen "priestesses of beauty" (para. 5)? What does this indicate about her opinion of them? Of American culture as a whole?

3. Reread paragraphs 9 and 10, in which Suh uses many examples of specialized language, or jargon, from the beauty industry — including "exfoliant," "ultra-hydrating complex," and "emulsifying immunage." What is the effect of Suh's use of such language? Describe in detail how Suh communicates her "reverie" in these paragraphs.

4. The saleswoman calls Suh "an Oriental" (para. 19). What does Suh achieve by using this word? What is the difference between this term and the currently more culturally acceptable term *Asian American*?

5. Reread the dialogue in paragraphs 12 through 16. What effect does this exchange have on your understanding of the essay's message?

RESPONDING TO THE WRITER

What is your response to Suh's makeover? What did you feel as you read the essay? How did you feel at the end after she scrubs off the makeup?

For a quiz on this reading, go to bedfordstmartins.com/mirror.

Beauty: When the Other Dancer Is the Self

ALICE WALKER

A bright young girl who considers herself the "prettiest" child in her family suffers an injury that scars her beauty and her childhood. When she is subjected to stares and derision at a new school, her family decides she should move back to a familiar neighborhood and live with her grandmother. This separation changes relationships at a critical time within her family as her mother becomes ill. Thirty years later, the author Alice Walker looks back at the incident and examines how it affected her image of herself and her experience of life, in both positive and negative ways. Can you point to an experience in your own childhood that seems to have colored every event that followed? With the benefit of hindsight, can you now interpret those events differently? How important is our own self-perception in determining the course of our lives?

Alice Walker was born in 1944 in Georgia, the youngest of eight children. She is best known for her novel *The Color Purple* (1982), which in 1983 won both the Pulitzer Prize for Fiction and the National Book Award. It was later made into a film nominated for eleven Academy Awards. A prolific and varied writer, Walker has produced eight novels, two collections of short stories, numerous volumes of poetry, and two collections of essays. Her work has been included in many anthologies. In 2002, she published an update of her early work, *Langston Hughes, American Poet*, a biography for children. Her most recent novel, *Now Is the Time to Open Your Heart*, was published in 2004. "Beauty: When the Other Dancer Is the Self" first appeared in her essay collection *In Search of Our Mothers' Gardens: Womanist Prose* (1983).

THINKING AHEAD

Think of a time when you or someone you know — a friend or a fictional character — suffered a disfiguring or debilitating injury. What was the person's response to this injury? How did that response change over time?

INCREASING VOCABULARY

faze (v.) (2)	penitentiary (n.) (16)
sassiness (n.) (4)	sullen (adj.) (17)
relegated (v.) (8)	crater (n.) (32)
makeshift (adj.) (9)	scandalous (adj.) (36)
cataract (n.) (13)	dashed (v.) (44)

It is a bright summer day in 1947. My father, a fat, funny man with beautiful eyes and a subversive wit, is trying to decide which of his eight children he will take with him to the county fair. My mother, of course, will not go. She is knocked out[1] from getting most of us ready: I hold my neck stiff against the pressure of her knuckles as she hastily completes the braiding and then beribboning of my hair.   1

My father is the driver for the rich old white lady up the road. Her name is Miss Mey. She owns all the land for miles around, as well as the house in which we live. All I remember about her is that she once offered to pay my mother thirty-five cents for cleaning her house, raking up piles of her magnolia leaves, and washing her family's clothes, and that my mother—she of no money, eight children, and a chronic earache—refused it. But I do not think of this in 1947. I am two and a half years old. I want to go everywhere my daddy goes. I am excited at the prospect of riding in a car. Someone has told me fairs are fun. That there is room in the car for only three of us doesn't faze me at all. Whirling happily in my starchy frock, showing off my biscuit-polished[2] patent-leather[3] shoes and lavender socks, tossing my head in a way that makes my ribbons bounce, I stand, hands on hips, before my father. "Take me, Daddy," I say with assurance, "I'm the prettiest!"   2

Later, it does not surprise me to find myself in Miss Mey's shiny black car, sharing the back seat with the other lucky ones. Does not surprise me that I thoroughly enjoy the fair. At home that night I tell the unlucky ones all I can remember about the merry-go-round,[4] the man who eats live chickens, and the teddy bears, until they say: that's enough, baby Alice. Shut up now, and go to sleep.   3

It is Easter Sunday, 1950. I am dressed in a green, flocked,[5] scalloped-hem dress (handmade by my adoring sister, Ruth) that has its own smooth satin petticoat and tiny hot-pink roses tucked into each scallop. My shoes, new T-strap patent leather, again highly biscuit-polished. I am six years old and have learned one of the longest Easter speeches to be heard that day, totally unlike the speech I said when I was two: "Easter lilies / pure and white / blossom in / the morning light." When I rise to give my speech I do so on a great wave of love and pride and expectation. People in the church stop rustling their new crinolines.[6] They seem to hold their breath. I can tell they admire my dress, but it is my spirit, bordering on sassiness (womanishness), they secretly applaud.   4

"That girl's a little *mess*," they whisper to each other, pleased.   5

Naturally I say my speech without stammer or pause, unlike those who stutter, stammer, or, worst of all, forget. This is before the word   6

---

[1] **ESL knocked out:** Fatigued; tired out; exhausted.
[2] **ESL biscuit-polished:** Greased with a biscuit and made shiny.
[3] **ESL patent leather:** Leather with a hard, shiny surface.
[4] **ESL merry-go-round:** An amusement park ride featuring brightly colored animals to sit on; a carousel.
[5] **flocked:** Having a raised velvety pattern.
[6] **crinolines:** Stiff petticoats designed to make a skirt stand out.

"beautiful" exists in people's vocabulary, but "Oh, isn't she the *cutest* thing!" frequently floats my way. "And got so much sense!" they gratefully add . . . for which thoughtful addition I thank them to this day.

It was great fun being cute. But then, one day, it ended.   7

I am eight years old and a tomboy.[7] I have a cowboy hat, cowboy boots,   8
checkered shirt and pants, all red. My playmates are my brothers, two and four years older than I. Their colors are black and green, the only difference in the way we are dressed. On Saturday nights we all go to the picture show, even my mother; Westerns are her favorite kind of movie. Back home, "on the ranch," we pretend we are Tom Mix,[8] Hopalong Cassidy,[9] Lash LaRue[10] (we've even named one of our dogs Lash LaRue); we chase each other for hours rustling cattle, being outlaws, delivering damsels from distress. Then my parents decide to buy my brothers guns. These are not "real" guns. They shoot "BBs," copper pellets my brothers say will kill birds. Because I am a girl, I do not get a gun. Instantly I am relegated to the position of Indian. Now there appears a great distance between us. They shoot and shoot at everything with their new guns. I try to keep up with my bow and arrows.

One day while I am standing on top of our makeshift "garage"—   9
pieces of tin nailed across some poles—holding my bow and arrow and looking out toward the fields, I feel an incredible blow in my right eye. I look down just in time to see my brother lower his gun.

Both brothers rush to my side. My eye stings, and I cover it with my   10
hand. "If you tell," they say, "we will get a whipping. You don't want that to happen, do you?" I do not. "Here is a piece of wire," says the older brother, picking it up from the roof; "say you stepped on one end of it and the other flew up and hit you." The pain is beginning to start. "Yes," I say. "Yes, I will say that is what happened." If I do not say this is what happened, I know my brothers will find ways to make me wish I had. But now I will say anything that gets me to my mother.

Confronted by our parents we stick to the lie agreed upon. They place   11
me on a bench on the porch and I close my left eye while they examine the right. There is a tree growing from underneath the porch that climbs past the railing to the roof. It is the last thing my right eye sees. I watch as its trunk, its branches, and then its leaves are blotted out by the rising blood.

I am in shock. First there is intense fever, which my father tries to   12
break using lily leaves bound around my head. Then there are chills: my mother tries to get me to eat soup. Eventually, I do not know how, my parents learn what has happened. A week after the "accident" they take

---

[7] **ESL tomboy:** A young girl who enjoys vigorous activities traditionally associated with males.
[8] **Tom Mix:** An actor in 1930s Western films.
[9] **Hopalong Cassidy:** An actor in Western films and television series from the 1930s through the 1950s.
[10] **Lash LaRue:** An actor in Western films in the 1940s, known as the King of the Bullwhip.

me to see a doctor. "Why did you wait so long to come?" he asks, looking into my eye and shaking his head. "Eyes are sympathetic," he says. "If one is blind, the other will likely become blind too."

This comment of the doctor's terrifies me. But it is really how I look   13
that bothers me most. Where the BB pellet struck there is a glob of whitish scar tissue, a hideous cataract, on my eye. Now when I stare at people—a favorite pastime, up to now—they will stare back. Not at the "cute" little girl, but at her scar. For six years I do not stare at anyone, because I do not raise my head.

Years later, in the throes[11] of a mid-life crisis, I ask my mother and sister   14
whether I changed after the "accident." "No," they say, puzzled. "What do you mean?"

What do I mean?   15

I am eight, and, for the first time, doing poorly in school, where I have   16
been something of a whiz since I was four. We have just moved to the place where the "accident" occurred. We do not know any of the people around us because this is a different county. The only time I see the friends I knew is when we go back to our old church. The new school is the former state penitentiary. It is a large stone building, cold and drafty, crammed to over-flowing with boisterous, ill-disciplined children. On the third floor there is a huge circular imprint of some partition that has been torn out.

"What used to be here?" I ask a sullen girl next to me on our way past   17
it to lunch.

"The electric chair," says she.   18

At night I have nightmares about the electric chair, and about all the   19
people reputedly "fried" in it. I am afraid of the school, where all the students seem to be budding criminals.

"What's the matter with your eye?" they ask, critically.   20

When I don't answer (I cannot decide whether it was an "accident" or   21
not), they shove me, insist on a fight.

My brother, the one who created the story about the wire, comes to   22
my rescue. But then brags so much about "protecting" me, I become sick.

After months of torture at the school, my parents decide to send me   23
back to our old community, to my old school. I live with my grandparents and the teacher they board. But there is no room for Phoebe, my cat. By the time my grandparents decide there *is* room, and I ask for my cat, she cannot be found. Miss Yarborough, the boarding teacher, takes me under her wing, and begins to teach me to play the piano. But soon she marries an African—a "prince," she says—and is whisked away to his continent.

At my old school there is at least one teacher who loves me. She is the   24
teacher who "knew me before I was born" and bought my first baby clothes. It is she who makes life bearable. It is her presence that finally helps me turn on the one child at the school who continually calls me

---

[11] **throes:** Difficult or painful struggles.

"one-eyed bitch." One day I simply grab him by his coat and beat him until I am satisfied. It is my teacher who tells me my mother is ill.

My mother is lying in bed in the middle of the day, something I have   25
never seen. She is in too much pain to speak. She has an abscess in her ear. I stand looking down on her, knowing that if she dies, I cannot live. She is being treated with warm oils and hot bricks held against her cheek. Finally a doctor comes. But I must go back to my grandparents' house. The weeks pass but I am hardly aware of it. All I know is that my mother might die, my father is not so jolly, my brothers still have their guns, and I am the one sent away from home.
    "You did not change," they say.   26
    Did I imagine the anguish of never looking up?   27

I am twelve. When relatives come to visit I hide in my room. My cousin   28
Brenda, just my age, whose father works in the post office and whose mother is a nurse, comes to find me. "Hello," she says. And then she asks, looking at my recent school picture, which I did not want taken, and on which the "glob," as I think of it, is clearly visible, "You still can't see out of that eye?"
    "No," I say, and flop back on the bed over my book.   29
    That night, as I do almost every night, I abuse my eye. I rant and rave   30
at it, in front of the mirror. I plead with it to clear up before morning. I tell it I hate and despise it. I do not pray for sight. I pray for beauty.
    "You did not change," they say.   31

I am fourteen and baby-sitting for my brother Bill, who lives in Boston. He   32
is my favorite brother and there is a strong bond between us. Understanding my feelings of shame and ugliness he and his wife take me to a local hospital, where the "glob" is removed by a doctor named O. Henry. There is still a small bluish crater where the scar tissue was, but the ugly white stuff is gone. Almost immediately I become a different person from the girl who does not raise her head. Or so I think. Now that I've raised my head I win the boyfriend of my dreams. Now that I've raised my head I have plenty of friends. Now that I've raised my head classwork comes from my lips as faultlessly as Easter speeches did, and I leave high school as valedictorian,[12] most popular student, and *queen*, hardly believing my luck. Ironically, the girl who was voted most beautiful in our class (and was) was later shot twice through the chest by a male companion, using a "real" gun, while she was pregnant. But that's another story in itself. Or is it?
    "You did not change," they say.   33

It is now thirty years since the "accident." A beautiful journalist comes to   34
visit and to interview me. She is going to write a cover story for her magazine

[12] **ESL** **valedictorian:** The student who has the highest rank in his or her class and delivers the graduation speech.

that focuses on my latest book. "Decide how you want to look on the cover," she says. "Glamorous, or whatever."

Never mind "glamorous," it is the "whatever" that I hear. Suddenly all I can think of is whether I will get enough sleep the night before the photography session: if I don't, my eye will be tired and wander, as blind eyes will.   35

At night in bed with my lover I think up reasons why I should not appear on the cover of a magazine. "My meanest critics will say I've sold out," I say. "My family will not realize I write scandalous books."   36

"But what's the real reason you don't want to do this?" he asks.   37

"Because in all probability," I say in a rush, "my eye won't be straight."   38

"It will be straight enough," he says. Then, "Besides, I thought you'd made your peace with that."   39

And I suddenly remember that I have.   40

I remember: 41

I am talking to my brother Jimmy, asking if he remembers anything unusual about the day I was shot. He does not know I consider that day the last time my father, with his sweet home remedy of cool lily leaves, chose me, and that I suffered and raged inside because of this. "Well," he says, "all I remember is standing by the side of the highway with Daddy, trying to flag down[13] a car. A white man stopped, but when Daddy said he needed somebody to take his little girl to the doctor, he drove off."   42

I remember: 43

I am in the desert for the first time. I fall totally in love with it. I am so overwhelmed by its beauty, I confront for the first time, consciously, the meaning of the doctor's words years ago: "Eyes are sympathetic. If one is blind, the other will likely become blind too." I realize I have dashed about the world madly, looking at this, looking at that, storing up images against the fading of the light. *But I might have missed seeing the desert!* The shock of that possibility—and gratitude for over twenty-five years of sight—sends me literally to my knees. Poem after poem comes—which is perhaps how poets pray.   44

On Sight
I am so thankful I have seen
The Desert
And the creatures in the desert
And the desert Itself.

The desert has its own moon
Which I have seen
With my own eye.
There is no flag on it.

---

[13] **ESL flag down:** To signal to stop.

Trees of the desert have arms
All of which are always up
That is because the moon is up
The sun is up
Also the sky
The stars
Clouds
None with flags.

If there *were* flags, I doubt
the trees would point.
Would you?

But mostly, I remember this: 45

I am twenty-seven, and my baby daughter is almost three. Since her 46
birth I have worried about her discovery that her mother's eyes are different from other people's. Will she be embarrassed? I think. What will she
say? Every day she watches a television program called *Big Blue Marble*.
It begins with a picture of the earth as it appears from the moon. It is
bluish, a little battered-looking, but full of light, with whitish clouds
swirling around it. Every time I see it I weep with love, as if it is a picture
of Grandma's house. One day when I am putting Rebecca down for her
nap, she suddenly focuses on my eye. Something inside me cringes, gets
ready to try to protect myself. All children are cruel about physical differences, I know from experience, and that they don't always mean to be is
another matter. I assume Rebecca will be the same.

But no-o-o-o. She studies my face intently as we stand, her inside and 47
me outside her crib. She even holds my face maternally between her dimpled
little hands. Then, looking every bit as serious and lawyerlike as her father,
she says, as if it may just possibly have slipped my attention: "Mommy,
there's a *world* in your eye." (As in, "Don't be alarmed, or do anything
crazy.") And then, gently, but with great interest: "Mommy, where did you
get that world in your eye?"

For the most part, the pain left then. (So what, if my brothers grew up 48
to buy even more powerful pellet guns for their sons and to carry real
guns themselves. So what, if a young "Morehouse man"[14] once nearly fell
off the steps of Trevor Arnett Library because he thought my eyes were
blue.) Crying and laughing I ran to the bathroom, while Rebecca mum-
bled and sang herself off to sleep. Yes indeed, I realized, looking into the
mirror. There *was* a world in my eye. And I saw that it was possible
to love it: that in fact, for all it had taught me of shame and anger and
inner vision, I *did* love it. Even to see it drifting out of orbit in boredom,
or rolling up out of fatigue, not to mention floating back at attention in

---

[14]**Morehouse man:** A student at Morehouse College, Atlanta, Georgia, the only all-male,
historically black institution of higher learning in the United States.

excitement (bearing witness, a friend has called it), deeply suitable to my personality, and even characteristic of me.

That night I dream I am dancing to Stevie Wonder's[15] song "Always" (the name of the song is really "As," but I hear it as "Always"). As I dance, whirling and joyous, happier than I've ever been in my life, another bright-faced dancer joins me. We dance and kiss each other and hold each other through the night. The other dancer has obviously come through all right, as I have done. She is beautiful, whole and free. And she is also me.   49

EXERCISING VOCABULARY

1. In paragraphs 12 and 44, Walker quotes her doctor as saying, "Eyes are sympathetic. If one is blind, the other will likely become blind too." In what other context do we generally use the word *sympathetic*? What does it mean?

2. Walker writes that "Miss Yarborough, the boarding teacher, takes me under her wing" (para. 23). What does it mean to offer someone board? What is the situation of the boarding teacher? What does it mean to take someone under one's wing? Where does this image originate?

PROBING CONTENT

1. What happens that causes Walker to stop being "cute" (para. 7)? What role do her brothers play in this incident?

2. Describe the author before the "accident." What are her outstanding characteristics? How does she relate to those around her?

3. Describe Walker after the accident. How does she change both physically and psychologically?

4. When did Walker begin to regain her confidence? What role does her brother Bill play in this?

5. In paragraph 47, Rebecca says, "Mommy, there's a *world* in your eye." What did the child mean? Where does Rebecca get this idea? How did the child's reaction affect her mother?

CONSIDERING CRAFT

1. What is the significance of the title? Why does Walker choose a dance metaphor?

2. Why does Walker insert the poem "On Sight" within her essay (para. 44)? How does this affect your reading?

---

[15] **ESL** **Stevie Wonder:** An African-American singer, pianist, and songwriter who is blind.

3. Why does the author repeat certain phrases throughout the essay? Find two or three examples and discuss their use in the essay.

4. Examine several examples of achronological order in Walker's essay. Why do you think she chooses to present her narrative in this manner?

RESPONDING TO THE WRITER

What did you think of Rebecca's reaction to her mother's eye? What can her response teach us about acceptance of the physical differences among people?

For a quiz on this reading, go to bedfordstmartins.com/mirror.

Meet Marnie

GABY WOOD

Plastic surgery used to be something people had done in secrecy. How has this practice become so publicly acceptable? Do extreme surgical makeovers really create happy endings, as they appear to do on TV? Do they transfer discontent to otherwise complacent viewers who might now consider surgical intervention? In "Meet Marnie," which appeared in the July 18, 2004, edition of *The Observer*, a London newspaper, writer Gaby Wood gets to know one of the contestants on Fox's makeover show, *The Swan*. In telling Marnie's story after she goes home and resumes her life, Wood punctures the premise of such shows, which she says promise to help "people find their 'true selves' " but actually reward an individual who, in the end, appears "least like her former self." She also wonders whether something uniquely American in the shows appeals to a country founded on the "pursuit of happiness" or reflects a democratic impulse to redistribute beauty to those who don't have it.

Gaby Wood was born in 1971. She has been a regular contributor to *The Guardian* and the *London Review of Books* and is currently a staff writer for *The Observer* in London. She is the author of a short work of nonfiction, *The Smallest of All Persons Mentioned in the Records of Littleness* (1998), and a full-length nonfiction book, *Edison's Eve: A Magical History of the Quest for Mechanical Life*, which was a finalist for the 2002 National Book Critics Circle Award.

THINKING AHEAD

How familiar are you with makeover shows like *The Swan* or *Extreme Makeover*? What is your opinion of them? What is their appeal for viewers? If you are not familiar with these shows, what is your opinion of plastic surgery?

INCREASING VOCABULARY

augmentation (n.) (2)

veneers (n.) (2)

timorously (adv.) (4)

splayed (adj.) (4)

protagonists (n.) (5)

depersonalize (v.) (5)

incisive (adj.) (6)

inflammatory (adj.) 7

overt (adj.) 9

cyborgs (n.) 10

normalized (v.) 11

barbaric (adj.) 11

advent (n.) 15

reciprocate (v.) 21

docile (adj.) 27

balk (v.) 39

androids (n.) 40

farcical (adj.) 40

inequitable (adj.) 44

inaugural (adj.) 45

On prime-time TV, Marnie Rygiewicz, a 35-year-old mother of two, faces the camera and tells nearly 10 million viewers what is wrong with her life. Her sons' father left 10 years ago and she hasn't had a date since. She's wiped out from making dinner and going to basketball games and cleaning up. Every morning, when she arrives at the office in Michigan where she works as a medical assistant, people ask if she's had any sleep. She has lost sight of herself.

The camera pulls back to reveal a panel of experts listening sympathetically to Marnie's story. The show's resident therapist mutters something about self-esteem, and the doctors prescribe a solution: a brow lift, a mid-face lift, a nose job, fat removal from under the eyes, a corner lip lift, lip augmentation, a chin lift, breast augmentation, liposuction on the stomach, thighs, calves and ankles, teeth bleaching, a bridge, and veneers. Marnie happily agrees to these procedures, and makes arrangements to leave home for four months. She will spend that time in a hotel in Los Angeles, without ever being allowed to look in a mirror.

Cut to[1] a bandaged figure. Marnie is in pain, and desperate to remove her uncomfortable chin strap. She seems depressed, and after three days without leaving her room she is visited by the show's "life coach" — a small producer named Nely Galan, who says she is very disappointed in Marnie, who is expected to be in the gym two hours a day, six days a week. The program makers have given her all this wonderful free surgery, and this is how she behaves?

Months later (or minutes, to a TV audience) Marnie has been perfected. Wearing a fuchsia-pink evening gown, she is ushered into a gothically lit room, where her creators stand in a circle. The surgeons voice their approval. The therapist and dentist applaud. She is shown a mirror for the first time, and, behind her timorously splayed fingers, she begins to weep.

The Swan is one of three major reality-TV shows Americans have witnessed in the past few months in which the patient-protagonists undergo cosmetic surgery in order to improve their lives. All three are due to be shown in Britain. Much like its sister program, *Home Front*, ABC's *Extreme Makeover* is a kind of interior design program. Dilapidated women and men are knocked through and rebuilt before receiving finishing touches that depersonalize them and increase their apparent market value. They are then presented to their families, who are delighted with the new product to variously convincing degrees. In MTV's *I Want a Famous Face*, people are surgically made over to look like a particular celebrity. There have been dark-haired, acne-scarred twins who want to look like Brad Pitt,[2] a pre-op transsexual who dreams of resembling J-Lo,[3] an Elvis impersonator who feels the competition in Vegas is getting

[1] **ESL** **cut to:** To switch from one film scene to another.
[2] **ESL** **Brad Pitt:** An American movie star.
[3] **ESL** **J-Lo:** Jennifer Lopez, a singer and actor from New York City who has clothing and perfume lines.

tougher. Only Fox's[4] *The Swan*, which is currently in casting calls for a second season, has its patients compete in a final beauty pageant, with swimsuits, lingerie and evening wear, pitting even the "new improved" versions against each other.

The programs vaunt[5] the idea that they are helping these people find   6
their "true selves," and yet the winner on *The Swan* is the woman who is thought to have undergone the greatest "overall transformation"—in other words, the one who appears least like her former self. It's reminiscent of a line in the incisive plastic surgery drama *Nip/Tuck*: "Be yourself. You know you can look better." Or perhaps of Lily Tomlin's[6] old gag: "When I was little I wanted to be somebody. Now I wish I'd been more specific."

These shows have provided some of the most popular and controver-   7
sial viewing of recent times. Up to 12 million Americans watched them every week; talk-show host Rosie O'Donnell said they had put women back 30 years. One weekly news magazine carried the cover line: "Make-over Nation: Why America's Obsession with Plastic Surgery Is Going Dangerously Out of Control," and even *People* magazine, which has embraced these sewn-up celebrities, asked: "Has TV Plastic Surgery Gone Too Far?" Indeed, few recipes for cultural anxiety could be more inspired than the marriage of two of the most inflammatory contemporary phenomena: cosmetic surgery and reality TV.

Yet these surgical scenarios are truly gripping, both for the reasons   8
their creators hope—the transformations are extreme, the family reunions can be strangely emotional, desperate people seem to become happier before our eyes—and in more nefarious[7] ways: the surgeons are laddish and overly prescriptive, the procedures are risky and irreversible, and there is always the sadistic hope that this week, someone will regret it.

It is 14 years since Naomi Wolf wrote in *The Beauty Myth* that we   9
were living in "the Modern Surgical Age." What this historical phase was doing to us, she argued, was "an overt re-enactment of what 19th-century medicine did to make well women sick and active women passive." Indeed, cosmetic surgery is the only form of surgery in which the patient is healthy beforehand. Now there are so many layers of simulation involved—televisual surgery as opposed to the real thing, the act of being turned into a copy of someone else—that you might say we have left the Modern Surgical Age and entered the Postmodern[8] one.

"When I wrote *The Beauty Myth*," Wolf says now, "plastic surgery   10
was an extreme choice for the few. Now it has become so normative[9] that

---

[4] ESL **Fox:** An American television network.

[5] **vaunt:** To boast about.

[6] ESL **Lily Tomlin:** An American actor and comedian.

[7] **nefarious:** Wicked; evil.

[8] **postmodern:** Relating to art, architecture, literature, or thinking developed after and usually in reaction to modernism, marked in architecture by a return to more traditional elements and techniques and in other art forms by new ironic combinations of elements.

[9] **normative:** Relating to rules or standards.

people will look odd in the near future if they aren't surgically altered. The reality shows I feel have a fair dose of sadism involved—really we have reached the point of creating cyborgs."

Elaine Showalter, author of *The Female Malady*, among other distin-   11
guished feminist tomes, disagrees. "It doesn't seem to me like it's something sadistic that doctors practice on women," she says. "I think women are choosing it. And that's very different. I think that we're living in an intermediate era, where women are certainly made aware of body image to a degree and with a degree of detail that they never were—it seems to me every year there's a new part of the body that's offered up for correction, and you never knew it had standards. But I have the feeling that we're moving towards a future in which these things will be more routine, and safer, and less expensive. And it will be normalized. Now, for many people this may seem like a horrible world. But I kind of feel that if it were more normalized, it would be just like anything else—that people could do it in moderation. . . . Maybe I'm wrong—maybe it's just a step into the barbaric, or the downfall of civilization, but I don't think so."

Terry Dubrow, one of the surgeons on *The Swan*, has asserted: "Plastic   12
surgery as entertainment is here to stay." But the reality shows have not just made a spectacle out of plastic surgery; they have turned it into something ordinary people feel comfortable having in their living rooms. Unlike many other reality shows here—*American Idol, The Bachelor*—*Extreme Makeover* and *The Swan* are aimed at a slightly older generation, one that has had time to brew[10] some world-weariness and low-grade self-hatred. As a result, TV plastic surgery has become more than entertainment—it has become a kind of blueprint.

Dr. Rod Rohrich, president of the American Society of Plastic Surgeons,   13
says: "The growth of plastic surgery has been nothing short of phenomenal. With all these reality shows, the interest has sky-rocketed.[11] I think they've increased the awareness that plastic surgery isn't just for the wealthy and for the famous—it can be for everybody, for anybody that wants it if they want to save for it."

ASPS statistics for 2003 show that its members performed 8.7 million   14
procedures last year, a 33 percent increase on those performed in 2002, and that nearly eight and a half billion dollars were spent. Banks now offer loans for plastic surgery, and credit cards render many procedures affordable (the average cost of a breast augmentation is $3,375). One divorcee I met recently is selling her engagement ring on eBay[12] in order to have a "Brazilian butt lift." And families with annual incomes under $25,000 now account for an astonishing 30 percent of all cosmetic surgery patients. Only 23 percent earn more than $50,000.

Since the advent of "reality surgery," Rohrich has seen two things   15
happen: "One is that patients now want to have a lot more done—they

[10] **ESL brew:** To produce by fermentation.
[11] **ESL sky-rocketed:** Climbed rapidly.
[12] **ESL eBay:** An online auction site.

want this 'extreme makeover'—everything done in one sitting, which is not realistic, nor is it safe, in many cases. And it's also spurred a whole new industry of people who call themselves cosmetic surgeons and aren't real plastic surgeons, because the interest and growth has been so high. In America, if you have an M.D., you can call yourself anything you want. So plastic surgery has become a 'buyer-beware' speciality. Not a day goes by where I don't get a call or an email or see a patient who's had a problem or has been misguided by a non-plastic surgeon."

Liposuction, the most popular invasive procedure, is also the most dangerous. Complications include blood clots, organ puncture and infection, all of which can be fatal. The most recent information puts the average death rate for liposuction at 20 in 100,000 (deaths from hernia operations, by comparison, stand at 2 per 100,000). Combining liposuction with a tummy tuck increases the risk 14-fold.   16

On May 14, as *The Swan* was nearing its bikini-clad finale, the prestigious Manhattan Eye, Ear, and Throat Hospital was fined $20,000 for "egregious violations" of safety procedures during cosmetic surgery which led to the deaths of two women, including the 54-year-old writer Olivia Goldsmith. The fine is equivalent to about four tummy tucks, or veneers on a mere 10 teeth. In Florida, a ban has been imposed on combined liposuction and tummy tucks after the deaths of eight patients in 18 months. The ban is only three months long. In February, the body of a 35-year-old investment banker was discovered in a suitcase, encased in cement, under the home of an unlicensed cosmetic surgeon. Her body was identified by the serial numbers on her breast implants.   17

Back at home in Chesterfield, Michigan, Marnie Rygiewicz has started her new life as a stunning blonde. She is selling her house, taking her kids to school again, and looking through the paper to try to pick up a job until something else comes along. She has called a couple of plastic surgeons' offices looking for work, and she wouldn't mind doing some modeling—just until she works out what it is she really wants to do.   18

"I don't think the surgery itself really changed me," she reflects, two months after *The Swan*'s televised beauty pageant. "I just feel like a more confident person. I never really considered myself, like, ugly, but I would look in the mirror and feel like I had wasted so much time, and I wished that I could somehow get some time back."   19

As it happens, Marnie only went to the *Swan* audition in order to accompany her sister, who was trying out. She was chosen, she believes, because she was clearly more of a "burn-out[13] mom," and in the end her sister looked after her two boys for the four months she was away. Now her sister is auditioning for the second season.   20

"I want her to go through what I went through," says Marnie, who plans to reciprocate the childcare arrangements. "I would love for her to have that experience."   21

---

[13] **ESL burn-out:** Exhausted.

When Marnie speaks about the things she's looking forward to, I am   22
surprised to find her laying stress on "ageing naturally," since she has been
so recently filled with artificial substances. I ask her to list the surgical procedures she has had. There seem to be a crucial few missing. Did she not
have a boob job? "Oh yes," she recalls, "I had a breast augmentation. And
I had my lips done." "But," she adds, "I don't think I would have needed all
that had I not let myself go. It was something that I did to myself."

Which single surgical procedure does she think made the biggest   23
difference?

"I would say the one that took the tired bags under my eyes."   24

So far, I suggest, none of the symptoms she describes—tiredness, regret,   25
loss of identity—are things for which one might automatically recommend cosmetic surgery.

"Yeah," she agrees, "but I did look bad because of the way my life   26
was." Has she ever been diagnosed with depression? "No." So she never
thought of taking a drug like Prozac? "No," Marnie says quietly, "I feel a
lot better now."

Marnie has a soft, monotonous, almost somnolent[14] voice. I am re-   27
minded of a novel called *The Eve of the Future*, in which the industrial
wizard Thomas Edison designs the perfect woman: her speech is recorded
on golden phonographs, and destined only to repeat preordained words of
love. It's not that I think Marnie is unreal, it's just that. . . . well, if you
were to invent a sweet, docile, beautiful woman, how far would she be
from Marnie Rygiewicz? How did she get to be so perfect?

Dr. Randal Digby Haworth, the man who operated on Marnie,   28
speaks to me between mouthfuls from his Beverly Hills office (he is so
busy lifting[15] Hollywood lovelies he needs to use these spare moments to
catch up on lunch).

"I always say there are two types of plastic surgeons," Haworth ex-   29
plains. "Doctors who become artists and artists who become doctors, and
I am pretty much among the latter."

Plastic surgery, he says, is "a tool. It can be used to customize your   30
appearance in the same way you customize your living environment
through interior design, the same way that you customize your car, or
your pets, or the way you dress in Prada[16] versus Dolce.[17] In the right
practitioner's hands, plastic surgery is an extension of that—it can allow
you to turn your physical fantasies into realities."

And in terms of his own fantasies, I ask (thinking of the fact that the   31
women on *The Swan* ended up looking so alike), is there a type of woman
he favors?

"I'm more attracted to brunettes," Haworth says, without hesitation.   32

---

[14] somnolent: Sleepy.
[15] **ESL** **lifting:** Surgically tightening the skin to create a younger appearance.
[16] **ESL** **Prada:** Italian fashion house located in Milan.
[17] **ESL** **Dolce:** Dolce and Gabbana, an Italian fashion house.

I actually meant in terms of surgical enhancement. . . .   33

"Oh, I see. Good plastic surgery is invisible. It's bad plastic surgery   34
that gets the attention. I mean, we live in LA, and I've oftentimes gone out
with girls here on whom I've noticed little discreet scars in more intimate
moments. I'd say about 80 percent of people here have had plastic surgery,
and yet no one can deny that Los Angeles and Hollywood is the home to
some of the most beautiful women in the world."

But let's say good plastic surgery as opposed to none at all.   35

"OK, well, speaking as a man here, if it's a girl with a natural 'A' ver-   36
sus a beautiful, er, artificial 'C'? I'd prefer an artificial 'C.' If somebody's
got a nice figure but has love handles[18] here and there? Call me twisted,
but I'd prefer a good figure versus one that's less good."

And has he operated on women he has been in relationships with?   37

"Oh, absolutely. I have. It's generally repairing stuff that's not very   38
good—they've had plastic surgery before. You know, the breasts don't
fall as well."

Many Americans would balk at the suggestion that reality cosmetic   39
surgery shows might offer any significant insights into their culture. But
the programs do, I think, illustrate a fundamental American belief: the belief in self-improvement, or self-invention.

The Stepford Wives remake, which is due out in Britain at the end of   40
this month, contains a troublesome new twist: Stepford, the town that
turns women into androids, was created by a woman. Perhaps the story,
played for laughs this time, is not so farcical after all. Why are women
doing this to themselves?

The United States, it might be remembered, is a country founded on the   41
pursuit of happiness, whereas Britain is a country wedded—rhetorically, at
least—to its failings. Self-deprecation is our style. As a result, cosmetic
surgery can be seen as constructive in America, while meeting with more
resistance elsewhere. (It's striking that liposuction, which was invented by
a French surgeon, is more popular in America than anywhere else, and
that cellulite, the problem it set out to combat, was a concept unknown to
Americans before 1973. Yet these words have been welcomed into a per-
fectionist's vocabulary with open arms.)

Happiness is a serious business. Jim Holt, the author of a forthcoming   42
book on the subject, recently wrote an article for the *New York Times* in
which he argued dryly that happiness may be bad for you. A professor at
the University of Pennsylvania wrote in to complain that the article was a
threat to public health. "In countries where happiness is considered to be
more important, you generally have higher divorce rates, and more sui-
cides," Holt explains, "because people feel the ideal is that people should
be happy almost all the time, and so some radical change is necessary."

One way of seeing cosmetic surgery is as a new form of equal oppor-   43
tunity. In 1993, two economists found that good looks increased hourly
income by five percent. "It's not just a matter of good-looking people

[18] **ESL love handles:** Excess fat around the waist; also called a spare tire.

going to work in Hollywood and bad-looking people digging ditches," one of them, Daniel Hamermesh, said. "Even within any given occupation, good-looking people make more."

Jim Holt thinks this is unlikely to dim the optimism of a self-improver. "The distribution of beauty in America is as imbalanced as the distribution of wealth," he says. "Americans don't mind the inequitable distribution of wealth very much because they all feel that it's possible to become rich here. And there's something of the same logic that might apply to the way you look." 44

Janice Dickinson, self-described "world's first supermodel" and a judge on another reality-TV show, *America's Next Top Model*, believes the addiction to perfection is a disease. She has even given it a name: "perfliction," and diagnosed herself as its inaugural victim. Her symptoms are detailed in a new memoir, *Everything about Me Is Fake . . . And I'm Perfect!* When I compliment Dickinson on her coinage, she tells me, by way of thanks: " 'Perfliction' has been trademarked. I'm going to use it for a cream—it comes out in September at Bendels[19] department store." It's not clear how well a cream named after a problem might sell, but there's no doubting the joie de vivre[20] in Dickinson's proclamations ("I'm Dorian Gray!" she was heard to screech at her book launch, as if Dorian Gray[21] were Cinderella), and who knows—as far as the pursuit of perfection is concerned, she's an expert. 45

"Plastic surgery is an epidemic in the States," Dickinson says. "But it's everywhere. They don't talk about it in England—it's more hush hush, like everything else is. But it's always been there. There have been face lifts and botched boob jobs and great boob jobs, starting with . . . I don't know—Lady Diana had surgery!" 46

Did she? 47

"Hell, yes—look at her face! I mean, she had a boob job—she wasn't that well-endowed. I guarantee you that she pumped up the volume." 48

What about the pursuit of happiness? Does Dickinson think the women on *The Swan* and *Extreme Makeover* will be happier? 49

"I don't know. I'm no one to judge. I can only speak for myself." 50

So has cosmetic surgery made her happier? 51

"Yes. No. I don't know." She thinks for a while, reminisces about her first boob job, and the trips to Tijuana for illegal wrinkle fillers. "I think plastic surgery does not give you fulfilment," she concludes, "true, godly, Zen[22] contentment." 52

A few hours after our last conversation, Marnie Rygiewicz calls back. She leaves a message on my answering machine which seems to hang in the air, filled with its own kind of simple haunting. "Hi, Gaby. This is Marnie. I just forgot to mention one thing. I wouldn't have plastic surgery again. I have had it this time, but I wouldn't have it again. OK, thanks. Bye." 53

---

[19] **ESL Bendels:** An expensive department store in New York City.
[20] joie de vivre: French for love of life.
[21] **ESL Dorian Gray:** Protagonist of *The Picture of Dorian Gray*, a gothic novel by Oscar Wilde. Through most of the novel, Dorian remains young while his portrait ages.
[22] Zen: Relating to a Japanese sect of Buddhism that relies on meditation for enlightenment.

EXERCISING VOCABULARY

1. In paragraph 5, the author writes, "Dilapidated women and men are knocked through and rebuilt before receiving finishing touches that depersonalize them and increase their apparent market value." Terms like "dilapidated," "knocked through," "rebuild," and "market value" are normally used to describe what kind of project? How effective is the author's word choice here?

2. In paragraph 44, the author uses the phrase "unlikely to dim the optimism of a self-improver." What does it mean to "dim" something? Give some examples of things you might dim. What does it mean to "dim [one's] optimism"?

PROBING CONTENT

1. Who is Marnie? What happens to her? Why does the article focus on her?

2. What is the supposed goal of *The Swan*? How is this ironic?

3. What has resulted from the increased popularity of "reality surgery" (para. 15)? Are the results positive or negative or both?

4. Who coined the term "perfliction"? What does it mean? How does it apply to Marnie?

CONSIDERING CRAFT

1. The author cites several authorities in her essay. Examine two or three of these in detail. How effective are these authority figures' voices? Why does Wood include them?

2. There are allusions to various films and fictional works in the essay. Find two or three examples. Why does the author include these references? How do they affect your reading of the essay?

3. How does knowing that this article was written for a British periodical affect your reading? Find several places in the essay in which a non-American viewpoint is evident.

4. Why does Wood end the essay as she does? How effective is this closing?

RESPONDING TO THE WRITER

Would you be willing to be the reclamation project on one of these cosmetic surgery shows? Why or why not?

For a quiz on this reading, go to bedfordstmartins.com/mirror.

Venus Envy

PATRICIA MCLAUGHLIN

Do you think men today are just as stressed out as women are about the way they look? Do the men you know obsess about whether they have a few extra pounds here or a little less muscle there or whether a particular color or style is well suited to the image they want to show the world? In "Venus Envy," first published in the *Philadelphia Inquirer Magazine* on November 5, 1995, Patricia McLaughlin reports on the increasing importance of appearance to a man's self-image, popularity, and career success. In this analysis, McLaughlin draws candid and often humorous parallels with women's long-standing worries about their looks.

Patricia McLaughlin has written the Style column in the *Philadelphia Inquirer Magazine* since 1983, and her column "Ask Patsy" has appeared on TotalWoman.com since its launch in April 2000. Her syndicated column appears in over two hundred newspapers nationwide. She has also published feature stories and essays in the *Washington Post, Mirabella*, the *American Scholar*, the *New York Times Magazine*, and *Rolling Stone*.

THINKING AHEAD

How much does gender influence people's concern with their personal appearance? Which specific things about appearance most concern men? Which things most concern women? Compare the amount of time you think men and women devote to looking their best.

INCREASING VOCABULARY

wince (n.) (2)   ogle (v.) (7)
vertiginous (adj.) (3)

It used to be that what mattered in life was how women looked and what men did—which, to many women and other right-thinking people, didn't seem fair. Now, thanks to the efforts of feminists (and a lot of social and economic factors beyond their control) what women do matters more. 1

Meanwhile, in a development that's almost enough to make you believe in the Great Seesaw of Being, how men look is also beginning to carry more weight. Men are having plastic surgery to get rid of their love handles[1] and tighten their eye bags and beef up their chins and flatten their bellies and even (major wince) bulk up their penises. They're dyeing 2

---

[1] **love handles:** Excess fat around the waist; also called a spare tire.

their hair to hide the gray. They're buying magazines to find out how to lose those pesky last five pounds.

Naturally, women who always envied the way men never had to suf- 3
fer to be beautiful think they're making a big mistake. (What next: too-small shoes with vertiginous heels?) But maybe they don't exactly have a choice.

The key to how men feel about how they look, says Michael Pertschuk, 4
who's writing a book about it, is social expectation: What do they think folks expect them to look like? And how far do folks expect them to go to look that way?

You think of anorexia and bulimia as disorders that strike teenage 5
girls, but men get them, too—not many, but "a bit more" than used to, according to Pertschuk, a psychiatrist who sees patients (including men) with eating disorders. Because eating disorders virtually always start with a "normal" desire to lose weight and look slimmer, the increase among men suggests that men are worrying about their looks more than they used to.

Pertschuk has also worked with the dermatologists and plastic sur- 6
geons at the Center for Human Appearance at the University of Pennsylvania to screen candidates for cosmetic surgery, and he says "there are certainly more male plastic surgery patients," which suggests the same thing: "It's become more culturally accepted or expected for men to be concerned about their appearance."

And no wonder, when you look at the media. Stephen Perrine, articles 7
editor at *Men's Health*, a magazine that in the last six years has built a circulation as big as *Esquire*'s and *GQ*'s put together, says the mass media "in the last five to seven years has really changed the way it portrays men." Whether you look at Calvin Klein's[2] underwear ads or that Diet Coke commercial where the girls in the office ogle the shirtless construction hunk, "men are more and more portrayed as sex objects. So they're feeling the way women have for many, many years: 'Oh, that's what's expected of me? That's what I'm supposed to look like?' " And they—some of them, anyway—rush to live up to those expectations.

Which—wouldn't you know?—turns out to be a heck of a lot easier 8
for them than it ever was for women: "It's easier for men to change their bodies," Perrine says, "easier to build muscle, easier to burn fat." Besides, the male physical ideal is more realistic to begin with: A man "who's healthy and works out . . . will look like Ken, but a woman can exercise till she's dead, and she's not going to look like Barbie," Perrine says.

Ken? Is that really what women want? 9

Maybe some women. Me, I get all weak in the knees when I see a guy 10
running a vacuum, or unloading a dishwasher without being asked. Not that Calvin Klein is ever going to advertise his underwear on a cute guy with a nice big electric broom.

---

[2] **ESL Calvin Klein:** An American fashion designer known for his classic style.

But what women want isn't the point.   11

Used to be, Pertschuk says, men who had plastic surgery said they   12
were doing it for their careers: They wouldn't get promoted if they looked
old and fat and tired. Now they say the same thing women do: "I want to
feel better about myself." In other words, they look at their love handles
or eyebags or pot bellies or saggy chins and feel inadequate and ugly and
unworthy, just the way women have been feeling all along about their
hips, stomachs, thighs, breasts, wrinkles, etc.

That's new: For more men, self-regard has come to hinge not just on   13
what they do, but on what they see in the mirror. And it's easier to change
that than the values that make them feel bad about it.

EXERCISING VOCABULARY

1. What does the adjective *pesky* (para. 2) mean? This word sounds like the noun *pest*. What characteristics do pests and pesky things share? In what way could the last five pounds of a diet be pesky?

2. Check your "Increasing Vocabulary" definition for *vertiginous*. Using that definition as a starting point, explain what a person who suffers from vertigo fears. How does the phrase "too-small shoes with vertiginous heels" (para. 3) relate to what McLaughlin is saying here?

PROBING CONTENT

1. According to McLaughlin, what three changes in men's behavior show that they are worrying more about their looks than they used to? How are these changes a reaction to what is happening in our society?

2. Why does McLaughlin say that it is easier for men to conform to a cultural ideal than it is for women? Where do these cultural ideals come from?

3. According to Michael Pertschuk, why did men in the past say they were altering their appearance by such methods as plastic surgery? How have the reasons men give for having plastic surgery changed? What does this change indicate about our culture?

CONSIDERING CRAFT

1. Who is Venus? How does knowing who she is help you to understand the deliberate play on words in this essay's title?

2. How do McLaughlin's quotes from Michael Pertschuk and Stephen Perrine help make her point? If she wanted to use other sources, what would she gain by quoting them directly instead of just summing up their opinions?

3. What is the effect of having paragraphs 9 and 11 each be only one sentence long? What makes this strategy successful?

4. In her conclusion, McLaughlin restates her thesis. How does this kind of conclusion benefit the reader? How does it benefit the writer?

RESPONDING TO THE WRITER

To what extent does McLaughlin's essay persuade you that men and women suffer equally when it comes to agonizing about personal appearance? What in your
personal experience and your knowledge of the opposite sex causes you to either
support or doubt her position?

For a quiz on this reading, go to bedfordstmartins.com/mirror.

My New Nose

DAN BARDEN

How often do you look at your face each day? Do you ever fantasize about changing one of your features? In "My New Nose," which appeared in *GQ* (*Gentleman's Quarterly*) magazine in May 2002, Dan Barden takes a humorous but candid journey "to the center of his face." Having lived with a botched nose surgery for most of his adult life, Barden grew to embrace the tough guy "thug" persona he felt his crooked nose evoked. But after marriage, he had a change of heart and decided he wanted to be a "leading man" rather than a "character actor" in the drama of life. So again he went under the knife, and again the rhinoplasty led to important changes in his life and mindset.

Dan Barden's fiction and essays have appeared in *GQ*, *Details*, and various literary magazines. His first long work, *John Wayne: A Novel*, was published in 1998. He is currently an assistant professor at Butler University in Indianapolis, where he teaches creative writing and fiction writing.

THINKING AHEAD

What do you think of men who have cosmetic surgery to improve their looks? How does your response compare to your opinion of women who have cosmetic surgery?

INCREASING VOCABULARY

cowl (n.) (8)

bulbous (adj.) (8)

aesthetically (adj.) (9)

persona (n.) (10)

emblem (n.) (11)

self-effacing (adj.) (11)

fixation (n.) (13)

Until several months ago, I had a thuggish nose. It looked like I got 1
hit real hard. Collapsed in the middle, it leaned a lot toward the
left. It made people think I was tougher than I was, or aiming to be.
Once, in a bar in San Francisco, an old drunk asked me if I'd been a boxer.
When I lied and said yes, he told me I must have lost a lot. That's the sort
of nose I had.

I got it from a run-in with a surgeon who was supposed to correct a 2
deviated septum, which made my breathing difficult. But the operation
was botched, and I came out looking like a prizefighter. That operation—
when I was 19—was the most pain I've ever experienced, hands down.
Months later I found that my breathing had only gotten worse.

Eventually, I made peace with my nose. I found that I *liked* looking 3
like a thug. The nose turned me into the kind of Irish Catholic guy who

131

might fit in at the squad room on *NYPD Blue*. Without the nose, I came to think, I might have been just another guy who missed the boat to blandly handsome by about twenty minutes. I believed my nose was my destiny—my dark, Irish, bar-fighting heritage somehow rising to the surface of my face. It didn't matter that I'd never been in a fistfight. The nose was a projection of who I might have been if I weren't, in fact, me. I was almost convinced I *was* the nose. I don't know how many times I've puffed up my chest in front of some fellow who could easily crush me, thereby avoiding a fight. That was the nose talking.

But then a few things happened that I think of as the beginning of the   4 end of the old nose. I married a good woman. I started—brace yourself—wearing loafers. I shaved my goatee. It was at that point that I started to wonder, What if I wanted to pretend to be something other than what I always thought I should be? I watch way too many movies, and I began to worry about the distinction between a character actor and a leading man. Most guys with faces like mine are character actors. What if I wanted to be a lead? When I say *lead*, I don't mean being out there fighting for the spotlight. I mean leading the way leading men do, almost invisibly. John Wayne used to say that being a lead was less fun than people thought: Everybody else got to show off, and he had to stand there, alone, at the center of it all. Being a lead is like being the straight man—the fellow who stands around and lets everyone else do their shtick.

My old nose was my shtick, a song and dance I did for years. I wanted   5 to drop it all and lead, for once. I wanted to be so out in front of things that I became invisible.

So I decided to get a nose job. Rhinoplasty. The big fix. I made an ap-   6 pointment with a cosmetic surgeon, telling him the precise sort of nose I wanted. Neurotically, I explained to him the difference between an "Irish" nose and a "Caucasian" nose. I can't believe I said that. The bottom line was that I didn't want a perfect little Anglican nose, but one that fit my rangy[1] face. I had walked around for twenty years with a sponge of meat above my mouth, but I was terrified of a perfect nose.

The surgery went smoothly this time. I had no real pain, just an un-   7 pleasant swollen feeling. As I recovered, I wondered, floating in the Vicodin[2] clouds, whether I had betrayed some cosmic rule by changing my flesh. A friend, talking about his wife's plastic surgery, once told me that our bodies were nothing more than vehicles for our souls. He asked me whether I would live my whole life in the same dented car just because I was born in it. Well, maybe I should. Even if I could, did I have the *right* to try to change myself from a character actor into a lead?

It was a week or so before I could see the thing. My doctor snipped at   8 some sutures, removed the splint and told me that my new nose had cartilage from one of my ears. I kept him talking for a while to postpone the

[1] **rangy:** With ample room.
[2] **ESL** Vicodin: A pain-killing medication.

moment of truth. After he removed the cowl, he held up a mirror—just like in the movies—and I was amazed by the absolute straightness of the thing though it was a little bulbous at the end, the way my ancestors would want it. It was, indeed, a leading man's nose.

In some ways, the new nose is bigger than the old nose, but this time like the prow of a ship that cuts through the world more neatly. As my nose settled (and I began to breathe through it as well as my doctor promised I would), I noticed something: I stopped looking at the nose, almost as soon as it arrived. It immediately stopped being the focus of my face—it disappeared as a concern to me. My doctor put it best: "It's not that it's aesthetically such a better nose," he said, "but trauma is no longer the first thing someone thinks when they look at your face."

Something else happened as I got used to the nose: I could feel my persona shifting. It was a little scary. Actually, it felt like I was shifting in the direction of *not* having a persona. This felt weirdly powerful. I was no longer looking at my nose but at the absence of two decades of built-up defenses.

Psychologically, my nose had become the emblem for all that held me back, and I had had to deal with it. Some people will tell you that's an inside job. Years of psychotherapy, spiritual growth—blah, blah, blah. Of course, they're right, but I believe rhinoplasty can also be a kind of spiritual growth. It has taught me how to be, or how to begin to be, self-effacing— the man who can lead and disappear at the same time. Certainly, it has helped me physically. After I settled into my new nose, I suddenly yearned to get into shape. I'd been swimming before the operation, but after the surgery it just kicked in. My stroke became this thing of beauty. Part of the reason I'm swimming, I'm sure, is vanity—I want a nice body to go with my nice face—but it's also more mystical than that. I feel like I'm being charmed back to some state before anything went wrong, before trauma. I'm starting over, in a way, but no one's looking at my face.

I saw my doctor again recently. He's a great man—both a technician and an artist—and people should write poems about him, the way Yeats wrote poems about Byzantine[3] goldsmiths. Who has more to say about the turn of this century than a man who gives people new faces?

When I tried to explain to him the way I feel about my new nose, he talked about a "fixation on structure," how the service he provides is often to eliminate the structure and therefore the fixation. I would have thought this a load of crap if it weren't now the story of my life.

In the same conversation, he also reminded me of the nineteenth-century fondness for dueling scars, which I had totally forgotten about. Once upon a time, when men dueled, it was so fashionable to have saber scars on your face that some men actually faked them. Maybe that's what happened to me. I'm just glad I don't need to fake it anymore.

[3]**Byzantine:** Relating to the ornate painting and decorative style developed during the Byzantine empire.

EXERCISING VOCABULARY

1. What does the idiomatic expression "missed the boat" mean (para. 3)? How might the writer have "missed the boat to blandly handsome" (para. 3)? How does the term "blandly" qualify the term "handsome" here?

2. In paragraph 4, the author writes, "Being a lead is like being the straight man — the fellow who stands around and lets everyone else do their shtick." In what

Losing the Trauma: The Author Before and After Surgery

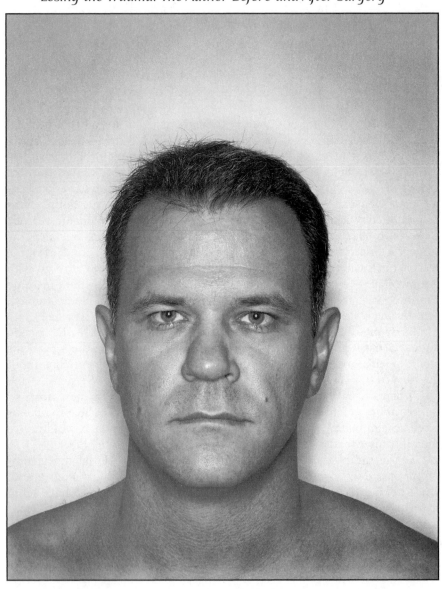

context do you normally hear the terms "lead," "straight man," and "shtick"? What is a straight man? What is shtick? What do these words mean as they are used in the essay?

PROBING CONTENT

1. What does the author mean when he says that "my nose had become the emblem for all that held me back" (para. 11)?

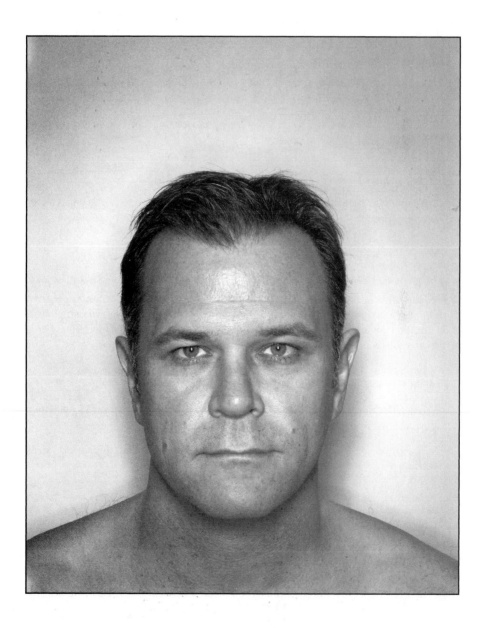

2. How does Barden describe what his nose looked like before surgery? What specific words does he use and why?

3. Describe what happened to make the author consider "the beginning of the end of the old nose"? What impact did the old nose have on the author's self-image?

4. How does the author react to his "new nose" directly after surgery? How does his reaction change later on? Why?

CONSIDERING CRAFT

1. The author alludes to actors and acting several times during the essay. Examine two or three examples. Why does the author include these references ?

2. The author quotes his cosmetic surgeon several times during the essay. Find two or three examples. Why does Barden use this strategy? How effective is it?

3. Why does the essay end with a discussion of dueling scars? How do they relate to the subject of the essay?

RESPONDING TO THE WRITER

Has your opinion of cosmetic surgery for men changed after reading this essay? Why or why not?

EXAMINING THE IMAGE

A large picture of the author with a bandaged face takes up most of the first page of Barden's article as it originally appeared in GQ. The two photographs shown on pp. 134–35 appeared on the second page of the article and were much smaller than the first image. The caption accompanying these two visuals in the original article reads "Losing the Trauma: The Author Before and After Surgery."

1. Where does Barden mention "trauma" in the essay? What exactly does he mean by the term?

2. What differences do you see between his *before* and *after* shots? How significant are these differences?

3. Why include the photographs with the essay? How do they affect your reading?

DRAWING CONNECTIONS

1. How would Dan Barden ("My New Nose") respond to Patricia McLaughlin's final assertion in "Venus Envy" that "For more men, self-regard has come to hinge not just on what they do, but on what they see in the mirror. And it's easier to change that than the values that make them feel bad about it" (para. 13)?

2. In "My New Nose," Barden says, "My old nose was my shtick, a song and dance I did for years. I wanted to drop it all and lead, for once. I wanted to be so out in front of things that I became invisible" (para. 5). How does Barden's rationale for having cosmetic surgery compare with those discussed in McLaughlin's essay "Venus Envy"? What would McLaughlin think of Barden's reasoning?

3. Compare the way plastic surgeons are portrayed in "Venus Envy" and "My New Nose." Be sure to use specific textual evidence in your response.

FOCUSING ON YESTERDAY, FOCUSING ON TODAY

In the early twentieth century, when the French Impressionist Auguste Renoir painted this nude, big was indeed beautiful. An ample, full-bodied woman was the feminine ideal; a thinner figure was suspect and suggested an impoverished existence. In the 1990s Body Shop ad, we again see the luscious curves of Renoir's beauty. However, this time we are no longer looking at a human model but at a plus-sized Barbie doll.

How has female body image changed since the Barbie doll was first introduced in 1959?

What do most supermodels look like today? How does today's feminine ideal of beauty differ from that presented in these two visuals? What message does The Body Shop, a body products company, send by using this image? What target audience is The Body Shop hoping to reach?

When Big Was Beautiful

A Real-Life Barbie Doll

REFLECTING ON THE WRITING

1. Using material from the essays in this chapter, as well as your own observations and experiences, write an essay in which you either support or refute the idea that people sometimes try to disguise what they consider to be an "ethnic" look so that they can display a more mainstream, homogenized "American" look.

2. Compare Patricia McLaughlin's ("Venus Envy") and Dan Barden's ("My New Nose") viewpoints about men's increased concern with their appearance. Which of these writers do you feel makes the most accurate observations? Explain your response.

3. People often go to extreme, even dangerous, measures to attain a certain ideal body or look. Using essays from this chapter and your own experience and observations, identify a dangerous trend—like steroid abuse, cosmetic surgery, fad diets, extreme makeovers, or eating disorders—that you would like to research further. Then write an essay in which you examine this trend and its effects on your peers.

4. H. D., Garry Trudeau, and Alice Walker chronicle the struggles that young people have with body image. Using their essays, others from this chapter, or examples from the media, write an essay about your own difficulties with growing up in a culture that privileges a certain nearly impossible ideal of beauty.

CONNECTING TO THE CULTURE

1. If, as McLaughlin ("Venus Envy") and Barden ("My New Nose") argue, men are now more concerned than ever before with their appearance, what elements in our society are most responsible for this heightened awareness? To what extent are the media (television, movies, magazines, newspapers, and the Internet) responsible? What consequences do you expect? What changes in advertising or new products support this thesis?

2. Think about the people who have helped shape your self-image, both inner and outer. These may be people you know personally or celebrities you have never actually met. These people may have been positive role models for you, helping you to set goals for yourself, or negative influences showing you what you did not want to become. In an essay, explore how one or several of these people have influenced you.

3. Different cultures have different ideals of beauty. Do some research on another country whose beauty ideals are different from those in the United States. In an essay, examine the differences you have found and relate how the standard of beauty affects the members of the culture you selected.

4. Ideals of beauty have changed throughout history in the United States. Pick a specific historical period and research how beauty was defined for men or women during that time. Then write an essay in which you compare the ideal body image of that historical period to today's ideal of beauty. Use specific examples and visuals from the time period you have researched.

CHAPTER 5

The Fabric of Our Lives
Fashion Trends and the Signals They Send

This photograph, "Do Clothes Really Make the Man?," was taken on June 29, 2004, at the prestigious Dolce and Gabbana men's fashion show in Milan, Italy. Showcasing D & G's Spring/Summer 2005 collection, this runway model is wearing the well-worn — some would say worn-out — look that is so popular today. Why are so many men, from celebrities to college students, eager to sport the fashion equivalent of what interior decorators call "shabby chic"? Why are many consumers willing to pay extravagant prices for ripped jeans and faded shirts?

- How interested are you or the men you know in male fashion trends?
- What impact have television makeover shows like *Queer Eye for the Straight Guy* had on male fashion?
- How does advertising affect male fashion trends?
- What other cultural forces affect male fashion trends and why?

Research this topic with TopLinks at bedfordstmartins.com/toplinks.

We are all consumers. Some of us buy only the bare necessities. Some of us regard shopping as an enjoyable pastime. Some of us are shopaholics whose uncontrollable shopping sprees threaten our financial and emotional well-being. In whichever category we fall, we are all consumers of everything from the food we eat and the clothes we wear to the shampoo we use, the CDs we listen to, and the books we read. Among all the products we consume, fashion items are among the closest to our hearts, not to mention our bodies. Although we cannot live without clothing, many of us want and often buy more, and more expensive, clothes than we need to shelter us from the elements and maintain our modesty. Why do our travel plans often include a stop at the local Hard Rock Cafe to buy a T-shirt we can show off when we get home? Do we buy different brands of jeans to portray certain images? What will people say if we get that extra piercing? How do we know what's in style? Will it still be "in" next month? Why do we care? How are we, as fashion consumers, manipulated by advertising and marketing executives who follow and create the latest trends? The essays in this chapter explore such questions and lead you to formulate some answers about your own consumer behavior and the consumer standards we accept.

GEARING UP

Think about the kind of fashion consumer you are. What do you buy? Where do you shop? Do you prefer shopping online or in a store? When do you go shopping? Do you go alone, or do you view shopping as a social activity? Do you buy on impulse or shop strictly from a list? How much are your buying choices influenced by advertising and peer pressure? Explain why you would rather have one designer shirt than two or three less expensive, no-name ones (or the opposite, if that is true for you).

COLLABORATING

In small groups, draw up a list of the hottest clothing trends among your peers. How do you explain these trends? How and where did they begin? What do they say about the consumers who participate in them? Discuss the lists from each group.

Swoosh!

READ MERCER SCHUCHARDT

Our culture lives by symbols. In fact, every day more and more of these symbols replace the words they represent. Look at traffic signs. You don't need to see the word *stop* to understand what the octagonal red sign means. And railroad tracks on a sign speak clearly for themselves. Computer screens are home to endless icons, as are designer clothes.

Read Mercer Schuchardt calls our world "postliterate." This doesn't mean we can no longer read and write. We can, and we do, as witnessed by the popularity of e-mailing, instant messaging, blogging, and text messaging. What Schuchardt argues here is that we read and write less frequently because we are required to do so less often. The author examines one of modern America's most successful icons, the Nike Swoosh, in this essay originally published in *Re:Generation Quarterly* and reprinted in the *Utne Reader* in 1997. The author is currently an Assistant Professor of Communication Arts at Marymount Manhattan College and has also published in the *Chicago Tribune* and the *Washington Times*.

THINKING AHEAD

Think about some products whose symbols or icons are so successful that consumers recognize them without seeing the product's actual name. How did these symbols become so familiar to us? Why do we understand their meaning without the help of words? How do they work to unite us in a common understanding?

INCREASING VOCABULARY

transected (v.) (1)	innovative (adj.) (4)
emulate (v.) (3)	analogue (n.) (6)

The early followers of Christ created a symbol to represent their beliefs and communicate with one another in times of persecution. The well-known Ichthus, or "Christian fish," consisted of two curved lines that transected each other to form the abstract outline of fish and tail. The word for *fish* also happened to be a Greek acronym wherein:

- Iota = Iesous = Jesus
- Chi = Christos = Christ
- Theta = Theos = God
- Upsilon = Huios = Son
- Sigma = Soter = Savior

1

Combining symbol and word, the fish provided believers with an inte-   2
grated media package that could be easily explained and understood.
When the threat of being fed to the lions forced Christians to be less explicit, they dropped the text. Without the acronym to define the symbol's
significance, the fish could mean anything or nothing, an obvious advantage in a culture hostile to certain beliefs. But to Christians the textless
symbol still signified silent rebellion against the ruling authorities. Within
three centuries, the faith signified by the fish had transformed Rome into a
Christian empire.

Today, in an electronically accelerated culture, a symbol can change   3
the face of society in about one-sixteenth that time. Enter the Nike Swoosh,
the most ubiquitous icon in the country, and one that many other corporations have sought to emulate. In a world where technology, entertainment, and design are converging, the story of the Swoosh is by far the most
fascinating case study of a systematic, integrated, and insanely successful
formula for icon-driven marketing.

The simple version of the story is that a young Oregon design student   4
named Caroline Davidson got $35 in 1971 to create a logo for then-
professor (now Nike CEO) Phil Knight's idea of importing and selling improved Japanese running shoes. Nike's innovative product line, combined
with aggressive marketing and brand positioning, eventually created an un-
breakable mental link between the Swoosh image and the company's name.
As Nike put it, there was so much equity in the brand that they knew it
wouldn't hurt to drop the word *Nike* and go with the Swoosh alone. Nike
went to the textless format for U.S. advertising in March 1996 and expanded
it globally later that year. While the Nike name and symbol appear together
in ads today, the textless campaign set a new standard. In the modern global
market, the truly successful icon must be able to stand by itself, evoking all
the manufactured associations that form a corporation's public identity.

In the past, it would have been unthinkable to create an ad campaign   5
stripped of the company's name. Given what was at stake — Nike's advertising budget totals more than $100 million per year — what made them
think they could pull it off?

First, consider the strength of the Swoosh as an icon. The Swoosh is a   6
simple shape that reproduces well at any size, in any color, and on almost
any surface — three critical elements for a corporate logo that will be reproduced at sizes from a quarter of an inch to 500 feet. It most frequently
appears in one of three arresting colors: black, red, or white. A textless
icon, it nevertheless "reads" left to right, like most languages. Now consider the sound of the word *Swoosh*. According to various Nike ads, it's
the last sound you hear before coming in second place, the sound of a basketball hitting nothing but net. It's also the onomatopoeic[1] analogue of
the icon's visual stroke. Reading it left to right, the symbol itself actually
seems to say "swoosh" as you look at it.

---

[1] **onomatopoeic:** Relating to a term whose name imitates the sound that it makes.

However it may read, the Swoosh transcends language, making it the 7
perfect corporate icon for the postliterate global village.

With the invention of the printing press, according to Italian semioti- 8
cian[2] Umberto Eco, the alphabet triumphed over the icon. But in an over-
stimulated electronic culture, the chief problem is what advertisers call
"clutter" or "chatter"—too many words, too much redundancy, too many
competing messages. Add the rise of illiteracy and an increasingly multicultural world and you have a real communications problem. A hyper-
linked global economy requires a single global communications medium,
and it's simply easier to teach everyone a few common symbols than to
teach the majority of non-English speakers a new language.

The unfortunate result is that language is being replaced by icons. 9
From the rock star formerly known as Prince to e-mail "smileys" to the
NAFTA[3]-induced symbolic laundry labels, the names and words we use to
describe the world are being replaced by a set of universal hieroglyphs.[4]
Leading the charge, as one would expect, are the organizations that stand
to make the most money in a less text-dependent world: multinational
corporations. With the decline of words, they now can fill in the blank of
the consumer's associative mind with whatever images they deem appropriate.

After watching Nike do it, several companies have decided to go 10
textless themselves, including Mercedes-Benz, whose icon is easily confused with the peace sign (an association that can only help). According
to one of their print ads, "right behind every powerful icon lies a powerful idea," which is precisely the definition of a global communications
medium for an accelerated culture. Pepsi's new textless symbol does not
need any verbal justification because it so clearly imitates the yin-yang[5]
symbol. In fact, a close look reveals it to be almost identical to the Korean national flag, which is itself a stylized yin-yang symbol in red, white,
and blue.

Never underestimate the power of symbols. Textless corporate sym- 11
bols operate at a level beneath the radar of rational language, and the
power they wield can be corrupting. Advertising that relies on propaganda methods can grab you and take you somewhere whether you want
to go or not; and as history tells us, it matters where you're going.

Language is the mediator between our minds and the world, and the 12
thing that defines us as rational creatures. By going textless, Nike and
other corporations have succeeded in performing partial lobotomies[6] on

[2] **semiotician:** A person who studies signs and symbols and the way that they operate in
everyday life.
[3] **NAFTA:** North American Free Trade Agreement, an agreement that in 1994 launched the
world's largest free-trade area.
[4] **hieroglyphs:** Characters in a system of picture writing.
[5] **yin-yang:** A black and white Chinese symbol that represents completeness by combining
both halves of the universe.
[6] **lobotomies:** Surgical procedures that sever nerves in the brain and that once were used to
control unruly psychiatric patients.

our brains, conveying their messages without engaging our rational minds. Like Pavlov's bell, the Swoosh has become a stimulus that elicits a conditioned response. The problem is not that we buy Nike shoes, but that we've been led to do so by the same methods used to train Pavlov's dogs.[7] It's ironic, of course, that this reflex is triggered by a stylized check mark — the standard reward for academic achievement and ultimate symbol for the rational, linguistically agile mind.

If sport is the religion of the modern age, then Nike has successfully   13 become the official church. It is a church whose icon is a window between this world and the other, between your existing self (you overweight slob) and your Nike self (you god of fitness), where salvation lies in achieving the athletic Nietzschean[8] ideal: no fear, no mercy, no second place. Like the Christian fish, the Swoosh is a true religious icon in that it both symbolizes the believer's reality and actually participates in it. After all, you do have to wear something to attain this special salvation, so why not something emblazoned with the Swoosh?

EXERCISING VOCABULARY

1. This essay begins with the history of an acronym. What is an acronym? Why are acronyms used? Give an example of an acronym that means something to you and explain what the letters mean. *Scuba*, for example, stands for "self-contained underwater breathing apparatus," and *CEO* stands for "chief executive officer."

2. The author refers to the Nike Swoosh as "ubiquitous" in paragraph 3. How accurate is this word in describing the popularity of the Nike symbol? Name at least five different places where the Swoosh appears.

3. In paragraph 4, Schuchardt says that Nike was able to drop the word *Nike* because "there was so much equity in the brand." What does it mean to have equity in something? Give two or three examples. What does using the word *equity* here imply about the Nike corporation?

PROBING CONTENT

1. Why did the early Christians adopt the Ichthus symbol? What significance did it hold for them?

2. Why, according to Schuchardt, must a successful advertising icon not need supporting language to be clearly understood by a wide range of people? How do you determine whether an icon is successful as a marketing tool?

---

[7] **Pavlov's dogs:** The animals that Russian scientist Ivan Pavlov (1849–1936) used in his experiments in predicting behavior under certain circumstances.

[8] **Nietzschean:** Referring to Friedrich Nietzsche (1844–1900), a German philosopher and author of *Man and Superman*.

3. What examples does the writer provide to support his position stated in paragraph 9 that "language is being replaced by icons"? What motive do companies have for replacing language with symbols?

4. What does this essay describe as the conditioned or predictable response to the stimulus of the Nike Swoosh? How effective is the Swoosh in generating this response?

CONSIDERING CRAFT

1. The writer chooses a complicated introduction. How well does the Christian fish symbol work as an introduction to this topic? Why do you think Schuchardt chose this symbol to introduce his essay?

2. This essay contains a number of unfamiliar references. If the writer knew that some readers would not understand these references, why did he include them? How do they improve or weaken the essay?

3. What does the final paragraph have in common with the introduction? What does the author want to accomplish by using this strategy? To what extent is he successful?

RESPONDING TO THE WRITER

Reread paragraph 11. What threat does the writer find in the growth of "textless corporate symbols"? Do you agree that his fear is justified? When you think about it carefully, to what extent do you feel surrounded by less language and more symbols? At what point might you become concerned?

For a quiz on this reading, go to bedfordstmartins.com/mirror.

The "Modern Primitives"

JOHN LEO

Body modification — whether by piercing, tattooing, scarring, or stretching — has been practiced for centuries by diverse cultural groups around the world. Only in recent years, however, has this phenomenon provoked serious popular attention in the United States. Body modification, initially taken to extremes by certain groups, has become much more mainstream. Multiple ear piercings are common, and people no longer stop and stare at nose and belly rings. Even Barbie once sported a butterfly tattoo. What is behind this renewed popularity in body modification? What kind of message are its practitioners trying to send?

In this essay from the July 31, 1995, edition of *U.S. News & World Report*, cultural critic and columnist John Leo tries to answer just these questions. Leo, whose weekly column appears in *U.S. News & World Report* and 150 newspapers, has written for the *New York Times* and *Time* magazine and is the author of *Two Steps Ahead of the Thought Police* (1998) and *Incorrect Thoughts: Notes on Our Wayward Culture* (2000).

THINKING AHEAD

When you think of body modification like piercing or tattooing, who comes to mind? A friend? A movie star? A musician? A gang member? What image do you have of people with piercings or tattoos? Do you have a piercing or tattoo, or have you considered getting one? What was your motivation? What effect did you want to achieve? What reactions did your piercing or tattoo elicit from other people?

INCREASING VOCABULARY

coveted (adj.) (1)
decry (v.) (2)
deviancy (n.) (4)
rationale (n.) (5)
centered (adj.) (5)
reclaiming (v.) (5)
pathological (adj.) (5)

bland (adj.) (7)
commodified (v.) (7)
faux (adj.) (7)
mortified (v.) (9)
repudiate (v.) (9)
latent (adj.) (11)
welling (v.) (11)

The days when body piercers could draw stares by wearing multiple earrings and a nose stud are long gone. We are now in the late baroque phase[1] of self-penetration. Metal rings and bars hang from eyebrows, noses, nipples, lips, chins, cheeks, navels and (for that coveted neo-Frankenstein[2] look) from the side of the neck.

"If it sticks out, pierce it" is the motto, and so they do, with special attention to genitals. Some of the same middle-class folks who decry genital mutilation in Africa are paying to have needles driven through the scrotum, the labia, the clitoris, or the head or the shaft of the penis. Many genital piercings have their own names, such as the ampallang or the Prince Albert. (Don't ask.)

And, in most cases, the body heals without damage, though some women who have had their nipples pierced report damage to the breast's milk ducts, and some men who have been Prince Alberted no longer urinate in quite the same way.

What is going on here? Well, the mainstreaming-of-deviancy thesis naturally springs to mind. The piercings of nipples and genitals arose in the homosexual sadomasochistic[3] culture of the West Coast. The Gauntlet, founded in Los Angeles in 1975 mostly to do master and slave piercings, now has three shops around the country that are about as controversial as Elizabeth Arden[4] salons. Rumbling through the biker culture and punk, piercing gradually shed its outlaw image and was mass marketed to the impressionable by music videos, rock stars and models.

The nasty, aggressive edge of piercing is still there, but now it is coated in happy talk (it's just body decoration, like any other) and a New Age[5]-y rationale (we are becoming more centered, reclaiming our bodies in an anti-body culture). Various new pagans, witches and New Agers see piercing as symbolic of unspecified spiritual transformation. One way or another, as Guy Trebay writes in the *Village Voice*, "You will never find anyone on the piercing scene who thinks of what he's doing as pathological."

The yearning to irritate parents and shock the middle class seems to rank high as a motive for getting punctured repeatedly. Some ask for dramatic piercings to enhance sexual pleasure, to seem daring or fashionable, to express rage, or to forge a group identity. Some think of it as an ordeal that serves as a rite of passage, like ritual suspension of Indian males from hooks in their chests.

Piercing is part of the broader "body modification" movement, which includes tattooing, corsetry, branding and scarring by knife. It's a sign of

---

[1] **late baroque phase:** A period of ornate, richly ornamented decoration.
[2] **ESL Frankenstein:** A monster created from parts of dead bodies by Dr. Victor Frankenstein in Mary Shelley's 1818 novel *Frankenstein, or The Modern Prometheus.*
[3] **sadomasochistic:** Relating to the association of sexual pleasure with the inflicting and receiving of pain.
[4] **Elizabeth Arden:** A company that produces beauty products and owns beauty spas.
[5] **ESL New Age:** A spiritual movement that stresses the unity and practice of all belief systems despite their differences.

the times that the more bizarre expressions of this movement keep pushing into the mainstream. The current issue of *Spin* magazine features a hair-raising photo of a woman carving little rivers of blood into another woman's back. "Piercing is like toothbrushing now," one of the cutters told *Spin*. "It's why cutting is becoming popular." Slicing someone's back is a violent act. But one of the cutters has a bland justification: People want to be cut "for adornment, or as a test of endurance, or as a sacrifice toward a transformation." Later on we read that "women are reclaiming their bodies from a culture that has commodified starvation and faux sex." One cuttee says: "It creates intimacy. My scars are emotional centers, signs of a life lived."

But most of us achieve intimacy, or at least search for it, without a   8
knife in hand. The truth seems to be that the sadomasochistic instinct is being repositioned to look spiritually high-toned. Many people have found that S&M[6] play "is a way of opening up the body-spirit connection," the high priest of the body modification movement, Fakir Musafar, said in one interview.

Musafar, who has corseted his waist down to 19 inches and mortified   9
his flesh with all kinds of blades, hooks and pins, calls the mostly twenty-ish people in the body modification movement "the modern primitives." This is another side of the movement: the conscious attempt to repudiate Western norms and values by adopting the marks and rings of primitive cultures. In some cases this is expressed by tusks worn in the nose or by stretching and exaggerating holes in the earlobe or nipple.

Not everyone who pierces a nipple or wears a tongue stud is buying   10
into this, but something like a new primitivism seems to be emerging in body modification, as in other areas of American life. It plugs into a wider dissatisfaction with traditional Western rationality, logic and sexual norms, as well as anger at the impact of Western technology on the natural environment and anger at the state of American political and social life.

Two sympathetic analysts say: "Amidst an almost universal feeling of   11
powerlessness to 'change the world,' individuals are changing what they have power over: their own bodies. . . . By giving visible expression to unknown desires and latent obsessions welling up from within, individuals can provoke change."

Probably not. Cultural crisis can't really be dealt with by letting loose   12
our personal obsessions and marking up our bodies. But the rapid spread of this movement is yet another sign that the crisis is here.

EXERCISING VOCABULARY

I. In paragraph 1, Leo speaks of "that coveted neo-Frankenstein look." What does it mean to covet something? What then does *coveted* mean? What does *neo* mean? Describe a neo-Frankenstein look.

[6] S&M: Sadomasochistic.

2. Paragraph 4 refers to "the mainstreaming-of-deviancy thesis." What does it mean to mainstream? How can you apply that meaning of mainstream to Leo's phrase?

PROBING CONTENT

1. In what cultures or among what groups of people did body piercing first become popular in the United States? What was its significance?

2. Explain the broader movement of which, according to Leo, body piercing is a part.

3. Before Leo explains what he means by the "new primitivism," (para. 10) he offers several other motives for body modification. What are these?

4. How effectively does the writer think body modification deals with "cultural crisis" (para. 12)? Why is this true?

CONSIDERING CRAFT

1. The title is an oxymoron, or a phrase made up of seeming opposites. Explain how people with tattoos or body piercings can be both modern and primitive.

2. Why does Leo mention several other motives for body modification and then dismiss them in favor of the idea that "a new primitivism" (para. 10) is the major motive?

3. What effect do Leo's many graphic examples of body modification have on you? Why does he include them?

4. Describe the writer's attitude toward his subject. What is the tone of this essay? How difficult is the vocabulary? Based on this information, for what audience do you think Leo is writing?

RESPONDING TO THE WRITER

You probably know several people who have body piercings or tattoos and might have them yourself. What were their or your motives for these body modifications? What images did they or you want to project? Did these body modifications produce the anticipated results?

For a quiz on this reading, go to bedfordstmartins.com/mirror.

EXAMINING THE IMAGE

Examine this contemporary ad for Body Rites, an Austin, Texas, "piercing, brand-ing, and scarification" center located inside a tattoo parlor. For some, to express oneself today requires more than wardrobe enhancement; it requires body modi-fication.

1. Why did the ad designer choose to use the split image?

2. What function does the text in this ad serve?

3. Why are so many people today exploring fashion trends beyond clothing, like piercing or tattooing?

Latino Style Is Cool. Oh, All Right: It's Hot.

RUTH LA FERLA

"Hispanic is hip. Right now, it's the thing to be," says Lisa Forero, a student whom Ruth La Ferla interviewed for the following article. What is Latino style? How are some Latinos using fashion to embrace their cultural heritage, and why are people outside Latino culture borrowing it? How is the fashion industry responding to the current fascination with all things Latino? And as leading apparel makers such as Ralph Lauren, Nike, Tommy Hilfiger, and the Gap attempt to mass-market provocative Latino styles, will cultural stereotyping result?

Ruth La Ferla explores these questions in "Latino Style Is Cool. Oh, All Right: It's Hot," which first appeared in the *New York Times* on April 15, 2001. A fashion writer for the *New York Times*, La Ferla has also written about style for *Mirabella* magazine, where she formerly served as fashion director.

THINKING AHEAD

The influence of the growing Hispanic population in the United States is increasing steadily in music, dance, language, education, and politics. What indicators of this growing influence do you see in the world around you? What future indicators do you expect to see?

INCREASING VOCABULARY

fret (v.) (2)	ostentatiously (adv.) (8)
clout (n.) (4)	insignia (n.) (9)
bemused (adj.) (5)	appropriated (v.) (10)
allude (v.) (6)	enamored (adj.) (14)
aping (v.) (6)	sultry (adj.) (16)
flaunting (v.) (6)	emulated (v.) (17)
solidarity (n.) (6)	bristle (v.) (19)
iconography (n.) (7)	besotted (adj.) (23)

On a recent Friday afternoon, Lisa Forero, her dark, shoulder-   1
length hair parted in the center, stalked the corridors of La Guardia High School of Performing Arts in Manhattan, perched on four-inch platform boots. Ms. Forero, a drama major, played up her curves in a form-fitting gray spandex dress and wore outsize gold hoops on her ears. Her fingertips were airbrushed in tints of pink and cream.

Did she fret that her image—that of a saucy bombshell—bordered   2
on self-parody? Not a bit. Dressing up as a familiar stereotype is Ms. Forero's pointedly aggressive way of claiming her Latino heritage, she

153

says. Ms. Forero, seventeen, acknowledged that she had not always been so bold. "Two or three years ago, I didn't usually wear gold," she said, "and I usually wouldn't get my nails done. But as I've gotten older, I've needed to identify more with my cultural background."

Her sandy-haired classmate Kenneth Lamadrid, seventeen, is just as brash. "Because of the way I look and because my parents called me Ken, a lot of people don't know that I'm Cuban," he said. But Mr. Lamadrid takes pains to set them straight. That afternoon, he was wearing a souvenir from a recent family reunion, a snug T-shirt emblazoned with the names of all of his relatives who have emigrated to the United States from Cuba. "I'm wearing my family history," he said. "You have to be proud of who you are." 3

Ms. Forero and Mr. Lamadrid are members of a population that, according to the 2000 census, seems on the verge of becoming America's largest minority group. Wildly heterogeneous,[1] its members come from more than twenty countries and represent a mixture of races, backgrounds and even religions. What Latinos share, as Ms. Forero well knows, is a common language—Spanish—and rapidly expanding cultural clout. 4

"Hispanic is hip," she observed dryly. "Right now, it's the thing to be." Indeed, in the last couple of years Latinos have been surprised and flattered to find themselves courted as voters, consumers, workers and entertainers. And now many are bemused to discover that, like hip-hop–influenced African Americans before them, they are admired as avatars[2] of urban chic. 5

"There is an emerging Latino style, and I think it appeals to more than just Latinos," said Clara Rodriguez, a professor of sociology at Fordham University in Manhattan and the author of *Latin Looks: Images of Latinas and Latinos in the U.S. Media* (Westview Press, 1997). Dr. Rodriguez made a point of distinguishing between pervasive archetypes—the smoldering vamp, the brilliantined Lothario[3]—and the fashion personas adopted by young urban Hispanics, which allude to those types without aping them. These Latin Gen X-ers[4] are rediscovering their roots and flaunting them, she said, while communicating solidarity by the way they dress. 6

Rodrigo Salazar, the editor of *Urban Latino*, a general interest magazine for young Hispanics, expressed a similar view. "As we stake our claim in the culture, we are starting to take control of our own images," Mr. Salazar said. Young, trend-conscious Latinos do that in part, he said, by experimenting with fashion and cultivating a street-smart style that is more overtly sensual than hip-hop and is at the same time heavily steeped in Hispanic iconography. 7

Flounces, ruffles and ear hoops are among the generic, ostentatiously Hispanic symbols being tossed into a pan-Latino blender these days. Even 8

[1] heterogeneous: Consisting of different kinds; varied.
[2] avatars: Embodiments in human form.
[3] Lothario: A man whose chief interest is in seducing women.
[4] ESL Gen X-ers: People who were born in the mid-1970s.

crosses are part of the mix, not as a symbol of faith but as a hip accessory. Mr. Salazar conceded that such items lend themselves to ethnic stereotyping but argued that perhaps that is all the more reason to flaunt them. For many young Hispanics, he said, they are a visual shorthand that signals their identity.

Latino style also incorporates the provocative cropped T-shirts, low-slung chinos, stacked heels and chains that are the fashion insignia of cholos, members of Latin street gangs. And it incorporates components of a style adopted by young Puerto Rican New Yorkers in the late 1970s: fitted shirts in phantasmagorial[5] patterns, hip-riding denims, cropped halters, blouses tied at the midriff, navel-baring T-shirts and platform shoes. Similar regalia survives as the style uniform of pop icons like Ricky Martin and Jennifer Lopez.

But the look is also indebted to the traditional garb favored by an earlier generation of Latino immigrants. On some days, for example, Mr. Lamadrid, the drama student, wears a guayabera, a loose multipocket shirt like the ones his Cuban grandfather used to wear. Nowadays, the shirts, worn by many young Hispanics as a badge of their heritage, have been appropriated by non-Hispanics as well.

"We take our lead from the things we've seen our parents wear and the things we've seen in movies," Mr. Salazar said, "but our style is evolving as our influence is growing. We're seeing ourselves in the street, and we're following the cues of our friends and celebrities who are Latino."

Mr. Salazar was describing a cultural pastiche[6] that has become increasingly identifiable—and some maintain, consummately marketable. Its potential mass appeal is surely not lost on Ms. Lopez, the singer and actress, who is negotiating with Andy Hilfiger, Tommy's younger brother, to market her own brand of Latina glam in a fashion line.

At the same time, Latina chic is being packaged for mass consumption by some leading apparel makers. In the last several months, Ralph Lauren, Nike, Tommy Hilfiger and the Gap have played to the current fascination with Latina exoticism in advertisements featuring variations on the full-lipped, south-of-the-border sexpot. Ralph Lauren's campaign showcases the Spanish film star Penélope Cruz in a snug top and a swirling skirt, performing what looks like flamenco. Both Guess and Sergio Valente display ads in which halter tops and rump-clutching denims encase Brazilian brunettes. And Vertigo, a midprice sportswear company, is showing its scarlet trouser suit on a raven-haired vamp, a ringer—it can't be coincidence—for a young Bianca Jagger.

"Our industry has become enamored with the dark, mysterious confidence that these women portray," said Steven Miska, the president of Sergio Valente.

---

[5] **phantasmagorial:** Relating to a shifting series of illusions.
[6] **pastiche:** A composition made up of several different parts.

Magazine editors, too, find the Latin look compelling. The March   15
issue of Italian *Vogue*, the fashionista's bible, has a feature in which
young Latino-Americans model the season's key looks.

Is the industry trying to market Latinness as a commodity? "Defi-   16
nitely," said Sam Shahid, the president and creative director of Shahid, a
New York advertising agency with fashion clients. Mr. Shahid employed
Hispanic models for the latest Abercrombie & Fitch catalog. "No one
moves as freely," he said, then added: "Selling a Latin look doesn't mean
it has to be a Carmen Miranda,[7] cha-cha type thing. 'Latin' can simply be
a sultry sex appeal."

Should Mr. Hilfiger and Ms. Lopez reach an agreement, industry in-   17
siders speculate that the collection will draw heavily on Ms. Lopez's Puerto
Rican heritage. "Her flash look, the stacked heels, the low-rise jeans—these
things are already being emulated by people well outside the Hispanic
community," said Tom Julian, a trend analyst for Fallon Worldwide, a
Minneapolis branding company.

Deliberately packaging an urban Hispanic look for mass consumption   18
makes sense to Mr. Julian. "Ethnicity is good in today's marketplace," he
said. "All of a sudden you are talking about hair, makeup, clothing and
accessories that are part of a lifestyle that is distinctive, that has a point
of view." Noting that so-called urban apparel—the streetwise casual
wear favored by young blacks and Hispanics—is a $5 billion-a-year busi-
ness, he ventured that a Latino subgenre could generate at least half that
amount.

Some Hispanics bristle at the reduction of their identity to a handful   19
of styling cues, which might then be peddled as Latin chic. They are un-
easy about being lumped by outsiders into an undifferentiated cultural
mass. "I think the world would often like to describe us as a bunch of hot
tamales," said Betty Cortina, the editorial director of *Latina*, a lifestyle
magazine for young women. "That happens to be the way many Latinas
see themselves," she conceded, "but if our cultural identity is all wrapped
up in a sexy sense of style, then we have a lot of work to do."

Others maintain that a degree of cultural stereotyping is inevitable   20
and may not be all bad. "It's important for people to understand that
within the Latin community there is range," said Elisa Jimenez, a New
York fashion designer and performance artist of part-Mexican descent. At
the same time, an attraction to certain cultural stereotypes can be positive,
she asserted, if "it inspires us to be happier, more expressive—any or all
of those things that we want to be more of."

Latino-influenced apparel and grooming are seductive to many non-   21
Latins intent on borrowing elements of a culture that they perceive as
more authentic, spontaneous and alluring than their own. "Latin equals

---

[7] **Carmen Miranda (1909–1955):** A Portuguese dancer, singer, and star of Brazilian and
Hollywood musicals, remembered particularly for her elaborate costumes and head-
dresses made from tropical fruit.

sexy," said Kim Hastreiter, the editor of *Paper*, a magazine that features a generous sampling of Latino artists, models, fashion, film and pop stars in its April issue. "It's heat and a certain aliveness."

Ms. Hastreiter might have been describing Cindy Green, a New   22
York performance artist and the graphic design director of the DKNY fashion house. Ms. Green flaunts acrylic-tipped nails airbrushed in hot pink and silver, a hyperfeminine look copied from the young Latina women she sees on her way to work. "I'm completely obsessed with my nails," she said, adding that she is just as much taken with the tight ponytails, dark lip liner and extreme makeup worn by many young Hispanic women. "I come from Ohio," she said, "and all this is very exotic to me."

Danielle Levitt, a New York City fashion photographer, is equally be-   23
sotted. "I can't explain my attraction to things that are Latin," she said. "I think it's the glamour." Ms. Levitt likes to pile on Latina-style gold bangles and heart-shaped pendants. At her throat she wears an elaborate gold nameplate, similar to those worn on the air by the stars of *Sex and the City*, a show that is arguably influenced by Latina style.

Ms. Jimenez had never designed clothes that were identifiably Latin   24
until Kbond, a vanguard Los Angeles clothing store, asked her recently for a look that was patently Hispanic. She responded by lopping the sleeves off a series of ruffled men's tuxedo shirts — "tricking them out," as she put it, into "sexy little halters" for women.

At the moment she is selling a line of sportswear steeped in Latin   25
kitsch[8] — "La Vida Loca" T-shirts, for example, printed with the characteristically Mexican images of a rose, a pair of dice and a skull. "It's time to get our heritage out there," Ms. Jimenez declared with mingled defiance and mirth. She envisions her designs teamed with uptight little handbags and immaculate white jeans.

Who's going to wear them?   26

"Are you kidding?" she said. "They're going to be the height of Upper   27
East Side[9] chic."

EXERCISING VOCABULARY

1. What relation does a parody have to the real thing? Why would someone consciously engage in the kind of "self-parody" La Ferla describes in paragraphs 1 and 2?

2. In paragraph 6, one of La Ferla's sources differentiates between young Hispanic trendsetters and "pervasive archetypes" of Hispanic culture. What is an archetype? How do the two archetypes mentioned in this paragraph fit this definition? What is significant about them?

[8] **kitsch:** Something that appeals to popular taste and is often of poor quality.
[9] **Upper East Side:** A neighborhood of expensive real estate in New York City that borders Central Park and includes portions of Park and Fifth Avenues.

3. In what sense are "flounces, ruffles and ear hoops" a type of "visual short-hand" (para. 8)? What do these accessories signify?

PROBING CONTENT

1. La Ferla compares young Latinos with "hip-hop–influenced African Americans before them" (para. 5). What similarities does she see?

2. Explain Rodrigo Salazar's statement "We're seeing ourselves in the street" (para. 11). What seems to account for the attraction of Hispanics and non-Hispanics alike to Latino style?

3. What evidence does La Ferla offer that "Latina chic" is significant enough to attract some serious interest from the business world?

4. What are the positive and negative aspects of associating young Latinos with certain obvious stereotypes?

CONSIDERING CRAFT

1. Interesting mental images and apparent contradictions are part of the title La Ferla has chosen for this essay. Are the two parts of the title really contradictory? How does the title predict the content of the essay?

2. This selection includes a number of direct quotations from a variety of sources. How does the author's selection of sources and quotations enhance her assertions? What other methods of proof does La Ferla employ to convince her readers?

RESPONDING TO THE WRITER

Have you seen the Latino style that La Ferla discusses? List some specific examples you have seen of clothing and accessories that typify this style. Your examples may come from everyday life or from movies and television. If you have not seen anyone expressing this style, why do you think you have not?

For a quiz on this reading, go to bedfordstmartins.com/mirror.

Belly-Baring Fad Not Cute as a Button

HAYLEY KAUFMAN

"Navels, no longer novel, have been embraced by the American mainstream," writes Hayley Kaufman. Bellybuttons—for centuries a private domain—are now being flaunted, pierced, and surgically altered to look more attractive. Have you embraced the bellybutton-baring fad? Have you noticed anyone with a less-than-perfect midsection wearing a midriff-baring outfit? What does the belly craze say about our culture? How far do you think the trend will go?

Kaufman has written for the *Boston Globe* since 1999 and currently serves as the newspaper's Deputy Arts Editor. "Belly-Baring Fad Not Cute as a Button" first appeared in the *Boston Globe* on February 11, 2002. Kaufman has contributed articles to a variety of Boston-based newspapers since graduating from the University of California at Davis, including *Boston* magazine, the *Cambridge Chronicle*, the *Tab*, and *Stuff at Night*. She has won a New England Press Association Award for environmental reporting.

THINKING AHEAD

They're pierced, peeking out from under short tops, and emerging over low-slung jeans. Should navels be functional or fun? Should everyone who wishes to do so be allowed to put his or hers on public display? Explain your response.

INCREASING VOCABULARY

obscured (adj.) (1)	feckless (adj.) (2)
whorled (adj.) (1)	ominously (adv.) (8)
perforate (v.) (2)	ubiquity (n.) (15)
oglers (n.) (2)	innovators (n.) (18)
taut (adj.) (2)	chagrin (n.) (22)

For centuries our collective navel was hidden from view, obscured first by animal pelts, later by togas[1] and Sans-a-Belt slacks.[2] The bellybutton—innie or outie, whorled or smooth—was a private domain, a shadowy vista to be meditated on by slack-jawed philosophers and prissy lint fiends. Like all good things, navel gazing was something best done alone.

The '90s changed all that, of course. No longer was the bellybutton something to cloak or conceal. Young, edgy, unwashed sorts—not content

---
[1] **ESL togas:** The loose outer garments worn by citizens of ancient Rome.
[2] **Sans-a-Belt slacks:** A type of pants that requires no belt.

merely to perforate their nostrils or eyebrows or tongues—began piercing their navels. Soon Britney Spears was cavorting through videos in skimpy hip-hugging ensembles, flaunting her flat belly for record execs and MTV oglers. The taut and the feckless (Jennifer Lopez, Sarah Jessica Parker, the Hilton sisters) followed suit. These days, you can't enter a mall without tripping over throngs of sixth-grade girls, their midriffs proudly bared.

Unfortunately, however, it's not just preteens. Navels, no longer novel, have been embraced by the American mainstream. They're protruding everywhere. Prime-time TV, general interest magazines, next to you in line at CVS.[3]   3

And the results, frankly, aren't pretty.   4

During the Super Bowl, AT&T Wireless shelled out millions on ads for its new mLife wireless service, one of which featured bellies and buttons of all shapes and sizes—blubbery, wrinkly, saggy, you name it. At least one New York plastic surgeon has begun practicing umbilicoplasty, fashioning prettier bellybuttons for the abdominally challenged—or those who think they are. The cost of the procedure? About $2,500 a pop.   5

Meanwhile, if you can't think of an instance when you've seen a midriff-baring outfit on someone who should have known better, you're not looking hard enough.   6

The belly craze "started out with crop tops and lowriders that you had to be young and fit to wear," said Sondra Grace, associate professor and head of fashion design at the Massachusetts College of Art. "Then, as the trend carried through and people started getting comfortable with it, some people thought you didn't have to be so young and fit."   7

She paused ominously. "It's an exposure that's not that flattering."   8

Indeed. But it is how real people look, said Mark Siegel, a spokesman for AT&T Wireless, when queried about the bellybutton ad, which aired during the third quarter of the Super Bowl. In it, wordless images of older people, overweight people, even newborns, their bellies bared, floated across the screen. The point? Our navels are evidence of our need to be connected and our need to be free.   9

"We wanted people to see themselves in these ads," Siegel said. "We wanted there to be recognizable human beings and not just fashion plates in them."   10

There's little chance the bellies popping up all over will be mistaken for the flat, artfully framed tummies of the models and starlets who launched the navel trend several years ago. But that's not stopping regular folks from trying to achieve a similar look.   11

New York plastic surgeon Bruce Nadler says requests for bellybutton-reshaping surgery have soared over the past couple of years. "With the latest trends in fashion, all of a sudden it's an area that's really come into focus," he said. Patients come in with pictures of navels they admire, "so they can look like their favorite pop star."   12

[3] **ESL** CVS: A pharmacy store chain.

Many umbilicoplasty patients are twenty- and thirty-somethings, says   13
Nadler, but not all.

"I'm 55, and I have a pierced navel," he said. "A lot of times older   14
women will come in with a pierced navel, and I'll ask them why they did
it. They say it's because their daughters look so well. They still have a
competitive thing going on. They've maintained themselves, and now they
get the final touch."

The clothing industry, meanwhile, has paved the way for belly ubiq-   15
uity. Skirts and pants have been cut to sit lower and lower, regardless of
whether the wearer can, or should, sport the hip-hugger look.

"You have people who normally would be wearing things to cover   16
their waist, but the clothes aren't made to do that anymore," said Jacque-
line Stathis, group exercise manager at Sports Club/LA in Boston's new
Ritz-Carlton Hotel. "So sometimes, whether you want to expose yourself
or not, you have to."

There is some good news, trend watchers say. Now that middle Amer-   17
ica has warmed to the American middle, the belly trend is officially on its
way out.

"The fashion innovators, the people onstage, they introduce a trend,"   18
Grace said. "When it gets oversaturated and the wrong people are doing
it, that's what kills it."

Anyone who's seen the recent perplexing Levi's ad—the one that fea-   19
tures a gaggle of bellybuttons singing like little toothless mouths—can attest that it's time to return the bellybutton to its rightful place: out of sight.

So what's the next hot body part—the one that teen queens will re-   20
veal years before the rest of the country would even consider it?

"The back and the leg," Grace said.   21

Those styles will be much to the chagrin of hip-hugger manufacturers   22
and crop-top wearers. But those of us who've seen one belly too many will
breathe a sigh of relief.

EXERCISING VOCABULARY

1. Kaufman says that models and starlets "launched the navel trend" (para. 11).
   What kinds of things are usually launched? How does another possible
   spelling of *navel* make this a play on words?

2. In paragraph 3, Kaufman writes that navels "have been embraced by the American mainstream." How is *embraced* usually used? What does it mean here?

PROBING CONTENT

1. According to the author, what is the problem with the belly-baring trend?
   What is a possible solution to this problem?

2. Why were navels chosen to play a large role in introducing AT&T's new mLife
   wireless service? What purpose do mLife and navels share?

3. According to New York plastic surgeon Bruce Nadler, why are many older women piercing their navels? How do his patients decide what their navels should look like?

4. What is "officially" ending the belly-baring trend? What body parts may take center stage next?

CONSIDERING CRAFT

1. After reading this essay, a reader has no doubt what the author thinks about the belly-baring trend, yet Kaufman never directly states her feelings. How then does she clearly convey her opinion? Give some specific examples to support your answer.

2. How does the double meaning in the title prepare the reader for Kaufman's style in this essay? Find another place where the author plays with language to achieve a humorous effect and make a serious point at the same time.

3. The word choice in this essay helps us visualize some very clear images. Identify one spot in the text where Kaufman's choice of words creates a strong image.

RESPONDING TO THE WRITER

Do you agree that certain fashion trends should be restricted to those who have the right figure for them? Name another fashion trend or style that looks best on a particular body type. Who should decide which people are eligible to wear new styles or follow new trends? Why do people sometimes wear something trendy even when it is unflattering?

For a quiz on this reading, go to bedfordstmartins.com/mirror.

On Covers of Many Magazines, a Full Racial Palette Is Still Rare

DAVID CARR

Halle Berry is famous for being the first African American woman to win an Academy Award for Best Actress. Would it surprise you to learn she is only the fifth black woman to appear on the cover of *Cosmo* magazine? Think of all the magazine covers you've observed over the years. Are you aware of how few nonwhite faces have stared back at you from them? In a November 18, 2002, article in the *New York Times*, David Carr examines how economics, consumer appeal, and presumed racism are intertwined in the conservative magazine industry. He also describes the slow process of change driven in part by young music lovers and the mainstream success of Oprah Winfrey's O magazine.

David Carr has worked as editor of the *Washington City Paper*, an alternative newspaper owned by the *Chicago Reader*. His articles have appeared in *Salon.com* and the *Atlantic Monthly*. He is currently the media critic for the *New York Times*.

THINKING AHEAD

What are you looking for when you look at a magazine's cover? How much does the cover influence your decision about whether to buy that magazine? How do you feel about nonwhite faces appearing on magazine covers?

INCREASING VOCABULARY

palette (n.) (title)	empowerment (n.) (10)
feat (n.) (1)	genre (n.) (11)
cadre (n.) (2)	misstep (n.) (15)
deemed (v.) (2)	indiscernible (adj.) (21)
incremental (adj.) (5)	stigma (n.) (22)
mainstream (n.) (6)	invariably (adv.) (29)
homogeneity (n.) (7)	fore (n.) (33)
transcends (v.) (10)	

Halle Berry, in her role as the sexy superspy Jinx in *Die Another Day*, helps James Bond save the world from certain doom. But Ms. Berry may be performing an even more improbable feat as the cover model of the December issue of *Cosmopolitan* magazine. 1

Ms. Berry became only the fifth black to appear on the cover of *Cosmopolitan* since the magazine began using cover photographs in 1964, and 2 she is the first since Naomi Campbell in 1990. Ms. Berry is evidently one of a tiny cadre of nonwhite celebrities who are deemed to have enough crossover appeal to appear on the cover of mass consumer magazines.

There are signs that the freeze-out may be beginning to thaw, as the continuing explosion of hip-hop has pushed many black artists into prominence, and as teenagers' magazines that are less anxious about race are bringing more diversity. But in many broad-circulation magazines, the unspoken but routinely observed practice of not using nonwhite cover subjects—for fear they will depress newsstand sales—remains largely in effect.   3

A survey of 471 covers from 31 magazines published in 2002—an array of men's and women's magazines, entertainment publications and teenagers' magazines—conducted two weeks ago by the *New York Times* found that about one in five depicted minority members. Five years ago, according to the survey, which examined all the covers of those 31 magazines back through 1998, the figure was only 12.7 percent. And fashion magazines have more than doubled their use of nonwhite cover subjects.   4

But in a country with a nonwhite population of almost 30 percent, the incremental progress leaves some people unimpressed.   5

"The magazine industry has been slow and reluctant to embrace the change in our culture," said Roy S. Johnson, editorial director of Vanguarde Media and editor in chief of *Savoy*, a magazine aimed at black men. "The change is broad and profound, and in many ways is now the mainstream."   6

The absence of cover-model diversity could reflect the industry's racial homogeneity. Four years ago, the trade publication *Mediaweek* found that only 6.1 percent of the magazine industry's professional staff was nonwhite.   7

"We do not see ourselves in magazines," said Diane Weathers, editor in chief of *Essence*, a monthly magazine for black women. "Considering what the country we live in looks like today, I think it's appalling."   8

The women's category has seen the most profound changes, largely as a result of *O*, the Oprah magazine, whose cover repeatedly hosts Oprah Winfrey[1] and has a large white readership.   9

Both *Cosmo* and *O* are published by Hearst magazines. As a newsstand giant, selling two million copies a month, *Cosmo* uses a near scientific blend of sex and Middle American beauty on its covers—a formula that does not seem to include black women. *O* magazine, in contrast, transcends race with a new, spiritually based female empowerment.   10

Publishing is a conservative industry, one that has been known to define risk as using a cover model with dark hair instead of blond. But a wave of Latina superstars like Jennifer Lopez, along with genre-breaking athletes like Tiger Woods[2] and the Williams sisters,[3] have redefined what   11

---

[1] **ESL Oprah Winfrey:** Successful television talk show host.
[2] **ESL Tiger Woods:** One of the top golfers in America today.
[3] **ESL the Williams sisters:** Serena and Venus Williams, American star tennis players.

a celebrity looks like. And the audience is changing as well. In the last five years, the nonwhite audience for magazines has increased to 17 percent from 15 percent, according to Mediamark Research Inc.

Yet, even as black and Hispanic women slowly make their way onto the covers of magazines of various genres, black males still find themselves mainly confined to a ghetto of music and sports magazines.   12

"When it comes to magazine covers, my client, who is one of the busiest guys in Hollywood, can't get arrested," said an agent for an A-list[4] Hollywood actor who declined to give her name or the name of her client for fear of making a bad situation even worse. "Magazines are in trouble and they are fearful of offending their audience of Middle Americans," she said. "But those same people are buying tickets to his movies."   13

Daniel Peres, editor of *Details*, a men's magazine owned by Fairchild Publications, said there was pressure to stick with outdated conventions because newsstands now display so many more titles competing for the consumer's attention.   14

"Everyone is terrified of a misstep," he said. "While most people in the business would prefer it go unspoken because they are horrified at being perceived as racist, it is a well-known legend that blacks, especially black males, do not help generate newsstand sales."   15

Christina Kelly, now editor in chief of *YM*, a teenagers' magazine owned by Gruner & Jahr USA, recalls a struggle with the circulation people when she worked as an editor in 1993 at the now-closed *Sassy* magazine.   16

"We wanted to put Mecca from the band Digable Planets on the cover because she was huge at the time and gorgeous," she recalled. "The circulation guys hated the idea, but we just went ahead and did it. The magazine was bagged with a separate beauty booklet, which was usually placed in the back, but this time, it was bagged in front. It just happened to have a picture of a blond, blue-eyed woman on it."   17

Today, magazines like *Teen People* and *YM* feature cover subjects of a variety of hues. In the last year, *YM* has had covers that included nonwhite artists like Ashanti and Enrique Iglesias. And in August, *Teen People* chose Usher, a black R&B singer, as its No. 1 "hot guy" and featured him on the cover.   18

"Race is a much more fluid concept among teens," said Barbara O'Dair, managing editor of *Teen People*.   19

Magazines for teenagers, because of their reliance on the heavily integrated music industry, use 25 percent nonwhite subjects on their covers. If white teenagers are crossing over to embrace minority artists, many artists are meeting them halfway in terms of style.   20

Fashion, previously a very segregated world, has become transracial, with young white women adopting street fashion while black artists wear   21

---

[4] **ESL** **A-list:** The most sought-after and hence most highly paid celebrities.

long, flowing tresses. Certain totems[5] of beauty—blond hair, among other things—can now be seamlessly situated on almost anyone regardless of race. The singers Shakira, Beyoncé Knowles, and Christina Aguilera, all nonwhite, have at times worn blond hair that is indiscernible from that of Britney Spears.

"There is virtually no stigma attached to black celebrities changing   22
their hair as there has been in the past," said Leon E. Wynter, author of *American Skin: Pop Culture, Big Business, and the End of White America* (Crown Publishers, 2002). "The hair thing is completely over."

And race itself has become more complicated and less definable, said   23
Mr. Wynter. He suggests that many of the Latin superstars like Jennifer Lopez are often seen not as minorities by young white teenagers, but as a different kind of white person. Very few of the breakout artists[6] featured on covers are dark skinned.

The growing acceptance of nonwhite cover subjects is not restricted to   24
teenaged girls. Men's magazines, for example, are not as racially mono-lithic[7] as they once were. *GQ*, which has a nonwhite readership of 18 per-cent, has always had more diverse images by featuring minority athletes and actors.

But a newer generation of men's magazines seem to find ethnicity   25
sexy. In the last year, five of the twelve women featured on the cover of *Maxim*, the spectacularly successful young men's magazine owned by Dennis Publishing USA, were other than white.

"It doesn't stem from any political motivation," said Keith Blanchard,   26
editor in chief of *Maxim*. His readers, mostly white young men, "are lis-tening to Shakira and Beyoncé. They are cheering for Lucy Liu kicking butt in *Charlie's Angels*. And I think there is a certain attraction to exotic women."

But there are those who would argue that equal opportunity objecti-   27
fication of women does not represent progress. "What is attractive is so-cially constructed," said Robin D. G. Kelley, a professor of history at New York University who has written extensively about race and black culture. "I think that race still matters, and many times what is happening is that these poly-racial figures are used to fulfill fantasies. It's the Jezebel[8] phe-nomenon."

As for the December *Cosmopolitan*, Kate White, the magazine's edi-   28
tor in chief, said Ms. Berry was on her cover simply because she meets all the criteria of a typical *Cosmo* girl. "She is beautiful, powerful, successful, and she can open a movie," Ms. White said, suggesting that Ms. Berry has the kind of wattage[9] that can draw people into a movie, or to buy a

---

[5] **totems:** Things treated with the kind of respect normally reserved for religious icons.
[6] **ESL breakout artists:** People who become stars quickly and sometimes unexpectedly.
[7] **monolithic:** Uniform in character and slow to change.
[8] **Jezebel:** In the Hebrew scriptures, a ninth-century B.C. queen who married Ahab and pro-moted idol worship; in general, an immoral woman.
[9] **ESL wattage:** Star power.

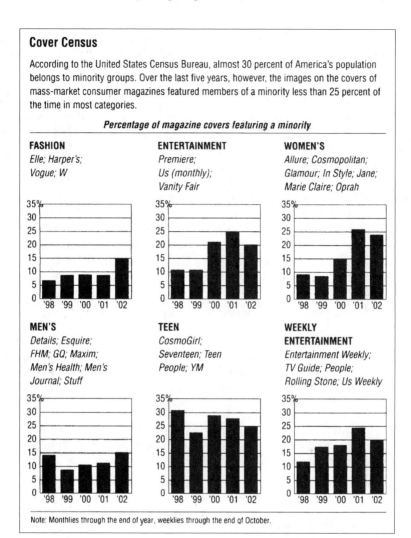

Cover Census

According to the United States Census Bureau, almost 30 percent of America's population belongs to minority groups. Over the last five years, however, the images on the covers of mass-market consumer magazines featured members of a minority less than 25 percent of the time in most categories.

Percentage of magazine covers featuring a minority

FASHION
Elle; Harper's; Vogue; W

ENTERTAINMENT
Premiere; Us (monthly); Vanity Fair

WOMEN'S
Allure; Cosmopolitan; Glamour; In Style; Jane; Marie Claire; Oprah

MEN'S
Details; Esquire; FHM; GQ; Maxim; Men's Health; Men's Journal; Stuff

TEEN
CosmoGirl; Seventeen; Teen People; YM

WEEKLY ENTERTAINMENT
Entertainment Weekly; TV Guide; People; Rolling Stone; Us Weekly

Note: Monthlies through the end of year, weeklies through the end of October.

magazine. Ms. White said the absence of nonwhite women on the cover of *Cosmo* reflected the celebrities that Hollywood produces, not the magazine's preferences.

Still, when the magazine uses a model instead of a celebrity, it almost 29 invariably chooses a white person. "We choose models who have already started to gain critical mass,[10] regardless of hair or eye color," said a Hearst spokeswoman in response. "We want the reader to have a sense of having seen them before."

It probably helps, in terms of both newsstand and advertising, that Ms. 30 Berry's face is everywhere now that she has been selected as a spokeswoman

---

[10] **critical mass:** The amount necessary to have a significant effect.

for the cosmetics company Revlon. There are important business, as well as cultural reasons, why after so many years that black, at least in some magazines, may be beautiful.

"Part of what is going on is that the beauty industry woke up and re-   31
alized there was a big market there," said Roberta Myers, editor in chief of *Elle*, a women's fashion magazine that is uncommonly diverse in cover selections. "The old assumptions that there was only one kind of beauty, the typical blond, blue-eyed Christie Brinkley[11] type, are gone."

While editors sweat over the consequences of diversifying their cover   32
mix, they may fall behind a coming generation of young consumers who have decided that race is much less important than how hot a given celebrity's latest record or film is.

"The list of who is acceptable or hot is slowly expanding," said   33
Mr. Wynter. "In the current generation, there is an underlying urge, an as-piration, to assert one's common humanity. You can't see it in the maga-zines that are on the shelves now, but it is coming to the fore."

EXERCISING VOCABULARY

1. In paragraph 12, the author writes that "black males still find themselves mainly confined to a ghetto of music and sports magazines." What is a ghetto? Why have people been confined to a ghetto in the past? What does the au-thor imply by his word choice here?

2. What does the author mean by the term "equal opportunity objectification of women" (para. 27)? Is this term positive or negative? Why? What does equal opportunity normally mean in the working world? Is it normally regarded as positive or negative? Explain your answer.

PROBING CONTENT

1. How has fashion become "transracial"? Give an example that illustrates this change.

2. What effect has the music world had on magazine covers? What target audi-ence has most directly influenced a change in magazine covers?

3. Why has the magazine industry been slow to reflect the growing numbers of nonwhite celebrities and readers? What kinds of magazines have been most likely to feature minorities on their covers? What evidence is there of change?

CONSIDERING CRAFT

1. This article originally appeared in the business section of the *New York Times*. What audience would have read this essay in its original form? How would the article differ if it had been written for the fashion section?

[11] **ESL Christie Brinkley:** American supermodel during the 1970s and 1980s.

2. What role do the bar graphs play? How do they enhance your reading of the essay?

3. Halle Berry is mentioned at the beginning and near the end of the essay. Why does the author use this strategy? How effective a choice is Berry for the writer's purpose? Why?

RESPONDING TO THE WRITER

How important is it to increase the appearance of nonwhite celebrities on popular magazine covers? Why? Explain your response.

For a quiz on this reading, go to bedfordstmartins.com/mirror.

Champagne Taste, Beer Budget

DELIA CLEVELAND

Have you ever splurged on an outfit you knew you couldn't afford? In "Champagne Taste, Beer Budget," Delia Cleveland compares herself to a recovering junkie whose drug of choice was designer clothing. She looks at the financial and intellectual drain of keeping her wardrobe current and shows how her addiction made her miss out on more rewarding experiences. Today, Cleveland vows "to seek the culture my designer clothes once implied I had."

"Champagne Taste, Beer Budget" first appeared in the March 2001 issue of *Essence* magazine. Cleveland wrote this essay while attending New York University as a media studies major and has had her work published in *Black Elegance* and *Spice* magazines.

THINKING AHEAD

Have you ever been obsessed with owning something, going somewhere, or doing some particular thing? How did this obsession affect you? How did you achieve the object of your desire? To what extent did reaching your goal satisfy you?

INCREASING VOCABULARY

paltry (adj.) (2)	stagnation (n.) (8)
façade (n.) (2)	tote (v.) (10)
	swaggering (v.) (10)

My name is Dee, and I'm a recovering junkie. Yeah, I was hooked 1
on the strong stuff. Stuff that emptied my wallet and maxed out
my credit card during a single trip to the mall. I was a fashion addict. I wore a designer emblem on my chest like a badge of honor and respect. But the unnatural high of sporting a pricey label distorted my understanding of what it really meant to have "arrived."

At first I just took pride in being the best-dressed female at my high 2
school. Fellows adored my jiggy style; girls were insanely jealous. I became a fiend for the attention. In my mind, clothes made the woman and everything else was secondary. Who cared about geometry? Every Friday I spent all my paltry paycheck from my part-time job on designer clothes. Life as I knew it revolved around a classy façade. Then slowly my money started getting tight, so tight I even resorted to borrowing from my mother. Me, go out looking average? Hell no! I'd cut a class or wouldn't bother going to school at all, unable to bear the thought of friends saying that I had fallen off and was no longer in vogue.

Out of concern, my mother started snooping around my bedroom to see where my paycheck was going. She found a telltale receipt I'd carelessly left in a shopping bag. Worse, she had set up a savings account for me, and I secretly withdrew most of the money — $1,000 — to satisfy my jones.[1] Then I feverishly charged $600 for yet another quick fashion fix.

"Delia, you're turning into a lunatic, giving all your hard-earned money to multimillionaires!" she screamed.

"Mama," I shrugged, "you're behind the times." I was looking fly,[2] and that was all that mattered.

Until I got left back in the tenth grade.

The fact that I was an A student before I discovered labels put fire under my mother's feet. In her eyes, I was letting brand names control my life, and I needed help. Feeling she had no other choice, she got me transferred to another school. I had screwed up so badly that a change did seem to be in order. Besides, I wanted to show her that labels couldn't control me. So even though everyone, including me, knew I was "smart" and an excellent student, I found myself at an alternative high school.

Meanwhile, I began looking at how other well-dressed addicts lived to see where they were headed. The sobering reality: They weren't going anywhere. In fact, the farthest they'd venture was the neighborhood corner or a party — all dressed up, nowhere to go. I watched them bop around[3] in $150 hiking boots — they'd never been hiking. They sported $300 ski jackets — never went near a slope. I saw parents take three-hour bus trips to buy their kids discount-price designer labels, yet these parents wouldn't take a trip to make a bank deposit in their child's name. Watching them, I was forced to look at myself, at my own financial and intellectual stagnation, at the soaring interest on my overused credit card.

That's when it all became clear. At my new high school I attended classes with adults — less emphasis on clothes, more emphasis on work. Although the alternative school gave me invaluable work experience, I never received the kind of high-school education I should have had — no sports, no prom, no fun. I realized I had sacrificed an important part of my life for material stuff that wasn't benefiting me at all.

That was twelve years ago. Today I'm enjoying a clean-and-sober lifestyle. Armed with a new awareness, I've vowed to leave designer labels to people who can truly afford them. I refuse to tote a $500 baguette[4] until I can fill it with an equal amount of cash. I'm not swaggering around in overpriced Italian shoes till I can book a trip to Italy. On my road to recovery, I have continued to purchase clothing — sensibly

[1] **ESL** **jones:** A craving for something.
[2] **ESL** **fly:** Cool; fabulous.
[3] **ESL** **bop around:** To go freely from place to place.
[4] **baguette:** A handbag shaped like a loaf of French bread.

priced. And every now and then, the money I save goes toward a Broad-way play or a vacation in the sun. I'm determined to seek the culture my designer clothes once implied I had. I no longer look the part—because I'm too busy living it.

EXERCISING VOCABULARY

1. Examine the title. What does the phrase "champagne taste" imply? How would such taste be in conflict with a "beer budget"? How well does this title work for this essay?

2. The author comments that in high school she couldn't bear the thought of not being "in vogue" (para. 2). What does it mean to be in vogue? How could being in vogue in one area of the United States mean being hope-lessly out of fashion in another area? Give several examples to illustrate your answer.

PROBING CONTENT

1. What was the author's obsession in high school? What effect did this have on her life?

2. How did Cleveland's mother find out about her daughter's problem? How did her mother's reaction to this discovery change Cleveland?

3. What event finally caught Cleveland's attention? What action did her mother take? Why was this an unexpected decision?

4. What important realizations did the author reach? How did she arrive at these conclusions?

5. What evidence does Cleveland offer to confirm that she has recovered from her addiction?

CONSIDERING CRAFT

1. When you begin reading this essay, you might think that Cleveland's obses-sion is going to be with drugs. What language does she use to encourage this misdirection? Cite several specific examples. Why does the author delib-erately allow the reader to be misled in this way? How does her use of such language affect the way you read the essay?

2. Throughout her essay, the author sprinkles slang that may be unfamiliar to you. Cite several examples of such language. Why would the author include these expressions if many readers and dictionaries would not be familiar with them? What would be lost if they were to be omitted or replaced by standard English?

RESPONDING TO THE WRITER

To what extent do you identify with the author's willingness to invest most of her money in clothes? Does the fact that her decisions caused her to miss much of the fun of high school make you sympathize with her? Did you know people like Delia Cleveland in high school, or do you know them now in college? What advice would you offer them?

For a quiz on this reading, go to bedfordstmartins.com/mirror.

The Tyranny of "Abercrappie"

DAMIEN CAVE

In the following essay, Damien Cave describes the horror he felt when his younger brother joined the millions of teenagers entranced by Abercrombie & Fitch's homogenized clothing. What do teenagers find so appealing about the brand? Are they drawn to A&F's sexually charged advertisements? Or have the brand's "frat-boy mentality" and image of freedom and excitement made the logo an essential part of today's teen uniform? Cave examines Abercrombie's marketing campaign and makes some interesting discoveries.

"The Tyranny of 'Abercrappie'" first appeared in *Salon.com,* where Damien Cave worked as a senior writer covering high-tech policy, economics, and international affairs. He has also written for *Washington Monthly, Rolling Stone,* the *Keene Sentinel, Takeoffs and Landings,* the *Bolivian Times,* and *Time Out New York.* Cave attributes his interest in fashion to his grandfather, the owner and primary designer of a men's outerwear company, and fondly remembers childhood excursions to department stores, where his grandfather lectured him on fabrics, styles, and changes in the industry. Cave is currently working as a reporter for the *New York Times.*

THINKING AHEAD

Do you shop for clothes and accessories at a particular store? Are there stores whose clothing you would never consider wearing? What has influenced you to make these decisions about what is right for you to wear?

INCREASING VOCABULARY

stumped (v.) (2)

banter (n.) (3)

manipulative (adj.) (4)

ogle (v.) (5)

irk (v.) (9)

self-deprecation (n.) (9)

staunching (v.) (10)

amplified (v.) (11)

trysts (n.) (11)

arbiter (n.) (11)

frugal (adj.) (12)

incensed (adj.) (12)

fervor (n.) (14)

brandishing (n.) (22)

incessant (adj.) (22)

smugness (n.) (24)

pedantic (adj.) (24)

trump (v.) (25)

savvy (adj.) (32)

A bercrappie" is what my youngest brother called Abercrombie &   1
Fitch after Ryan, our fifteen-year-old sibling, begged for the worn-
looking, overpriced clothes du jour.

Shirts, pants, sweaters, socks—Ryan wanted Abercrombie every-   2
thing and he stumped for the stuff like a wide-eyed activist. In the
kitchen, tossing punches at Josh and me, he used the word "quality."
When I walked away, he chased me with a speech about owning "just a
few things that you love to wear." He even suggested that I pick up some
Abercrombie—"It might help you get a girlfriend," he offered with very
little tact.

Christmas was only a few days away and the smart-alecky banter—"I   3
want X" vs. "So what, you can't have it"—rang typical, as much a part
of our family's holiday tradition as egg nog. But a specific brand request:
That was new.

I remembered longing for Air Jordans,[1] Champion sweatshirts, even   4
Ralph Lauren Polo shirts. But my parents shamed me into either buying
them myself or squeezing them out of relatives. On occasion, Mom or
Dad gave in, but they always had a choice. Never, strong as my longing
was, had one designer inspired the single-branded passion I heard in
Ryan's voice. Somehow, Abercrombie was different: more manipulative
and more coveted than both its past and present rivals.

That drug-like draw angered me. After watching packs of pimply   5
teenage boys in Massachusetts malls ogle the boobs and brands of the opposite sex, I couldn't help but want Ryan to swim against the current in
this sea of conformity.

I swore I would never buy him the Abercrombie clothing I saw his   6
peers wearing like a uniform. In fact, I decided I would play with his re-
pulsive desire by putting a "Just kidding!" note inside an Abercrombie
gift-certificate envelope.

First, though, I tried to fight back with words.   7

"Why would you want to be a billboard?" I asked. "They're not pay-   8
ing you to advertise their name."

Ryan went for finely tuned sarcasm. "But it's just so cool," he said, try-   9
ing to irk me in the short term while offering the kind of self-deprecation
that just might convince me to give him what he wanted later on.

By that time, my question was largely rhetorical. I already knew the   10
real reason he was lusting after these clothes. Only two months earlier,
Ryan had begun fusing himself to Nicole, a blond A student who won our
family's favor by staunching Ryan's class-clown tendencies.

But while she kept his bragging to a minimum, Nicole also amplified   11
Ryan's navel-, chest- and shoulder-gazing. When I picked her up on
Christmas night, she wore a yellow Abercrombie T-shirt, and as I drove
the magnetic couple back to our family's house, A&F earned at least as
much air time as the latest gossip about teachers and other high school

---

[1] **ESL** **Air Jordans:** Expensive sneakers named for famous basketball player Michael Jordan.

trysts. Nicole, like many women present and past, had become the arbiter of her man's taste. And in her court, Abercrombie was king.

"I think it's all she wears," said my mother that same afternoon, chuckling. She had already decided that Nicole passed muster, so her criticism remained light. Still, as a frugal New Hampshire native who stocks her shelves with generic foods and her closets with closeouts, my mom became easily incensed when discussing Abercrombie's prices.   12

"Seventy dollars for pants! It's outrageous."   13

What's more, as a mother who objects to premarital sex with a puritanical fervor, she also objected to the company's marketing campaign. Essentially, it sexualizes America's love of the aristocratic golden boy and girl—the blond, WASPish,[2] Ivy League[3] party animals most recently represented by Jude Law and Gwyneth Paltrow in *The Talented Mr. Ripley*.   14

Ads for Ralph Lauren, Tommy Hilfiger and Nautica have played on similar themes for years, but Abercrombie's models look younger, more collegiate. And Abercrombie plays closer to the frat-boy mentality, plastering naked male chests in most of its 205 store windows, while selling 300-page, quarterly catalogs that cost $6 and include interviews with porn stars and articles about drinking.   15

Indeed, women appear in the ads as well, but the boys rule. When they're not baring their asses to clamber naked aboard a dock or lying prostrate in the grass, the models huddle, flex and pose in store foregrounds like ten-foot trophies, a fact that most teens couldn't help but notice and want to copy in their own lives.   16

My mother didn't much care about whether the bare butts were male or female. She objected to what she perceived as the encouragement of sex. In so doing, she was in cahoots with[4] Illinois Lt. Gov. Corinne Wood, who called for a consumer boycott of Abercrombie because of the sexually explicit nature of its holiday "Naughty or Nice" catalog.   17

But as I tried to decide what to buy Ryan and my two other adolescent siblings for Christmas, the sex didn't bother me. The brand's dominance did. That dominance, in my opinion, has less to do with skin than with the company's fusion of two settings: the city of hip-hop lore, and the college of the frat-inspired free-for-all. The former can be seen in the company's baggy, urban-inspired designs; clean-cut models on grassy fields embody the latter.   18

Sex is a mythical part of these settings, but parents often fail to realize that these places—and thus Abercrombie—symbolize more than the longing to get naked. Ultimately, they represent freedom, excitement—a wide array of adventures that remain off-limits to the teenage children of today's SUV-driving parents.   19

The Reynoldsburg, Ohio, company has posted twenty-nine consecutive quarters of record sales and earnings, making it one of the world's   20

---

[2] **ESL** **WASPish:** Characteristic of a White Anglo-Saxon Protestant.
[3] **ESL** **Ivy League:** A group of prestigious universities located in the eastern United States.
[4] **ESL** **in cahoots with:** Cooperating with.

best-performing retail brands. Surveyed teenagers repeatedly rank it near the top in terms of "coolness." To see that success only in terms of sex implies that teenagers are nothing more than their hormones, and that they are the company's only customers.

Neither implication is correct. I know adults who wear Abercrombie 21 clothing, if only the shirts that carry the company name on the inside label. And as for sex: Yes, many teenagers' bodies insist that the subject come up, and often. But hormones affect more than sexual desire. As adults, in our own lives, we know this. But when we eye our sons and brothers, amnesia[5] strikes.

Somehow we have forgotten—probably because of our fears—that 22 the hormone-inspired energy of youth leads most often to neither sex nor violence. The brandishing of bare chests by teenage boys and their incessant raunchy[6] chatter represent a healthy desire to learn, to push against adult boundaries, to discover the art of living. It's the same force that can be heard on the first Beck[7] album, completed before he was old enough to vote.

Even though Abercrombie taps into this pent-up energy with controver- 23 sial content, the images don't matter. The company is "cool" not because of the sex or the beer, but because these subjects signify a much wider idea, namely the freedom to live as the kid—not the parent—sees fit.

Opining on Abercrombie's appeal, however, didn't much change my 24 decision to boycott the store. I still wanted Ryan to be above it all. But after putting my note in the gift certificate envelope, my smugness stung me. I already had bought books and movie passes. I feared the trick certificate placed me at risk of becoming the pedantic big brother.

So I gave in. On Christmas Eve, I bought Ryan a fleece jacket, marked 25 down from $49.99 to $29.99. I justified it by remarking that the name "Abercrombie" only appeared on the inside tag and on the zipper. Ryan had been getting good grades, so I figured he deserved it. I figured my love should trump my politics. I figured his tastes mattered more than mine.

Much to my surprise, my parents did the same thing. On Christmas 26 morning, Ryan opened not just my Abercrombie box, but several others. We had resisted the call of the $70 pants, but ultimately we had given in. We had conformed, accepting Ryan's argument for "quality" and "clothes worth loving." And we all knew it. Mom, Dad and I glanced at Ryan as he stripped to try on each jersey, then stared guiltily back at each other.

"I can't believe it," Dad said. 27

"The little twit got what he wanted," I added. "And Abercrappie 28 won. They got us."

Then and now, I continue to fight back. I explain to Ryan how he's 29 been made a pawn, a cookie-cutter version of youth. I'm hoping that he'll

[5] **amnesia:** A loss of memory.
[6] **ESL raunchy:** Sexually explicit or obscene.
[7] **ESL Beck:** Beck Hansen, a songwriter and performer who blends folk, electronic, punk rock, and rap influences.

learn to dress and live for himself, not his peers or his girlfriends. I'm hoping he'll rebel against Abercrombie and his peers.

If and when he does, we'll still have other battles to fight. Joshua, my thirteen-year-old brother, coiner of the term "Abercrappie," didn't get any of the company's clothing for Christmas. But when he opened the surf sweatshirt I got him, his first question was: "Where did you get it?" And as he watched Ryan open box after box from Abercrombie, Josh's eyes opened wide with yearning. Later, he dropped hints that maybe Abercrombie wasn't so bad. 30

Ultimately, I'm not surprised. When Hannibal Lecter[8] asked, "What do we covet?" he couldn't have been more right in answering, "We covet what we see." 31

My only wish is that suburban, teenaged style looked less like a dress code. I wish Abercrombie had stiffer competition; that kids would demand more from their merchants. But most of all, I wish Ryan, Nicole and so many other teenagers would act as smart and savvy as I know they are. 32

Until then, I'll buy them what they want—then try and convince them to hate it. 33

EXERCISING VOCABULARY

1. Restaurants often offer a *soupe du jour*, or "soup of the day." In the first paragraph, the author refers to Abercrombie & Fitch's offerings as "clothes du jour." What does this usage imply?

2. In paragraph 14, Cave states that Abercrombie & Fitch's advertising campaign "sexualizes America's love of the aristocratic golden boy and girl." Since America has no aristocracy, what does Cave mean by this? In what sense are such young people "golden"?

PROBING CONTENT

1. What had happened in the past when the author wanted specific name-brand clothing? How was Ryan's desire different?

2. What are Cave's objections to Ryan's wearing Abercrombie & Fitch clothing? What started Ryan's obsession and kept it going?

3. What are the main objections of the author's mother to Abercrombie & Fitch? How valid are her objections?

4. What does the author find objectionable about Abercrombie & Fitch's marketing campaign? What does he think is the message behind the ads that makes A&F a "cool" company?

[8] **ESL** **Hannibal Lecter:** Cannibalistic serial killer of Thomas Harris's novels *Red Dragon*, *The Silence of the Lambs*, and *Hannibal* and their film versions.

5. How does Cave justify his Christmas gift for his brother Ryan? What does Christmas morning lead Cave to conclude?

CONSIDERING CRAFT

1. Cave uses an extended example from his own family to argue a much larger point in this essay. Why is this personalized method more effective than simply developing more objective steps in a logical argument?

2. Near the end of this essay, the author quotes Hannibal Lecter, the cannibalistic murderer in the films *The Silence of the Lambs, Hannibal,* and *Red Dragon.* Lecter's desires are certainly far more deviant than a desire for a particular clothing brand. Why does Cave choose this quotation from this character? What point is Cave making?

RESPONDING TO THE WRITER

Damien Cave wants teenagers to take more control of their lives, to have higher expectations, and to overcome the status quo. How is his desire at odds with current teenage culture?

For a quiz on this reading, go to bedfordstmartins.com/mirror.

DRAWING CONNECTIONS

1. Compare the reactions of Delia Cleveland's and Damien Cave's mothers to their children's obsession with what they wear. What circumstances might account for the differences in their reactions?

2. Do you think that Cave's younger brother Ryan will become the kind of "junkie" that Cleveland was? Offer evidence from "The Tyranny of 'Abercrappie' " and "Champagne Taste, Beer Budget" to support your position.

FOCUSING ON YESTERDAY, FOCUSING ON TODAY

The Hathaway Man, pictured here in a print advertisement from the 1960s, was a debonair icon of men's fashion, reminiscent of a leading man from the Golden Age of Hollywood. Sporting an eye patch, holding fencing equipment, and wearing the "Rolls Royce" of shirts, this gentleman is as self-assured as James Bond.

The Hathaway Man

Five ways to identify a Hathaway shirt—at a glance

IT'S AS EASY to recognize a Hathaway shirt as a Rolls Royce—if you know these subtle signs:

1. Notice how generously the shirt is cut. More cloth than you get in a mass-produced shirt. Ergo, more comfortable.

2. Look at the *buttons*. They are unusually large. And the *stitches*—unusually small.

More than 30,000 stitches in one shirt.

3. Now look at our *cuffs*. They have square corners. This applies to our French cuffs *and* to the kind you button.

4. Where the front tail joins the back tail, you always find our hallmark—the letter **H** discreetly embroidered in scarlet.

5. The men who wear HATHAWAY

shirts are individualists, so they seldom wear *white* shirts.

The shirt illustrated above is a fine Karnac cotton from Egypt, woven for Hathaway in Wauregan. The rectangular checks are copied from a rare French original. Retails at $8.95. Write C. F. Hathaway, Waterville, Maine. In New York, call MUrray Hill 9-4157.

In this ad for Skechers sneakers, we move from the Hathaway Man's eye patch and fencing equipment to music icon Christina Aguilera's fishnet stockings and boy toys. Displacing Britney Spears as the "Skechers girl," Aguilera, raised in New York and Philadelphia by parents of Irish and Ecuadorian descent, gives a new edge and a new global appeal to the advertising campaign for this popular brand of shoes.

What changes in our culture explain the differences between the Hathaway ad and the Skechers ad? Consider changes in gender roles, the boom in young consumers, and the effect of the music industry on advertising. What selling strategies do these advertisements use? Consider the use of text, celebrity endorsement, cobranding, sex appeal, and target audience. Do these two ads represent a way of fitting in or a way of standing out?

Sex and the Sneaker

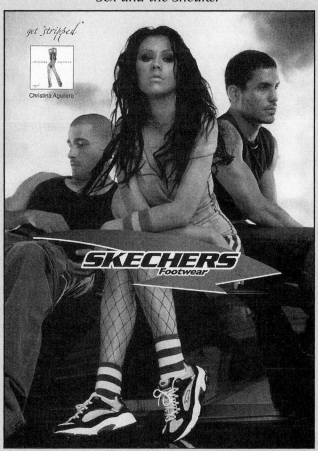

REFLECTING ON THE WRITING

1. Write an essay in which you examine the role that shopping for clothes plays in your life and in the lives of your peers. Make sure to examine both positive and negative aspects.

2. Pick a popular fashion trend, as John Leo, Ruth La Ferla, and Hayley Kaufman did in their essays, and write an essay in which you trace its popularity. Explain the reasons behind that popularity. You may wish to use magazine articles, the Web, and interviews for source material.

3. As La Ferla does in her essay, choose one group within our larger culture and write an essay in which you examine fashion trends or styles that can be directly linked to that group. Be sure to select a trend or style that has permeated our culture. Include an explanation of why that trend or style has become popular among many people.

4. Design an advertising campaign for an imaginary fashion product such as a piece of clothing or an accessory. Devise a logo and write advertising copy for your product. Present your campaign to a hypothetical fashion buyer who is looking for a new advertising agency.

CONNECTING TO THE CULTURE

1. Pick a popular fashion trend like body piercing, nail art, or popped collars, and write an essay in which you examine the reasons, both direct and indirect, behind the trend's popularity. You may consult magazine articles and the Web and conduct interviews to gather material for your essay. Make sure that you properly document your sources.

2. Think about what kind of fashion consumer you are. What do you spend your money on and why? Do you feel pressured to buy—or to avoid—certain brands? Write an essay in which you examine your consumer habits and what they say about you and the culture in which you live.

3. Study the different fashions worn by people on your campus. Divide people into groups according to the clothes and accessories they wear. In an essay, give names to each of these groups, describe the fashion statements they make, and speculate on what messages they are trying to send by their unique styles.

4. Choose one brand of clothing and examine its advertising campaign. Be sure to look at ads in newspapers, in magazines, on billboards, on television, and on the Internet. What consumers do the ads target? What models are used? What message lies behind the advertising? How successful is the advertising strategy? Have there been any legal issues concerning the campaign? Consider these questions in an essay in which you analyze the ad campaign for your brand of clothing.

CHAPTER 6

Fantasies for Sale
Marketing American Culture

Watch out for this independent woman. She's patriotic. What's more American than denim and the flag? She's natural, she's free, she's focused. No boundaries visible. No artificiality. Just a girl and a field and—a bottle of cologne.

- What is the message of this advertisement?

- Why is the cologne bottle placed where it is?

- The product in the ad is Tommy Girl cologne, but what is really being sold?

- Who is in the target audience for this ad?

- Are you buying what this ad is selling? Why or why not?

Research this topic with TopLinks at bedfordstmartins.com/mirror.

> I remember the exact day. I was thirteen, and I saw this big billboard on
> Decatur Street, not far from my house, had this big, lean black guy, re-
> ally good-looking, with his jeans rolled up, splashing water on a beach,
> cigarette in one hand and a slinky black chick on his back. All smiles. All
> perfect teeth. Salem menthols. What great fun. I thought to myself, Now
> there's the good life. I'd like to have some of that. So I went home, went
> to my drawer, got my money, walked down the street, and bought a
> pack of Salem menthols.

The speaker is Angel Weese, a young character in John Grisham's best-
selling novel *The Runaway Jury*. Our own encounters with advertising
may not cause such immediate and direct responses, but we do respond.
Most of us want what Angel wants—some of the good life. And if those
jeans, that cologne, that car, that deodorant, or those sneakers help get
us to the good life, we're there. Advertising is so much a part of our lives
that we may not notice its pervasive, subtle effect. How are ads created?
What messages are ads sending? Why do some ad mascots like the Geico
gecko, the Energizer Bunny, and the AFLAC duck become our friends?
Why do some jingles or famous ad phrases—like "Because I'm worth it,"
"Just do it," "For everything else, there's MasterCard," "What happens
in Vegas stays in Vegas," or "Obey your thirst"—stay in our heads?
How do ad agencies find the perfect pitch, the best "hook," the winning
slogan?

What do the ads that get our attention and send us to the stores say
about us as consumers? We are advertising targets not just as individual
consumers but also collectively. Of the groups you belong to—college
students, men or women, particular racial or ethnic backgrounds—which
ones seem to have been targeted by manufacturers' ad campaigns? "One
size never fits all" in strategic advertising. When we move beyond asking
what product an ad is selling and instead demand to know what the ad is
really saying about our culture and ourselves, we may be surprised by the
insights we gain and the savvy consumers we become.

COLLABORATING

In groups of three or four students, list five phrases, symbols, jingles, or slogans associated with widely advertised products. Collect these lists and play an Advertising IQ game based on the *Jeopardy* model. Choose a host to read the clues aloud and to call on teams to guess the product. For example, if the clue read aloud is "I'm lovin' it," the correct response would be "What is an advertising slogan for McDonald's?"

After the game, discuss why you can easily supply questions for these advertising answers when it's so difficult to remember other things — like historical dates or the Periodic Table of the Elements.

Mad Ave.

JOHN FOLLIS

Do you ever wonder if advertising people have a conscience? How can they do their best to convince us we must have things we can't afford, don't really need, and may even suffer for having used? Based on John Follis's assertion — "I can't imagine how anyone could be part of a campaign like Joe Camel, even if they smoke. It utterly amazes me that anyone can say with a straight face that a campaign featuring a cartoon camel is not directed at kids" — at least one person in the advertising business has given this some serious thought. And his conclusions have put him at odds with many others in his profession. An insider in the world of advertising for over twenty years, Follis has won over eighty awards, including nine Clios for creative excellence in advertising. His book, *Mad Ave.*, takes a critical look at the advertising industry and has been called "a collection of Seinfeldesque vignettes from Madison Avenue." Follis's insights give us an entirely different picture of the glib world of slogans and jingles. The following essay first appeared in the Winter 1998 issue of *Adbusters.*

In addition to managing his own ad agency, Follis Inc., John Follis is a contributing columnist to *Adweek* and an adjunct professor at the Fashion Institute of Technology in New York City. Away from magazine shoots and television spots, Follis participates in Outward Bound Wilderness Survival courses — where he sees very few ads.

THINKING AHEAD

Imagine that you work for an advertising company. Your boss orders you to develop a credible advertising campaign for a product you hate. What would such a product be? Why do you hate it? How would you begin work on your new assignment?

INCREASING VOCABULARY

erudite (adj.) (1)   provocative (adj.) (18)
vindication (n.) (11)

I remember a day, early in my career, when I was young and naive and on staff at a large agency. On this particular day management had gathered the troops to screen the agency reel for one of those "Aren't-We-Great" morale-boosting meetings. As the lights dimmed, the hushed crowd gazed at beautifully shot images of puppies and children and Kraft marshmallows seductively blended with seamless editing and incredibly composed music. The lights came back up and, after a rousing hand, the

1

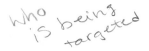

erudite CEO,[1] pipe in hand, took the stage and opened the floor for questions.

After listening to him answer inquiries like, "Gee, how'd you get that   2
puppy to lick the little girl's face," I decided to take advantage of this unexpected opportunity to "Ask the Cheese." Eventually, The Cheese nods in my direction and I spit it out:

"Do you have any reservations about advertising a product like   3
marshmallows—which is almost 100 percent sugar with zero nutritional value—and targeting mothers and young children?"

As if a party guest had just knocked over the host's best crystal vase, a   4
sudden uncomfortable silence filled the room. A few heads turned to see which of their coworkers was so bold, or stupid, to put the agency CEO on the spot in front of his entire staff. The CEO calmly paused, took a few slow puffs on his pipe, and with carefully measured words, responded:

"It is my belief that it's the government's role to decide which prod-   5
ucts should or shouldn't be advertised. And as long as the product is legal, it's the agency's responsibility to do the best job possible to advertise its clients' products." I suddenly had visions of the corporate Gestapo[2] quickly escorting me out of the room and beating me senseless.

As the days passed, I never second-guessed the legitimacy of my ques-   6
tion. I just began to second-guess the timing of it. I also began to wonder how much it affected my termination several months later.

I can't imagine how anyone could be part of a campaign like Joe Camel,   7
even if they smoke. It utterly amazes me that anyone can say with a straight face that a campaign featuring a cartoon camel is not directed at kids.

Obviously, some people just see it as a job they're paid (very well, no   8
doubt) to do. Maybe it's no different than being a criminal lawyer:

> *Judge*: We have 14 witnesses that claim they saw your client shoot the woman. His fingerprints are on the gun and we have it on videotape. How does your client plead?
> *Defense attorney*: Not guilty.

A copywriter buddy of mine is one of the most talented writers in the   9
business. The guy's amazing. After moving around a bit he settled into a high-level, well-paying job at a huge agency. He's got a couple of young kids and a nice home in a fancy neighborhood. I called him the other day just to catch up. When I asked about his job, I sensed a slight tone of resignation. He told me he's working on a battery account which features a fictitious family called "The Puttermans."

The Puttermans can only be described as a plastic-coated, alien-   10
looking, TV family-from-hell, with giant batteries fused to their spines.

---

[1] **CEO:** Chief executive officer, the highest officer in a business or corporation.
[2] **ESL Gestapo:** Nazi Germany's secret police.

The spots consist of bad sitcom-like shenanigans.[3] By the time you read this The Puttermans will probably have been put to rest with the other ill-fated ad characters.

It doesn't seem so long ago that my writer buddy and I sat around   11
talking about the advertising hacks who sell out for the money to do the dreck we both hated. Now, with a family and mortgage, my friend has new priorities. Before our chat concluded, he shared what seemed like an attempt at vindication. The five-year-olds at his daughter's birthday party wanted his autograph when they heard he was the guy who did the Putterman commercials.

During my career I've had to work on some challenging assignments (in-   12
fant anal thermometers comes to mind) but never anything that I've really had a problem with—like Spam[4] or Barney.[5] I have, however, been in-volved with a few products that seemed a bit, shall we say, questionable.

I had to struggle to keep a straight face when a marketing consultant   13
started going into a little too much detail about a high-tech toilet seat called the "Santi-Seat."

Apparently, I'm not alone. I've heard similar tales of woe from other   14
agency owners. In one such case, the agency was approached by a company called Burial at Sea. Apparently, if your dearly departed was so inclined, a burial at sea could be arranged. When the company was asked how they used their boats when business was slow, we were told, "porno movies."

For every advertisable product on the market there's a hidden army of   15
trade salespeople. Everyday, these people pack their suitcases with pencil erasers or GI Joe Battle Action accessories or whatever it is they're selling and take off on the road to places like Wilmington and Boise and Greenville trying to make quota to keep their jobs so they can do the same thing for another year. In the Great Sales War these men and women are the in-fantry, the front-line grunts. Compared to them, ad people are the air force, the glamorous flyboys who get the credit. The ad agency, equipped with the latest high-tech weaponry, goes in for the kill with a blitzkrieg[6] campaign. But even if it's a stupid product, most ad people don't have to devote too big a part of their lifetime trying to sell it.

One of my clients was an umbrella company. They made good quality   16
umbrellas—they didn't break with the first gust of wind. The guy I dealt with was the sales director. Nice guy. Smart guy. But basically, the guy was an umbrella salesman. He'd travel around the country with a bag full of umbrellas: the standard, the mini, the micro-mini, the full-size, the golf, the automatic, the semi-automatic, the designer line, the cane-style, the water-resistant.

---

[3] shenanigans: Tricky or mischievous behavior.
[4] ESL Spam: A processed, canned meat product.
[5] ESL Barney: A large, friendly purple dinosaur that stars in a children's television program.
[6] blitzkrieg: German for lightning war, an attack waged with great speed and force.

This guy spent about 80 percent of his waking hours dealing with um- 17
brellas. Don't get me wrong. Umbrellas are certainly an important and necessary part of society. I just wouldn't want to devote my life to selling
them.

Thirteen years after the "Marshmallow Incident," I find myself having 18
lunch with the very man to whom I addressed my provocative question.
When I bring up the incident he confesses to a lack of recollection. Prefac-
ing it with how young and naive I was, I recall the scene.

"Hmmm . . . so what did I answer?" he asks curiously. 19

"You said that it's the government's role to determine which products 20
should or shouldn't be advertised and that as long as a product is legal it's
the agency's responsibility to do the very best job possible to advertise its
clients' products."

With hardly a pause the ex-CEO speaks in a soft but certain manner, 21
"I think my answer would be different today."

He goes on to say how we all must be willing to accept more social re- 22
sponsibility for the decisions we make in business. I feel vindicated.

A year later, I notice a blurb in the trades about my converted CEO 23
pal. He has just passed away.

In the agency business there's always pressure. The creatives feel it to get 24
great work produced. The account people feel it to keep their clients
happy and spending their money. The president feels it to be winning new
business. The chairman feels it to be making a profit and keeping his
Board happy. And the Board feels it to keep its stockholders happy. If you
work in an agency, there's the additional pressure of never-ending dead-
lines, demanding bosses, and corporate politics. And if the agency loses a
client, which happens all the time, you could be out of a job.

When people are subjected to that kind of pressure they can do some 25
strange things. I once knew an art director who physically attacked an account exec with a metal T-square just for being asked to make the logo
bigger.

There's a saying, "It's only advertising." It's true. It's not like finding 26
a cure for AIDS. However, if you're serious about the business, and most
are, it can feel like mortal combat. I've worked with many whose philoso-
phies are Survival of the Fittest, and The End Justifies the Means.

Somewhere there was some kind of survey done about which careers the 27
public respected most. I'm not sure which ranked the highest, but I know
"Advertising Executive" ranked somewhere at the bottom. I think it was
between "Lawyer" and "Used Car Salesman." I guess the American public figures that being saved from ring-around-the-collar isn't like being
saved from cancer or nuclear war.

How soon they forget about those cute little Dancing Raisins. And 28
Clara Peller and her "Where's the beef?" Don't tell me that didn't have

some socially <u>redeeming</u> value. Even President Bush used that line. And does anyone actually watch the Super Bowl for the game?

But I have to admit, it does seem a bit weird when some woman 29 working on a cure for AIDS is in some lab cubicle somewhere making 25K while the guy who came up with "It's Bubblicious!" is sitting in some corner office making a half mil.

Hey, welcome to Mad Ave. 30

Hey this is our crazy world

EXERCISING VOCABULARY

1. In paragraph 1, Follis describes the head of an agency as an "erudite CEO." What kind of person might you associate with the word *erudite*? Does Follis mean this sincerely? How do you know? What makes the CEO appear to be erudite?

2. If a person needs to make "an attempt at vindication" (para. 11), what might you conclude about his or her previous behavior? Why might someone continue in a job that requires vindication?

PROBING CONTENT

1. What reaction does the writer's question to the CEO receive? Why is this so? What does the question indicate about the writer?

2. Follis's copywriting friend once felt as Follis does about ethics in advertising. What changed his friend's priorities? How does Follis make it clear that his friend feels some guilt about changing his attitude?

3. Follis asks, "And does anyone actually watch the Super Bowl for the game?" (para. 28). What does he mean? How valid is his question? Why?

CONSIDERING CRAFT

1. Identify some of the military words and images that Follis uses in paragraph 15 to create an extended metaphor that compares a life in marketing to one spent fighting a war. How effective is this comparison? What does it say about Follis's attitude toward his subject?

2. The title is a deliberate play on words, since many ad agencies in New York City have Madison Avenue addresses. What does Follis's shortening this address to "Mad Ave." in his title allow the reader to predict about his essay's theme?

RESPONDING TO THE WRITER

People in many professions sometimes have to do things that make them uncomfortable. Lawyers sometimes must defend people they would like to see behind bars; military personnel sometimes must carry out orders they do not support.

Advertisers sometimes must design effective sales campaigns for unnecessary or poorly made products or even products that are potentially harmful (like alcohol or cigarettes). How sympathetic are you toward these advertisers, who may just be doing their jobs? Should advertisers be held accountable for the effects of their clients' products? Explain your answer.

For a quiz on this reading, go to bedfordstmartins.com/mirror.

Illusions Are Forever

JAY CHIAT

Do you think advertisements often show products that seem too good to be true? According to marketing executive Jay Chiat, ads are indeed full of lies — but not the lies you might expect. It's the "situations, values, beliefs, and cultural norms" that constitute "the real lie in advertising" by creating a false reality and telling us how we should look, feel, and act. Should we accept the version of truth offered by media makers, or can we find our own truth? Do you buy into the vision of the world created for you by advertising executives?

When Chiat died in 2002, he was remembered as a creative genius who revolutionized the advertising industry. In 1967, he founded the Chiat/Day ad agency, which quickly grew into one of the industry's most prestigious companies. Chiat was the mastermind behind many ground-breaking advertising campaigns, including the battery ads featuring the famous Energizer Bunny and the original Apple computer ads launched in 1984, featuring striking images from George Orwell's novel *1984*. He was also responsible for making the Super Bowl into the advertising showcase that it is today. In 1997, Chiat left the marketing industry to lead ScreamingMedia, a provider of information management services. "Illusions Are Forever" was first published in the October 2, 2000, issue of *Forbes* magazine.

THINKING AHEAD

What image of the world does advertising present to us as consumers? How can this image affect us? How attainable is this world for most of us?

INCREASING VOCABULARY

sobriety (n.) (1)
piety (n.) (1)
transgressor (n.) (1)
unrelenting (adj.) (5)
pervasiveness (n.) (5)
acculturated (adj.) (5)
arbitrary (adj.) (6)
preposterous (adj.) (6)

infinitely (adv.) (7)
patently (adv.) (8)
pernicious (adj.) (8)
culprit (n.) (9)
obscuring (v.) (9)
plausible (adj.) (9)
inviolable (adj.) (11)

[handwritten: tries to build Trust]

[handwritten margin: Trust honesty]

I know what you're thinking: That's rich,[1] asking an adman to define truth. Advertising people aren't known either for their wisdom or their morals, so it's hard to see why an adman is the right person for this assignment. Well, it's just common sense—like asking an alcoholic about sobriety, or a sinner about piety. Who is likely to be more obsessively attentive to a subject than the transgressor?

[handwritten margin: everything]

Everyone thinks that advertising is full of lies, but it's not what you think. The facts presented in advertising are almost always accurate, not because advertising people are sticklers[2] but because their ads are very closely regulated. If you make a false claim in a commercial on network television, the FTC[3] will catch it. Someone always blows the whistle.[4]

[handwritten margin: in full of lies]

The real lie in advertising—some would call it the "art" of advertising—is harder to detect. What's false in advertising lies in the presentation of situations, values, beliefs, and cultural norms that form a backdrop for the selling message. *[handwritten: + definition]*

[handwritten margin right: weasel words]

[handwritten margin: definition of Advertisement]

Advertising—including movies, TV, and music videos—presents to us a world that is not our world but rather a collection of images and ideas created for the purpose of selling. These images paint a picture of the ideal family life, the perfect home. What a beautiful woman is, and is not. A prescription for being a good parent and a good citizen.

The power of these messages lies in their unrelenting pervasiveness, the twenty-four-hour-a-day drumbeat that leaves no room for an alternative view. We've become acculturated to the way advertisers and other media-makers look at things, so much so that we have trouble seeing things in our own natural way. Advertising robs us of the most intimate moments in our lives because it substitutes an advertiser's idea of what ought to be—What should a romantic moment be like?

You know the De Beers diamond advertising campaign? A clever strategy, persuading insecure young men that two months' salary is the appropriate sum to pay for an engagement ring. The arbitrary algorithm[5] is preposterous, of course, but imagine the fiancée who receives a ring costing only half a month's salary? The advertising-induced insult is grounds for calling off the engagement, I imagine. That's marketing telling the fiancée what to feel and what's real.

Unmediated is a great word: It means "without media," without the in-between layer that makes direct experience almost impossible. Media interferes with our capacity to experience naturally, spontaneously, and

---

[1] **ESL** **That's rich:** Sarcastic expression meaning amusing and ironic.
[2] **ESL** **sticklers:** People who enforce discipline and order.
[3] **FTC:** The Federal Trade Commission, an organization that regulates trade between the United States and other countries.
[4] **ESL** **blows the whistle:** Reports unfavorable information or alerts authorities to illegal or dangerous practices.
[5] **algorithm:** A procedure for solving a mathematical problem in a finite number of steps, often involving repetition of the same basic operation.

genuinely, and thereby spoils our capacity for some important kinds of personal "truth." Although media opens our horizons infinitely, it costs us. We have very little direct personal knowledge of anything in the world that is not filtered by media.

Truth seems to be in a particular state of crisis now. When what we watch is patently fictional, like most movies and commercials, it's worrisome enough. But it's absolutely pernicious when it's packaged as reality. Nothing represents a bigger threat to truth than reality-based television, in both its lowbrow and highbrow versions—from *Survivor*[6] to A&E's *Biography*.[7] The lies are sometimes intentional, sometimes errors, often innocent, but in all cases they are the "truth" of a media-maker who claims to be representing reality.

The Internet is also a culprit, obscuring the author, the figure behind the curtain, even more completely. Chat rooms, which sponsor intimate conversation, also allow the participants to misrepresent themselves in every way possible. The creation of authoritative-looking Web sites is within the grasp of any reasonably talented twelve-year-old, creating the appearance of professionalism and expertise where no expert is present. And any mischief-maker can write a totally plausible-looking, totally fake stock analyst's report and post it on the Internet. When the traditional signals of authority are so misleading, how can we know what's for real?

But I believe technology, for all its weaknesses, will be our savior. The Internet is our only hope for true democratization,[8] a truly populist[9] publishing form, a mass communication tool completely accessible to individuals. The Internet puts CNN on the same plane with the freelance journalist and the lady down the street with a conspiracy theory,[10] allowing cultural and ideological pluralism[11] that never previously existed.

This is good for the cause of truth, because it underscores what is otherwise often forgotten—truth's instability. Truth is not absolute: It is presented, represented, and re-presented by the individuals who have the floor,[12] whether they're powerful or powerless. The more we hear from powerless ones, the less we are in the grasp of powerful ones—and the less we believe that "truth" is inviolable, given, and closed to interpretation. We also come closer to seeking our own truth.

---

[6] **ESL** *Survivor:* A television program that shows participants using survival skills to compete for a one-million-dollar prize.

[7] **ESL** A&E's *Biography:* A television program that profiles celebrities and historical figures.

[8] democratization: The process of placing a country under the control of its citizens by allowing them to participate in government or decision-making processes in a free and equal way.

[9] populist: Advocating the rights and interests of ordinary people in politics or the arts.

[10] **ESL** conspiracy theory: A belief that a particular event is the result of a secret plot and not the result of chance or the actions of an individual.

[11] pluralism: The existence of groups with different ethnic, religious, or political backgrounds within one society.

[12] **ESL** have the floor: Have permission to speak.

That's the choice we're given every day. We can accept the very com-   12
pelling, very seductive version of "truth" offered to us daily by media-
makers, or we can tune out its influence for a shot at finding our own
individual, confusing, messy version of it. After all, isn't personal truth the
ultimate truth?

EXERCISING VOCABULARY

1. Chiat states that advertising gives us "a prescription for being a good parent and a good citizen" (para. 4). Who usually gives us a prescription? For
   what reason? Explain how and why advertising's prescriptions may be different.

2. The author tells us that most of our knowledge of the world is "filtered by
   media" (para. 7). What does it mean to filter something? What can you think
   of that is filtered? How can the media filter our knowledge of the world? Why
   do the media do this?

3. In paragraph 8, Chiat speaks of "lowbrow and highbrow versions" of reality-
   based television. Examine his examples and think of some of your own. What
   is the difference between lowbrow and highbrow?

PROBING CONTENT

1. What did Jay Chiat do for a living? Why is this important to know when you
   read this essay?

2. In Chiat's opinion, what is "the real lie in advertising"? What truth does advertising represent? Explain your response.

3. Why is advertising so effective, according to this author? In what ways is this
   either beneficial or harmful for consumers?

4. According to Chiat, what will be "our savior" (para. 10)? From what will it
   save us? How will this be accomplished?

CONSIDERING CRAFT

1. In the first sentence of this essay, the author addresses the reader directly.
   Why does he do this? How do you respond to his introduction? Is this an effective opening strategy? Why or why not?

2. Chiat uses an extended example in paragraph 6. Describe this example. Why
   did the author choose this particular example to support his argument? How
   effective is his choice? Defend your response.

3. The author ends his essay with a rhetorical question. Explain what a rhetorical question is and how one might be used. Find one of the other rhetorical

questions Chiat uses. How effective is his use of this writing strategy through-out the essay, including in the conclusion?

RESPONDING TO THE WRITER

In his concluding paragraph, Chiat suggests that we "tune out" the influence of media to find our own version of "truth." To what extent is this possible? Explain your conclusion.

For a quiz on this reading, go to bedfordstmartins.com/mirror.

The Selling of Rebellion

JOHN LEO

According to the adage "Sex sells," sex is supposedly the sure-fire way to sell any product from alcohol to automobiles. But John Leo identifies another common hook for advertising—the idea of rebellion against the dominant culture. According to Leo and the Spice Girls, "The message is everywhere—'the rules are for breaking.'" Is this merely the latest advertising approach, or is there a much more serious issue involved here? If there are truly "no rules," then what governs actions and responses? Is this selling or selling out? Leo exposes a wave of advertising that may inadvertently do much more than influence our decisions about which restaurant to choose or which jeans to wear.

John Leo wrote this essay for the "On Society" column in the October 12, 1998, issue of *U.S. News & World Report*. Leo, whose weekly column appears in that magazine and 150 newspapers, has written for the *New York Times* and *Time* magazine and is the author of *Two Steps Ahead of the Thought Police* (1998) and *Incorrect Thoughts: Notes on Our Wayward Culture* (2000).

THINKING AHEAD

List as many products as you can that have advertising associated with breaking rules, dissolving boundaries, ignoring culturally accepted behavior, or reaching beyond the ordinary. What messages do these ads deliver? Why do these ads seem dangerous to some people?

INCREASING VOCABULARY

satirical (adj.) (3)	mantra (n.) (6)
drivel (n.) (3)	decorum (n.) (7)
repressive (adj.) (4)	motif (n.) (8)

Most TV viewers turn off their brains when the commercials come on. But they're worth paying attention to. Some of the worst cultural propaganda is jammed into those sixty-second and thirty-second spots.

Consider the recent ad for the Isuzu Rodeo. A grotesque giant in a business suit stomps into a beautiful field, startling a deer and jamming skyscrapers, factories, and signs into the ground. (I get it: Nature is good; civilization and business are bad.) One of the giant's signs says "Obey," but the narrator says, "The world has boundaries. Ignore them." Trying to trample the Rodeo, the hapless giant trips over his own fence. The Isuzu zips past him toppling a huge sign that says "Rules."

Presumably we are meant to react to this ad with a wink and a nudge,   3
because the message is unusually flat-footed[1] and self-satirical. After all,
Isuzus are not manufactured in serene fields by adorable lower mammals.
The maddened giant makes them in his factories. He also hires hip ad
writers and stuffs them in his skyscrapers, forcing them to write drivel all
day, when they really should be working on novels and frolicking with
deer.

But the central message here is very serious and strongly antisocial: 4
We should all rebel against authority, social order, propriety, and rules of
any kind. "Obey" and "Rules" are bad. Breaking rules, with or without
your Isuzu, is good. Auto makers have been pushing this idea in various
ways since "The Dodge Rebellion" of the mid-1960s. Isuzu has worked
the theme especially hard, including a TV ad showing a bald and repres-
sive grade-school teacher barking at kids to "stay within the lines" while
coloring pictures, because "the lines are our friends."

A great many advertisers now routinely appeal to the so-called post-   5
modern sensibility, which is heavy on irony (wink, nudge) and attuned to
the message that rules, boundaries, standards, and authorities are either
gone or should be gone. Foster Grant sunglasses has used the "no limits"
refrain. So have Prince Matchabelli perfume ("Life without limits"),
Showtime TV (its "No Limits" campaign) and AT&T's Olympics ads in
1996 ("Imagine a world without limits"). No Limits is an outdoor-
adventure company, and No Limit is the name of a successful rap record
label. Even the U.S. Army used the theme in a TV recruitment ad. "When
I'm in this uniform I know no limits," says a soldier—a scary thought if
you remember Lt. William Calley[2] in Vietnam or the Serbian Army today.

Among the ads that have used "no boundaries" almost as a mantra   6
are Ralph Lauren's Safari cologne, Johnnie Walker scotch ("It's not tres-
passing when you cross your own boundaries"), Merrill Lynch ("Know
no boundaries"), and the movie *The English Patient* ("In love, there are
no boundaries").

Some "no boundaries" ads are legitimate—the Internet and financial   7
markets, after all, aim at crossing or erasing old boundaries. The antisocial
message is clearer in most of the "no rules" and "antirules" ads, starting
with Burger King's "Sometimes, you gotta break the rules." These include
Outback steakhouses ("No rules. Just right"), Don Q rum ("Break all the
rules"), the theatrical troupe De La Guarda ("No rules"), Neiman Marcus
("No rules here"), Columbia House Music Club ("We broke the rules"),
Comedy Central ("See comedy that breaks rules"), Red Kamel cigarettes
("This baby don't play by the rules"), and even Woolite (wool used to be
associated with decorum, but now "All the rules have changed," an ad
says under a photo of a young woman groping or being groped by two

---

[1] **flat-footed:** Clumsy and too direct.
[2] **Lt. William Calley:** A U.S. Army officer who was held responsible for a massacre of civilians during the Vietnam War.

guys). "No rules" also turns up as the name of a book and a CD and a tag line for an NFL video game ("No refs, no rules, no mercy"). The message is everywhere — "the rules are for breaking," says a Spice Girls lyric.

What is this all about? Why is the ad industry working so hard to use   8
rule-breaking as a way of selling cars, steaks, and Woolite? In his book *The Conquest of Cool*, Thomas Frank points to the Sixties counterculture. He says it has become "a more or less permanent part of the American scene, a symbolic and musical language for the endless cycles of rebellion and transgression that make up so much of our mass culture ... rebellion is both the high- and mass-cultural motif of the age; order is its great bogeyman."

The pollster-analysts at Yankelovich Partners Inc. have a different   9
view. In their book *Rocking the Ages: The Yankelovich Report on Generational Marketing*, J. Walker Smith and Ann Clurman say rule-breaking is simply a hallmark of the baby boom generation: "Boomers always have broken the rules. . . . The drugs, sex, and rock 'n roll of the '60s and '70s only foreshadowed the really radical rule-breaking to come in the consumer marketplace of the '80s and '90s."

This may pass — Smith says the post-boomers[3] of Generation X[4] are   10
much more likely to embrace traditional standards than boomers were at the same age. On the other hand, maybe it won't. Pop culture is dominated by in-your-face transgression now and the damage is severe. The peculiar thing is that so much of the rule-breaking propaganda is largely funded by businessmen who say they hate it, but can't resist promoting it in ads as a way of pushing their products. Isuzu, please come to your senses.

EXERCISING VOCABULARY

1. What is satire? How is the Isuzu ad "self-satirical" (para. 3)?

2. In what sense has the expression "no boundaries" become a mantra for advertisers? With what groups are mantras usually associated? Why are mantras usually repeated? What characteristics of mantras would be helpful to advertisers?

PROBING CONTENT

1. According to Leo, what is the central message in the Isuzu ad using the giant? What is the probable intent of the Isuzu company?

2. Which automaker does the essay say introduced the "breaking rules" ad approach? When was this? Why is the timing significant?

---

[3] **ESL** **post-boomers:** Those born after the baby boom, a noticeable rise in the U.S. birthrate following World War II.
[4] **ESL** **Generation X:** People who were born in the mid-1970s.

3. Name three products besides the Isuzu Rodeo that Leo says have been marketed under the banner of rebellion. If the "no boundaries" hook is widely
   used in advertising, it must work. Why does the idea of "no limits" appeal to
   many people?

4. According to Thomas Frank, author of *The Conquest of Cool*, what is the "great
   bogeyman" of this age in history (para. 8)? What does the term "bogeyman"
   mean? How did the 1960s promote this idea?

CONSIDERING CRAFT

1. Explain this essay's title. Why is it so appropriate?

2. What is the writer's own opinion about the use of "no boundaries" and "no
   rules" advertising? Cite specific references from the essay to support your answer. Does the writer expect most of his audience to agree or disagree?
   Why?

3. To what does Leo return in the final paragraph to bring his essay to a satisfying conclusion? Why is this method of ending an essay generally so successful?

RESPONDING TO THE WRITER

In the last paragraph, Leo refers to a book whose authors believe that "the post-
boomers of Generation X are much more likely to embrace traditional standards
than boomers were at the same age." Do you agree or disagree with this assertion? Why? Based on your position, describe the future of "no rules" advertising
campaigns.

For a quiz on this reading, go to bedfordstmartins.com/mirror.

Lunchbox Hegemony? Kids and the Marketplace, Then and Now

DAN COOK

What if a child's first words after *Mama* and *Dada* were *Coke, Nike,* and *Chevy*? If those seem unlikely, how about *Disney*? What difference is there to a child between these brand names and unbranded words like *soda* or *pop, sneaker,* and *car*? Author Dan Cook traces a century of increasingly sophisticated and aggressive marketing to children, from the 1915 department store innovation to separate children's sizes in their own department to our modern-day expectation "to see video monitors flashing images of Britney Spears, oversized replicas of teddy bears, and primary-colored display fixtures everytime we walk into a Kids 'R' Us." Cook makes some disturbing observations about the psychological and sociological effects that all these branded messages have on children's self-expression and sense of autonomy, and he challenges adults to examine their participation in children's consumer culture. This article first appeared in *poppolitics.com* on December 5, 2001.

Dan Cook is an assistant professor of advertising and sociology at the University of Illinois in Champaign. His articles have appeared in *poppolitics.com* and *LiPmagazine.com.* He is the editor of *Symbolic Childhood: Popular Culture and Everyday Life* (2002) and the author of *The Commodification of Childhood: The Children's Clothing Industry and the Rise of the Child Consumer* (2004).

THINKING AHEAD

When you were a child, what was one thing that you nagged your parents to buy for you? What caused you to want that one item so much? Did you get it? Why? What difference did getting it — or not getting it — make?

INCREASING VOCABULARY

hegemony (n.) (title)

unimpeded (v.) (3)

procure (v.) (4)

omnipotence (n.) (6)

dichotomies (n.) (7)

saturated (v.) (8)

docile (adj.) (8)

incursion (n.) (8)

rapacious (adj.) (9)

reciprocal (adj.) (13)

fuses (v.) (15)

cohort (n.) (16)

insidious (adj.) (16)

cumulatively (adv.) (16)

commodified (adj.) (17)

benign (adj.) (18)

artifacts (n.) (18)

infamous (adj.) (18)

rampant (adj.) (20)

toiled (v.) (21)

foibles (n.) (26)

autonomy (n.) (29)

devoid (adj.) (31)

arbiters (n.) (34)

tweaked (v.) (34)   blatant (adj.) (38)
barrage (n.) (35)   usurped (v.) (39)
                                     appeases (v.) (39)

I f you want to catch a glimpse of the gears of capitalism grinding away   1
in America today, you don't need to go to a factory or a business
office.

Instead, observe a child and parent in a store. That high-pitched whin-   2
ing you'll hear coming from the cereal aisle is more than just the pleadings
of a single kid bent on getting a box of Fruit Loops into the shopping cart.
It is the sound of thousands of hours of market research, of an immense
coordination of people, ideas and resources, of decades of social and economic change all rolled into a single, "Mommy, pleeease!"

"If it's within [kids'] reach, they will touch it, and if they touch it,   3
there's at least a chance that Mom or Dad will relent and buy it," writes
retail anthropologist, Paco Underhill. The ideal placement of popular
books and videos, he continues, should be on the lower shelves "so the little ones can grab Barney[1] or Teletubbies[2] unimpeded by Mom or Dad,
who possibly take a dim view[3] of hyper-commercialized critters."[4]

Any child market specialist worth their consulting fee knows that the   4
parental "dim view" of a product most often gives way to relentless pes-
tering by a kid on a quest to procure the booty of popular culture. Officially,
marketers refer to the annoyance as children's "influence" on purchases;
unofficially, it is the "nag factor." The distinction is important because
businesses are discouraged from explicitly inciting children to nag their
parents into buying something, according to advertising guidelines from
the Better Business Bureau.

Do Kids Use Products, or Vice Versa?

One strain of academic thought asserts that media and consumer products   5
are just cultural materials, and children are free to make use of them as
they will, imparting their own meanings to cartoons, toys, games, etc.

There's little doubt that children creatively interpret their surround-   6
ings, including consumer goods. They color outside the lines, make up
rules to games, invent their own stories, and make imaginary cars fly. If
we lose sight of children's ability to exercise personal agency[5] and to
transform the meanings imposed on them by advertising (as well as those
imparted by parents), we will forever be stuck in the belief structure which
grants near-omnipotence to the corporate realm.

[1] **ESL Barney:** A large, friendly purple dinosaur that is the star of a children's television
show.
[2] **Teletubbies:** Characters on a British cartoon show for young children.
[3] **ESL take a dim view:** Disapprove.
[4] **ESL critters:** Animals.
[5] **agency:** Power or influence.

[handwritten: objects form on imaginations]

Granting children magical transformative powers of the imagination, however, only further romanticizes an already oversentimentalized view of childhood. Children are human. Imaginations can be colonized. The materials they use to create their own meanings are preprogrammed with brand identification, gender, race, and class clichés, and standard good-bad dichotomies. And, as any marketer will tell you, exposure to target market is nine-tenths of the brand battle.

It's Not Just the Corporations

[handwritten: It is easy to blame corp. but really it is the parents that let the kids get away with]

How has this kid consumer world come to be? Easy explanations abound, from spoiled children to overindulgent or unengaged parents. Easiest of all is to accuse corporations of turning kids into blank-faced, videogame-playing, violence-saturated, sugar-mongering, overweight, docile citizens of the future. Pundits[6] and politicians from far-left to far-right have found ideologically comfortable soapboxes[7] from which to voice their opposition to the corporate incursion into childhood.

Soulless advertisers and rapacious marketers alone, however, cannot account for the explosion of the kids' four to twelve market, which has just about tripled since 1990, now raking in around $30 billion annually, according to latest estimates. 9

Don't get me wrong; the target of the critique is on track. What is troubling, though, is not just that kids demand goods by brand name as early as two years old. It's the habit of thought which conveniently separates children from economic processes, placing these spheres in opposition to one another, and thereby allowing anyone—including corporations—to position themselves on the side of "innocent" children and against "bad" companies or products. 10

[handwritten: consumers give what the children want]

Marketers and advertisers tell themselves—and will tell you if you ask—that they are giving kids what they "want," or providing educational devices or opportunities for "self-expression." 11

The thing of it is, on some level, they are right. What is most troubling is that children's culture has become virtually indistinguishable from consumer culture over the course of the last century. The cultural marketplace is now a key arena for the formation of the sense of self and of peer relationships, so much so that parents often are stuck between giving into a kid's purchase demands or risking their child becoming an outcast on the playground. 12

The relationship is reciprocal. Childhood and consumer capitalism inform and co-create each other. It is not just that the children's market is the Happy Meal version of a grown-up one. It stands apart from others because childhood is a generative[8] cultural site unlike any other. 13

Children consumers grow up to be more than just adult consumers. They become mothers and fathers, administrative assistants and bus drivers, 14

---

[6] **pundits:** Experts.
[7] **soapboxes:** Platforms from which speakers deliver their speeches.
[8] **generative:** Able to create.

nurses and realtors, online magazine editors and assistant professors—in short, they become us who, in turn, make more of them. Childhood makes capitalism hum over the long haul.

Kids' consumer culture takes a most intimate thing—the realization   15
and expression of self—and fuses it with a most distant system—the production of goods, services, and media in an impersonal market.

Cumulatively, this fusion has been forged cohort by cohort and gener-   16
ation by generation over the 20th century, making each of us a small conspirator in its reproduction. The process is so insidious that by the time a child gains the language and capacity to grasp what is occurring, his or her attention patterns, preferences, memories and aspirations cannot be neatly separated from the images and poetics of corporate strategy.

The History We Are

Adults are the living legacies of commodified childhoods gone by. Our   17
memories, our sense of personal history are, to some extent, tied to the commercial culture of our youth: an old lunchbox with television characters on it; a doll, a comic book or a brand of cereal; a sports hero, perhaps; certainly music of one sort or another.

These may seem like benign artifacts of a fading past, harmless enough,   18
slated to wind up as pieces of nostalgia at junk shops and yard sales. They might seem particularly benign when viewed against the backdrop of today's hyper-aggressive children's marketing strategies, which target children who eat branded foods and play in branded spaces, who are exposed to television in school courtesy of Channel One and who, to take one infamous example, learn geometry by measuring the circumference of Oreo cookies.

The "hegemonic power" of that Starsky and Hutch[9] lunchbox of yes-   19
teryear seems almost laughable by comparison.

But the joke unfortunately is on us, in part, because the Teletubbies   20
and Pokemon of the '90s would not have been possible without the Starsky and Hutch of the '70s, and those crime-fighting hunks would not have been possible in some measure without the Mouseketeers of the '50s, whose apple-pie[10] smiles would not have been possible without the Lone Ranger of the radio days of the '30s. If we are to intervene in the rampant commodification of childhood, we need to balance the impulse to place exclusive blame on corporations for polluting children's minds and bodies with a larger, historical perspective.

Creating the Child's Point of View

At the opening of the 20th century, working-class children still toiled in the   21
factories or worked the streets of the rising industrial city as bootblacks,[11]

---

[9] **Starsky and Hutch:** The main characters in a crime-fighting TV show from the 1970s.
[10] **ESL apple-pie:** All-American; innocent.
[11] **bootblacks:** People who polished boots.

newsies,[12] and helpers. They (mostly boys) spent their money on food and candy, in the new nickelodeon theaters, pool halls and restaurants. Aside from these amusements, there was no children's consumer market to speak of.

Enter the "bourgeois[13] child" at the end of the 19th century, whose value was no longer economic, but sentimental. Liberated from direct, industrial labor and placed into school, this child was trained in the technical skills and social posture appropriate for a new bureaucratic order. His (again, usually his) childhood was to be full of fancy, not preoccupied with factory or farm work; his first school, a "children's garden," as close to Eden as possible. 22

The image of the bourgeois child would spread beyond the confines of a rising urban, white, middle class to become the model for virtually all childhoods in industrialized nations by the millennium. 23

During the second decade of the 20th century, department stores began to recognize and welcome the bourgeois child, providing separate, modest toy departments with play spaces where mothers could "check" their children while they shopped. Prior to about 1915, there were also no separate infants' and children's clothing departments in department stores—clothes tended to be stocked by item, not size. One could find children's socks in hosiery, children's shirts in the men's or women's department, etc. 24

A Chicago manufacturer of baby garments, George Earnshaw, hit upon something when he began to convince department store management to devote separate space to children's clothing and furnishings. Mothers and expectant mothers were to be served by this new arrangement, which would have "everything they needed" in one place. 25

Much ink was spilled in the trade and consumer journals throughout the '20s, '30s, and '40s in the attempt to discern the tastes, priorities, and foibles of "Mrs. Consumer," a caricature[14] which continues today as something of an icon of consumer society. (How else would we know that "Choosy mothers choose Jif"?)[15] The first children's retail spaces were built, located, staffed, and stocked with the consuming mother, not the child, in mind. 26

By the 1930s, however, individualized clothing and toy departments in department stores gave way to entire "floors for youth" complete with child-size fixtures, mirrors, and eye-level views of the merchandise. Merchants hoped to provide children with a sense of proprietorship over the shop or area by visually, acoustically and commercially demonstrating that it was a space designed with them in mind. 27

The basic arrangement was to display older children's clothing and related furnishings at the entrance to a floor or department. As kids moved 28

---

[12] **newsies:** Boys who sold newspapers on the streets.
[13] **bourgeois:** French word meaning middle class.
[14] **caricature:** A picture that exaggerates what is odd or funny.
[15] **ESL Jif:** A brand of peanut butter.

through the department, they encountered progressively younger styles until reaching the baby shop in the back. A designer of one such floor explained in a 1939 issue of the *Bulletin of the National Retail Dry Goods Association*:

> Older children . . . are often reluctant to shop on a floor where "all those babies" are shopping. The younger children are delighted to see the older children shopping as they go through these departments, for all children want to be older than they are. The little boy and little girl seeing the big boys and big girls buying will long for the day when he [sic] too can come to these departments and buy. . . . In this way a valuable shopping habit is created.

Note here how the child's viewpoint, agency, and emergent autonomy   29
are transformed into exchangeable, marketable values. What's new is the way that the child's perspective is invoked as legitimate authority within the context of commercial enterprise.

This was the beginning of a fundamental shift in the social status of   30
children from seen-and-not-heard, wait-till-you-grow-up dependency to having retail spaces, shelving in stores, and media messages tailored to their viewpoint, making it the basis of economic action. Today, we expect to see video monitors flashing images of Britney Spears, oversized replicas of teddy bears, and primary-colored display fixtures every time we walk into a Kids 'R' Us.[16]

And Now a Word from Our Sponsored Kids

Over a number of generations, children and younger adults became key   31
arbiters of kid-taste in the US. Children moved to the front-and-center of popular culture with the early successes of Shirley Temple and others like Mickey Rooney[17] in the '30s. Their images provided a foundation for the publicly shared persona[18] of the bourgeois child as one who moves in a world virtually independent from adult concerns and preoccupations — one that makes sense only in reference to its own child-logic. Think of the Peanuts characters whose world is totally devoid of adults of any consequence: All framing is child-eye level, only the legs of adults are shown, and when adults speak their voices are non-linguistic trombone-like notes.

Meanwhile, back in the marketplace, children were also acquiring   32
status as spokespersons for goods throughout the 20th century — from fictional icons like Buster Brown[19] (1910s) and the Campbell's Soup Kids (1920s), to actors like Cowboy Bobby Benson (1950s), to voice-overs for commercials during the Saturday morning "children's" television time (1960s). By the '60s, the child spokesperson had become such a fixture that

[16] **ESL** **Kids 'R' Us:** A children's clothing store chain.
[17] **Shirley Temple and . . . Mickey Rooney:** Child actors in the 1930s.
[18] **persona:** An image.
[19] **Buster Brown:** A young boy who is the mascot for a children's shoe company.

market researchers felt comfortable enough to query children directly for their product preferences, giving them a "voice" in the market sphere.

Children—or to be precise, media-massaged images of children—now   33
routinely and aggressively hawk almost any kind of product, from car tires to vacations to refrigerators to grape juice, as advertisers make use of both "cute appeal" and safety fears.

Kids frequently serve as peer arbiters in newspapers, magazines, and   34
websites, reviewing movies, videogames, toys, and television shows—as it is assumed, often correctly, that they have more intimate knowledge about the detail and appeal of these things than adults do. This is a world under continuous construction and it is theirs: oriented around their "desires," retrofitted to their physical size, and tweaked in just the right way to produce that all-important feeling of inadequacy if this or that product is not in their possession.

Factoring in the Nag

Kids not only want things, but have acquired the socially sanctioned   35
right to want—a right which parents are loath to violate. Layered onto direct child enticement and the supposed autonomy of the child-consumer are the day-to-day circumstances of overworked parents: a daily barrage of requests, tricky financial negotiations, and that nagging, unspoken desire to build the lifestyle they have learned to want during their childhoods.

Sometimes the balancing act is overwhelming. "Moms have loosened   36
nutritional controls," enthuses Denise Fedewa, a vice president and planning director at Leo Burnett in Chicago. "They now believe there are so many battles to fight, is fighting over food really worth it?"

Unsurprisingly, mainstream media provides few correctives. A recent   37
Time cover story on kids' influence on parents gushes over the excesses of the upper-middle-class in typical fashion, successfully detracting from the larger, more generalized problem of struggling parents.

Slipping the Parent Trap

If kid marketing tactics were merely blatant, their power would not be so   38
great, but consumption is enfolded into daily existence. Places like zoos and museums are promoted as "educational," toys are supposed to "teach," clothing allows for "individuality," and who can suggest that there is something wrong with "good ol' family fun" at, say, Dollywood?

The children's market works because it lives off of deeply-held beliefs   39
about self-expression and freedom of choice—originally applied to the political sphere, and now almost inseparable from the culture of consumption. Children's commercial culture has quite successfully usurped kids' boundless creativity and personal agency, selling these back to them— and us—as "empowerment," a term that appeases parents while shielding marketers.

Linking one's sense of self to the choices offered by the marketplace 40 confuses personal autonomy with consumer behavior. But, try telling that to a kid who only sees you standing in the way of the Chuck-E-Cheese-ified[20] version of fun and happiness. Kids are keen to the adult-child power imbalance and to adult hypocrisy, especially when they are told to hold their desires in check by a parent who is blind to her or his own materialistic impulses.

We have to incite children to adopt a critical posture toward media 41 and consumption. A key step in combating the forces eating away at childhood is to recognize our own place as heirs of the bourgeois child and thus as largely unwitting vehicles of consumer culture. The mere autocratic vetoing of children's requests will only result in anti-adult rebellion.

The challenge facing us all—as relatives, teachers, friends, or even 42 not-so-innocent bystanders—is to find ways to affirm children's personal agency and their membership in a community of peers while insisting that they make the distinction between self-worth and owning a Barbie or a Pokemon card. Or anything, for that matter.

EXERCISING VOCABULARY

1. In paragraph 3, Cook cites Paco Underhill, whom Cook calls a "retail anthropologist." What work does an anthropologist do? How could this be done in retail?

2. Cook believes that kids are on a mission to acquire "the booty of popular culture" (para. 4). What is the original meaning of *booty*? Why would Cook argue that it is not overstatement to use the word in this context?

3. In paragraph 7, Cook writes that children's "imaginations can be colonized." Define *colonize*. How can this verb be applied to the effect that marketing may have on children's imaginations?

4. Cook states that today's kids assume "the socially sanctioned right to want" (para. 35). What does it mean to sanction something? What has caused kids to have this opinion?

PROBING CONTENT

1. Explain "the 'nag factor.'" How do businesses refer to this? Why is this distinction important?

2. What are some of the reasons that marketing to children has become such a profitable corporate activity? How do advertisers rationalize their techniques?

3. How may advertising influence a child's perspective of himself or herself? Of others?

---

[20] **ESL Chuck-E-Cheese:** A pizza restaurant chain featuring toys and games for children.

4. At the end of this essay, what solution does Cook offer? What must adults do before this solution will work?

CONSIDERING CRAFT

1. Why does Cook title his essay "Lunchbox Hegemony"? What entire category of objects is he using lunchboxes to represent? How well does the title prepare you for the content?

2. Cook devotes considerable space in this essay to tracing the rise of children as a commercial force. To what extent is this space well used? How does this history lesson support the central ideas of the essay?

RESPONDING TO THE WRITER

Cook asserts that the problem with advertising is not that it is obvious and direct but that "consumption [has been] enfolded into daily existence" (para. 38). Is he exaggerating? Give several examples that support your response.

For a quiz on this reading, go to bedfordstmartins.com/mirror.

EXAMINING THE IMAGE

1. Where has the boy in this cartoon gotten the idea that some sneakers will enable him to "run faster or jump higher"?

2. What is his mother's reaction?

3. How does her reaction affect his desires?

4. How does this cartoon reinforce the ideas that Dan Cook expresses in "Lunchbox Hegemony"?

Triumph of the Shill

JENNIFER POZNER

After Charlize Theron raced through *The Italian Job* in a Mini Cooper, BMW sold thirty thousand of the cars before the film made it to DVD. When the Fonz applied for a library card on the television show *Happy Days*, applications for library cards shot up 500 percent. In the film *Sideways*, the cranky main character refuses to attend a dinner if merlot wine is going to be served; after the movie was released, merlot sales dropped. The same character praises pinot noir wine, and sales increased. This report on the power of product placement appeared in the April 25, 2005, *U.S. News & World Report*. Are we really inclined to react positively to products smoothly embedded into the movies and television shows we watch? Absolutely, asserts Jennifer Pozner in her essay. There has always been some degree of interaction between products and content, but Pozner believes that "advertiser-controlled content is more threatening today than at any prior point because of the sheer breadth and inescapable power of our modern mediated landscape." This article first appeared in the spring 2004 issue of *Bitch: Feminist Response to Pop Culture*.

Jennifer Pozner is a media critic, feminist journalist, and public speaker. She is currently president of Women in Media and News, which she founded in 2002. She has worked for the national media watch group FAIR (Fairness and Accuracy in Reporting) and Sojourner: The Women's Forum. Her freelance writing has appeared in numerous print and online publications — including *Ms.*, *Women's Review of Books*, *Newsday*, the *Chicago Tribune*, *Salon*, *AlterNet.org*, and *Bitch* — and in several anthologies. She has also appeared as a commentator on Comedy Central's *The Daily Show with Jon Stewart* and Fox News Network's *The O'Reilly Factor*.

THINKING AHEAD

Have you ever bought a product because you saw it drunk, eaten, plugged in, turned on, or worn on a television show or in a film? What was it? Why did you feel that you needed or wanted it? How do you think product placement on television shows or in movies affects sales? Why?

INCREASING VOCABULARY

diva (n.) (2)	blatantly (adv.) (5)
salaciously (adv.) (2)	ubiquitous (adj.) (5)
ceded (v.) (2)	tout (v.) (7)
squelch (v.) (4)	brazen (adj.) (8)
deem (v.) (4)	smitten (adj.) (8)
demographics (n.) (4)	cavorting (v.) (10)
exacerbates (v.) (4)	mused (v.) (10)

instigator (n.) (12)

exponentially (adv.) (12)

unabashed (adj.) (13)

harangued (v.) (13)

reap (v.) (13)

proponents (n.) (15)

disingenuous (adj.) (15)

mandate (n.) (16)

unabated (adj.) (17)

degraded (v.) (17)

clout (n.) (18)

slew (n.) (19)

replicating (v.) (20)

precursor (n.) (21)

mainstay (n.) (22)

nominally (adv.) (22)

euphemism (n.) (24)

compensate (v.) (24)

vapidity (n.) (26)

permeated (v.) (26)

specious (adj.) (29)

apathy (n.) (31)

benevolent (adj.) (33)

H ere's how you make an Absolut Hunk martini: Add four parts famous-brand vanilla vodka, one part simple syrup, one part fresh lime juice, a splash of pineapple juice, and one giant heaping of product placement. [1]

Last year, on *Sex and the City*, PR[1] diva Samantha landed her aspiring-actor lover a starring role in an ad campaign for a well-known liquor company. Samantha and her friends salaciously sipped Absolut Hunk martinis as the campaign took off, and a beefcake[2] shot of the boy toy stripped down, oiled up, and wearing nothing but a strategically placed vodka bottle was plastered on billboards and bus shelters all over the show's New York setting. Just as Steven Spielberg used real-life firm 3 Ring Circus to craft futuristic commercials for Lexus, Reebok, and other sponsors for use in *Minority Report*, according to *Newsday, Sex and the City*'s producers approached Absolut—not the other way around—and ceded the creative process to the vodka peddler's ad shop, TBWA/Chiat/Day. [2]

The resulting publicity was all too typical of the merging of news, entertainment, and public relations in today's media market. Headlines such as the *Arizona Republic*'s " 'City' Slickers; Bid Adieu to Carrie & Co. with Your Own Sippin' Party" helped the Absolut Hunk martini travel from the boob tube[3] to the bar scene, while the *Washington Post, Newsday*, and other outlets printed the recipe so readers could make the cocktail at home. And without spending one red cent for prime-time spots or print spreads, Absolut managed the ultimate score: During Katie Couric's interview with Absolut Hunk actor Jason Lewis, NBC's *Today* mimicked *Sex and the City* and digitally inserted the hottie's ad in Times Square as if it were an actual, real-life billboard. [3]

Corporate sponsors have long lorded their lucre[4] over television networks, using their purchasing power to promote programs they consider [4]

---

[1] **ESL PR:** Public relations.
[2] **ESL beefcake:** Muscular males.
[3] **ESL boob tube:** Derogatory term for television from *boob* (meaning "fool").
[4] **lucre:** Money.

worthy and threatening to withhold ad buys to squelch content they deem controversial (or geared toward the nonwhite, low-income, or aging demographics undesirable to them). But product placement exacerbates advertisers' already-active influence over what we watch, see, and hear in sitcoms, dramas, and reality TV—not to mention radio, film, video games, and even broadcast journalism. With the arrival of brand integration, advertisers no longer have to rely on veiled financial blackmail—or even commercial breaks—to get their messages through. Instead, marketers are weaving their products and services directly into the plots of popular TV shows, where not even the most careful TiVo[5] jockey can fast-forward through them.

It's not just that sets and characters are subtly dressed with recogniz-   5 able brands, as in years past. This sort of scenic plug certainly still exists, more blatantly than ever: Close-ups of Sydney Bristow's Nokia cell phone are common on ABC's *Alias*, while over on Fox, Kiefer Sutherland's *24* character drives a manly Ford Expedition; shots of sponsors' goods are ubiquitous on almost all reality shows, from *The Bachelor*'s fridge full of Pepsi to the picture phones used by aspiring singers on *American Idol* and lovelorn losers on *Joe Millionaire*.

But product placement also makes its way into dialogue, as when the   6 romantic lead of the WB's short-lived 2000 series *Young Americans*, whose production was funded by Coca-Cola, interrupted a tender moment to ask the object of his puppy love,[6] "Will you pass me a Coke?" The ever-popular makeover genre gives *Queer Eye for the Straight Guy*'s Fab Five the perfect platform to pose, praise, and primp with Neutrogena sunless tanner, Norelco nose-hair trimmers, Redken pomade,[7] and a wide range of other name-brand beauty, fashion, and interior-design products, all of which are aggressively promoted in "shopping guides" on Bravo's website. (Apparently, all this shilling is motivating men to the malls: As reported in several newspapers, a survey by PR firm Jericho Communications, unaffiliated with the show, found that "men were five times more likely than women to go shopping" on a Wednesday after a new *Queer Eye* episode aired, and respondents said they'd be most likely to purchase products endorsed by Carson Kressley, *QE's* fashion expert, than any other celebrity.)

Daytime TV, meanwhile, resembles nothing so much as the Home   7 Shopping Network. Viewers can wake up to Katie Couric telling NBC audiences where they can buy must-have fall fashions; then listen to Ellen DeGeneres read promotional copy for cruises, home spa treatments, and other gifts she bestows on her talk-show audience; and spend the afternoon watching Oprah chow down on Costco's chicken pot pies and gush over Isaac Mizrahi's clothing line for Target. And, most dangerously,

[5] **TiVo:** Device to pause, record, and speed up live television programming.
[6] **ESL** **puppy love:** An infatuation between young people.
[7] **pomade:** A scented cream for hair.

celebrities are being stealthily hired to tout branded drugs and risky medical procedures on the talk-TV circuit—as when Carnie Wilson hyped gastric-bypass surgery on *Good Morning America* without disclosing that she was paid for her endorsement.

The last several years have seen brand integration rise to brazen new levels. Entire episodes of popular programs are being crafted for companies that aren't satisfied with simple set dressing or one-off dialogue plugs. A January 2000 episode of *Friends* revolved around Rachel's desire to sneak mass-produced pseudo-antiques past roommate Phoebe, who objected to chain furniture franchises sucking individuality from people's homes. By the close of the half hour, Pottery Barn's name was plugged (and praised) more than a dozen times, and Phoebe was so smitten with their tables, lamps, linens, and tchotchkes[8] that she just had to buy more. 8

Even those producers who refuse to sell their sets or scripts to corporate sponsors can find, over time, that resistance is futile. The ad industry is fighting back against TiVo and other ad-skip technology by altering preexisting content in ways that could threaten the visual and editorial integrity of programming. Products that didn't originally exist, such as a soda can in a cop's hand or a logo on a high-schooler's t-shirt, can be digitally inserted into TV reruns. A rep from Princeton Video Imaging, the tech gurus[9] behind "virtual advertising," told the *Detroit News*, "Our technology allows you to insert Coke in one episode, then Pepsi [the next time it shows], then Dr. Pepper in the third. It gives the seller the chance to monetize that real estate over and over again." 9

Even more disturbing than marketers plundering our programming for "monetizing opportunities" is the newest trend: content created for the sole purpose of pushing products. On the premiere of ABC's *Extreme Makeover: Home Edition*, a group of designers were given a week to remodel the house of a suburban, middle-class family whose rosy-cheeked little daughter survived leukemia. Cameras captured the family cavorting at a name-brand vacation resort while the team, led by *Trading Spaces* toolmaster Ty Pennington, renovated their home with Craftsman tools, stocked their kitchen with Kenmore appliances, and filled their living room with electronics from Toshiba, Panasonic, and Sony—all of which were available for purchase from a Sears-sponsored, link-filled "As Featured On" section of ABC.com (which viewers were prompted to visit at the end of the program). The sentimental climax came when the young cancer survivor gasped with glee at the life-size dollhouse Pennington had built for her. The happiness on that brave little girl's face, Pennington mused, is what this was all about. 10

Well . . . not quite. *EM: Home* is about what most reality TV series are about: manufacturing poor excuses for entertainment around sponsors' goods. According to the *New York Times*, *EM: Home* was the most 11

---

[8] **tchotchkes:** Knickknacks; trinkets.
[9] **gurus:** Advisers.

lucrative branded-entertainment deal ABC has ever inked, with Sears paying more than $1 million for narrative integration in each of the six episodes, as well as purchasing commercials during each hour.

Brand integration is largely responsible for the reality-TV genre as we   12 know it today, and not vice versa. Widely acknowledged as the instigator of both the current reality craze and the ubiquity of product placement, *Survivor* was only greenlighted after executive producer Mark Burnett explained to CBS that instead of the network paying actors, advertisers would pay the network for a starring role. In the words of *Advertising Age*, Burnett "envision[ed] *Survivor* as a commercial vehicle as much as a TV drama." The adventure theme is simply a pretext for contestants to interact with brands such as Doritos, Mountain Dew, Bud Light, and Saturn, to the tune of more than $3.7 million each for the initial series and $12 million for the second installment, with the price tag rising exponentially each season. That may seem pricey, but as the head of sales for CBS told *Advertising Age*, it was "one of the best bargains in TV history." In addition to months of prime-time exposure to viewers who can't tune out product plugs without losing track of the action, advertisers use *Survivor* imagery in their marketing campaigns and get added exposure from countless clips played on news and infotainment programs.

This phenomenon was even more unabashed on NBC's *The Restau-*   13 *rant*, an "unscripted drama" that followed celebrity chef Rocco DiSpirito as he harangued waitstaff, trained line cooks, and schmoozed[10] customers in a carefully edited quest to launch a Manhattan eatery over six prime-time hours in the summer of 2003. (The show will return this summer.) The series was crafted by Burnett, conceived by Ben Silverman (the self-described "media synergist"[11] responsible for ABC's product-laced *Who Wants to Be a Millionaire?*), and produced by Silverman's production company, Reveille, and Magna Global Entertainment, a branded-entertainment development wing of media giant Interpublic that is "dedicated to the creation of original television programming that is funded by and serves the needs of Interpublic's clients." In this case, according to the *New York Post*, Magna clients Coors, American Express, and Mitsubishi paid between $4 and $6 million in development and advertising for story-driving presence in *The Restaurant*. NBC didn't have to pay a dime for the series—all the networks had to do was save half the commercial time during the show's run for the sponsors, and reap cross-promotional benefits from AmEx ads starring DiSpirito.

No wonder the main item on *The Restaurant*'s menu was a hot, steam-   14 ing plate of product placement. Logo-studded opening credits featured an AmEx[12] "Open" sign on the door, along with customers charging meals to their AmEx cards. DiSpirito talked shop in his Mitsubishi Endeavor,

---

[10] schmoozed: Engaged in idle conversation.
[11] synergist: Someone who cooperates with others to achieve a greater effect.
[12] ESL AmEx: American Express credit card company.

invited the bouncy Coors Twins to the restaurant's opening, and issued stilted commands to his employees—some reportedly dubbed in[13] by producers—such as "Don't come back without Coors for all these people." ("I will forever be trained to hold a Coors Light bottle by the neck with the label facing outwards," Albert Davis, the restaurant's espresso maker, told the *Baltimore Sun*.)

Despite the heavy-handed dialogue and conspicuously brand-conscious   15 camera work, *Restaurant* insiders spun the shilling as seamless. Silverman told the *Hollywood Reporter* that product placement was "organic to the concept," "fit in naturally," and "even lent credibility to the environment." But like most product placement proponents, their enthusiasm was disingenuous: In one interview, Burnett defended the series' creative purity ("The whole show was unscripted. Every story line was organic and raw," he told *Newsday*); in the next, he admitted to the *Hollywood Reporter* that brand integration is "a very good business move" because it offers "a great opportunity for sponsors to have more control" over content. Burnett told *Daily Variety* that his "future is dramatic television like this," because these shows are "the next evolution of storytelling." Magna's Robert Riesenberg sang the same tune in the *St. Louis Post-Dispatch*: "The kind of organic product integration found in *The Restaurant* represents a bold new era in television."

This bold new era may soon define scripted programming as well.   16 That's the theory behind a sit-com pilot[14]—produced for close to a million bucks by Viacom, Sony Entertainment, and Anonymous Content— which would star Plato, the puffy purple creature from Sony Walkman commercials, as he tries to fit in at college. If any network picks up the series, it will probably be due to the show's appealingly discounted licensing fee, made possible by Sony's investment. Still, executive producer Lenny Bekerman insists that there is "no mandate" to put Sony gadgets in the show. "It's not a 22-minute commercial," he told NPR's *Marketplace*. "It's a stand-alone television series." But if an alien from an electronics ad gets his own series, how can it possibly be anything but a sitcom-length commercial? Official mandate or no, if produced, *Plato* will exist primarily to sell the Sony-product lifestyle to young adults, as Bekerman explained: "We're not going to see [Sony electronics] because they're blatant or they're product placement; we're going to see them because . . . every college student would wear a Walkman or have a stereo in their room or have a laptop."

If these trends continue unabated, entertainment crafted around com-   17 mercial messages will replace traditional narrative. Eric Yaverbaum, president of Jericho, the firm that conducted the *Queer Eye* shopping survey, can't wait. "Sitcoms are not blatant ads, which makes them much better sales vehicles. Look at a Target or a Wal-Mart—why don't they have their

---

[13] **ESL dubbed in:** Added new sound to a film or tape.
[14] **ESL sit-com pilot:** A sample episode for a television situation comedy used to determine if a new show will attract an audience.

own show? I don't know if it will take another decade for it to happen, but it will happen," he said in a phone interview. The line between commerce and content has degraded to such a degree that by 2002, BMW had launched a DirecTV channel on which all programs feature BMW automobiles.

In their March 2003 *Monthly Review* essay "The Commercial Tidal Wave," Robert W. McChesney and John Bellamy Foster note that because 80 percent of U.S. ad spending is funneled through the eight largest conglomerates that own advertising agencies, the clout of companies like Interpublic—which brought us *The Restaurant*—has grown, "which gives them considerable ability to name their tune with corporate media firms more than willing to play ball." Among many examples McChesney and Foster point to is a series of top-level meetings held in 2000 by USA Network, in which major advertisers were invited to "tell the network what type of programming content they wanted." When networks manufacture content to meet advertisers' needs and advertisers give content to networks for free, it's a win-win for marketers and big media—but viewers are losing big. "We're trying to create marketing platforms through television for our clients," Riesenberg told the *Philadelphia Daily News*. "It's not at all about making better television. We don't profess to be able to do it better. It's really about finding that right fit, and then integrating them into that fit."

The biggest of all the myths promoted by reality TV is that these programs exist simply because the public demands them, as "proven" by ratings. It's not nearly that simple: Behind *Survivor*'s long-term, landscape-shifting impact was the relentless promotion of the series by CBS's parent company, Viacom. To generate buzz,[15] more than 100 affiliate radio stations ran segments, including dozens of drive-time interviews with Burnett (which folks could listen to while driving past Viacom-owned billboards for the show), while 16 of CBS's TV stations and Viacom's MTV and VH1 covered *Survivor* as if its ins and outs were news. Eventually, *Entertainment Tonight* and a slew[16] of other infotainment programs jumped on the bandwagon,[17] interviewing booted contestants (after they had appeared on CBS's *Early Show*, of course), a practice that has become de rigueur[18] for broadcast tabloids and respected news outlets alike.

The PR blitzkrieg[19] made it appear as though there were overwhelming yet spontaneous popular interest in the show; all the biggest reality series have achieved their spectacular popularity by replicating *Survivor*'s strategy of multiplatform media attention, product integration, and public relations. That's the dirty little secret behind the corporate media contention

[15] **ESL buzz:** Excited talk.
[16] **slew:** A large number.
[17] **ESL jumped on the bandwagon:** Joined a popular cause.
[18] **de rigueur:** French for required, expected.
[19] **blitzkrieg:** German for lightning war; an attack waged with great speed and force.

that they are bombarding us with ad-rich, quality-poor reality shows simply because that's supposedly what the public wants.

This cross-promotional strategy extends not only to the shows them-   21
selves but to their stars. Take, for example, Eden's Crush, a 2001 marketing scheme–turned–WB show–turned–girl group created to test the power of the AOL Time Warner empire. The show was *Popstars*, and girls at home were encouraged to identify with the hundreds of contestants competing to become Spice Girls clones. Though the show also pushed Salon Selectives hair-care products, on this *American Idol* precursor the wanna-be pop stars themselves were the ultimate product placement. "You can't buy that kind of advertising," producer David Foster told the *St. Petersburg Times*, not acknowledging that the entire series was one long ad. Warner Music Group chairman Roger Ames saw it slightly differently, calling the WB tie-in "a huge running start" for future record sales and a "dream come true," because "even if you could buy all the advertising in the world, there's the difference between advertising and editorial, and this is editorial." The value of the media time given to the yet-unformed group was estimated to be at least $20 million. Because of the built-in fan base sure to result from so many hours of "editorial" exposure on network TV, Warner's London/Sire Records inked a recording contract before the band had a name—or even singers. Not until the songs were written, the show placed in the prime-time lineup, and the pre- and post-production planned were the artists plugged in, like an afterthought. Once selected, Eden's Crush appeared on WB affiliate news stations in New York and Chicago, guest-starred on the WB's *Sabrina, the Teenage Witch*, were featured on the Warner Brothers–syndicated infotainment show *Extra*, and conducted an AOL live chat. The group's first single sold more than 200,000 copies right out of the gate.[20]

By the time this format was rehashed with *American Idol*, the infotain-   22
ment circuit, primed by several seasons of reality hype, was hungry for any information Fox would give. Outtakes[21] ran on every channel, seemingly at every hour, for months—especially on Fox itself—with clips, contestant interviews, and *Idol* gossip as a daily mainstay. Hundreds of kids were humiliated, insta-celebrity was bestowed upon several nominally talented contestants, millions of home viewers subscribed to AT&T wireless to vote for their favorite singer, and eventual winner Kelly Clarkson appeared everywhere. All that cross-promotion guaranteed both ratings gold for Fox and an astonishing debut for Clarkson's single, which broke the Beatles' record for fastest-ever rise to number one on the *Billboard* charts. "I was like, How did that happen?" Clarkson exclaimed, a bit dazed, on an *Idol* reunion show.

Gee, I wonder.   23

Watching *American Idol* is like sitting through an endless, commercial-   24
ized hall of mirrors—it's a real-life version of the over-the-top product

---

[20] **ESL out of the gate:** A horseracing term that refers to horses being released to begin a race; immediately.
[21] **outtakes:** Short, discarded scenes for television or film.

placement in *Josie and the Pussycats*. Fox has reaped millions by making *Idol* wanna-bes literally do backflips over corporate logos, gulp Coke, shampoo with Herbal Essences, and drive Ford Focuses in mini-commercials disguised as music videos. The contestants who succeed are as much commodities as the products they hawk: Clarkson's humble, aw-shucks personality helped her win the *Idol* title, but by the time she promoted her single "Miss Independent" during the show's second season, the producers attempted to remake her hair, makeup, and persona in Christina Aguilera's sexed-up image. "Image" was the euphemism mean-spirited judge Simon Cowell used every time he told Kimberly Locke, an African-American contestant who made it to third place during *Idol*'s second season, that her great voice couldn't compensate for her too-big body and "weird" (read: black) hair. (Cowell didn't stop haranguing Locke until she relaxed her hair.)

If current trends continue, this tyranny of image — and the way it   25 seeks to strip away what little diversity exists in mass media — will only worsen. Media insiders say the future of scripted television is an immediate, interactive model in which viewers will be able to instantly purchase products they see on their favorite shows. For six months in 2002, *Days of Our Lives* and *Passions* fans who admired, say, the nightie some soap vixen[22] wore while she seduced her evil twin's fiancé could score one of their very own by tuning into ShopNBC's "Soap Style," a pilot arrangement in which items featured on the soaps were sold on NBC's shopping channel and website, helped along by guest appearances from soap stars. Jericho's Yaverbaum told *Bitch* he predicts "a scrolling ticker at the bottom of every show. It'll be like this: You like the bed Frasier's sleeping in? Buy it at x furniture store." His advice to marketers: "It's obvious. Television has this captive audience — people think these people are *real*, they want to be like them. Let them know directly that these characters are wearing your fashions and you'll sell like crazy the next day. Cut the network in on your sales and everybody will make a whole lot of money."

Brilliant from a business standpoint, this model has serious implica-   26 tions for programming. One-look-fits-all casting will worsen, as will the homogeneity[23] and vapidity of storylines. Considering how steadfastly fashion advertisers cling to young anorexics as the female ideal, average-size and older actresses will find it even harder to score roles once shows are designed to sell clothes off characters' backs. Let's say Pottery Barn creates a family drama that revolves around a set full of their furniture: What are the chances that abortion or racial profiling would be discussed by characters whose main function is to showcase a trendy couch? Dozens of years and mergers ago, before commercialism so thoroughly permeated every aspect of media content, television occasionally gave difficult social issues the dramatic treatment they deserved. But a

[22] **vixen:** A sexy woman.
[23] **homogeneity:** Sameness.

groundbreaking miniseries like *Roots* wouldn't happen in the TV future Yaverbaum imagines, since advertisers aren't interested in the horror of slave owners branding human beings — they're only interested in positive branding opportunities.

Potentially quality content is already being pushed out of the way to make room for programming built around embedded ads. By February 2003, Fox had devoted 41 percent and ABC a third of its sweeps offerings to reality shows. Scripted shows other than established franchises like *Law & Order* and *CSI* are finding it increasingly difficult to survive. Sally Field's 2002 series *The Court*, about a female Supreme Court justice, was yanked after only three episodes; the laugh track–less *Andy Richter Controls the Universe* was canned before it was ever allowed to develop an audience. The same fate befell last fall's detective drama *Karen Cisco*, which many critics felt had promise; it was replaced by *Extreme Makeover, EM: Home, The Bachelorette*, and *Celebrity Mole*. Discussing the greed that governs such programming decisions, *Bernie Mac* producer Larry Wilmore told *Entertainment Weekly* that despite his show winning an Emmy and a slate of other awards in its first season, Fox has regularly preempted *Mac* in favor of ratings draws like *Joe Millionaire*. "Now, this is an award-winning, groundbreaking show. Let alone, when was the last time a black show has been in that position?" Wilmore asked. "They don't care. . . . They'll pull us for whatever reality show brings that 30 share." And even when a reality series is likely to be a ratings flop (anyone remember *Are You Hot?*), the comparatively small investment involved means that networks still consider such fodder[24] less risky than nurturing expensive scripted fare.

As advertisers seek broader, deeper, and more direct control over media content than they had even in the early days of television (when soap operas actually sold soap to housewives), defenders of brand integration claim their opponents are misguided Chicken Littles, fearing falling sky where no danger exists. According to Madison Avenue[25] execs and network reps, we needn't worry our pretty little heads about the ads that populate our programs because TV is simply returning to its golden age. Since branded entertainment wasn't so bad in the '50s, they ask, what real harm could it possibly pose today?

Though seductive, this argument is not just factually specious but historically unsophisticated. For example, tobacco advertising contributed to widespread health problems among the TV-watching and moviegoing population during those "simpler days" when the Marlboro Man was a trusted friend. The real difference between then and now is one of scope: Advertiser-controlled content is more threatening today than at any

27

28

29

---

[24] **fodder:** Something of little value.
[25] **Madison Avenue:** A street in New York City where many advertising agencies are located.

prior point because of the sheer breadth and inescapable power of our modern mediated landscape. Yesteryear's housewives could turn off "their stories" if they were annoyed by silly soap jingles. Today, it's nearly impossible to tune out the commercials woven into hundreds of TV shows, blockbuster films, music and talk-radio programs; thousands of mass-market magazines and newspaper stories; and millions of Internet sites. Media consolidation compounds the problem, as corporate media owners increasingly consider artistic vision and cultural relevance extraneous to their pursuit of astronomical profits.

Yet among the most disturbing aspects of brand integration is the ho-hum response it too often fetches. Why should we care about product placement degrading content, we wonder, when TV has become so bland, risk-free, and hackneyed[26] that a show like *According to Jim* is an ABC mainstay? It's an understandable reaction to media that have so consistently frustrated, alienated, and disappointed us. But if we care at all about independent thought and cultural diversity, we must demand that programming improve, not accept its commercial erosion with a sigh.   30

Advertisers are banking on our apathy in their slow quest to condition us to become the very shopping-obsessed drones[27] parodied in *Josie and the Pussycats*. As one product-placement expert told the *Boston Globe*, viewers will grow accustomed to hypercommercialism before, during, and after TV shows because "it's a matter of time. . . . What may seem intrusive today will likely be normal five years from now." This is deeply disturbing, and not only in terms of its negative effects on entertainment. Advertising is profoundly manipulative at its core. Its imagery strives to deprive us of realistic ideas about love, beauty, health, money, work, childhood, and more in an attempt to convince us that only products can bring us true joy; numerous studies show that the more ads we view, the worse we feel about ourselves. How much worse will this psychological exploitation become when woven directly into our narratives?   31

The stronger a foothold advertisers gain over entertainment—whether they peddle their influence through old-school ad buys or new-school product placement—the more power they have to define our collective values, and the more poisonous media images of women are becoming. Nothing demonstrates this more blatantly than the piggish reality genre: *Joe Millionaire*'s entire premise is that women are evil gold diggers who deserve to be lied to and humiliated for our enjoyment; on *America's Next Top Model*, nearly nude teen girls are berated by judges for sounding too smart when they speak and being "plus size" at 5'10" and 135 pounds.   32

Mike Darnell, Fox's reality guru and the brains behind *Joe Millionaire* and its progenitor,[28] *Who Wants to Marry a Multi-Millionaire*, once told   33

[26] **hackneyed:** Overused, worn out.
[27] **drones:** People who repeat the same actions mindlessly.
[28] **progenitor:** Something that comes before and is related to something that follows.

Entertainment Weekly that his dream project would be a beauty pageant featuring female prisoners: "You give them a chance to get a makeover, and it's a 40-share special." I can see it now: Corporations using prison labor could present themselves as socially responsible businesses rehabilitating incarcerated women via telemarketing and product-assembly skills. Connie Convict, an unkempt, underfed inmate who spends her day booking American Airlines reservations and bagging Starbucks espresso beans, could emerge as a beauty queen, with a little help from some benevolent cosmetics line: "Maybe she found it behind bars . . . maybe it's Maybelline!"

Unless we get serious about product placement — collectively, and quickly — we shouldn't be shocked if "Miss San Quentin" sashays[29] her way to prime time.   34

EXERCISING VOCABULARY

1. In paragraph 4, Pozner uses the term "brand integration." What is a brand, in this sense? With what does she say brands have been integrated?

2. What does an "infotainment" program offer (para. 21)? From what two words is this new word derived? What does the need for this word to have been created indicate?

3. Pozner uses the word *shill* in the title and several times in the essay. What is the denotative meaning of this word? How does using it in the title set the tone for her essay?

PROBING CONTENT

1. According to a survey by Jericho Communications, what effect has the television show *Queer Eye for the Straight Guy* had on men's shopping habits? What difference does it make that this public relations firm is unaffiliated with the show?

2. What was the original purpose of soap operas? How has daytime television begun to resemble the Home Shopping Network? Give specific examples. When does this trend become alarming to Pozner?

3. How do shows like *Extreme Makeover: Home Edition* signal a new and disturbing trend in the link between television and advertising? What does this represent for ABC? For Sears?

4. Ads have been intermingled with television programs before, but Pozner claims that this practice is more dangerous now than it was in the past. How does she support her argument? What changes have occurred since the early days of soap operas?

---

[29] **sashays:** Walks with exaggerated swaying.

CONSIDERING CRAFT

1. In paragraph 4 ("long lorded their lucre"), paragraph 6 ("pose, praise, and primp"), and paragraph 15 ("spun the shilling as seamless"), Pozner uses alliteration. What is alliteration? What does Pozner achieve by using this type of figurative language? What effect does its use have on the tone of these paragraphs?

2. Reread the first sentence of paragraph 14. After the words "hot, steaming plate of," what word does the reader expect to see? What does the author do instead? Why? Why in this paragraph?

3. Pozner uses a number of sources to support her essay. Select two or three of these sources and explain why the author chose those people or those publications to cite in her essay. What does their inclusion contribute to Pozner's argument?

RESPONDING TO THE WRITER

How often have you noticed product placement in television shows or movies? Name some products you have seen. How have you been influenced by this advertising tactic? Has Pozner raised a legitimate concern, or is she making too much of this? Explain your opinion.

For a quiz on this reading, go to bedfordstmartins.com/mirror.

Custom-Made

Tara Parker-Pope

"I'll take a beer and a Big Mac, please."
"Make that pizza a large with pickled herring and reindeer."
"I'll have a double scoop of vanilla on a cone with corn sprinkles."

McDonald's and Pizza Huts may now serve diners in many major cities outside of the United States, but, if you are ever in one of these restaurants, you will notice that the menu may not be what you're used to. We may marvel at these unusual variations on some of the most popular foods in the American diet, but the people responsible for international marketing cannot afford the luxury of being surprised when it comes to pleasing local tastebuds. It's their job to study the preferences of the target population and then to market what people in India, England, or Russia will buy.

Tara Parker-Pope takes us on a fascinating trip around the world and behind the scenes where marketing decisions are made to see what's hot and what's not about American favorites. Parker-Pope has been a *Wall Street Journal* reporter since 1993 and writes a weekly health column. She is the author of a book titled *Cigarettes: Anatomy of an Industry from Seed to Smoke* (2001). This essay was first published in *Wall Street Journal Europe* on September 30, 1996.

THINKING AHEAD

What's the strangest food or combination of foods you have ever tasted? Why did you eat this? Where were you? What did you learn from the experience? What foods would you like to try that you have never tasted? Why?

INCREASING VOCABULARY

sequentially (adv.) (2)

tweaked (v.) (5)

globalizing (v.) (8)

ubiquitous (adj.) (24)

concoct (v.) (28)

quintessential (adj.) (28)

quirky (adj.) (29)

laconic (adj.) (30)

slew (n.) (31)

P ity the poor Domino's Pizza Inc. delivery man. 1

    In Britain, customers don't like the idea of him knocking on 2
their doors—they think it's rude. In Japan, houses aren't numbered sequentially—finding an address means searching among rows of houses numbered willy-nilly.[1] And in Kuwait, pizza is more likely to be delivered to a waiting limousine than to someone's front door.

[1] **ESL** willy-nilly: In random order.

"We honestly believe we have the best pizza delivery system in the world," says Gary McCausland, managing director of Domino's international division. "But delivering pizza isn't the same all over the world." 3

And neither is making cars, selling soap, or packaging toilet paper. International marketers have found that just because a product plays in Peoria, that doesn't mean it will be a hit in Helsinki. 4

To satisfy local tastes, products ranging from Heinz ketchup to Cheetos chips are tweaked, reformulated, and reflavored. Fast-food companies such as McDonald's Corp., popular for the "sameness" they offer all over the world, have discovered that to succeed, they also need to offer some local appeal—selling beer in Germany and adding British Cadbury chocolate sticks to their ice-cream cones in England. 5

The result is a delicate balancing act for international marketers: How does a company exploit the economies of scale that can be gained by global marketing while at the same time making its products appeal to local tastes? 6

The answer: Be flexible, even when it means changing a tried-and-true recipe, even when consumer preferences, like Häagen-Dazs green tea ice cream, sound awful to the Western palate. 7

"It's a dilemma we all live with every day," says Nick Harding, H. J. Heinz Co.'s managing director for Northern Europe. Heinz varies the recipe of its famous ketchup in different markets, selling a less-sweet version in Belgium and Holland, for instance, because consumers there use ketchup as a pasta sauce (and mayonnaise on french fries). "We're looking for the economies from globalizing our ideas, but we want to maintain the differences necessary for local markets," says Mr. Harding. 8

For those who don't heed such advice, the costs are high. U.S. auto makers, for instance, have done poorly in Japan, at least in part because they failed to adapt. Until recently, most didn't bother even to put steering wheels on the right, as is the standard in Japan. While some American makers are beginning to conform, European companies such as Volkswagen AG, Daimler-Benz AG, and Bayerische Motoren Werke AG did it much sooner, and have done far better in the Japanese market as a result. 9

For Domino's, the balancing act has meant maintaining the same basic pizza delivery system world-wide—and then teaming up with local franchisers[2] to tailor the system to each country's needs. In Japan, detailed wall maps, three times larger than those used in its stores elsewhere, help delivery people find the proper address despite the odd street numbering system. 10

In Iceland, where much of the population doesn't have phone service, Domino's has teamed with a Reykjavik drive-in movie theater to gain access to consumers. Customers craving a reindeer-sausage pizza (a popular flavor there) flash their turn signal, and a theater employee brings them a cellular phone to order a pizza, which is then delivered to the car. 11

---

[2] **franchisers:** People who pay for the right to use a company's name and market its products.

Local Domino's managers have developed new pizza flavors, including   12
mayo jaga (mayonnaise and potato) in Tokyo and pickled ginger in India.
The company, which now has 1,160 stores in 46 countries, is currently trying to develop a nonbeef pepperoni topping for its stores in India.

When Pillsbury Co., a unit of Britain's Grand Metropolitan PLC,   13
wanted to begin marketing its Green Giant brand vegetables outside the
United States, it decided to start with canned sweet corn, a basic product
unlikely to require any flavor changes across international markets. But to
Pillsbury's surprise, the product still was subject to local influences. Instead of being eaten as a hot side dish, the French add it to salad and eat it
cold. In Britain, corn is used as a sandwich and pizza topping. In Japan,
school children gobble down canned corn as an after-school treat. And in
Korea, the sweet corn is sprinkled over ice cream.

So Green Giant tailored its advertising to different markets. Spots   14
show corn kernels falling off a cob into salads and pastas, or topping an
ice-cream sundae.

"Initially we thought it would be used the same as in the United   15
States," says Stephen Moss, vice president, strategy and development, for
Green Giant. "But we've found there are very different uses for corn all
over the world."

And Green Giant has faced some cultural hurdles in its race to foreign   16
markets. Although vegetables are a significant part of the Asian diet,
Green Giant discovered that Japanese mothers, in particular, take pride in
the time they take to prepare a family meal and saw frozen vegetables as
an unwelcome shortcut. "Along with the convenience comes a little bit of
guilt," says Mr. Moss.

The solution? Convince moms that using frozen vegetables gives them   17
the opportunity to prepare their families' favorite foods more often. To
that end, Green Giant focused on a frozen mixture of julienned[3] carrots
and burdock root, a traditional favorite root vegetable that requires several hours of tedious preparation.

The company also has introduced individual seasoned vegetable serv-   18
ings for school lunch boxes, with such flavors as sesame-seasoned lotus
root. Although fresh vegetables still dominate the market, Green Giant
says its strategy is starting to show results, and frozen varieties now account for half the vegetable company's sales in Japan.

The drive for localization has been taken to extremes in some cases: 19
Cheetos, the bright orange and cheesy-tasting chip brand of PepsiCo Inc.'s
Frito-Lay unit, are cheeseless in China. The reason? Chinese consumers
generally don't like cheese, in part because many of them are lactose-
intolerant.[4] So Cheetos tested such flavors as Peking duck, fried egg, and
even dog to tempt the palates of Chinese.

---

[3] julienned: Sliced into thin strips.
[4] lactose-intolerant: Unable to properly digest lactose, the sugar in milk and certain other
    dairy products.

Ultimately, says Tom Kuthy, vice president of marketing for PepsiCo   20
Foods International's Asia-Pacific operations, the company picked a but-
ter flavor, called American cream, and an Asianized barbecue flavor called
Japanese steak. Last year, Frito rolled out its third flavor, seafood.

In addition to changing the taste, the company also packaged Cheetos   21
in a 15-gram size priced at one yuan, about 12 cents, so that even kids
with little spending money can afford them.

The bottom line: These efforts to adapt to the local market have paid   22
off. Mr. Kuthy estimates that close to 300 million packages of Cheetos
have been sold since they were introduced two years ago in Guangzhou.
Cheetos are now available in Shanghai and Beijing as well.

Frito isn't through trying to adapt. Now the company is introducing a   23
33-gram pack for two yuan. Mr. Kuthy also is considering more flavors,
but dog won't be one of them. "Yes, we tested the concept, but it was
never made into a product," he says. "Its performance was mediocre."

Other PepsiCo units have followed with their own flavor variations.   24
In Thailand, Pizza Hut has a tom yam-flavored pizza based on the spices
of the traditional Thai soup. In Singapore, you can get a KFC Zinger
chicken burger that is hot and spicy with Asia's ubiquitous chili. The Sin-
gaporean pizza at Pizza Hut comes with ground beef, green peppers, and
chili. Elsewhere in Asia, pizzas come in flavors such as Mongolian, with
pork, chili, and garlic; salmon, with a creamy lobster sauce; and Satay,
with grilled chicken and beef.

Coming up with the right flavor combinations for international con-   25
sumers isn't easy. Part of the challenge is building relationships with customers in far-flung markets. For years, the founders of Ben & Jerry's
Homemade Inc. had relied on friends, co-workers, and their own taste
buds to concoct such unusual ice-cream flavors as Chunky Monkey and
Cherry Garcia.

But introducing their ice cream abroad, by definition, meant losing   26
that close connection with their customers that made them successful.
"For Ben and me, since we've grown up in the United States, our customers were people like us, and the flavors we made appealed to us," says
co-founder Jerry Greenfield, scooping ice cream at a media event in the
Royal Albert Hall in London. "I don't think we have the same seat-of-the-
pants feel for places like England. It's a different culture."

As a result, one of the company's most popular flavors in the United   27
States, Chocolate Chip Cookie Dough, flopped in Britain. The nostalgia
quotient of the ice cream, vanilla-flavored with chunks of raw cookie dough,
was simply lost on the Brits, who historically haven't eaten chocolate-chip
cookies. "People didn't grow up in this country sneaking raw cookie-
dough batter from Mom," says Mr. Greenfield.

The solution? Hold a contest to concoct a quintessential British ice   28
cream. After reviewing hundreds of entries, including Choc Ness Monster
and Cream Victoria, the company in July introduced Cool Britannia, a
combination of vanilla ice cream, strawberries, and chocolate-covered

Scottish shortbread. (The company plans to sell Cool Britannia in the United States eventually.)

And in a stab at building a quirky relationship with Brits, the duo   29
opted for a publicity stunt when Britain's beef crisis meant farmers were left with herds of cattle that couldn't be sold at market. Ben & Jerry's creative solution: Use the cows to advertise. The company's logo was draped across the backs of grazing cattle, and the stunt made the front page of major London newspapers.

The company has just begun selling ice cream in France but isn't sure   30
whether the company will try contests for a French flavor in that market. One reason: It's unclear whether Ben & Jerry's wry humor, amusing to the Brits, will be understood by the laconic French. "We're going to try to get more in touch, more comfortable with the feel of the French market first," says Mr. Greenfield.

But for every success story, there have been a slew of global market-   31
ing mistakes. In Japan, consumer-products marketer Procter & Gamble Co. made several stumbles when it first entered the market in the early 1970s.

The company thought its thicker, more-absorbent Pampers diapers in   32
big packs like those favored in America would be big sellers in Japan. But Japanese women change their babies twice as often as Americans and prefer thin diapers. Moreover, they often have tiny apartments and no room to store huge diaper packs.

The company adapted by making thinner diapers packaged in smaller   33
bags. Because the company shifted gears quickly, Procter & Gamble is now one of the largest and most successful consumer-goods companies in Japan, with more than $1 billion in annual sales and market leadership in several categories.

EXERCISING VOCABULARY

1. According to the article, Ben & Jerry's Chocolate Chip Cookie Dough ice cream failed to appeal to the British because in England that flavor has no "nostalgia quotient" (para. 27). What does *nostalgia* mean? What other foods have a high nostalgia value for Americans? Why is this true?

2. What does the verb *opted* mean in paragraph 29? In answering, consider what the noun *option* means.

PROBING CONTENT

1. According to Parker-Pope, why must companies custom-market American products to suit the tastes of international consumers?

2. Choose one of the author's examples and discuss the changes made to the product to market it in another country. Explain why the effort failed or succeeded.

3. Not only are the ingredients in American products often varied for international markets, but sometimes whole products are put to entirely different uses outside the United States. What examples does Parker-Pope give of such products?

4. What kind of pizza topping is Domino's trying to develop for its Indian market? Why would such a product sell in India?

CONSIDERING CRAFT

1. This essay first appeared in the World Business section of the *Wall Street Journal Europe*. Knowing this, how might you characterize Parker-Pope's audience? Why would this essay also appeal to readers outside that audience?

2. Why does this author need to provide specific examples of marketing campaigns or custom-made products? How do you think Parker-Pope determined how many examples to use?

3. How does the writer use the example in the final paragraph to create a satisfying conclusion? How else might the author have ended this essay?

RESPONDING TO THE WRITER

Think about the essay's content from the other direction. What foods that originated in other countries are popular in the United States? How have those foods been adapted to look more acceptable or taste better to Americans?

For a quiz on this reading, go to bedfordstmartins.com/mirror.

India Call Sites Teach Lessons
on America

DAVID STREITFELD

Have you ever been rude to a telemarketer? Did you just assume that the caller shared your cultural values? If a computer help-desk technician is seated across an ocean from you, do you change your responses and manner to cross the cultural divide? Should you? In "India Call Sites Teach Lessons on America," reporter David Streitfeld shows us what happens when telemarketers, technicians, and bill collectors from India learn how to deal with American customers. To start, they change their names for American ears, from "Arjun" to "Aaron" and "Sangita" to "Susan." The Indian workers' complaints about the job sound very American: bad hours, minimal job satisfaction, few creative opportunities, and little advancement potential. Streifeld thinks it's time we heard ourselves from the other end of the conversation.

David Streitfeld has been a staff writer for the *Los Angeles Times* since 2001, and he worked for many years before that as a reporter for the *Washington Post*. His freelance work has appeared in publications as varied as *Wired* and *Vogue*.

THINKING AHEAD

Have you ever dialed a toll-free number for help with your computer, your Gameboy, or your cell phone and found yourself speaking with someone in a foreign country? How do you feel about American companies locating their help desks outside the United States? What advantages and disadvantages do you see for the companies, the employees, and the consumers?

INCREASING VOCABULARY

recession (n.) (7)
abrasive (adj.) (9)
plummeted (v.) (11)
embarked (v.) (12)

attrition (n.) (17)
coarse (adj.) (24)
obnoxious (adj.) (24)

In a sleek new office building, two dozen young Indians are studying the customs of a place none of them has ever seen. One by one, the students present their conclusions. 1

"Americans eat a lot of junk food. Table manners are very casual," says Ritu Khanna. 2

"People are quite self-centered. The average American has 13 credit cards," says Nerissa Dcosta. 3

"Seventy-six percent of the people mistrust the government. In the near future, this figure is expected to go up to 100 percent," says Sunny Trama.   4

The Indians have been hired to take calls from Americans whose computers have gone haywire.[1] To do this, they need to communicate in a language that is familiar but a culture that is foreign.   5

"We're not saying India is better or America is better," says their trainer, Alefiya Rangwala. "We just want to be culturally sensitive so there's no disconnect when someone phones for tech support."   6

Call centers took root here during the 2001 recession, when U.S. companies were struggling to control expenses. By firing American workers and hiring Indians, the companies slashed their labor costs by 75 percent.   7

At first, training was simple. The centers gave employees names acceptable to American ears, with Arjun becoming Aaron and Sangita becoming Susan.   8

But whether Aaron and Susan were repairing computers or selling long-distance service, problems cropped up. The American callers often wanted a better deal or an impossibly swift resolution, and were aggressive and sometimes abrasive.   9

The Indians responded according to their natures: They were silent when they didn't understand, and often committed to more than their employers could deliver. They would tell the Americans that someone would get back to them tomorrow, and no one would.   10

Customer satisfaction plummeted. U.S. clients grew alarmed. Some even returned their business to U.S. call centers.   11

Realizing that a new multibillion-dollar industry with 150,000 employees was at risk, Indian call centers have embarked on much more comprehensive training. New hires are taught how to express empathy, strategies to successfully open and close conversations and how to be assertive.   12

Khanna, Dcosta, Trama and their new colleagues work for Sutherland Global Services, a New York company that is one of the larger outsourcing companies here. They've been put through a three-week training session where they research hot-button issues, pretend they are American anchors reporting the latest news and imitate celebrities.   13

"What they know about Americans is just the tip of the iceberg," says the teacher, Rangwala. "Violence and sex, this is not what America is about. Or it's not the only thing America is about."   14

This is the students' last day of cultural and voice training. Rangwala warns them that at least half a dozen might wash out.[2]   15

As they slip away to make a short recording that will test their pronunciation skills, K. S. Kumar, Sutherland's director of operations for   16

---

[1] **ESL haywire:** Out of control.
[2] **ESL wash out:** Fail.

India, gives a little graduation speech. "You're shortchanging yourself if you don't stick with this," he advises.

It would certainly help Kumar if they remained with Sutherland.   17
While many people apply for call-center jobs, those who get hired tend not to stick around. Sutherland's annual attrition rate is 40 percent.

In part, it's the hours. Tomorrow night, the students will get their first   18
taste of the night shift. By the time they move across the hall to the call center itself, they'll be starting around 2 a.m.—early afternoon in Los Angeles.

But miserable hours aren't the only reason for quitting.   19

"I worked in a modern-day sweatshop," says Amith Shetty, 26.   20
"There was air-conditioning, comfortable seats, good food, but the work was tough and the targets unrealistic. To cope, I started smoking more and drinking more."

Indians who did outbound telemarketing tended to have a particu-   21
larly difficult time. "We were told the Americans were going to be angry," says Aarti Angelo, 24, who sold long-distance plans for AT&T. "Some would take you to the end and then hang up. Sometimes, you would break down."

That's when things could get really ugly. "There are some reps who   22
would yell back," remembers Dexter Fernandes, Angelo's former colleague.

Some customers figured it out anyway. "They became slower, patron-   23
izing," Shetty says. "They'd say, 'My name is John. That's J.O.H.N.'"

Not all the callers were coarse or abusive. But if you're answer-   24
ing 100 calls a day and five to ten of them are obnoxious, it becomes wearying.

One reason so many employees like Angelo, Fernandes and Shetty   25
have been quitting is that there's nowhere to move up.

"Don't expect us to just sit here and take people's lousy work and   26
leave the creative work to the U.S.," says Jeroen Tas, vice chairman of call center firm Mphasis. "We have a lot of well-educated, smart, ambitious, eager people here, and they all want to move up."

Mphasis, based in Bangalore, has started doing collection work, a job   27
that is considered highly creative.

Originally, the ever-agreeable Indian agents had a hard time getting   28
people to pay bills that were six months overdue. Too often, says trainer Deepa Nagraj, the calls would go like this:

"Hi," the Indian would say. "I'd like to set up a payment to get your   29
account current. Can I help you do that?"

"No," the American responds.   30

"OK, let me know if you change your mind," the Indian says and   31
hangs up.

Now, says Nagraj, the agents take no excuses.   32

EXERCISING VOCABULARY

1. In paragraph 12, Streitfeld writes that new employees at the Indian call center learned "how to express empathy." What is empathy? Why would it be an important part of such a training program?

2. Amith Shetty compares working for Sutherland to working "in a modern-day sweatshop" (para. 20). What is the history of the word *sweatshop*? How accurate is the use of the word in this context?

PROBING CONTENT

1. Why did some American companies originally relocate their call centers to India? What were conditions like in the United States at that time?

2. What problems arose with the company's early training program? What changes were made?

3. Why is the attrition rate at Sutherland Global services so high? Which employees had the most difficult assignment? Why was this assignment so difficult?

4. What problem occurred when collection firms like Mphasis used Indian workers? How was this problem resolved?

CONSIDERING CRAFT

1. What is ironic about the title of this essay? How do the title and the first four paragraphs work together to introduce the author's topic?

2. Who made up the original target audience for this piece? What do the author's word choices, sentence length, and complexity of ideas tell you about the expected average reader?

3. Why did Streitfeld choose to write this article to express the viewpoint of the Indian employees instead of the viewpoint of the American consumers?

RESPONDING TO THE WRITER

This essay is written from the viewpoint of the Indian workers. What issues might arise if the same subject — call centers for American businesses in India — were addressed from the viewpoint of American clients?

DRAWING CONNECTIONS

1. Tara Parker-Pope writes, "Part of the challenge is building relationships with customers in far-flung markets" (para. 25). According to David Streitfeld, how

would representatives of Sutherland Global Services react to this statement? Cite evidence from "India Call Sites" to support your answer.

2. One lesson learned by both Sutherland Global Services ("India Call Sites") and Domino's Pizza ("Custom-Made") is that business as usual may require unusual strategies in other countries. Describe one unusual strategy that each of these companies has adopted to be successful with foreign customers.

Wrapping Up Chapter 6

REFLECTING ON THE WRITING

1. Using materials from any of the selections in this chapter, write an essay explaining the extent to which you believe advertisers and corporations should be held accountable for the results of the use of their products.

2. Write an essay that draws connections between how certain people (distinguished by age, gender, or cultural identity) experience their own self-image and cultural image and how they are portrayed in advertising. Research your topic by finding advertisements either online or in hard copy that support your argument. Refer to the essays in Chapters 3 and 4 on cultural identity and body image to generate some initial ideas.

3. As a consumer advocate who protects the public's rights, write an essay that alerts consumers to the different kinds of advertising manipulation mentioned in this chapter. Illustrate your argument with detailed descriptions of ads from some actual advertising campaigns.

CONNECTING TO THE CULTURE

1. Locate ads for at least five different products that try to sell a product by using the same hook. Consider sex, celebrities, unusual art, shock value, children, or animals as possible hooks. Analyze each ad, explaining how the same advertising angle is used differently to sell each product. Explore the real message each ad sends to consumers. Review Chapter 2, Deconstructing Media: Analyzing an Image, to help you organize your essay.

2. Choose one group of people (for example, Latinos, the elderly, teenagers, women, parents, or African Americans) and develop a hypothesis about how they are portrayed in advertising. Then go to magazines, television, or the Internet to locate ads featuring that group. If the evidence you find supports your hypothesis, you have a thesis. If the evidence contradicts your hypothesis, develop a new thesis based on the evidence. Write an essay using your examples to fully support your thesis.

3. Watch a movie or several television shows and make notes about all the specific product brands that are featured or mentioned. Are these brands essential to the plot or to character development? Why are they used? What message does their use convey to viewers?

4. Invent a product and create an advertising campaign for it. Include details such as how the print and Web ads will look, where the print ads will be placed, how a short script for a television ad will read, who will star in the commercials, what background music will play in the ads, and who the target audience will be.

FOCUSING ON YESTERDAY, FOCUSING ON TODAY

Mixing Pancakes with Social Change

All you need for perfect pancakes

Sweet milk ready mixed in it! So rich it needs no eggs! Just add water—and in two minutes you have hot golden-brown pancakes on the table. America's favorite all-year-'round breakfast

Few cultural icons have reflected social and political change in American culture—and sold so much pancake mix in the process—as this smiling face. Aunt Jemima, whose earliest real-life counterpart was a former slave, first appeared on pancake boxes early in the 1890s. By the 1950s, she was criticized as a negative image of African American women. Her image underwent several changes throughout the 1950s and 1960s and was last updated in 1989. The bandana was shed long ago, but through it all, Aunt Jemima has kept her trademark smile.

So Cool, It's Hot

What a difference a few decades makes. Advertising food products in the twenty-first century demands models who wouldn't dare eat a pancake. In fact, do you believe that this woman ever eats the incredibly rich, calorie-laden Häagen Dazs ice cream she's fondling? Although there's artistry in her pose, sex is the selling point. Nothing essential is actually revealed, which only serves to heighten the ad's sexuality. Why would sex sell ice cream?

Analyze the appeal of these two very different ads. Make a list of adjectives that come to mind when you see Aunt Jemima; then make a list of adjectives that come to mind when you see the Häagen Dazs model. In what kinds of magazines might each ad appear? Who would be the target audience for each? How effective is each ad for its target population? Why?

CHAPTER 7

Flickering Illusions

Television and Movie Messages

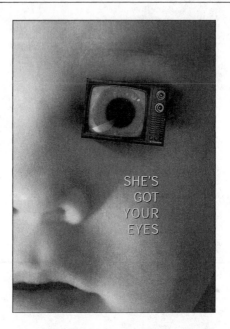

This arresting image, titled "She's Got Your Eyes," first appeared in Kalle Lasn's *Culture Jam*, a 2000 study of the negative effects of the media. The book, authored by the founder of *Adbusters* magazine, details how culture jammers attempt to fight against what they consider to be the harmful effects of media such as TV, film, radio, music, and the Internet. Since television is probably the most powerful media influence on us throughout our lives, this visual asks the question: How exactly and to what extent does television impact us from birth to death?

- Why is a television set superimposed on the child's eye in this image?

- What is the significance of the text? What do people usually mean when they say these words to a parent?

- How might the message be modified if an adult were pictured in this visual?

- What reaction might culture jammers desire to elicit in those who see this visual? Why?

Research this topic with TopLinks at bedfordstmartins.com/mirror.

What do the messages bouncing off our satellite dishes say about us? If our movies and television shows were the only evidence of our existence, what could they lead an outsider to assume about our culture? Are we projecting the best and the brightest our society has to offer? Or are we celebrating voyeurism, violence, and dysfunction? Do our television and movie screens simply reflect our popular culture, or do they go beyond mirroring and actually cause us to behave in certain ways?

Even while they are sending mixed messages, the people, places, and situations presented in television shows and movies provide us with a common bond. No matter how diverse the people are in a classroom, on a plane, or at a party, most of them can connect through a conversation about a sitcom episode or a film. Phrases from television and movies — "Is that your final answer?," "The tribe has spoken," "You're fired!," and "May the force be with you" — are a large part of our shared discourse. But just how diverse are the faces and families we watch? Do the stereotypes we fail to question divide us even as they give us a common ground for conversation?

As children, young people, and adults, we are influenced by the moving images we see in television shows and films. Even the most independent-minded of us have to admit that in some areas, movies and television shows influence who we are and who we feel we should be. Did you ever consider having plastic surgery after watching *Nip/Tuck* or *Extreme Make-over*? Promise to work harder on your relationship after seeing an episode of *Desperate Housewives*? Consider adopting forensic chemistry as a profession after watching an episode of *C.S.I.?* Resolve to stay away from deserted houses, dark woods, or the water after biting your nails through a horror film? Beyond these seemingly inconsequential influences, our notions of beauty, self-worth, security, and justice are all shaped by the bright images that flash before our eyes. To what extent are you influenced by movies and television shows?

Reconsidering Friends

JAMES PONIEWOZIK

Do you accept behavior in your friends that you don't accept from strangers? In fact, isn't that part of what it means to be a friend? And when you grow accustomed to a certain behavior in your friends, are you more tolerant of that behavior in people you don't know? In "Reconsidering *Friends*," *Time* media critic James Poniewozik ponders the cultural significance of *Friends*, the popular but lightweight sitcom that ended in 2004 after ten seasons. He notes that within "all the musical-chairs dating" and weekly comical hijinks typical of romantic comedies, *Friends* had a consistent fixation with alternative families. "None of the Friends has had a baby the 'normal' way — in the Bushian sense — through procreative sex between a legally sanctioned husband and wife." Poniewozik concludes that "the message of *Friends* . . . is that there is no normal anymore," a notion apparently accepted by the millions of Americans viewers who made the show a hit.

James Poniewozik has been the media and television critic for *Time* magazine since 1999. Previously, he was the media critic at *Salon.com*. His writing has also appeared in *Fortune, Rolling Stone, New York*, the *New York Times Book Review, Suck.com*, and *Talk*. He is heard on the radio as a commentator for NPR's *On the Media* and *All Things Considered*.

THINKING AHEAD

How much do you know about the televison show *Friends*? Do you believe it should be considered an icon of TV history? Why or why not?

INCREASING VOCABULARY

grandiose (adj.) (2)	jilting (v.) (7)
court (v.) (3)	exercised (adj.) (8)
nihilism (n.) (3)	propagate (v.) (9)
bland (adj.) (4)	plurality (n.) (10)
innocuous (adj.) (4)	discredit (v.) (10)
mediocre (adj.) (5)	scant (adj.) (10)
ratify (v.) (5)	rendered (v.) (10)
aspirations (n.) (6)	

I n the *Friends* episode "The One Where No One Proposes" — in which Rachel Green has had Ross Geller's baby after a one-night stand — Ross's father gazes at the tiny girl in the hospital. "My first grandchild," he purrs. "What about Ben?" asks Ross, referring to his son by his lesbian ex-wife, born in the first season. "Well, of course Ben," Mr. Geller covers up. "I meant my first granddaughter."

Is it farfetched that a man would forget his own grandson? Sure. But   2
the gag works, because many of us also forgot Ben existed, even though
he figured heavily in the sitcom's first two seasons. Jokes on *Friends* often
involve characters' reminding us of basic details about their lives (say, that
Monica and Ross are brother and sister) or forgetting details about one
another (in Season 7, Chandler gets glasses, and everyone, including his
fiancé Monica, believes he has always had them). *Friends* is like that:
content to be funny and forgettable. Even the episode titles—"The One
Where . . ."—suggest that even if the titles were more grandiose, you
wouldn't remember them.

Friends underestimates itself. But that's understandable, because we   3
underestimate it too. The highly popular show, which signs off after ten
seasons on May 6, has not inspired the kind of cultural hand wringing
about its existential[1] meaning that *Seinfeld* did—despite NBC's hubristically[2] plugging *Friends* as the "best comedy ever"—and its proud-to-be-
shallow attitude may be the reason. Beginning in the Norman Lear 1970s,
we decided that great sitcoms must not be simply funny; they must also be
important. That is, they must court controversy (*All in the Family*). They
must document social progress (*Mary Tyler Moore*). They must have a
sense of satire (*M*A*S*H*) or mission (*The Cosby Show*). They must be
about something. Even *Seinfeld*, the "show about nothing," was about
being the show about nothing; its nihilism was so well advertised as to beg
cultural critics to read deep meaning into it.

Friends, on the other hand, is simply about being a pleasant sitcom.   4
The bland, it-is-what-it-is title, the innocuous theme song "I'll Be There
for You"—everything about it screams that it would rather be liked than
respected. Its comments about the outside world are kept to the background. (Literally. After 9/11 rocked New York City, the Magna Doodle
board on Joey's apartment door had the initials "FDNY" written on it.)
What do people talk about when they talk about *Friends*? Jennifer Aniston's hair. Jennifer Aniston's husband. The Ugly Naked Guy across the
street. The Smelly Cat song. "We were on a break!"

But perhaps we need to redefine "important TV." When Aniston,   5
Courteney Cox (later Cox Arquette), Lisa Kudrow, Matt LeBlanc, Matthew
Perry and David Schwimmer arrived en masse,[3] controversy was still a
mark of great sitcoms (*Roseanne*); however, it also allowed mediocre ones
(*Ellen*, *Murphy Brown*) to act important. *Friends* went out of its way to
be lightweight. But it may have done more to show how American values
and definitions of family have changed—and to ratify those changes—
than its peers, precisely because it was so innocuous.

---

[1] **existential:** Relating to a twentieth-century philosophical movement that denies that the
universe has any intrinsic meaning or purpose and requires individuals to take responsibility for their own actions and shape their own destinies.
[2] **hubristically:** With extreme pride or egoism.
[3] **en masse:** French for "in a mass" or as a group.

Back in 1994—that *Reality Bites*,[4] Kurt Cobain[5] year—the show   6
wanted to explain people in their 20s to themselves: the aimlessness, the
cappuccino drinking, the feeling that you were, you know, "always stuck
in second gear." It soon wisely toned down its voice-of-a-generation aspirations and became a comedy about pals and lovers who suffered comic
misunderstandings and got pet monkeys.

But it stuck with one theme. Being part of Gen X[6] may not mean you   7
had a goatee or were in a grunge[7] band; it did, however, mean there was a
good chance that your family was screwed up and that you feared it had
damaged you. Only Ross and Monica have a (relatively) happy set of parents. Phoebe's mom (not, we later learn, her biological mother) committed suicide, and her dad ran out. When Chandler was nine, his parents
announced their divorce at Thanksgiving—Dad, it turned out, was a
cross-dresser, played by Kathleen Turner. Joey discovered his father was
having an affair. Rachel's mom left her dad, inspired by Rachel's jilting
her fiancé at the altar.

For ten years, through all the musical-chairs[8] dating and goofy college-   8
flashback episodes, the characters have dealt with one problem: how to replace the kind of family in which they grew up with the one they believed
they were supposed to have. One way was by making one another family.
But they also found answers that should have, yet somehow didn't, set off
conniptions[9] in the people now exercised over gay marriage and Janet
Jackson's nipple.

There was, of course, all the sleeping around, though that's not ex-   9
actly rare on TV today. More unusual was *Friends*' fixation—consistent
but never spotlighted in "very special episodes"—with alternative families. Like all romantic comedies, *Friends* tends to end its seasons with
weddings or births. And yet none of the Friends has had a baby the "normal" way—in the Bushian sense—through procreative sex between a
legally sanctioned husband and wife. Chandler and Monica adopt. Ross
has kids by his lesbian ex-wife and his unwed ex-girlfriend. Phoebe carries
her half brother and his wife's triplets (one of the funniest, sweetest and
creepiest situations ever—"My sister's gonna have my baby!" he whoops).
As paleontologist Ross might put it, *Friends* is, on a Darwinian level,
about how the species adapts to propagate itself when the old nuclear-
family methods don't work.

---

[4] *Reality Bites*: A 1994 film comedy directed by Ben Stiller about Gen-Xers facing life after
college and looking for work and love in Houston.
[5] Kurt Cobain: The lead singer of the rock group Nirvana, who committed suicide in 1994.
[6] ESL Gen X: The group of people born in the mid-1970s.
[7] grunge: A variety of rock music that emerged in the 1980s in America and owes much to
punk and heavy metal.
[8] ESL musical-chairs: A children's game in which music plays as participants circle a group
of chairs and one chair is removed from the group. When the music stops, all sit down
wherever they are, and the person left standing is eliminated. The game is won when
two people remain and one sits in the sole remaining chair.
[9] conniptions: A display of excessive emotion.

The message of *Friends*, in other words, is that there is no normal   10
anymore and that Americans—at least the plurality needed to make a sitcom No. 1—accept that. (To the show's discredit, it used a cast almost
entirely of white-bread[10] heteros to guide us through all that otherness.)
In January 1996, when Ross's ex-wife married her lesbian lover, the episode
raised scant controversy, and most of that because Candace Gingrich—the
lesbian sister of Newt, then Speaker of the House—presided over the ceremony. "This is just another zooey[11] episode of the justifiably popular
Friends," yawned *USA Today*. Sure, sitcoms like *Roseanne* had introduced
gays earlier—but it's not as though that had rendered gay marriage un-
controversial, then or now. The bigger difference was in attitude, both the
show's and the audience's.

What was radical about *Friends* was that it assumed these situations   11
were not shocking but a fact of life. Maybe your dad wasn't a drag queen,
Friends says, but maybe your parents split up, or maybe you had a
confirmed-bachelor uncle whom the family, whatever its politics, had
come to accept. If it was important for *Murphy Brown* to show that a
single woman could have a baby in prime time—and spark a war with a
Vice President—it was as important that *Friends* showed that a single
woman could have a baby on TV's biggest sitcom, sparking nothing but
"awwws."

In the end, the characters are approaching something like traditional   12
happy endings: Phoebe married, Chandler and Monica becoming parents,
Ross and Rachel headed for whatever closure the writers have devised,
Joey going west for the Valhalla of spin-off-dom. Still, what a weird route
they took. *Friends* may not have been as artistically great as NBC says,
but it may have been more important than the show itself seemed to believe. If, as the headlines keep screaming, the culture war is not over, for
half an hour a week over 10 years, we were able to forget it existed. What
else are friends for?

EXERCISING VOCABULARY

1. The author declares that *Friends* "has not inspired the kind of cultural hand
   wringing about its existential meaning that *Seinfeld* did" (para. 3). Under
   what circumstances do people wring their hands? What emotional state
   does this action indicate? What does Poniewozik mean by "cultural hand
   wringing"?

2. In paragraph 5, Poniewozik writes that "*Friends* went out of its way
   to be lightweight." How can a television show be described as "lightweight"? What would be the opposite of a lightweight show? Give several
   examples.

---

[10] **white-bread:** Referring to middle-class North American Caucasians.
[11] **zooey:** Strange; off-beat.

PROBING CONTENT

1. According to the author, who underestimates the value of *Friends*? What are the reasons for this?

2. Poniewozik gives several examples of how *Friends* is different from other television shows. Name these shows. In what ways does *Friends* differ from them?

3. Why does Poniewozik think we need to "redefine 'important TV'" (para. 5)? What has *Friends* shown its viewers? Give some examples to support your response.

4. In the author's opinion, what was radical about *Friends*? How does he support his opinion?

CONSIDERING CRAFT

1. Why does Poniewozik open the essay with a reference to a specific episode of *Friends*? What does he achieve by using this particular episode?

2. The author ends the essay with a question that is a play on words. Why does he choose this ending? How effective is this strategy?

RESPONDING TO THE WRITER

How do you respond to the author's assessment of the importance of *Friends*? Has your thinking about this series changed as a result of having read this essay? Is there another television show that you feel is more worthy than *Friends* of iconic status? If so, what is it? Defend your response.

For a quiz on this reading, go to bedfordstmartins.com/mirror.

Searching for a Real Gay Man

HEMAL JHAVERI

Twenty years ago, a popular song claimed that it was "hip to be square," and society finally has given the nerdy pocket-protector types a second look. Today, judging by the increasing numbers of gay characters appearing on television — on the sitcom *Will and Grace*, the makeover show *Queer Eye for the Straight Guy*, and the drama *Queer as Folk*, is it now "hip to be gay"? In "Searching for a Real Gay Man," which first appeared in poppolitics.com on October 22, 2002, writer Hemal Jhaveri acknowledges that gay male characters are now an entertainment staple. "Unfortunately, by only reinforcing perceptions that viewers are already comfortable with, a vast majority of these shows preserve the status quo rather than challenge it," she writes. Especially notable is the absence of gay male sexuality in the form of the touching and kissing often observed in straight characters. Even on the reality show *The Amazing Race*, which Jhaveri points to as a compelling look into the life of a "married" gay couple, she notes the two men traversed the world with nary a kiss shown on television.

Hemal Jhaveri is a Washington, D.C.–based writer and Web designer. She currently blogs about television and pop culture on the Web site DCist.com.

THINKING AHEAD

Which television shows do you know that feature gay characters? How are these characters represented? What do you think of these TV shows? Why?

INCREASING VOCABULARY

harbor (v.) (2)

staple (n.) (3)

ubiquitous (adj.) (3)

disconcertingly (adv.) (3)

status quo (n.) (3)

genre (n.) (4)

wooed (v.) (4)

affable (adj.) (7)

disarming (adj.) (7)

asexual (adj.) (9)

volatile (adj.) (11)

voyeuristic (adj.) (12)

dysfunction (n.) (14)

taboo (n.) (17)

caricatures (n.) (19)

static (adj.) (21)

contrived (adj.) (21)

crass (adj.) (21)

Afew weeks ago, over a mostly liquid Sunday brunch of Bloody
Marys[1] and Mimosas,[2] a friend of mine leaned across the table and
exclaimed, "You so wish you were a gay man." The comment, while
a little out of the blue, was not entirely off target.

There are plenty of straight women, who, like me, harbor some version of the same fantasy. With the current media frenzy over gay culture
presenting images that are irresistible, can you blame us?

Gay male characters on television are something of a hip staple these
days, but despite their ubiquitous presence, the representations of gay men
have been disconcertingly one-dimensional. Few shows, if any, and certainly none on network TV, have presented well-defined, complicated gay
characters that might challenge existing perceptions of gay culture and
masculinity. Unfortunately, by only reinforcing perceptions that viewers
are already comfortable with, a vast majority of these shows preserve the
status quo rather then challenge it.

When it debuted this summer, jumping into an already over-crowded
genre, the "make better, not over" reality show *Queer Eye for the Straight
Guy* brought the joys of being gay to a whole new audience. Carson,
Thom, Kyan, Jai and Ted, the queer eyes who seem to have kicked off the
current cultural infatuation with gayness, function like ambassadors of
homosexuality to the straight world. They seem to have wooed an entire
nation (or at least a large portion of straight women) with their charm
and wit, as if daring Middle America to dislike them.

The men are bitingly funny and catty[3] and snarky[4] in the way that
your best girlfriends are, but with much better punch lines.[5] In one
episode Thom snipes[6] about the décor of a straight guy's apartment:
"You've heard of minimalism right? Well . . . this is bleak." And then
there's Carson on a newly made over space: "Oh look! You put a living
room where the crack den used to be." Watching the show, you can't help
but giggle along.

Queer Eye treads lightly when it comes to acknowledging the stereotypes to which all five guys play. Kyan (the grooming guy) approached the
topic with make-over candidate John, as he received a day at the spa.
Kyan asks, "What would your friends back in Virginia say if they saw you
like this?" The fully wrapped and relaxed John replies, "That probably
can't be repeated on TV." Indeed, while John appears genuinely grateful
to have the experience, he acknowledges the perception that it seems
"kind of girly."

With *Queer Eye*, the underlying message seems to be that "if you
just got to know us, you'd love us," and this strikes me as being quite

1
2
3
4
5
6
7

---

[1] **ESL** **Bloody Marys:** Drinks containing vodka and tomato juice.
[2] **ESL** **Mimosas:** Drinks containing champagne and orange juice.
[3] **ESL** **catty:** Gossipy.
[4] snarky: Witty.
[5] **ESL** **punch lines:** The final parts of jokes, which make them funny.
[6] snipes: Criticizes.

possibly true. With its affable hosts, disarming charm and bitchy, but well-meaning, wit, *Queer Eye* feels like an especially well-executed marketing campaign for homosexuality. I'll admit that I've been won over. *Queer Eye* makes for great television viewing, but it's wholly dismissive (and far too easy) to assume that's where gay culture begins and ends.

By clinging to existing stereotypes, and mainly seeing all gay people as savants[7] of style, we marginalize and dilute the complicated lives of many. In ignoring gay men's sexuality, we project a condescending tolerance of a lifestyle, implying that homosexuality is all well and good, unless it actually involves sex.   8

Queer Eye seems to be the rule for gay men on TV: cute, white, charming and totally asexual. But there are a few, though not very prominent, exceptions that challenge the rules.   9

Keith, from HBO's *Six Feet Under*, is one of the most compelling and well-developed gay characters on TV. A gay, African American, ex-cop with a mean temper, he hardly fits into the mold that is currently being fashioned via *Queer Eye*. While Keith's sexuality is important in defining him, it isn't the only characteristic we view him with. We're shown the complete picture of a man, with depth, dimension and ambiguity. In addition to being gay, Keith is also a loving father figure, a son, and an officer with his own authority issues.   10

In a scene from last season, Keith and his partner David attended a brunch with mostly other gay men, where they play a party game called Leading Ladies. The game embodies a stereotypical camp[8] factor, asking party-goers to guess the names of various Hollywood starlets. David, Keith's partner, quickly dispenses with his turn, while Keith struggles. By the end, Keith is so uncomfortable and obviously out of place, that a woman mockingly asks, "Are you sure you're gay?" The brunch scene underscores tensions already building up in David and Keith's volatile relationship, but we're subtly shown that there exists an established culture that not everyone fits into. It's this depiction of a gay character existing outside of his sexuality and the stereotypes that come with it that is fascinating to watch and so rarely seen on television.   11

Cable networks like HBO and Showtime have embraced the same-sex relationship, but one of the rare instances on network TV was found, surprisingly enough, on CBS's reality show *The Amazing Race*. While *Will & Grace* gets credit for breaking the genre wide open, and NBC now runs half-hour versions of *Queer Eye* in a prime time slot, neither of these shows presents an extended look at a committed same-sex relationship (although Will does try periodically). *The Amazing Race* flew in under the radar this summer and offered viewers the voyeuristic pleasure of spying on relationships under pressure.   12

---

[7] **savants:** Wise or scholarly persons.
[8] **camp:** Exaggerated, affected, overdone, or tasteless.

Chip and Reichen, the gay couple that won the race around the world,   13
were identified as "married." Whether the labeling was a calculated move
to generate interest in the show or not, it caused a ripple of controversy
with conservative action groups like the American Decency Association
and sparked more than a few heated discussions on Internet forums about
the validity of such a claim.

Despite some grumbling, viewers had the opportunity to see the inter-   14
nal dynamics of a committed gay relationship, and, surprise surprise, it
wasn't that different from what we'd expect from a heterosexual one. If
anything, Reichen and Chip's relationship differed in that it was annoy-
ingly perfect and—except for a brief incident involving Reichen's foot
being run over—conflict-free. They exhibited none of the dysfunction
(Mille and Chuck) and bickering[9] (Kelly and Jon) that marked almost
every other romantic couple on the race. At one point, describing his relationship with Reichen, Chip sweetly said: "Reichen and I are just clicking[10] without even asking, which is a really nice thing. We just do things
for each other and don't step on each other's toes and realize that it's all
for the same goal."

Filtered through the magic of editing or not, what viewers were left   15
with on screen was a portrait of a healthy, supportive, loving and mutu-
ally respectful relationship. We should all be so lucky. The show presented them as fiercely competitive, aggressive in nature and physically fit.
Reichen and Chip challenged the stereotypes that all gay men are good for
is fashion advice and snarky remarks.

While Reichen and Chip are married, though, we never saw them ex-   16
change a kiss. The gay-themed programming we're seeing now offers up a
straight sanitized version of homosexuality, one that excludes all mention,
of, well, sex. Bravo, for example, kept *Boy Meets Boy* as asexual as possible. It may be the only dating show that had an explicit "no sex" rule.
Participants were allowed to kiss each other, but a few episodes in and
viewers had yet to see a simple smooch[11] between any of the gay (or
straight, when that turned out to be the case) participants and James. The
only person James repeatedly kissed was gal pal Andra.

The social taboo that exists between same-sex couples kissing or   17
showing any kind of physical affection towards each other is so strong
that it's presented a somewhat warped perspective on homosexuality. The
current line of programming seems to suggest that gay men are only different from heterosexual men in that they have a better sense of style and
a better sense of humor. While acts of lesbian sexuality have held a more
accepted and erotic image in the sexual mythology of American culture,
there still exist strong social taboos surrounding men kissing other men.
Showtime's *Queer as Folk*, a series about a group of gay men, can be

[9] **bickering:** Quarreling.
[10] **ESL** **clicking:** Communicating easily.
[11] **ESL** **smooch:** Kiss.

intimidating with its aggressive sexuality, but the explicit portrayals present an honest look at the characters' lives, one that viewers aren't always comfortable with.

By prime-time standards, gay sexuality is something that audiences 18
don't seem to be ready for. Yet, if networks continue to ignore the topic and treat sex as the dirty little secret of homosexuality, that's best not seen or heard of, it sends the message that homosexuality is indeed something best swept under the rug[12] and not discussed honestly.

This inequality between what's presented on TV and accepted in real 19
life is all the more apparent when the issue of legalizing gay marriages comes up. One of the reasons I so enjoyed watching Chip and Reichen on *The Amazing Race* was seeing them interact as a couple and realizing that behind the label of being gay, there existed two individuals, not caricatures, which is what a lot of shows seem to present us with.

This current trend in programming may just be a passing fad, or it 20
could lead to a more lasting, even-handed reflection of the gay community (one that may actually include a lesbian), but as of now they do little to combat people's preexisting prejudices.

Unfortunately, it looks like this static trend in programming will con- 21
tinue into the new fall season. ABC's new sitcom *It's All Relative* has two gay parents at the center of its show, but it, too, is contrived and stereotypical. As expected, the gay men are shown as uptight, flamboyant,[13] neat freaks paired with equally stereotypical Irish in-laws, presented as loud, crass, buffoonish[14] drunks. Bring on the laughs!

The number of gay-themed programs and gay characters on television 22
continues to grow, but how effective they are at changing and challenging long-held stereotypes is debatable. The problem now isn't one of exposure, but of seeing more complicated and varying depictions of gay men and women. The representations of gay men on TV, with so few exceptions, risk railroading[15] an entire minority group into an egregious[16] asexual (but certainly well-groomed) cliché.

EXERCISING VOCABULARY

1. In paragraph 6, Jhaveri writes that "*Queer Eye* treads lightly when it comes to acknowledging the stereotypes to which all five guys play." What does it mean when a person treads lightly? What does the author suggest about this television show by using this expression?

2. According to the author, "By clinging to existing stereotypes, and mainly seeing all gay people as savants of style, we marginalize and dilute the complicated

[12] **ESL swept under the rug:** Hidden from view.
[13] **flamboyant:** Flashy.
[14] **buffoonish:** Clownlike.
[15] **railroading:** Forcing.
[16] **egregious:** Blatant; ridiculous.

lives of many" (para. 8). Where is something placed if it is marginalized? What does it mean to dilute something? Name some things you can dilute. How then can you dilute people's lives by stereotyping them?

3. In paragraph 16, Jhaveri claims that "gay-themed programming . . . offers up a straight sanitized version of homosexuality." Why do you sanitize something? What is a sanitized version of homosexuality?

PROBING CONTENT

1. What is the author's main complaint about how TV shows represent gay men? Which television show does she single out for criticism? Why does she choose that show?

2. What does Jhaveri think of *Six Feet Under*? What does the character Keith contribute to the show?

3. How was Chip and Reichen's relationship represented on *The Amazing Race*? What does the author see as positive about that representation? As negative?

4. What does Jhaveri hope for the future of gay-themed television programs? How hopeful is she?

CONSIDERING CRAFT

1. The author uses many specific examples of TV shows and characters in her essay. Find two or three instances of this strategy. How does this use of specific examples affect your reading?

2. Jhaveri uses several similes and metaphors in her text. What do phrases like "out of the blue" (para. 1), "like ambassadors of homosexuality" (para. 4), and "flew in under the radar" (para. 12) add to your reading experience?

3. Why does the author tell you that she is a straight female? Why does she mention this early in the essay? In what ways does this knowledge affect your reaction to her essay?

RESPONDING TO THE WRITER

Have you watched any of the television shows mentioned in this essay? Why? Do you agree or disagree with Jhaveri's assessment of television shows featuring gay men? Defend your answer.

For a quiz on this reading, go to bedfordstmartins.com/mirror.

Crazy for Dysfunction

DOUGLAS CRUICKSHANK

Is your family more like the Simpsons, the Osbournes, or the people who appear on *The Jerry Springer Show*? Which of those family representations are truly dysfunctional in the psychological meaning of the term? Are these shows creating models for your ideal family? As surprising as it may seem, Douglas Cruickshank's essay, "Crazy for Dysfunction," which appeared in *Salon.com* on May 3, 2002, identifies the Simpsons and the Osbournes as basically functional, healthy families, even if they are nontraditional (of course, one is a cartoon). The many dysfunctional families on television, in movies, and in literary memoirs provide both positive and negative references for the audience, Cruickshank reports. Programs like *Jerry Springer*, for example, hold seeds of destruction because they package dysfunction as entertainment, rewarding the "most messed-up person," while *The Oprah Winfrey Show*'s approach creates a sense of connection with viewers who are also struggling with difficult problems.

Douglas Cruickshank is a senior writer for *Salon.com*, where he has been contributing essays since 1997. His writing has also appeared in the *San Francisco Chronicle*, *San Francisco Examiner Magazine*, and *Readerville Journal*.

THINKING AHEAD

What is your definition of a dysfunctional family? Which shows do you watch on television that feature these families? In what ways are they dysfunctional? How do these shows affect you and your expectations for your own family?

INCREASING VOCABULARY

aberration (n.) (1)	venue (n.) (14)
entity (n.) (1)	ostensibly (adv.) (14)
shunned (v.) (1)	formative (adj.) (15)
daunting (adj.) (2)	pathological (adj.) (20)
profane (adj.) (3)	jargon (n.) (22)
viable (adj.) (3)	taboo (n.) (24)
niche (n.) (6)	reverts (v.) (28)
lucrative (adj.) (6)	

Once upon a time, the dysfunctional family was an aberration, an entity feared and shunned by normal families—good families—who modeled themselves on the Cleavers, the Nelsons, the Andersons, and the Stones[1] (as in Donna Reed,[2] not Mick and Keith[3]). The designation was uttered almost exclusively by experts in the dreaded "professional help" category. And such was the shame of dysfunction that the dysfunctional would go to extreme lengths to hide their flaws in function, believing an appearance of normalcy might actually move them closer to it, or at the very least make life easier for everyone, most of all the neighbors.

Which brings us, several decades later, to *The Osbournes*, a TV family of daunting popularity that features drug-addled dinosaur rocker Ozzy Osbourne and his real-life wife, son and daughter. They go about their daily business before cameras, flipping each other off[4] and peppering their conversations with the F-word. Much to the satisfaction of MTV, every obscenity, drug reference and unadorned outburst of intrafamilial angst[5] brings more viewers, making the weekly Ozzyfest the second most popular show on cable (wrestling is first) and a favorite of President Bush.

Clearly, the dysfunctional family has been rehabilitated. What was once considered dark and unmentionable now constitutes high-quality entertainment. Profane kooks and apprentice psychopaths have become endearing TV stars, while televised confessions of supposed stigmas—incest, drugs, alcohol, emotional abuse, and relationships without civility—have become a viable path to fame, wealth and warm societal acceptance.

"Lovable but dysfunctional families have been a trademark for Fox going back to the days of *Married . . . with Children*," wrote Nellie Andreeva recently in the *Hollywood Reporter*. "The network hopes to keep that string alive." Indeed, Fox has at least five new shows in the works based on the dysfunctional-family premise, Andreeva reports. But the upstart network, which kicked things off with *Married . . .* in 1987, now faces stiff competition.

And that's just what can be found in *TV Guide*. The dysfunctional family is a star of stage and screen, as well as a cavalcade[6] of memoirs that take the very idea of a damaged family dynamic out of the shadow land it inhabited when it was mined only by a handful of high-culture writers such as Eugene O'Neill[7] and Tennessee Williams,[8] whose dysfunctional

[1] **the Cleavers, the Nelsons, the Andersons, and the Stones:** The families portrayed on four popular television sitcoms in the 1950s and 1960s.
[2] **Donna Reed:** The actor who played the female lead in a popular television family sitcom in the 1950s and 1960s.
[3] **ESL Mick and Keith:** Mick Jagger and Keith Richards, members of the rock group the Rolling Stones.
[4] **ESL flipping each other off:** Making a rude hand gesture.
[5] **angst:** Anxiety; worry.
[6] **cavalcade:** A flood; a great number.
[7] **Eugene O'Neill:** A twentieth-century American dramatist who authored *Long Day's Journey into Night*, *The Iceman Cometh*, and *Desire under the Elms*.
[8] **Tennessee Williams:** A twentieth-century American dramatist who authored *A Streetcar Named Desire*, *The Glass Menagerie*, and *Cat on a Hot Tin Roof*.

backgrounds served as source material, and into the down-market glare of the popular mass media. Most recently on the big screen, *The Royal Tenenbaums*, a film about a tortured clan of social misfits, though not a blockbuster, has—as of early April—grossed nearly $52 million—more than twice its production budget.

Meanwhile, intimate memoirs overflowing with kink and confession, such as Mary Karr's *Liar's Club* and its follow-up, *Cherry*, as well as Kathryn Harrison's *The Kiss*, have given amazing firepower to the literary market niche in recent years. Last and loudest, daytime TV shows such as those hosted by Jerry Springer, Jenny Jones and Sally Jesse Raphael have turned the most revealing personal confessions into a lucrative, if ethically questionable, entertainment product.

But then perhaps we never really understood the meaning of the word *dysfunctional* in the first place. Like a whole passel[9] of other therapeutic terms, this is an adjective that seems to have slipped into the layman's language via the sloppy phenomenon known as psychobabble. Yet just as it is vague when used in everyday conversation, so does the "dysfunctional family" lack a precise definition even in the realm of psychology. The phrase encompasses a vast range of behaviors and can mean most anything the person using it wants it to, but a broad, generally accurate definition is: *a family that functions poorly or not at all and communicates or behaves in ways that are emotionally unhealthy; a family that creates a negative environment that can be detrimental, or even catastrophic, to the development of its members.*

Great, but what's a family? The nuclear family—mom, dad, kids— now constitutes a minority of the adult/child groups living together in the United States. So, not only has "dysfunctional" undergone an apparent transmogrification,[10] the term "family" has outgrown its original meaning. At the same time that the emotional tangles of family life have begun to see the light of day, the nature of families has radically changed to include a growing cast of characters, making the entanglements more complex.

A brief history of semantics doesn't necessarily explain our fondness for families, whatever their composition, that are rife with "issues," as they are now called. But the morphing of the nuclear family surely has a role in the media celebration of messed-up domestic groups. If television means to offer a reflection of real life—or, more recently, real life itself— dysfunction is going to pop up, now perhaps more than ever. Beaver, Bud, Princess and Kitten[11]—every episode of their fictional lives involved a crisis, but it was a crisis fit for the times. Telling a fib was big news in the world of Ricky Nelson;[12] it could be that Ozzy badgering his daughter

---

[9] **passel:** A large number.
[10] **transmogrification:** A change from one form to another.
[11] **Beaver, Bud, Princess, and Kitten:** The names of children in the families portrayed in 1950s and 1960s family television shows *Leave It to Beaver* and *Father Knows Best*.
[12] **Ricky Nelson:** The star of the 1950s and 1960s family show named after his parents, *Ozzie and Harriet*.

Kelly about a gynecologist's appointment is the moral equivalent. What was dysfunctional in the old sense is still called dysfunctional, but these days it is also typical, much to everyone's relief.

Robert J. Thompson, founding director of the Center for the Study   10
of Popular Television at Syracuse University, says that even what many consider the most dysfunctional TV families are "very functional at their roots." Of the three shows with the most beloved dysfunctional families — *The Simpsons, Roseanne* and *Married . . . with Children* — only the last had a family "that was really, truly dysfunctional," says Thompson.

"You could make the argument that all four of the people in that   11
show would've been better off if they were not in that family," he says. "But in the case of *Roseanne* and *The Simpsons*, for all the trashy qualities on the surface, they are basically families that love each other, support each other, and all the rest of it, though not necessarily in traditional fashion."

(Thompson says he doesn't address the pioneering *All in the Family,*   12
which first aired in 1971, because the show featured no young children among the core performers.)

"*The Osbournes,*" Thompson adds, "proves that even a guy like Ozzy   13
Osbourne, once best known for biting the head off a bat during a concert, has absorbed himself in what amounts to a bizarre, kooky and relatively foul-mouthed family, but it's a family nevertheless. People are together, they're coming home every night, it's completely functional. So, ironically enough, on one level, pop-culture entertainment has really not let go of the notion of the ideal family."

In the venue of publishing, as in the realm of issue-obsessed daytime   14
TV, where the raw confessional memoir — on the page or in front of the camera — dominates, the ideal family has been dismissed as myth. Nothing is forbidden, nothing is particularly embarrassing, all of it — literate accounts of incest, shouting matches about paternity — is aired ostensibly in the pursuit of mental health. And it may well be mentally healthy for the writer and the blurter[13] as well as for their audiences. These are vehicles, Thompson says, "that introduce us to things going on with our fellow citizens that we may not be aware of."

Carl Pickhardt, a psychologist and novelist, calls the function of books   15
like Karr's and Harrison's "a memoir catharsis." The writing has "allowed the expression of the dark side of family life to come to the surface," he says. "And I think that's good. It's also allowed some people to talk about and identify behavior that they previously took for granted and never thought had any particular formative effects."

In the process, Pickhardt says, "we've re-normed our view of family   16
life. When we look at it now, we say that every family is a mix: The old notion of the idealized TV family isn't exactly true, but by the same

---

[13] **blurter:** A person who speaks without thinking.

token,[14] the extraordinarily painful and traumatic vision given by a lot of these memoirs is not the whole story either."

Pickhardt, who has a private practice in Austin, Texas, thinks there's also been a shift in how therapists see troubled family relations—and a change in their approach to helping. In the past, he says, "there was a view [on the part of therapists] of what wasn't there but should have been there, of negative things going on that were having destructive effects, and the power of the past. That needed to be investigated in order to help people heal from what had happened."   17

"That's still of therapeutic concern," Pickhardt adds, "but there's been somewhat of a shift so that now there's also an appreciation of taking a look at what *is* there, what is positively present, and focusing on what can be done in the present."   18

Therapists also tend to use the term *dysfunctional* with much more restraint than civilians. "We describe families in terms of what their specific issues or problems are," says Dr. Leigh Leslie, a psychologist, family therapist and associate professor of family studies at the University of Maryland. "We have our diagnostic manuals. But [the language in them] is not what's common to the general public. That's not to say that professionals don't use the term, but when they do, they talk about what *kind* of dysfunctional family. It's not a term professionals use a lot."   19

Meanwhile, plain folks toss around the word with abandon. "Psychological terms are second nature to us because psychologists are part of our everyday dialogue," says Deborah Tannen, the author of *I Only Say This Because I Love You* and a professor of linguistics at Georgetown University. The downside of this trend, Tannen says, "is what I see as a tendency to pathologize. Sometimes we over-apply these psychological interpretations: We're calling people pathological when in fact they just have a different style.   20

"So, for example, the New Yorker who talks to the Californian is accused of being hostile when maybe she's just being blunt," Tannen continues. "Or you're accused of being pathologically secretive because you don't think it's right to talk about your personal life. You try to say what you want in an indirect way, you're called passive aggressive, you're called manipulative."   21

At first, some mental health professionals thought that incorporating psychological terms in common conversation was a good thing. "It showed some awareness," Leslie says. "But it does get to the point where now if someone tells me, 'I'm an enabler,' I have to ask, 'What do you mean by that?' Because it's come to mean so many different things, it loses its meaning for professionals. Psychological jargon has infiltrated our culture. I don't know that it always helps us communicate any better, but at least there's an openness to it."   22

---

[14] **ESL by the same token:** In the same fashion; likewise.

There is no disputing the dysfunction and pathology of those who oc- 23
cupy the hot seats on *The Jerry Springer Show*, *Jenny Jones Show* and
others like them. They're programs, Thompson says, in which viewers see
"the real nuts and bolts of family dysfunction . . . you actually look into
the heart of darkness of where a real American family can go, as opposed
to a fictional one.

"What they've done," he says, "are two things: one very healthy, one 24
perverse. The healthy part is what has brought a lot of this stuff out of the
closet. That's a good thing—they've taken the taboo out of speaking
about this."

But the unhealthy part, Thompson says, "is that in packaging dysfunc- 25
tion as a form of entertainment it's become the only way in which a lot of
people could ever achieve celebrity. By simply confessing, letting go, and
paying the price of your self-respect and privacy, one is able to instantly get
this kind of recognition that, of course, human beings long for."

This is, in Thompson's words "a little bit sick." But more important, 26
it takes the confessional catharsis beyond the constructive point, when it
demonstrates that we all have similar problems, to a place in which dysfunction becomes a badge of legitimacy. Suddenly, the most messed-up
person wins the prize. Dysfunction, says Thompson, "turns out to be
something that is valued in its own right as a means to keep the *Springer*
show and the *Jenny Jones* show going. And that's the disturbing part."

Says Tannen, "People watch *The Jerry Springer Show* and think, 27
'Those people are really sick. I can't believe they're on TV.' It's very different from what Oprah did, which in my mind was the opposite thing—
creating a sense of connection: 'Oh, there's someone talking about her
problem. I had the same problem and I thought I was the only one. This is
such a load off my mind. I'm *not* the only one.'" Jerry Springer, she says,
"breaks that connection."

By the same token, though, shows like Springer's offer more selfish re- 28
lief. The viewer might say, "I am so glad I don't have that problem. I'm
better off than I thought I was." At that point, "dysfunctional family" re-
verts to its old definition, reserved for the truly hopeless and lost. Judging
from the popularity of the Springer-like shows, that meaning maintains its
charm as a nifty[15] means of establishing superiority.

"People who use the term 'dysfunctional family' have no idea what 29
they're talking about," Leslie says. "They know what their definition is,
but is it a shared definition? Well, there is no shared definition other than
it's a family that is having, or has had, some kind of severe problems.

"What people have become aware of is this notion that all families 30
have problems, that it's normal to have problems, and the problem-free
ideal family doesn't exist," she continues. "Terms like 'dysfunctional family' are not at all helpful to anybody, because it describes nothing and
everything."

---

[15] **ESL** **nifty:** Good; clever.

EXERCISING VOCABULARY

1. The author quotes psychologist Dr. Leigh Leslie, who says that the term "enabler" has "come to mean so many different things, it loses its meaning for professionals" (para. 22). What does the term mean in the psychological sense? Does it have a positive or a negative connotation? What other meanings does the term "enabler" have?

2. In paragraph 23, Cruickshank quotes Robert Thompson who says that *The Jerry Springer Show* and *The Jenny Jones Show* reveal "the real nuts and bolts of family dysfunction. . . . you actually look into the heart of darkness of where a real American family can go." What does the phrase "nuts and bolts" mean here? What literary reference is Thompson alluding to when he speaks of "the heart of darkness"? Why does he use this reference?

3. In paragraph 26, the author writes that "dysfunction becomes a badge of legitimacy." Name some groups of people who normally receive badges. Why do they receive them? When is something legitimate? What then does Cruickshank mean when he describes dysfunction as a "badge of legitimacy"?

4. In paragraph 15, Carl Pickhardt refers to the function of books that feature dysfunctional families as "memoir catharsis." Why do people write memoirs? What is a catharsis? How does this phrase apply to books like Karr's and Harrison's?

PROBING CONTENT

1. Why is the dysfunctional family now so popular on television shows? Give some examples of popular shows that feature this kind of family.

2. Besides television, where else are dysfunctional families showcased? Provide examples to defend your response.

3. Does the author believe that there is a single definition of *dysfunctional*? Why or why not? What definition or definitions does he provide in his essay?

4. What are some of the positive aspects of ordinary people using language best understood by psychologists? What harm may result?

CONSIDERING CRAFT

1. Why did the author title his essay "Crazy for Dysfunction"? Explain the irony in this title. How does Cruickshank's title announce the content of the essay to follow? How effective is it? Why?

2. Throughout the essay, the author cites a number of authorities. Examine three of these passages in detail. Why did Cruickshank choose to use these sources? What effect does their inclusion have on the essay?

3. Locate several passages in which Cruickshank uses comparison and contrast in his essay. How does this rhetorical strategy help the author support his thesis?

4. Examine the final two quotations in the essay. Why does Cruickshank choose to end the essay with these particular quotations? What kind of conclusion do they provide? Why?

RESPONDING TO THE WRITER

What do you think are the effects of watching dysfunctional families on television or reading about them in memoirs? Which points do you agree with in the essay? With which do you disagree?

For a quiz on this reading, go to bedfordstmartins.com/mirror.

Barrier Between Adults' and Children's Entertainment Is Breaking Down

Louise Kennedy

Is there a way to create art that speaks to both children and adults? Is the line between what's made for children and what's made for adults becoming harder to define today? In this essay, Louise Kennedy examines several recent films that are popular with viewers of all ages. Are *Harry Potter and the Sorcerer's Stone*, *Shrek*, and *Monsters, Inc.* really as family friendly as marketers make them out to be? In Kennedy's opinion, they're not: "It's not about what will satisfy or enlighten children and their parents; it's about what will open their wallets." This kind of marketing, she argues, harms both children and adults. Do you agree with the author's assessment, or do you feel more positively about this line blurring? Could it bring parents and children closer together?

Louise Kennedy began working as an editor for the *Boston Globe* in 1988 and is now a columnist for the *Boston Globe Magazine*, where this essay first appeared on January 13, 2002. She has also worked as a freelance reporter for both the *New Haven Register* and the *New Haven Advocate* and has published in *New England Monthly*. She cowrote *The Between the Lions Book for Parents: Everything You Need to Know to Help Your Child Learn to Read* (2004) with Linda K. Rath.

THINKING AHEAD

What is the difference between adults' and children's entertainment? In what ways can children's television shows, movies, games, or books appeal to adults? In what ways can adult entertainment appeal to children? Give specific examples.

INCREASING VOCABULARY

allusions (n.) (5)	mainstream (adj.) (8)
incisive (adj.) (5)	ceded (v.) (8)
provoke (v.) (5)	graphic (adj.) (8)
panders (v.) (7)	succumbing (v.) (8)
cynical (adj.) (7)	consign (v.) (8)
freighted (adj.) (7)	

L et's imagine two people. One loves *Harry Potter*, collects *Scooby-*   1
Doo action figures, spends hours every week playing computer
games, and couldn't wait to see *The Lord of the Rings*.

The other trades stocks online, watches *The Sopranos*, wouldn't be   2
caught dead at any movie rated G, and is thinking of starting his own
Web-based business. Now, let's say one of these people is forty-nine, and
the other is twelve.

Which one is which?   3

And what does it mean that we can't tell? Clearly, something is hap-   4
pening to the line between children and adults. Adults play children's
games, read children's books, and watch children's movies more than ever
before; children, meanwhile, surf freely through the adult world online
and on TV, encountering images and ideas that only fifty years ago would
have been strictly off-limits. Adults try to look younger and children try to
look older; sometimes it feels as if the whole world wants to be sixteen.

Meanwhile, the distinction between items created for adults and those   5
intended for kids seems harder and harder to make. Is *SpongeBob Square-*
Pants really a cartoon for kids, and is *Fear Factor* really aimed at grown
men and women? Who's meant to watch professional wrestling? And if
Daniel Handler is writing his Lemony Snicket books strictly for children,
why do they include allusions to Sunny von Bulow[1] and Albert Camus?[2]
Sometimes, as in Lemony Snicket's case, the blurring of boundaries results
in a delightful entertainment for all ages; sometimes it even goes on to create powerful art. The first installment of *The Lord of the Rings*, to the
surprise of those of us who had lumped it in with Dungeons & Dragons,[3]
combines sweeping action and grand themes to reach all but the youngest
audiences. *The Simpsons* remains fresh and incisive, still managing to provoke both adult thinking and childlike glee. And, in my house at least,
everybody loves the big heart and big laughs of *Malcolm in the Middle*.

But let's consider the three top-grossing movies of 2001: *Harry Potter*   6
and the Sorcerer's Stone, *Shrek*, and *Monsters, Inc.* Are they for children
or for adults? The industry skirts that question by calling them "family
films," a term that marketers love because it means they can sell to everybody. And, given the success of *Harry Potter* and *The Fellowship of the*
Ring, Hollywood is already racing to work on a whole new crop of
family-friendly flicks, based on such old favorites as *Curious George*, *The*
Cat in the Hat, and *Where the Wild Things Are*.

The hype would have you believe that this is a golden age for chil-   7
dren's movies, but the bottom line is the bottom line: These familiar titles
make it easy to cross-market and cross-promote the books, movies, and

---

[1] **Sunny von Bulow:** The diabetic wife of Claus von Bulow. She has been in a coma since
December 1980, when her husband allegedly tried to kill her with an overdose of in-
sulin.
[2] **Albert Camus (1913–1960):** Algerian-born French existential novelist, essayist, and dramatist.
[3] **Dungeons & Dragons:** A role-playing game invented in the 1970s.

action figures all at once. It's not about what will satisfy or enlighten children and their parents; it's about what will open their wallets. Just look at, say, *Shrek*, with its weird mix of gross-out potty humor and nasty Hollywood in-jokes. This isn't art that appeals simultaneously to the deepest longings of children and adults; it's a marketing vehicle that panders to adults' lowest impulses and at the same time asks of children a cynical knowingness that they'd be better off waiting years to acquire. *Monsters, Inc.*, though it's lighter and less freighted with insider baggage, also contains too much winking at adults to make real sense to young kids, and too little thematic depth or sophistication to hold lasting meaning for adults. No wonder everyone's wild about *Harry*—even though it's far too frightening for any child under eight.

If it sounds old-fashioned or overprotective to make that kind of blanket statement, maybe that's an indication of where we are. The mainstream culture has ceded to conservatives the idea that some things are too graphic, too frightening, or just too much for young children; to draw the line is to mark ourselves as squares. But isn't it possible to say that we want children to be children, and adults to be adults, without succumbing to a sugarcoated fantasy of childish innocence on the one hand and a wisecracking dystopia⁴ of aging cynics on the other? For one of the strangest things about the current blurring of childhood and adulthood is that it presents, as the sole alternative, a rigid and oversimplified division of the world. Either take your child to a movie that's too adolescent for either of you, or consign him to the pastel paradise of *Dragon Tales* while you dive into *Hannibal*, with its soullessly jokey gore. But surely there's a way to make art that speaks to both children and adults—that enriches our sense of what it means to be human, no matter how old a human we happen to be.

"There is a category of brilliance which is neither stupid and innocent nor winking and blinking," says the artist and author Maurice Sendak. "It's very hard to walk that line." . . .

Crossing a Line

Even as children move into the adult realm, adults drift back into the entertainments of their childhood. They collect toys, watch cartoons, play games. That's a shift that goes back at least to the 1950s, says Henry Jenkins, who directs comparative media studies at MIT and is the editor of *The Children's Culture Reader*. After World War II, fathers were encouraged to come home and play with their kids—not just for the kids' sake, but because it was good for the dads, too. And the kids who grew up with more playful dads, Jenkins says, "have become a generation of adults who want to hold on to play even later, and even if they have no children." Can you say "baby boomers"? The generation that began

⁴ **dystopia:** An invented society with debased and oppressive living conditions.

by refusing to trust anyone over 30, with all its members now past that milestone, still insists on acting forever young. "A lot of the crossover happened in the '60s, early '70s," says Michael Patrick Hearn, because teen culture became infantilized. "They didn't want to grow up," says Hearn, whose *Annotated Wizard of Oz* and *Annotated Huckleberry Finn* appeal as much to adults as to children, "so you stay within the child's culture." Young adults then read *The Velveteen Rabbit* and *The Little Prince*, J.R.R. Tolkien and *Alice in Wonderland*; on the radio, they listened to "White Rabbit" or *House at Pooh Corner*.

Now, "there's a lot of crossover" again, Hearn says. These same people 11 are returning to Tolkien, rediscovering picture books, picking up comics and buying tickets to *Scooby-Doo in Stage Fright*—playing downtown right now. While he thinks some adult interest in children's literature arises from the universal desire for compelling narratives and vivid characters, which modern adult literature has often scanted, he's blunt about another cause for the blur: "I think it's a marketing tool," he says. "They're trying to get as many markets as they can."

Film writer David Thomson agrees that the influence of marketing is 12 pervasive. "It constantly amazes me," he says, "how much television has advertising aimed at children," with the result that the "purchasing ambition" of children "has just been building steadily through the 20th century." Thomson also cites the growing tendency to market movies to teenagers. And beyond that, he says, "'Teenager' is a thing that seems to me to be reaching back into childhood. I have a twelve-year-old; he's been a teenager since he was ten. Children are sort of getting into that act earlier. Teenism, or whatever you want to call it, is extending forward and backward."

Culture Medium?

So will we all, in fact, end up acting sixteen forever? And if we do, what 13 happens to the genuinely free spirit of child's play and the genuinely complex pleasures of adult seriousness? It might sound like a marketer's dream to have everyone going back to see *Shrek* twelve times, then marching in lockstep to the next big thing, but surely it's possible to create a culture that's deeper, richer, and wilder than that. . . .

EXERCISING VOCABULARY

1. In paragraph 7, Kennedy states that *Monsters, Inc.* is "lighter and less freighted with insider baggage" than *Shrek*. How can one movie be lighter than another? What is insider baggage? What does the author imply about these two movies by using this phrase?

2. In paragraph 8, Kennedy mentions a "sugarcoated fantasy of childish innocence." What does it mean to sugarcoat something? How can childish innocence be described as a sugarcoated fantasy?

PROBING CONTENT

1. According to Kennedy, what is happening to adults' and children's entertainment? What evidence does she provide to support her argument?

2. What does Kennedy think of popular children's movies today? What two major examples does she use to drive her point home? What does she say about these two films?

3. According to the essay, what have adults desired since the 1950s? What part has marketing played in capitalizing on these desires?

4. How has marketing influenced children? What does Kennedy think of the "crossover" between adults' and children's entertainment?

CONSIDERING CRAFT

1. Reread the first three paragraphs. What is unusual about the way the author begins her essay? How does her opening writing strategy affect your reading?

2. Kennedy asks many questions in her essay. Find several examples, beginning with the fourth paragraph. Why does she include so many questions? Does she expect answers? What part do these questions play in the development of her argument?

3. The author uses many specific examples of movies, television shows, books, and games in her essay. Locate several of these examples. How do they function in the essay? From your perspective as a reader, how well do these examples serve the writer's purpose?

RESPONDING TO THE WRITER

Do you consider the crossover between adults' and children's entertainment to be beneficial, problematic, or a combination of the two? Answer the question by considering your own experiences and those of your friends and family.

For a quiz on this reading, go to bedfordstmartins.com/mirror.

Why We Crave Horror Movies

STEPHEN KING

An old English prayer—"From ghoulies and ghosties, long-leggedy beasties, and things that go bump in the night, Lord God protect us"—suggests that people have worried about "things that go bump in the night" for a long time. If ghouls and ghosts frighten us so, why do so many of us love scary movies? Fantastic, otherworldly monsters, knife-wielding psychopaths, lunatics with pitchforks or chain saws—the scarier, the better. What kind of civilization produces people who are thrilled by on-screen murder, torture, and gruesome evil?

A fairly normal and fun-loving one, insists the famous author of this essay. Stephen King needs no introduction to either readers or film buffs around the world. He is the creator of such frightening tales as *Carrie* (1973), *The Shining* (1977), *Misery* (1987), *The Eyes of the Dragon* (1987), *Bag of Bones* (1998), *Hearts in Atlantis* (1999), and *Riding the Bullet* (2000), an e-book available only on the Internet. King repopularized the serial novel with *The Green Mile*, published in six installments from March through August 1996. He has also authored many short stories and screenplays and has played cameo roles in several films based on his works. The king of horror's prolific writing career nearly came to an end in 1999, when he was struck by a van and critically injured while walking near his summer home in western Maine. The author chronicles this painful period of both his personal and professional life in *On Writing: A Memoir of the Craft* (2000). His most recent book, written with Stewart O'Nan, is *Faithful: Two Diehard Boston Red Sox Fans Chronicle the 2004 Season* (2004). "Why We Crave Horror Movies" is King's attempt to explain why we love it when he scares us to nightmares. The essay was first published in *Playboy* in December 1981.

THINKING AHEAD

Do you like horror movies? Which ones terrify you? Why? If they frighten you, why do you watch them?

INCREASING VOCABULARY

grimaces (n.) (1)	status quo (n.) (9)
depleted (v.) (3)	sanctions (n.) (10)
innately (adv.) (4)	remonstrance (n.) (10)
voyeur (n.) (6)	recoil (v.) (11)
penchant (n.) (7)	

I think that we're all mentally ill; those of us outside the asylums only
hide it a little better—and maybe not all that much better, after all.
We've all known people who talk to themselves, people who sometimes
squinch their faces into horrible grimaces when they believe no one is
watching, people who have some hysterical fear—of snakes, the dark, the
tight place, the long drop . . . and, of course, those final worms and grubs
that are waiting so patiently underground.

When we pay our four or five bucks and seat ourselves at tenth-row
center in a theater showing a horror movie, we are daring the nightmare.

Why? Some of the reasons are simple and obvious. To show that we
can, that we are not afraid, that we can ride this roller coaster. Which is
not to say that a really good horror movie may not surprise a scream out
of us at some point, the way we may scream when the roller coaster
twists through a complete 360 or plows through a lake at the bottom of
the drop. And horror movies, like roller coasters, have always been the
special province of the young; by the time one turns forty or fifty, one's
appetite for double twists or 360-degree loops may be considerably
depleted.

We also go to reestablish our feelings of essential normality; the horror movie is innately conservative, even reactionary. Freda Jackson as the
horrible melting woman in *Die, Monster, Die!* confirms for us that no
matter how far we may be removed from the beauty of a Robert Redford
or a Diana Ross, we are still light-years from true ugliness.

And we go to have fun.

Ah, but this is where the ground starts to slope away, isn't it? Because
this is a very peculiar sort of fun indeed. The fun comes from seeing others
menaced—sometimes killed. One critic suggested that if pro football has
become the voyeur's version of combat, then the horror film has become
the modern version of the public lynching.

It is true that the mythic, "fairy-tale" horror film intends to take away
the shades of gray. . . . It urges us to put away our more civilized and
adult penchant for analysis and to become children again, seeing things in
pure blacks and whites. It may be that horror movies provide psychic relief on this level because this invitation to lapse into simplicity, irritational-
ity, and even outright madness is extended so rarely. We are told we may
allow our emotions a free rein . . . or no rein at all.

If we are all insane, then sanity becomes a matter of degree. If your insanity leads you to carve up women like Jack the Ripper or the Cleveland
Torso Murderer, we clap you away in the funny farm (but neither of those
two amateur-night surgeons was ever caught, heh-heh-heh); if, on the
other hand, your insanity leads you only to talk to yourself when you're
under stress or to pick your nose on your morning bus, then you are left
alone to go about your business . . . though it is doubtful that you will
ever be invited to the best parties.

The potential lyncher is in almost all of us (excluding saints, past and
present; but then, most saints have been crazy in their own ways), and

every now and then, he has to be let loose to scream and roll around in the grass. Our emotions and our fears form their own body, and we recognize that it demands its own exercise to maintain proper muscle tone. Certain of these emotional muscles are accepted—even exalted—in civilized society; they are, of course, the emotions that tend to maintain the status quo of civilization itself. Love, friendship, loyalty, kindness—these are all the emotions that we applaud, emotions that have been immortalized in the couplets of Hallmark cards and in the verses (I don't dare call it poetry) of Leonard Nimoy.[1]

When we exhibit these emotions, society showers us with positive reinforcement; we learn this even before we get out of diapers. When, as children, we hug our rotten little puke of a sister and give her a kiss, all the aunts and uncles smile and twit and cry, "Isn't he the sweetest little thing?" Such coveted treats as chocolate-covered graham crackers often follow. But if we deliberately slam the rotten little puke of a sister's fingers in the door, sanctions follow—angry remonstrance from parents, aunts, and uncles; instead of a chocolate-covered graham cracker, a spanking. 10

But anticivilization emotions don't go away, and they demand periodic exercise. We have such "sick" jokes as "What's the difference between a truckload of bowling balls and a truckload of dead babies?" (You can't unload the truckload of bowling balls with a pitchfork . . . a joke, by the way, that I heard originally from a ten-year-old.) Such a joke may surprise a laugh or a grin out of us even as we recoil, a possibility that confirms the thesis: If we share a brotherhood of man, then we also share an insanity of man. None of which is intended as a defense of either the sick joke or insanity but merely as an explanation of why the best horror films, like the best fairy tales, manage to be reactionary, anarchistic, and revolutionary all at the same time. 11

The mythic horror movie, like the sick joke, has a dirty job to do. It deliberately appeals to all that is worst in us. It is morbidity unchained, our most base instincts let free, our nastiest fantasies realized . . . and it all happens, fittingly enough in the dark. For those reasons, good liberals often shy away from horror films. For myself, I like to see the most aggressive of them—*Dawn of the Dead*, for instance—as lifting a trapdoor in the civilized forebrain and throwing a basket of raw meat to the hungry alligators swimming around in that subterranean river beneath. 12

Why bother? Because it keeps them from getting out, man, it keeps them down there and me up here. It was Lennon and McCartney who said that all you need is love, and I would agree with that. 13

As long as you keep the gators fed. 14

[1] **Leonard Nimoy:** An actor who played Commander Spock in television's original *Star Trek* series.

EXERCISING VOCABULARY

1. At the end of paragraph 11, King asserts that really good horror movies "manage to be reactionary, anarchistic, and revolutionary all at the same time." Define these three adjectives. Usually these words have a political meaning and are used to refer to governments. Explain their meaning when King applies them to horror movies.

2. In paragraph 12, King describes the "mythic horror movie" as "morbidity unchained." Define *morbidity* and explain King's use of it here.

PROBING CONTENT

1. To what is King referring when he mentions "those final worms and grubs that are waiting so patiently underground" (para. 1)? How does this reference contribute to the main point of this essay? How does it establish the author's tone?

2. How is watching a horror movie "daring the nightmare" (para. 2)? Why, according to King, do we do this?

3. In what sense, according to the essay, do horror movies encourage us to think like children? Why might adults want an opportunity to think like children again?

4. Which emotions does the writer say "tend to maintain the status quo of civilization itself" (para. 9)? Why are these emotions so important to society?

5. What "dirty job" does King think horror movies perform for us? Why is it important that something assume this job?

6. What do "the hungry alligators" in paragraph 12 represent? How do horror movies feed these alligators?

CONSIDERING CRAFT

1. Does King literally "think that we're all mentally ill" as he says in paragraph 1? Why does he write this? What does such a statement add to King's essay?

2. Describe the effect of the single-sentence paragraphs 5 and 14. How does this effect aid the overall impact of each point? How does it aid the essay's main idea?

3. Some of the language and references deliberately chosen by King are not polite — "to pick your nose" (para. 8), "rotten little puke of a sister" (para. 10), and the joke about dead babies in paragraph 11. What do you expect audience reaction to these references to be? What is your own reaction? Why does King include these?

RESPONDING TO THE WRITER

From your own experience, evaluate King's explanation of why we like horror movies. How accurate is it to assume that a dark side is lurking in each of us just beneath our civilized skins? What difference does it make in your relationships with other people if you accept or reject this notion?

For a quiz on this reading, go to bedfordstmartins.com/mirror.

Three Cheers for Reality TV

HEATHER HAVRILESKY

Admit it. You love reality TV. Let those nay-saying critics be silent — the American viewing audience has clearly spoken, judging by the popularity and proliferation of such shows. But don't silence Heather Havrilesky. She is one media expert who praises the best of the so-called reality television offerings. In "Three Cheers for Reality TV," which first appeared in *Salon.com* on September 13, 2004, Havrilesky defends the genre, noting that viewers who have been watching the same episodic sitcom plot structures for decades feel that shows like *Survivor* offer something fresh and new. She lauds famed *Survivor* producer Mark Burnett for his high standards of human drama and visual appeal and says Jerry Bruckheimer's *The Amazing Race* is even a notch higher in quality. However, she blasts shows like *Elimidate, The Ultimate Love Test,* and *The Swan,* saying, "the lowest rung on the reality ladder has nothing to do with the sharp, fascinating shows at the top."

Heather Havrilesky is television critic for *Salon.com* and writes a Web log called *Rabbit Blog.* She cocreated *Filler,* a long-running cartoon on *Suck.com,* with illustrator Terry Colon, and her work has appeared in *New York Magazine, Spin,* and the *Washington Post* and on National Public Radio's *All Things Considered.*

THINKING AHEAD

Describe your general reaction to reality television. Are you a fan? Why or why not? Which are your favorite shows? Your least favorite shows? Explain your responses.

INCREASING VOCABULARY

puerile (adj.) (2)
stigma (n.) (6)
bemoan (v.) (7)
genre (n.) (8)
lowbrow (adj.) (9)
implemented (v.) (10)
whittled (v.) (10)
provocateur (n.) (13)
aesthetically (adv.) (14)
vicarious (adj.) (14)
confidante (n.) (14)
meandering (adj.) (15)
cliques (n.) (16)
belligerent (adj.) (16)

aficionados (n.) (17)
mesmerizingly (adv.) (17)
epitomized (v.) (17)
improvization (n.) (18)
bellicose (adj.) (19)
overtly (adv.) (21)
narcissistic (adj.) (22)
sociopathic (adj.) (22)
savvy (adj.) (23)
posturing (n.) (23)
preening (n.) (23)
rampant (adj.) (23)
veneer (n.) (24)
heedlessly (adv.) (25)

propagate (v.) (25)　　　　　　　foibles (n.) (25)
crass (adj.) (25)　　　　　　　　 devoid (adj.) (26)
loathsome (adj.) (25)

S ifting through so-called reality TV has become like rummaging through   1
a landfill: There seems to be no end to the quantity and types of trash
you'll find. . . . [I]f we're going to start setting taste standards for reality TV, there's going to be a lot of dead air time." [*Myrtle Beach Sun
News*, 9/2/04]

"This is not just bad television in the sense that it's mediocre, point-   2
less, puerile even. It's bad because it's damaging." [BBC journalist John
Humphrys, in a speech to U.K. TV executives, *Reuters U.K.*, 8/27/04]

"Reality TV is so cheap because you don't need writers, actors, direc-   3
tors . . . it is killing off new talent and we are all worse off for that." [Re-
becca of Cambridge, U.K. posting on *BBC News*, 8/28/04]

"Reality TV, in particular, mocks committed relationships and makes   4
trust seem foolish, some teens said. So teens tend to 'hook up' with friends
to get a sexual fix without the responsibility of a relationship." [*Rich-
mond Times-Dispatch*, 9/7/04]

"Sarah Austin occasionally watches reality TV, but finds it sad, rather   5
than engaging." [*The Age*, 9/5/04]

Welcome to the modern world, where we're all sucking on the same   6
pop cultural crack pipe, but only the unrefined among us will admit that
they inhale. Reality TV earns its reputation as the dangerous street drug
du jour[1] mostly by aiming its lens at human behavior—we're far less pho-
togenic than we imagine ourselves to be. While shows run the gamut[2]
from high-quality, dramatically compelling work to silly, exploitative
trash, pundits[3] consistently point to programs at the bottom of the barrel
and cast aspersions[4] on those foolish enough to watch them. Thanks to
this stigma, it's not always easy to get a clear picture of how many people
genuinely enjoy reality shows and aren't about to give them up.

Instead, every few months, a new survey announces that reality is on   7
its way out. Last March, an Insider Advantage survey found that "67 percent of Americans" were "becoming tired of so-called reality programs."
This year, a survey by Circuit City concluded that 58 percent of viewers
are "getting tired" of reality TV. (What are they excited about? Why,
HDTV, of course—they just can't wait to purchase their new HDTV-
capable sets!) Can you expect accurate results when you ask people if
they're "getting tired" of anything? But even while many people take their
cue from the media and bemoan the evils of reality, they're still watching.
Just as there are those who claim to read *Penthouse* for the fine articles,

---
[1] **du jour:** French for "of the day."
[2] **run the gamut:** To range from one extreme to the other.
[3] **pundits:** Critics or authorities on a particular subject, especially in the media.
[4] **cast aspersions:** To attack someone's character or reputation.

no matter how "sad, rather than engaging" reality TV might be, audiences have yet to drop off as predicted.

"Reality TV is not going away," says Marc Berman, television analyst   8
for *Mediaweek.* "This summer, reality dominated. In terms of total viewers during the regular season, three of the top five shows [*The Apprentice,* *American Idol* and *Survivor*] were reality shows." Berman predicts that we'll see these same reality shows pull in big numbers in the fall, along with frequent time-slot winners like *The Bachelor* and whichever new reality programs draw in big audiences. "The bottom line is that the genre is absolutely exploding," Berman says.

Instead of writing off millions of viewers as the unenlightened con-   9
sumers of lowbrow entertainment, shouldn't we ask why they're attracted to reality TV in the first place?

First of all, viewers have been exposed to the same half-hour and   10
hour episodic plot structures, implemented in roughly the same ways, for decades now, setting the stage for a less conventional format. Even once-groundbreaking, high-quality dramas like *ER* and *The West Wing* have evolved into parodies of themselves, with all the usual suspects striding through halls and corridors, spitting out the same clever quips until the next big tragedy hits. Meanwhile, traditional sitcoms are faring even worse, as the networks spend millions each fall to develop shows that don't stick. While those in the industry bemoan the fact that the networks have whittled their sitcom offerings down to two or three shows, that makes perfect sense when you recognize how bad TV executives have been at locating genuinely good shows, and how expensive it is just to develop a handful of episodes. *Two and a Half Men,* one of the only new sitcoms from last fall to make it to another season, is considered a hit, yet it's not remotely funny. And the best sitcoms—*Everybody Loves Raymond, Will & Grace* and *That '70s Show*—are all winding down, with one-half (*Raymond*) to two years left in them, at most.

That's not to say that the world of scripted entertainment is dead—   11
far from it. Instead, new formats are taking hold: one-camera sitcoms like *Arrested Development* and *Entourage,* sketch comedies like *Chappelle's Show* and *Da Ali G Show,* and unconventional twists on old formulas like *Deadwood* and *The Wire.* But unconventional means risky, which is why none of those shows are on the Big Three networks, which seem as faithful to old-formula fiction as Joanie was to Chachi.[5]

Ultimately, though, it's not the basic format of the traditional sitcom   12
or drama that's to blame; it's the lack of original, high-quality writing. By now everyone knows that HBO, a channel not poisoned by the copycat mentality of the networks, is behind most of the best shows on television. Many producers and writers report that quality scripts and ideas are out there, but the networks aren't necessarily looking for quality. What seems

---

[5]**Joanie . . . Chachi:** Two characters on the TV sitcom *Happy Days,* which ran from 1974 to 1984.

familiar about those wisecracking[6] characters on their couches isn't the setting or the format; it's the mediocre jokes and story lines that simply mimic the story lines of other better—but not necessarily great—shows. Sadly, as the networks continue the impossible search for guaranteed hits and sure things, they limit their scope to the sorts of shows that have succeeded before instead of seeking original voices with something to say. This is why we'll end up watching soggy star vehicles[7] like John Goodman's *Center of the Universe* and Jason Alexander's *Listen Up* (It worked with Charlie Sheen, right?) this fall instead of encountering truly original comedies with fresh, surprising characters.

Will we be watching? The truth is, the best reality shows feature exactly the kinds of fresh, surprising characters that most sitcoms and dramas lack. For those who care about the quality of reality shows they produce, the bar has been set very high by Mark Burnett. At a time when reality TV appeared to be shackled to the somewhat shallow teenage-bitch-slap tradition of *The Real World*, Burnett insisted on bringing the same intelligent editing and beautiful cinematography to *Survivor* that he brought to *Eco Challenge*. He recognized that, beyond painstakingly careful casting and crafting of dramatically compelling story lines, viewers would want to get a real feel for the show's exotic setting. As fleeting as those aerial and wildlife shots can seem, they add an inestimable dimension to the viewer's experience. Anyone who watched the first few episodes of *Survivor* knew that the show was bound to be a hit, and the reason for that had more to do with sparkling shots of cornflower-blue water than it had to do with Richard Hatch (although having a naked, backstabbing provocateur around certainly helped). 13

If reality offerings were limited to claustrophobic, repetitive, aesthetically irritating shows like *Elimidate* or *The Bachelor*, it would be easy to write off the entire genre as the work of sensationalistic producers churning out trash for a quick buck. Instead, a few sharp producers like Burnett saw the enormous potential of the form and approached it with a passion, creating a vicarious experience for the viewer. They recognized that reality TV could truly engage audiences, pulling them into a time and place, populated by real human beings. As long as the cast and the settings were a little larger than life, as long as the stories were edited to make the viewer feel like a personal confidante to each of the competitors, audiences would find themselves swept into the action, investing far more of their emotions in the competition than they imagined was possible. 14

The Amazing Race followed in the footsteps of *Survivor* in terms of quality, but conquered the most difficult production challenges imaginable. Ten teams of two scamper across the globe, racing to complete various 15

---

[6] **ESL** **wisecracking:** Joking.
[7] **ESL** **soggy star vehicles:** Unoriginal, unsuccessful television shows designed to showcase a star.

tasks, but you never, ever spot a single camera, not when several teams are running across a beach to the finish line, not when they're hang gliding or walking teams of dogs or eating two pounds of Russian caviar. Produced by Jerry Bruckheimer and edited with so many suspense-inducing tricks it's impossible not to get caught up in the action, *The Amazing Race* took Burnett's high standards of human drama and visual appeal and built on them. Lumping together an intensely difficult, expensive, painstakingly produced show like *The Amazing Race* with meandering, silly shows like *The Ultimate Love Test* is an insult to the sharp, talented people who seem to set the bar higher each season.

Of course, meandering, silly shows have a certain charm of their own.   16
Fox's *Paradise Hotel* stumbled on accidental genius with its hyperaggressive cast of frat boys and neurotics. Originally intended as a sleazy dating show where those guests who didn't "hook up" would get thrown out of Paradise *"forever!"* as the voice-over put it, *Paradise Hotel* evolved into a nasty battle between two cliques, with the producers scrambling to mold their "twists" and promos to fit the bizarre clashes arising on the set. There's something to be said for a show that evolves based on the strange behavior of its cast, thanks mostly to the fact that its cast is made up of belligerent drunks. Sadly, *Paradise Hotel*'s success was purely accidental. The producers foolishly moved the show away from its original location, a gorgeous Mexican resort with brilliant white walls that lit every scene beautifully, making all of the inhabitants appear larger than life. They renamed the show, cast it with bland, empty-headed Neanderthals,[8] added an even-more-awful host and some pointless twists, and the magic was over. The ironically titled *Forever Eden* was canceled before the season ended.

But part of the joy of watching, for true reality aficionados, is witness-   17
ing such false starts and mesmerizingly entertaining mistakes. While those who've never seen much of the genre bemoan the foolishness of most shows, it's the newness of the form that makes it so exciting. When not even the producers can predict how the characters on a show will react, audiences feel like they're a part of something that's evolving before their eyes. The second season of *The Joe Schmo Show*, titled *Joe Schmo 2*, epitomized this state. The show lures two individuals into thinking that they're contestants on a dating show called *Last Chance for Love*, when in fact, their fellow contestants are really actors, paid to create absurd, funny scenarios.

To the dismay of the show's producers and crew, a few episodes in,   18
one of the two Schmos named Ingrid figured out that something was very wrong and kept asking the actors around her if they had memorized the things they were saying, or there was "some kind of *Truman Show*[9] thing

---

[8] **Neanderthals:** Early humans thought to have limited intelligence.
[9] **The Truman Show:** A film starring Jim Carrey about a man who does not realize that he has been the unwilling star of a reality show for his entire life.

going on." Instead of declaring the show a failure, the producers chose to reveal the truth to Ingrid and then enlisted her as an actor for the rest of the show. This kind of behind-the-scenes, seat-of-the-pants[10] improvisation is such completely new territory, it's not hard to understand why audiences are intrigued.

Furthermore, if our obsession with celebrities tends to rise and fall and rise again in cycles, then it makes sense that reality TV would become popular in the wake of the late '90s, when celebrity obsession reached new levels of absurdity. Audiences bored with Brad and Jennifer[11] or Jennifer and Ben[12] or Paris and Nicole[13] suddenly found themselves with more knowable, less remote personalities to root for. Instead of focusing all their attention on those far too privileged to comprehend or relate to, audiences could embrace no-nonsense, surprisingly open-minded Rudy of *Survivor* or despise the outspoken-but-bellicose Susan Hawk. Reality "stars" like lovable couple Chip and Kim from *The Amazing Race* or country-boy Troy from *The Apprentice* offer us a chance to admire real people for qualities that go beyond choosing the perfect dress for the Oscars or smiling sweetly for the cameras.

Plus, now that magazines like *InStyle* make it clear that a major celebrity's image and personality are essentially created by a team of stylists, interior designers, assistants, managers and publicists, it's no wonder we crave an exploration of the little quirks and flaws of ordinary people. And when it comes to making enemies, anyone can throw a temper tantrum and then stalk offstage, but how many ordinary humans can manage the messy explosion of insults and accusations set off by Omarosa of *The Apprentice*? Who knew that "Now *there's* the pot calling the kettle black!" was a racial slur?

Many have argued that self-consciousness will be the death of the genre. As more and more contestants who appear on the shows have been exposed to other reality shows, the argument goes, their actions and statements will become less and less "real." What's to blame here is the popular use of the word "reality" to describe a genre that's never been overtly concerned with realism or even with offering an accurate snapshot of the events featured. In fact, the term "reality TV" may have sprung from *The Real World*, in which the "real" was used both in the sense of "the world awaiting young people after they graduate from school," and in the sense of "getting real," or, more specifically, getting all up in someone's grill[14] for eating the last of your peanut butter.

---

[10] **ESL** **seat-of-the-pants:** Unplanned; with no preparation.
[11] **ESL** **Brad and Jennifer:** Brad Pitt and Jennifer Aniston, celebrities who were married but are now divorced.
[12] **ESL** **Jennifer and Ben:** Jennifer Lopez and Ben Affleck, celebrities who were once engaged to each other.
[13] **ESL** **Paris and Nicole:** Paris Hilton and Nicole Richie, daughters of a hotel heir and a musician, Lionel Richie, respectively, and stars of the first season of the television show *The Simple Life*.
[14] **ESL** **getting all up in someone's grill:** Slang term for confronting someone in an angry manner.

The truth is, part of the entertainment offered by reality TV lies in   22
separating the aspects of subjects' behavior that are motivated by an
awareness of the cameras from the aspects that are genuine. You can't expect someone who's surrounded by cameras to act naturally all of the
time, and as the genre has evolved, editors and producers have become
aware that highlighting this gap between the real self and the camera-
ready self not only constitutes quality entertainment, but may be the easiest shortcut to creating the villain character that any provocative narrative
requires. When *Big Brother 5*'s Jason pouts his lips, flexes his muscles and
adjusts his metrosexual[15] headband in the mirror, then confides to the
camera that every idiotic thing he's done in the house so far has been part
of a master plan to confuse his roommates, he not only makes a great
enemy for the more seemingly grounded members of the house, but he also
hints at narcissistic and sociopathic streaks that reality TV has demonstrated may be a defining characteristic of the modern personality. Either
an alarming number of reality show contestants are self-obsessed and
combative, or the common character traits found in young people have
shifted dramatically.

In our self-conscious, media-savvy culture, such posturing and preen-   23
ing are a worthy subject for the camera's gaze, documenting as they do the
flavor of the times. When young kids talk about marketing themselves
properly and "breaking wide," it makes perfect sense to shine a light on
the rampant self-consciousness and unrelenting self-involvement of these
characters. When we see Puck of *The Real World* screeching at the top of
his lungs or Richard Hatch of *Survivor* confiding to the cameras that he
considers the other players beneath him, we may be glimpsing behavior
that's more true of the average American than any of us would like to believe.

But then, no matter how premeditated many of the words and ac-   24
tions of reality show stars can be, the proper events and tasks eventually
conspire to create cracks in the shiny veneer, revealing flaws and personality tics they'd clearly wish to hide. If even the smooth operators of *The
Apprentice* stumble on their words, bare their claws and show their less
polished selves regularly, you have to figure that keeping your true self
hidden from the camera is more difficult than it looks. Katrina, for example, started the first season appearing smooth and polished, then
slowly unraveled as the personalities and tactics of the players around
her seemed to erode her sense of self. And who can forget Rupert on *Survivor*, who went from lovable teddy bear to snarling grizzly whenever
someone crossed him? Real people are surprising. The process of getting
to know the characters, of discovering the qualities and flaws that define
them, and then discussing these discoveries with other viewers creates
a simulation of community that most people don't find in their everyday

---

[15] **ESL** **metrosexual:** Relating to a heterosexual man's adoption of characteristics some-
    times stereotypically attributed to gay men.

lives. That may be a sad commentary on the way we're living, but it's not the fault of these shows, which unearth a heartfelt desire to make connections with other human beings. Better that we rediscover our interest in other, real people than sink ourselves into the mirage of untouchable celebrity culture or into some überhuman,[16] ultraclever fictional *Friends* universe.

Naturally, there will always be those shows that heedlessly propagate   25 crass televised stunts without any socially redeeming qualities. *The Swan*, which turns normal, attractive women into hideous plasticized demons with lots of pricey plastic surgery, then pits the demons against each other in a beauty contest, is more freakishly dehumanizing than anything George Orwell[17] could've dreamed up. *Gana La Verde*, a *Fear Factor*-style competition where immigrants compete for a green card, or at least for the use of lawyers who might win them a green card, makes you wonder if we're not one step away from feeding the underprivileged to the lions on live TV. But the lowest rung on the reality ladder has nothing to do with the sharp, fascinating shows at the top. The best reality shows transform ordinary places and people into dramatic settings populated by lovable heroes and loathsome enemies, and in the process of watching and taking sides and comparing the characters' choices to the ones we might make, we're reacquainted with ourselves and each other. Great fictional TV has the power to engage us, too, but the networks aren't creating much of that these days. When was the last time *CSI* sparked a little self-examination? Does *Still Standing* make you giggle in recognition at life's merry foibles?

Lowbrow or not, all most of us want from TV is the chance to glimpse   26 something true, just a peek at those strange little tics and endearing flaws that make us human. While the networks' safe little formulas mostly seem devoid of such charms, reality shows have the power to amuse, anger, appall, surprise, but most of all, engage us. Isn't that the definition of entertainment?

EXERCISING VOCABULARY

1. In paragraph 15, Havrilesky describes Mark Burnett as one of the people who "set the bar higher each season." Where does the phrase originate? What does it mean? How does it apply to Burnett?

2. The author quotes the aphorism "Now *there's* the pot calling the kettle black!" (para. 20). What does this phrase mean? How could Omarosa consider this a racial slur?

3. In paragraph 9, the author mentions "lowbrow entertainment." What is the origin of the word *lowbrow*? What does it mean? How is it used here?

---

[16] überhuman: Superhuman.
[17] **George Orwell:** The author of the dystopian novel *1984*, in which Big Brother regulates and monitors all human activity.

PROBING CONTENT

1. Why are reality shows dismissed by some people? Who criticizes the genre? What do they say?

2. What question does the author think it is important to ask about reality television? Why?

3. According to the author, what are the best reality TV shows? What do these shows have to offer the viewer?

4. What effect has the American public's obsession with celebrities had on reality television programming? Why?

CONSIDERING CRAFT

1. The author uses several allusions to popular culture in her essay. Examine the first sentence in paragraph 6. What situation and individual is she referring to when she says that "only the unrefined among us will admit that they inhale"? Why does she include this reference?

2. Why does Havrilesky open her essay with a series of quotations? Examine the quotations in detail and compare them. What point is the author trying to make? How effective is her writing strategy?

3. Find several points in the essay where the author cites media authorities or research studies. Why does she include this material? How does it affect your reading?

4. Havrilesky names numerous celebrities and television shows from both the past and the present in her essay. Find several examples in the essay. What does this strategy accomplish?

RESPONDING TO THE WRITER

Do you agree with Havrilesky that reality shows have redeeming social value? Defend your position.

For a quiz on this reading, go to bedfordstmartins.com/mirror.

Greeting Big Brother with Open Arms

EMILY EAKIN

Remember when it was fun to watch people who didn't know they were being observed, like those on the television show *Candid Camera*? Why are we now interested in watching people who do know they are being watched? In "Greeting Big Brother with Open Arms," which appeared in the January 17, 2004, edition of the *New York Times*, Emily Eakin casts an eye on our fascination with surveillance as entertainment, otherwise known as reality TV. It turns out there may be something hidden behind the camera after all. She talks to expert Mark Andrejevic, who believes that the reality genre "is essentially a scam: propaganda for a new business model that only pretends to give consumers more control while in fact subjecting them to increasingly sophisticated forms of monitoring and manipulation." For example, TiVo allows people to watch television shows when they want to, but in return, TiVo watches what these viewers watch and gets "valuable information" about their preferences.

Emily Eakin is currently on the staff of *The New Yorker*. She has been a culture reporter for the *New York Times*, a fashion features writer at *Vogue*, and a contributor to *The Economist*, *Interview*, the *New York Times Book Review*, and *Vanity Fair*.

THINKING AHEAD

What do you think of reality TV shows that peer into the private lives of people? Do you watch any of these shows? Would you participate in one? Why or why not?

INCREASING VOCABULARY

malignant (adj.) (1)	revere (v.) (5)
telling (adj.) (2)	scam (n.) (6)
surveillance (n.) (2)	banality (n.) (9)
voyeurism (n.) (3)	benign (adj.) (10)
unseemly (adj.) (3)	conceded (v.) (11)
rhapsodizing (v.) (4)	inducement (n.) (12)
therapeutic (adj.) (4)	detrimental (adj.) (12)
aesthetic (n.) (5)	contrivance (n.) (13)

For 50 years, Big Brother[1] was an unambiguous symbol of malignant   1
state power, totalitarianism's all-seeing eye. Then *Big Brother* became a hip reality television show, in which 10 cohabiting strangers
submitted to round-the-clock camera monitoring in return for the chance
to compete for $500,000.

That transformation is telling, says Mark Andrejevic, a professor of   2
communication studies at the University of Iowa at Iowa City. Today,
more than twice as many young people apply to MTV's *Real World*
show than to Harvard, he says. Clearly, to a post–cold-war generation of
Americans, the prospect of living under surveillance is no longer scary
but cool.

Media critics have frequently portrayed the reality show craze in un-   3
flattering terms, as a sign of base voyeurism (on the part of viewers) and
an unseemly obsession with fame (on the part of participants). But Mr.
Andrejevic's take, influenced by the theories of Theodor Adorno[2] and
Michel Foucault,[3] is at once darker and more subtle.

Reality shows glamorize surveillance, he writes, presenting it "as one   4
of the hip attributes of the contemporary world," "an entree into the
world of wealth and celebrity" and even a moral good. His new book, *Reality TV: The Work of Being Watched* (Rowman & Littlefield), is peppered with quotes from veterans of *The Real World*, *Road Rules* and
Temptation Island, rhapsodizing about on-air personal growth and the
therapeutic value of being constantly watched. As Josh on *Big Brother* explains, "Everyone should have an audience."

At the same time, Mr. Andrejevic (pronounced an-DRAY-uh-vitch)   5
argues, the reality genre appears to fulfill the democratic promise of the
emerging interactive economy, turning passive cultural consumers into active ones who can star on shows or vote on their outcomes. (The series
Extreme Makeover takes this promise literally, he notes, "offering to rebuild 'real' people via plastic surgery so that they can physically close the
gap between themselves and the contrived aesthetic of celebrity they have
been taught to revere.")

As seductive as this sounds, in Mr. Andrejevic's view reality television   6
is essentially a scam: propaganda for a new business model that only pretends to give consumers more control while in fact subjecting them to increasingly sophisticated forms of monitoring and manipulation.

As he put it in a telephone interview: "The promise out there is that   7
everybody can have their own TV show. But of course, that ends up being
a kind of Ponzi scheme.[4] You can't have everybody watching everybody
else's TV show. And since that's not possible, in economic terms, the way

---

[1] **Big Brother:** The leader of the totalitarian government in George Orwell's 1949
dystopian novel *1984*; government surveillance.
[2] **Theodor Adorno:** Twentieth-century German philosopher and sociologist.
[3] **Michel Foucault:** Twentieth-century French philosopher and social critic.
[4] **Ponzi scheme:** An investment swindle in which high returns, allegedly profits, are made to
early investors using funds from later investors.

it's going to work is according to this model of a few people monitoring what the rest of us do."

Think of TiVo or Replay, he said. These digital recorders allow   8
people to watch the television shows they want when they want to. But in return, he points out, the recorders' manufacturers get a stream of valuable information about viewer preferences. The same principle, he argues, holds true for online shops that offer custom CD's in exchange for data on personal musical tastes. Or Web sites that use "cookies" to track users' movements on the Internet.

Marketers aren't interested in exceptional behavior, he added. They   9
want to know about the routine aspects of daily life, the same material that shows like *The Real World* and *Big Brother*—in which banality passes as authenticity—strive to capture on film.

In short, Mr. Andrejevic said, reality television's true beneficiaries are   10
not the shows' cast members (who can wind up making little more than minimum wage for the hours—or months—they spend before the camera) or ordinary viewers (who don't really choose what happens on their television screens) but the marketers, advertisers and corporate executives who have a large stake in seeing surveillance portrayed as benign.

Of course, he conceded, his students don't necessarily see it this way.   11
Raised on Web logs, Google, cellphones and instant messaging, they "divulge much more information about themselves on a daily basis than previous generations," he said, and they don't associate the idea of surveillance with a totalitarian Big Brother.

"The concern I have is that self-expression gets confused with the in-   12
ducement to assist in marketing to yourself," Mr. Andrejevic said. "But my students say they've got nothing to hide. And until there are some consequences they perceive as detrimental, they're not going to be concerned."

At least in one respect, he added, reality television does conform to real   13
life. "It portrays the reality of contrivance, the way consumers are manipulated," he said. "I look at it with the fascination of somebody watching a car wreck."

EXERCISING VOCABULARY

1. In her opening paragraph, the author describes Big Brother as a symbol of "malignant state power, totalitarianism's all-seeing eye." What is totalitarianism? From what root word does it stem? How can an eye be "all-seeing"?

2. In paragraph 4, Eakin writes that Mark Andrejevic's book is "peppered with quotes." Under what circumstances do you normally pepper something? What action does peppering something imply? What does it mean when an author peppers a book with quotations?

PROBING CONTENT

1. What do Americans today think about living under surveillance? What is the proof of this, according to the author?

2. Who is Mark Andrejevic? What is his view of reality shows? How does he support his argument?

3. According to Andrejevic, who really profits from reality television shows? Why is this so?

4. How did Professor Andrejevic's students react to his theory of reality TV? Why did they react the way they did?

CONSIDERING CRAFT

1. Why does the author open the essay with an allusion to George Orwell's dystopian novel *1984*? How does this prepare the reader for the essay's thesis?

2. Eakin devotes most of her essay to discussing Mark Andrejevic's view of reality television. Why does she choose this strategy? How effective is this method of developing an essay?

RESPONDING TO THE WRITER

Has Emily Eakin's article altered your opinion of reality television? If so, in what ways? If not, why not?

For a quiz on this reading, go to bedfordstmartins.com/mirror.

DRAWING CONNECTIONS

1. Heather Havrilesky asserts in "Three Cheers for Reality TV" that "The best reality shows transform ordinary places and people into dramatic settings populated by lovable heroes and loathsome enemies, and in the process of watching and taking sides and comparing the characters' choices to the ones we might make, we're reacquainted with ourselves and each other" (para. 25). How would Emily Eakin, author of "Greeting Big Brother with Open Arms," respond to Havrilesky's claim?

2. How would Heather Havrilesky, author of "Three Cheers for Reality TV," respond to this quotation from media critic Mark Andrejevic, who is cited in Emily Eakin's "Greeting Big Brother with Open Arms": The reality genre "is essentially a scam: propaganda for a new business model that only pretends to give consumers more control while in fact subjecting them to increasingly sophisticated forms of monitoring and manipulation" (para. 6)? Make sure to support your answer with specific examples.

FOCUSING ON YESTERDAY, FOCUSING ON TODAY

PSYCHO *Scream*

Screams, from both the actors and the audience, have always been associated with horror movies. The actors responsible for two of the most famous film screams are shown here: Janet Leigh's in the Alfred Hitchcock classic *Psycho* (1960) and Drew Barrymore's in the first movie in Wes Craven's popular *Scream* series (1996). *Psycho* is the tale of Norman, a seemingly nice young man turned serial killer who runs the Bates Motel, where guests check in and then check out permanently. This photo from the movie shows

SCREAM *Scream*

Janet Leigh's character, Marion Crane, as she encounters her killer in the infamous shower scene. The *Scream* photo shows a terrified Drew Barrymore listening to the person who has just murdered her boyfriend in the backyard and will soon murder her.

What exactly do these two images convey? What part of each woman's face is featured most prominently? How has the depiction of women changed from classic horror movies to contemporary ones? Based on these two images alone, how do you think horror films have changed since the 1960s? Do the same elements frighten us today?

REFLECTING ON THE WRITING

1. Read the essay by Louise Kennedy, "Barrier Between Adults' and Children's Entertainment Is Breaking Down," paying particular attention to the final paragraph. Then write an essay in which you answer her question: "So will we all, in fact, end up acting sixteen forever? And if we do, what happens to the genuinely free spirit of child's play and the genuinely complex pleasures of adult seriousness?" (para. 13). Make sure to include examples drawn from recent television shows, films, books, video games, music, music videos, and Internet Web sites to support your argument. You may also wish to refer to essays in Chapters 6, 7, 8, and 9.

2. Using the essays in this chapter, as well as your own observations and experiences, write an essay in which you discuss how the self-image of men or women is handled or mishandled in movies or on television shows. Include several specific examples from movies or television. You may also refer to other essays in this book, such as those in Chapters 3, 4, and 5.

3. Watch several episodes of *Will and Grace*, *Queer Eye for the Straight Guy*, or any other television show that features gay characters or deals with gay themes. Write an essay in which you analyze the way in which the characters are portrayed and certain issues are explored. Consider questions like the following: Are negative stereotypes reinforced? If so, in what ways? Do the characters seem like real people or caricatures? How do the gay characters on these shows interact with the straight characters? You may wish to refer to Heather Havrilesky's "Three Cheers for Reality TV" and Hemal Jhaveri's "Searching for a Real Gay Man."

CONNECTING TO THE CULTURE

1. Watch several different reality television shows during one week. Use specific examples from what you watch to prove or disprove the idea that reality television has "the power to amuse, anger, appall, surprise, but most of all, engage us," as Heather Havrilesky asserts in "Three Cheers for Reality TV" (para. 26).

2. During a one-week period, view a variety of television shows that feature families. Write an essay in which you describe three or four of the different kinds of families featured on these shows. Use specific examples from what you watch to prove or disprove the idea that "the term 'family' has outgrown its original meaning," as Douglas Cruickshank asserts in "Crazy for Dysfunction" (para. 8).

3. Reread Stephen King's "Why We Crave Horror Movies." Write an essay in which you agree or disagree with his argument that horror films allow a safe release for what would otherwise be expressed as insane or even criminal behavior. You may extend your argument to include other forms of "dangerous" leisure-time activities like playing violent video or computer games,

watching violent television shows, reading violent novels, or listening to violent music.

4. Write an essay in which you argue for the iconic status of one particular film or television show. You may refer to James Poniewozik's "Reconsidering *Friends*." First consider what qualifies as an iconic movie or TV show. Then make a list of at least five films or shows, past or present, that could be the subject of your essay. Make your final choice, watch several episodes of the show or watch the movie, and take notes as you are watching it. You may also wish to consult Internet sources like the IMDb (the Internet Movie Database) or the Web site for the film or television show you have chosen.

CHAPTER 8

Stop! Listen. What's That Sound?

How Music and Culture Mix It Up

The biggest sensation at the 2003 MTV Music Video Awards wasn't Justin Timberlake or Coldplay, both of whom won awards. The shocker was Madonna's liplock with Britney Spears after their opening performance of "Like a Virgin" and "Hollywood." Later Madonna and Christina Aguilera re-enacted the same kiss.

- What do you think these performers were hoping to accomplish?
- How do you think most of the fans reacted? Why?
- In the opening act, Madonna wore black while Spears and Aguilera wore white lingerie. What might these costume and color choices represent?
- Do you think that this behavior increased CD sales? Why?

Research this topic with TopLinks at bedfordstmartins.com/mirror.

GEARING UP

What kinds of music do you listen to? When do you listen? Where? What effect does listening have on you? What songs do you associate with special occasions, events, or memories? Who are your favorite musical performers? What would influence you to listen to a kind of music you haven't heard or liked before?

What medium other than music is as completely bound up in the culture that creates it? The sounds change as the instruments do, the lyrics and language keep pace with our fears and our ambitions, and rhythm and meaning continue to be created. Music, like other forms of communication, is both personal and communal. Our powerful response to music comes from deep within us and may sometimes surprise us with its intensity. Like smells or photographs, songs have the power to recreate significant events and even entire periods of our lives. The kinds of music we like and the songs that reside in our heads, refusing to go away, are as indicative of who we are as the clothes we wear, the books we read, and the causes we support. Jazz great Quincy Jones, writing in the April 18, 2005, issue of *Time* magazine, writes, "Music has a magic no other medium possesses. I have seen firsthand how it can cross all boundaries, whether they are cultural, linguistic, political or geographical."

We react to a song individually, but when many of us react positively to the same songs, musical success happens. Of course, it's not all magic; our musical tastes, like our tastes in fast food or jeans, endure constant bombardment by the media. And just as fashions recycle themselves, so do musical trends. What's old suddenly becomes hot again; what was hot yesterday is cold today. Recycled musical trends are a little different from their sources and may be distinguished by new instruments, new voices, new rhythms, and new times. But it's worth a glance backward to see where the sounds have been heard before.

COLLABORATING

In groups of three or four, discuss why music is important to each of you. Find out everyone's favorite kind of music and what has influenced these choices. Then try to explain why some music maintains its popularity from one generation to the next but other musical groups and songs fail to last from one Grammy season to another.

Same Old Song

Lorraine Ali

In "Same Old Song," first published in *Newsweek* on October 9, 2000, Lorraine Ali writes that pop music essentially stays the same, despite changing, and that whichever decade since the 1950s you consider, its music is often designed to make elders angry. Music's shock value, however, gets "ratcheted up a notch with every generation," and today, lyrics with themes of sex and violence are increasingly dominating the charts. The new frontier in music is a rebellion against political correctness; women are debased and degraded, and "excess and greed are extolled as worthy attributes." The result? Pop is as predictable as an action movie. Is shock value being used as a selling tool — a substitute for musical innovation and originality?

Ali is a general editor at *Newsweek* who covers music for the magazine's Arts and Entertainment section. She has written about everything from Christian alternative rock to Latino Lone Star rap and has interviewed musicians from Dolly Parton to Marilyn Manson. Named 1997's music journalist of the year, Ali was a senior critic for *Rolling Stone,* has contributed to the *New York Times* and *GQ,* and was regularly interviewed on VH-1's 2002 to 2003 series *One Hit Wonders.* Her piece on Palestinian rappers, "West Bank Hardcore," was included in *Da Capo Best Music Writing 2001.*

THINKING AHEAD

Why is some of today's music offensive to some adults? Are they upset in the same way and for the same reasons that adults in the past were upset by Elvis Presley or the Beatles? Which elements are the same? Which elements are different?

INCREASING VOCABULARY

avid (adj.) (1)	retool (v.) (6)
esthetic (adj.) (2)	vilest (adj.) (6)
irk (v.) (2)	revitalized (v.) (7)
saturated (adj.) (5)	misogyny (n.) (7)
proliferate (v.) (5)	homophobia (n.) (7)
precursor (n.) (6)	jaded (adj.) (8)
induced (v.) (6)	desensitized (adj.) (8)
debased (v.) (6)	vacuous (adj.) (9)
extolled (v.) (6)	withers (v.) (9)

All the controversy, criticism and praise surrounding Eminem's recent release *The Marshall Mathers LP* finally caused a fiftyish coworker of mine to go out and buy the album to see what all the commotion was about. It's not as if he was treading on totally foreign terrain—he did, after all, love N.W.A.'s *Straight Outta Compton* when it came out a dozen years ago, and has avid interest in most anything that rubs people the wrong way. He just needed to know what the newest source of outrage was all about. He locked himself in his office and came out an hour later. "Wow," he said. "This sure isn't for adults."

He was right. And that's the point: pop music is an esthetic and consumer product targeted at kids between grade school and grad school, and often designed to irk their elders. It's been that way since young Frank Sinatra crooned[1] to screaming girls in the 1940s, Little Richard camped and gyrated in the '50s, the Beatles championed free love in the '60s, the Sex Pistols spat on fans in the '70s and Public Enemy instilled fear of a black planet in 1990. Throughout each trend and era, parents have been deeply concerned and kids have done their best to keep them that way.

Things get ratcheted up a notch with every generation. You're not rebelling if you're listening to the same stuff your parents did; you're embarrassing yourself. Remember Jim Morrison's hammy Oedipal[2] psychodrama[3] in the Doors' "The End" (1967): "Father, I want to kill you! Mother, I want to . . . arrgh!" Eminem's cartoonish "Kill You" moves the ball forward by collapsing both parents into a single Bad Mommy to be raped and murdered. Those parental warning stickers may really be for parents, as if to say, "Hey, there's stuff in here your kid will understand and you won't."

There's a hitch. As every book about raising kids will tell you, children need limits—in part to protect them, and in part to give them boundaries to smash and trample. Generation after generation of iconoclasts,[4] from Joyce and Picasso to Elvis and Marilyn to punks and gangstas, have gradually pushed the limits a little further. When N.W.A. dropped "F—k Tha Police" in 1988, it was a shocking moment. When DMX conveys essentially the same sentiments, who really notices? Even N.W.A.'s raps about killing rivals "like it ain't no thang" weren't so far from Johnny Cash's in "Folsom Prison Blues," where he sang of shooting a man in Reno "just to watch him die."

But in some ways, it is different. Johnny may have sung about doing hard time—and other things you wouldn't want your mama to know about—but his fantasy seems tame compared with the sex-and-violence-saturated lyrics that proliferate and dominate the *Billboard*[5] charts today.

---

[1] **crooned:** Sang in a gentle, murmuring manner.
[2] **Oedipal:** Characterized by sexual attraction of a son toward his mother and hostile or jealous feelings toward his father.
[3] **psychodrama:** A dramatic narrative or event characterized by psychological overtones.
[4] **iconoclasts:** People who attack settled beliefs or institutions.
[5] **ESL** *Billboard*: A weekly magazine of the music industry.

It's a change that hasn't gone unnoticed. With hip-hop's current debate over whether rap has gone too far, insiders are once again trying to decipher what the dividing line is between true artistic value and provocative schlock.[6] The answers will come in retrospect, but in order for the genre to continue growing, it's an important debate that needs to start now.

At the moment, the new frontier of rebellion seems to be against political correctness—the well-intentioned fear of offending any person or "group." In the 1960s and '70s, the fashionably rebellious attitude was to celebrate differences, to elevate the condition of women, minorities and gays ("Come on people now, smile on your brother"). That precursor to the P.C.[7] ethos has now become the cultural mainstream; this election year, Democrats with their many-colors-of-Benetton[8] constituency and Republicans with their many-colors-of-Benetton convention are eagerly trying to top each other in their respect for each and every group that might be induced to vote for them. But in popular entertainment, and especially music, women are being debased in ever more degrading ways, excess and greed are extolled as worthy attributes and gay-bashing serves as a mark of deep-down daring. To be a counterculture rebel now, all you have to do is retool the vilest prejudices of your grandparents' day in the vilest language of your own. What's being promoted as the slaughter of sacred cows is McBigotry, with a state-of-the-art beat and no beef at all.

The result? Mainstream rap and hard rock, addicted to ever-escalating doses of defiance, can now feel as predictable as bad Hollywood action flicks. Part of the problem is that no really new style or scene has busted out of the gate since gangsta rap revolutionized hip-hop in the late '80s and grunge revitalized rock back in the early '90s. If there was anything out there in whatever today's equivalents might be of Compton, Calif., or Seattle, the entertainment corporations would have ferreted it out by now, exploited it and stamped it with their own trademarks. True, the Internet offers the promise of an under-the-radar musical bohemia[9] where an alternative sound might lie low long enough to flourish—the trouble is, most stuff on the Web is so far under the radar that a potentially supportive fan base can't find it. So pop music has fallen back on the tried-and-true attention-getters—sex, violence, sex, consumerist excess and sex—and added the latest kinks in the Zeitgeist:[10] misogyny and homophobia as expressions of free-floating countercultural rage and anxiety.

Another part of the problem is that we risk becoming jaded and desensitized. When—as rappers and deliberately obnoxious bands like Limp Bizkit are proving every day—you can say absolutely anything you want, what's

---

[6] schlock: Something of low quality or value.
[7] **ESL** P.C.: Politically correct.
[8] many-colors-of-Benetton: Slogan used by Benetton clothing to indicate wide appeal of its products.
[9] bohemia: A community of people such as writers or artists living an unconventional life.
[10] Zeitgeist: The general intellectual, moral, and cultural climate of an era.

the point of saying anything? And how can you be outrageous enough to get anybody's attention when everybody is shouting at the same volume?

Of course, today's most vacuous pop—from bling-bling[11] to Britney to Blink-182—will pass away, either because it collapses under the weight of its own decadence like disco of the '70s and the hair bands of the '80s, or because it withers from sheer neglect. This happens to the vacuous pop of most every generation: the musical equivalents of Chia Pets give way to the musical equivalents of Razor scooters. The kids to whom these fads are marketed outgrow them and are replaced by new ranks of kids, snickering at yesterday's amusements and suckered in by tomorrow's. The great hope of pop music has always been that in these ruthless revolutions and counter-revolutions a terrible beauty will be born. It was with Public Enemy, with Nirvana—and with Elvis, too. We can only hope we'll get lucky again.

9

EXERCISING VOCABULARY

1. In paragraph 3, Ali asserts that, with popular music, "Things get ratcheted up a notch with every generation." What is the literal meaning of this expression? In what professions is it most frequently used in a literal sense? What does it imply as used here with regard to music?

2. What is an icon? What is an iconoclast (para. 4)? What role have iconoclasts played in the development of popular music?

3. What are some of the characteristics and habits of a ferret? Why has the word *ferret* become a verb, as in "ferreted it out" (para. 7)? What does this verb imply?

4. In paragraph 6, Ali refers to "the slaughter of sacred cows" and "McBigotry." What famous company does this language call to mind? What about today's rock music does Ali consider bigotry? Why?

PROBING CONTENT

1. Why did Ali's coworker buy an Eminem album? What was the coworker's re-action after listening to the album? Who is the target audience for pop music?

2. What twofold purpose do boundaries serve for children? What has tradition-ally been the relation of music to those boundaries? How is today's music both similar to and different from the traditional relationship?

3. In the 1960s and 1970s, what marked rebellious attitudes? What is necessary for an artist to be referred to as "a counterculture rebel" today (para. 6)? What has resulted from this difference?

4. According to the author, what will happen to "today's most vacuous pop" music (para. 9)? Why is she so certain about this eventual outcome?

[11] **bling-bling:** Hip-hop slang for showy jewelry.

CONSIDERING CRAFT

1. In paragraph 9, Ali labels some pop music of yesterday and today "the musical equivalents of Chia Pets" and "Razor scooters." Describe these two objects. What do they have in common? What is the author saying about pop music by using this unusual analogy?

2. There is an element of hope and positive thinking in the last paragraph of Ali's essay that is lacking earlier. Why does she choose to end this way? Is this ending out of character with the rest of her essay? Why or why not?

RESPONDING TO THE WRITER

Ali asserts that the real attention grabbers in music since the 1950s have always been the same, no matter how musical styles change. Chief among these attractors are sex and violence. To what extent do you agree with her evaluation? What other factors in music are equally important to its popularity and success? Give some specific examples to support your ideas.

For a quiz on this reading, go to bedfordstmartins.com/mirror.

A Voice for the Lonely

STEPHEN COREY

Can you recall a memorable song from a certain time in your life—a song that meant everything to you during the beginning or the ending of a relationship, for instance? Did you apply the lyrics of the song to your own emotional state? In the following personal account, Stephen Corey examines the link between music and memory, thinking back to a time when he learned that much of music is about "love—lost, found, hoped for, and despaired of." When Corey learns of singer Roy Orbison's death, he reflects on how music at times cannot be distinguished from feeling. What do you think he means by this? What is it about music that can transport us back to emotions we experienced years earlier?

Stephen Corey is a widely published poet and essayist. He is currently an editor of the *Georgia Review* and has written nine collections of poetry, including *Stephen Corey: Greatest Hits 1980–2000* (2000) and *There Is No Finished World* (2003). His poems and essays have appeared in *American Poetry Review, Kenyon Review, Republic,* and *Shenandoah,* and his work has also been widely anthologized. He has three times been named Georgia Author of the Year by the Georgia Council of Writers and Journalists. This piece first appeared in *In Short: A Collection of Brief Creative Nonfiction* (1996).

THINKING AHEAD

Think of a time in your life when one special song seemed to capture your feelings exactly. What made that song so appealing? How did you react when you heard the song? Were you more moved by the lyrics or the tune? How does hearing this song affect you today?

INCREASING VOCABULARY

sundry (adj.) (1)

jolt (v.) (4)

flurry (n.) (5)

ranting (adj.) (11)

implications (n.) (11)

roused (v.) (12)

modulations (n.) (13)

camaraderie (n.) (15)

errant (adj.) (16)

commendable (adj.) (18)

erratic (adj.) (18)

The right silence can be a savior, especially in these days of motorcycles, leaf blowers, and malls that thrum with a thousand voices and dozens of sundry machines. Five or six days a week, I get up pretty early—generally around 4 A.M.—and one of the things I like most about those last hours of darkness is their stillness. The house is quiet, the streets

1

are quiet, and (except on weekends, when some of the serious drunks are hanging on) the all-night restaurants are quiet. Reading and writing and thinking come more easily when you know you won't be interrupted, and over the past twenty years I've never found a better mental bodyguard than the hours before dawn.

I got my first serious training as an early riser when I acquired a news-   2
paper delivery route in seventh grade: three miles of widely scattered houses on the edge of Jamestown, New York, and beyond—just me, the moon, darkness, and the various faces of silence. I recall stopping my brisk walk sometimes, especially in winter when every step squeaked and crunched on the snow that nearly always covered the ground, and mar-veling at how there were no sounds except those of my own making. But just as often, that quiet made me nervous, even though my hometown was awfully safe in those days. I learned to offset the urge to look over my shoulder by carrying a pocket-sized transistor radio.

The music helped me to cope with more than just the empty morning   3
streets—I was, as I said, in seventh (and then eighth, and finally ninth) grade during those lone marches. In short, I was just learning something of what much of that music was about: love—lost, found, hoped for, and despaired of.

Most habits die hard, and old ones can seem immortal. Last week, I   4
was up as usual at 4 A.M., and I headed out in the car toward the nearest newspaper box. As always during these quick runs, I flipped on the radio for some wake-up rhythms to jolt my system for the solitary work time soon to come back at the house.

Instead of music, I caught the voice of the all-night deejay[1] just as she   5
was saying, "We have tragic news in over the wire: singer Roy Orbison is dead . . ." She gave a quick flurry of details (heart attack, Hendersonville, North Carolina, hospital), repeated the central fact— "Roy Orbison, dead at fifty-two" —and then (my heart applauds her still for this) said not a word but cut straight into "Only the Lonely."

There I was, cruising down the abandoned city street with the radio   6
now up as loud as I could stand it, mouthing the rising and falling words, rocking side to side as I held the wheel, and riding Orbison's waiting, nearly-cracking voice back twenty-four years to the passenger seat of Jon Cresanti's Volkswagen Beetle.

We're told these days that the hottest and fastest wire into memory is   7
our sense of smell, but music must run a close second. Some songs carry us into a certain mood, some to a general region of our past lives, and some to a very particular moment and situation in time. Jon and I were brought together by chance and loneliness for a couple of months during our sophomore year in high school. The alphabetical seating in our home-room put us next to each other in the back row, and Jon was a talker. We hadn't known each other before: we came from different parts of town,

---

[1] **ESL** deejay: Slang for disc jockey, one who plays recorded music for the public.

had different friends, and moved through different sequences of classes. But for a while we found a bond: my girlfriend had recently dropped me after more than a year of going steady, and Jon had eyes for a girl who had none for him.

I had time—all the time I was no longer spending with my girl. Jon had a car and was old enough to drive it, having failed a grade and thereby become a crucial year older than the typical sophomore. I signed on board, and we cruised day after day, weekend after weekend, killing time and eating at the wondrous new "fast food restaurant" that had just opened. We sat in his car eating fifteen-cent hamburgers and twelve-cent french fries near the real golden arches,[2] the kind that curved up and over the entire little structure (no inside seating, no bathrooms)—and, naturally, listening to the radio. The Four Seasons were with us, as were The Beach Boys, Nat King Cole, The Supremes.   8

But in those two desperate months of shotgunning[3] for Jon, there was only one song that really mattered, one song we waited for, hoped for, and even called the radio station and asked for: Roy Orbison's "Pretty Woman."   9

That opening handful of heavy guitar notes (a lovesick teenager's equivalent of Beethoven's Fifth) carried us into a world of possibility, a world where a moment's fancy could generate love, where losers could be winners just by wishing for success. The pretty woman walks on by, and another failure has occurred—but suddenly, the downward sweep of the wheel is reversed as the woman turns to walk back, and there is nothing in the world but fulfillment of one's dreams.   10

Pop songs are full of such stuff, of course, and have been for as long as the phonograph record and the radio have been with us; we get all kinds of talk about the importance of television in modern life, but I think we need more examination of the ways we have been encompassed by music. I'm not talking about ranting "discussions" of the immorality of certain strains of pop music, but some real studies of the much wider and deeper implications of growing up in a world awash with radio waves.   11

Needless to say, I wasn't concerned about such matters there in the McDonald's parking lot. I wouldn't even have thought about what it was in Orbison's singing that made him so important to me. I took the words of the song's story for their relevance to my own emotional state, and I floated with those words inside a musical accompaniment that both soothed and roused my fifteen-year-old body.   12

When I heard of Orbison's death, I found myself wanting to figure out just what it was in that strange voice that might have been so compelling for me and others across the years. I think it might be in the way the voice itself often seems about to fail: in Orbison's strange and constant modulations,   13

[2] **ESL golden arches:** Symbol of McDonald's restaurants.
[3] **ESL shotgunning:** Riding in the front seat of a car on the passenger side.

from gravelly bass-like sounds to strong tenor-like passages to piercing falsetto[4] cries, there is the feeling for the listener that the singer is always about to lose control, about to break down under the weight of what he is trying to sing. Never mind that this is not true, that Orbison's style was one carefully achieved; what we are talking about here is emotional effect, the true stuff of pop and country music.

If Roy could make it, we could make it. And if Roy could stand fail- 14
ing, so could we.

This feeling of camaraderie with the faraway record star increased for 15
me, I think, the first time I saw him. He was so ordinary-looking—no, he
was so *homely*, so very contrary to what one expects romantic musical heroes to look like. He was *us*.

The right singer, the right sadness, the right silence. The way I heard 16
the story of the death of Orbison's wife in 1966 (and the way I'll keep believing it) was that the two of them were out motorcycling when an errant
car or truck hit them from an angle. She was riding just a few feet to the
side of and behind him, so the other vehicle clipped the back of his cycle
but caught hers full force. I've never gotten over this chilling illustration of
the forces of circumstance and the fate of inches, so much so that over the
years I have regularly found the story called to mind for retelling in classrooms or at parties.

I graduated from high school the year of the accident, and Orbison 17
disappeared from the national music scene. (It wasn't until recently that I
heard how the death of two sons by fire in 1967 compounded Orbison's
private tragedies.) Oddly, there is a way in which the disappearance or the
death of a singer these days doesn't really matter to his or her listeners,
since that person is still present in exactly the same way as before. All the
songs take on a slightly new cast, but the singer still lives in a way that
one's own deceased relatives and friends cannot.

When my girl wanted me back, I dropped Jon's friendship and never 18
tried to regain it—a not-very-commendable way to be. But we were glued
for a while by those banging Orbison notes and those erratic vocals, and
maybe that was enough, or at least all that one could hope for.

Music can block out silence, on dark scary roads and in moments of 19
loneliness. But there's also a sense or two in which a song can create silence: when we're "lost in a song" the rest of the world around us makes,
for all practical purposes, no sound. And in an even more strange way, a
song we love goes silent as we "listen" to it, leaving us in that rather primitive place where all the sounds are interior ones—sounds which can't be
distinguished from feelings, from pulsings and shiverings, from that gut
need to make life stronger than death for at least a few moments.

When "Only the Lonely" faded, that wonderful deejay still knew 20
enough not to say a word. She threw us straight forward, 4:15 A.M., into
"Pretty Woman."

[4] **falsetto:** An artificially high voice used by singers.

EXERCISING VOCABULARY

1. What responsibilities does a bodyguard have? Why does the author refer to the predawn stillness as a "mental bodyguard" (para. 1)? What does the stillness guard against?

2. It's easy to understand how "music can block out silence" (para. 19). But how is it possible, as Corey continues, for music to "create silence," when silence means the absence of sound?

PROBING CONTENT

1. How and where did Corey first learn of Roy Orbison's death? What did the author admire about the way the message was delivered? What was the immediate effect of the news on Corey?

2. What circumstances brought Corey and Jon Cresanti together? What further circumstances solidified their relationship? What part did music in general and Roy Orbison's music in particular play in their friendship?

3. According to the author, what is at the core of Orbison's musical appeal? What message does his music transmit? Why is this message important?

4. What does Corey mean when he writes that "the death of a singer these days doesn't really matter" (para. 17)? How is this a change from Corey's youth?

CONSIDERING CRAFT

1. As a reader, you may strongly identify with the author's feelings in this essay even though you may be unfamiliar with, or not attracted to, the music of Roy Orbison. How does Corey accomplish this? How does his writing give a sense of universality to this piece through his personal connection with one artist's music?

2. In the last paragraph of the essay, Corey returns the reader to the time when Corey first learned of Orbison's death. How does this recalling of the past function in the structure of the essay? What might be accomplished by modeling this technique in your own writing?

RESPONDING TO THE WRITER

Do you agree with Corey that music may open a direct channel into our memory (para. 7)? Choose one song that always moves you backward in time and causes you to refocus on a particular person, place, or event. Explain why this song has such a powerful effect on you.

For a quiz on this reading, go to bedfordstmartins.com/mirror.

Rock of Ages

RICHARD LACAYO

"Pop music is no longer mostly a way that one generation defines itself against its elders," writes Richard Lacayo in "Rock of Ages," first published in the February 26, 2001, issue of *Time* magazine. In fact, Lacayo says, music can bring generations together by encouraging communication between parents and children. Conversations about music allow parents to discuss pop culture with their kids and give children the opportunity to let parents into their world. But how can parents be "cool" with the music their kids listen to without explicitly endorsing lyrics that glorify sex, drugs, and profanity?

A senior writer for the Nation section of *Time* magazine, Lacayo often covers controversial topics including abortion, gun control, and the right to privacy. His work has also been published in the *New York Times*, and he is the coauthor of *Eyewitness: 150 Years of Photojournalism* (1990).

THINKING AHEAD

What kinds of music do your older friends or your parents listen to? What do you think of their choices? Do they listen to the music you like? What similarities and differences do you hear between the music they listen to and the music you choose?

INCREASING VOCABULARY

fevered (adj.) (1)
toddling (adj.) (2)
bonding (n.) (2)
incest (n.) (2)
taboo (n.) (2)
collaborate (v.) (3)
supplanted (v.) (5)

gouging (v.) (5)
decrepitude (n.) (7)
endorse (v.) (8)
pun (n.) (8)
complicit (adj.) (8)
splintered (v.) (10)
unflinching (adj.) (11)

Let's all get up
And dance to a song
That was a hit before
Your mother was born
            —The Beatles

Remember when that song was about your mother? You do? Too   1
bad. In that case, now it's about you. The very thought is enough to
send a chill down the spines of most baby boomers,[1] who already
have plenty of reasons to wonder if they haven't started looking as old as
Paul McCartney. (And remember, he was the Cute Beatle.) At one time it
probably seemed that rock music was entirely yours, a thing that you
could imagine grew out of your own fevered brain. Now a good slice of it
apparently belongs to somebody else, somebody who likes gangsta rap
and tinny kid pop and fight songs from WWF Smackdown![2] It doesn't
help that this week the Grammy for album of the year may go to Eminem,
the white rapper who wants to rape his mother, or at least he says he does
on the album that may get the Grammy. Hey, you're probably old enough
to be his mother. For that matter, so is Elton John, who is taking the risk
of performing a duet with him at the Grammys.

To make things worse, pop music is otherwise going through one of   2
those moments when the general run of things is so toddling—Britney
Spears, Backstreet Boys—that skinny white boys who talk a little tough,
meaning Eminem, get to seem like a big deal. So if you happen to be a
parent in, say, your forties or fifties, nobody would blame you if you just
turned away from pop music altogether. And if you happen to be a
teenager, of course, you might not mind if they did. But the funny thing is,
at the same time that the hard edge of pop gets harder and the soft edge
gets softer, it's plain that rock has also become one of those things, like
pets and baseball, that lets parents and kids find a shared passion. It may
be that Eminem doesn't provide much opportunity for parent-child bonding, unless you're trying to explain why the incest taboo is not just some
stupid rule that Mom invented to be mean. But a lot of baby boomers
have figured out that it's a short trip from the Pink Floyd they once loved
to the Radiohead their kids love now. And a lot of their kids have likewise
found their way back to the music of their parents.

This explains Emily Curtin, twenty-two, who now plays guitar in a   3
New York City rock band. When she was in her late teens in Worcester,
Mass., Emily used to collaborate with her twin younger brothers to make
rock-music-compilation tapes—they called them Kids' Pix—for her parents. The idea was to educate the folks, who already understood the rock
music of their own warmly remembered youth, about newer stuff. "They

---

[1] **ESL** **baby boomers:** People who were born in the United States during a high-birth-rate
    period immediately after World War II.
[2] **ESL** **WWF Smackdown!:** A World Wrestling Federation championship competition.

listened to the tapes all the time," she says. "My mom got into the Magnetic Fields. Dad got into My Bloody Valentine."

In Marshfield, Wis., John Spellman and his wife Jeanne are fiftysome-   4
things who reawoke to rock music as the older ones among their four kids discovered the Beatles, the Grateful Dead and Pink Floyd. "Now we spend time talking about things like how the Dead are not really a rock band," says John. "How they come out of a tradition of classic American blues, from Appalachia and the South." In return, he has picked up from his kids a taste for the Dave Matthews Band and U2, a group he finds "inspirational." Spellman's children even introduced him to music from his youth that he had missed the first time it came along. Through them he discovered Bob Marley, the reggae[3] star whose supreme moment was in the 1970s.

Even if guitar-band rock is a niche market now, supplanted by hip-   5
hop as the reigning format of pop music, it still qualifies as the lingua franca[4] of pop culture. Roughly a half-century after Elvis recorded "Heartbreak Hotel," nearly everybody under seventy has some emotional attachment to electrified music with a beat. As a consequence, pop music is no longer mostly a way that one generation defines itself against its elders. The baby boomers' own parents grew up with Frank Sinatra, Rosemary Clooney and Nat "King" Cole. Rock was such an unmistakable break with that creamy tradition that teenagers of the 1960s and '70s understood it right away as music to fight Mom and Dad to, especially since their parents usually hated the stuff. Now kids have to accept that most of their own music is not so different from what their parents had, parents who grew up on Lou Reed, to say nothing of Iggy Pop, a guy who was gouging his skin with broken glass when Marilyn Manson was still sticking thumbtacks in his tricycle tires.

But that also makes it easier for them to comprehend the music their   6
parents used to love. This helps explain the watershed[5] success of the *Beatles 1* album, which topped *Billboard*'s album charts for eight weeks and has sold more than 20 million copies worldwide. You don't score numbers like that just from the middle-aged Beatlemaniacs still shaking their imaginary moptops.[6] It requires massive sales to the teenagers and twentysomethings who buy most records. The phenomenon of that album followed the success of Santana's *Supernatural*, which paired a survivor of the '60s with up-to-the-minute acts like Lauryn Hill, Everlast and Rob Thomas from Matchbox 20. And before Santana, there was Aerosmith and Eric Clapton, Neil Young and Tina Turner, Sting and Cher, David Bowie and Bruce Springsteen. All of them sustained long careers by adding younger fans to the ones who remember them from before they got reading glasses.

---

[3] **ESL reggae:** Popular music of Jamaican origin that combines native styles with elements of rock and soul music.
[4] **ESL lingua franca:** Latin for common or shared language.
[5] **watershed:** Indicating a significant change.
[6] **ESL moptops:** Mop-like haircuts that were popularized by the Beatles.

What all this means is, simply by pointing out to your children that   7
you understand that Phish owes a lot to the Grateful Dead, you can distract them briefly from your otherwise evident decrepitude. There are already institutions that have positioned themselves to benefit from that fact,
adapting rock to the family-theme-park phenomenon. The Experience
Music Project in Seattle, which opened last year, aims to be a place where
parents can explain to their kids that James Brown is the old guy who
sounds like Mystikal, and kids can tell their parents that Mystikal is the
young guy who sounds like James Brown. The Rock 'n' Roll Hall of Fame
in Cleveland, Ohio, even offers guidance to local high school teachers on
how to work rock history into their lesson plans. This will make it easier
for parents to talk to their kids about the music of their own youth,
though it also opens the way to a day when sophomores will get detention
for not turning in their term papers on Frank Zappa.

All the same, as a means to reach kids, rock is more complicated than   8
pets and baseball. It has never been completely domesticated by age and
commercial calculation. One way that rock bands keep their distance
from respectability these days is by shouting "F—" a few dozen times on
every album. (Or even "I wanna f—you like an animal," as Trent Reznor
famously offered on one of his Nine Inch Nails albums.) Rock is still all
tied up with sex and drugs, and it's a supremely subtle parent who can
share all kinds of music with her kids without also seeming to endorse the
troubling stuff. On this past New Year's Eve, the Experience Music Project sponsored a sold-out dance party that attracted 1,200 people, including parents, teenagers and even younger children. The aim was to provide
something with the feel of a rave[7] party but without the drug scene that
goes with it. Then again, the main stage attraction was the band Crystal
Method, whose name is an obvious pun on crystal meth, the amphetamine-
based party drug. "A band can call itself what it wants to call itself," says
Robert Santelli, deputy director of public programs at EMP. Which is
true, of course. But the adults who offer the band to kids are inescapably
complicit in any message the band conveys. It all gets complicated.

The skanky[8] side of pop music is something that Sheila Brown turns   9
to her advantage. Brown is an executive secretary at Tribune Interactive,
part of the Tribune Co., the Chicago-based media empire. Her daughters
Nnyla, twenty-three, and Rayna, thirteen, love some kinds of rap. So does
she. And the parts she doesn't love—the trash talk, the relentless treatment of women as nothing more than walking booties[9]—give her a chance
to discuss with her daughters just why she doesn't love them. "We discuss
things openly about sex and relationships," says Brown. "What's tacky[10]
and what's not tacky. Sometimes the kids are more embarrassed by things
they see in music videos than I am." Nnyla agrees that music provides a

---

[7] **ESL rave:** A party or dance, usually featuring electronic music.
[8] **ESL skanky:** Slang word for "disgusting."
[9] **ESL booties:** Slang word referring to the buttocks.
[10] **ESL tacky:** Tasteless or of low quality.

way for her and her mother "to talk about sex more than we might otherwise. Mom will say she doesn't like a song because it makes women look like sex objects, that rap music and rap videos take women back twenty to thirty years. I thought about it, and I can see that."

Even when you like the music you hear them listening to, there are reasons why it takes hard work to share music with kids. Pop-music turnover is faster than ever. The group that gets two or three successful albums in a row is harder to find. No sooner do you figure out who Blink-182 is, than Blink-183 takes its place. And music is more splintered into niche markets and tribal followings. It can be tricky to navigate the by-ways of postpunk and trip-hop, ambient techno and speed metal. But remember, there was a time when you had no trouble telling the difference between surf music and Merseybeat.

And what do you do when your kids find their way back to the very music you always hated as a kid? You try to steer them to the iconoclas-tic[11] New York Dolls; they stumble into the cheesy pyrotechnics[12] of Kiss. You send them off to discover early Chicago; they come back with Kansas. And what if, after all your careful guidance, they still love Limp Bizkit and Papa Roach? What if they still go out and buy that stuff by Eminem? At that point only the wisdom of age will do. Go back and take an unflinching look at your old record collection. There's probably a Black Sabbath album in there somewhere.

EXERCISING VOCABULARY

1. In paragraph 5, Lacayo suggests that guitar-band rock is only "a niche market now." In paragraph 10, the author states that music is now more divided into "niche markets." What is a niche? How significant is something in a niche? If certain types of music are confined to niches, what does this say about their popularity and visibility?

2. The author argues that popular music "has never been completely domesti-cated" (para. 8). What does it mean to domesticate something? To what or whom is the term usually applied? What are its implications? What does this mean with regard to rock music?

PROBING CONTENT

1. What is it about today's music that is opening up conversations between parents and children? Why is this surprising?

2. According to the authors, what kind of music dominates today's popular music? What kind of music still forms the most common basis for popular culture? Why is there a difference between the two?

---

[11] **iconoclastic:** Attacking beliefs or institutions.
[12] **pyrotechnics:** A fireworks display.

3. How have older musicians and groups retained their audiences? Why is the ability to do this essential to their continued success? What evidence do the authors offer to prove that this is happening?

4. What was ironic about the dance sponsored by the Experience Music Project? What dilemma did that present for the adult sponsors of the event?

CONSIDERING CRAFT

1. When the author refers to the example of Sheila Brown and her two daughters in paragraph 9, why does he suddenly shift language patterns to use words like *skanky, trash talk,* and *walking booties*? What effect does this shift in language have on you? How does it affect the impact of his example? What would be lost if the writer had simply continued using standard English?

2. This essay is filled with the names of musicians and music groups. You probably are not familiar with every one of them. Do you think that the author expects every reader to be? Why are so many of these references included? What effect does their inclusion have on your reading?

RESPONDING TO THE WRITER

In your experience, do people of different generations seem to be drawn to the same musical styles and performers? Cite specific examples to reinforce your answer. How tolerant are people of music they may not appreciate or approve of? Why do you think this is true?

For a quiz on this reading, go to bedfordstmartins.com/mirror.

Does Sex Still Sell?

KEITH GIRARD AND LIZ SKINNER

Why are sexy images such an important part of music marketing, especially for female artists? Has it always been that way, or has the power of sex to sell music gradually been increasing? In "Does Sex Still Sell?," which appeared in *Billboard* magazine on January 21, 2004, Keith Girard and Liz Skinner make a surprising claim: There is such a thing as "too sexy," at least in our post-September 11 world. Mediocre record sales of highly provocative artists like Britney Spears and Pink may attest to this. "In times of trouble, strong, stable, supportive people are favored," said one researcher who studies how social and economic factors influence human preferences. "When times are good, we tend to favor the fun person." This may be good news for those female performers who chafe at the sexual marketing thought to be necessary for strong CD sales.

Keith Girard was editor in chief of *Billboard* magazine when this piece was published. Previously, he wrote for *Crain's* of New York. Liz Skinner is a reporter for *Bloomberg News*, based in Washington, D.C.

THINKING AHEAD

Who is your favorite female vocalist? What makes her popular? Who buys her music? What part does sexuality play in her music, her appearance, her performances, and the way her music is marketed?

INCREASING VOCABULARY

divas (n.) (2)	abating (v.) (16)
edgy (adj.) (3)	demographic (adj.) (17)
mediocre (adj.) (4)	indulgences (n.) (22)
alluring (adj.) (10)	resurgence (n.) (24)
nuances (n.) (11)	introspective (adj.) (26)
crass (adj.) (12)	exudes (v.) (26)
bemoans (v.) (14)	blatantly (adv.) (29)
	hype (n.) (32)

Christina vamps like a burlesque stripper. Britney's gone from school-girl to slut. Pink is punk. 1

    Many of music's reigning divas are partying like it's 1999, even though the world has become a darker, more uncertain and more anxious place since September 11, 2001. 2

With the economy in a funk[1] and record sales down for three years   3
running, even established artists are sexing it up—no doubt encouraged
by edgy industry executives.

The problem is, the public just doesn't seem to be in the mood for it,   4
and the recent mediocre album sales by Spears, Pink and similar artists
may reflect a classic case of mismarketing.

"When social and economic times are more threatening and pes-   5
simistic, we actually prefer others with more mature facial, body and personality characteristics," says Terry Pettijohn, a Ph.D. social psychologist
at Mercyhurst College in Erie, Pennsylvania.

If Pettijohn's observations are accurate, then industry executives who   6
are pushing artists to "tart it up"[2] are miscalculating the market and could
be damaging careers.

"Audiences are listening to lyrics more," says Ron Vos, president/chief   7
executive of Hi Frequency Marketing in North Carolina. "They're focused
on content and story line, not dancing and having fun, and they want the
artist to reflect that."

Indeed, female artists who are succeeding on the radio and on the   8
charts have tapped into the nation's post-September 11 soul-searching.

Vos, whose firm worked with Avril Lavigne and Norah Jones, says   9
these artists are writing music that's about being in touch with your values. They portray themselves as self-made people who write about their
feelings, he says.

Sex certainly sells. The concept has been around as long as advertis-   10
ing. But Lavigne and Jones reflect a different kind of sexuality that's much
subtler, more genuine and thus more alluring in a time of crisis.

Given the national mood, such nuances could easily be the difference   11
between strong and mediocre sales.

One of the hottest breakthrough groups of last year, rock band   12
Evanescence, is fronted by Amy Lee, who is appalled by the crass marketing of some pop stars. "Talking bad about Britney is like beating a dead
horse; I won't even go there," she says.

But what really bothers Lee are female artists who are good writers or   13
good singers but have gone from being "really classy and cool to just
stripping it all away."

Jewel, for example, has gone from folk songstress to cover girl, and 40-   14
something Sheryl Crow struts onstage in hot pants even as she bemoans
that other artists are being marketed like "porn stars."

"Obviously, sex is the most basic thing that you can sell," Lee says. "I   15
mean, you sell yourself, and I just hate it."

From Spears' kiss with Madonna at the MTV Video Music Awards to   16
Pink's onstage antics at the Billboard Music Awards, the trend toward
trampiness shows no signs of abating.

---

[1] **funk**: A state of depression.
[2] ESL **tart it up**: Increase emphasis on sex; dress or act provocatively.

But some academic research suggests that it runs counter to current   17
economic, social and demographic trends.

Last spring, Pettijohn and University of Georgia professor Abraham   18
Tesser presented a paper to the American Psychological Society in Atlanta
that examined how the social and economic environment affects human
preferences.

"In times of trouble, strong, stable, supportive people are favored," he   19
says. "When times are good, we tend to favor the fun person."

To reach that conclusion, the researchers studied the public's prefer-   20
ences for actresses between 1932 and 1995.

Individuals preferred smaller eyes, thinner cheeks and larger chins in   21
bad times, and women with larger eyes, fuller cheeks and smaller chins in
good times, the study found.

"The U.S. is always going back and forth between our puritan[3] val-   22
ues and our need for indulgences," says Sharon Livingston of the Livingston Group, a Windham, New Hampshire, marketing and research
firm.

Currently, songs with a mellow, introspective approach are finding a   23
receptive U.S. audience, in part because of the confusion and sense of
change in the wake of September 11, according to Ball State University
pop culture expert Richard Aquila.

That mood plays into the resurgence of the singer/songwriter, where   24
audiences are eager to hear what the individual has to say, he says.

"There's been a turn toward traditional values," Aquila adds.   25

Alicia Keys is representative of the trend. Her songs are introspective   26
and soulful. Her image, while sexual, also exudes strength and character.
Not surprisingly, her latest album is doing well on the charts.

Norah Jones is sexy, Livingston says. But "she's using libido[4] in a   27
gentle way and talking about relationships. It's a more constructive use of
her libido, but she's still creating interest and intrigue."

She's saying, " 'Come be with me, and you'll feel good about   28
yourself,' " she explains.

Spears, of course, has played the sex card most often and most bla-   29
tantly in the face of declining sales.

Her biggest single, ". . . Baby One More Time," cut when her image   30
was more wholesome, spent 39 weeks on the singles charts in 1998, including seven weeks in the top spot.

Her last single to hit No. 1 on the charts was "I'm a Slave 4 U" in   31
2001. It spent one week at the top.

Despite massive hype, Spears' latest album is posting only so-so sales.   32
And Pink's latest release is suffering as well. Sales of "Try This" have
fallen far short of her previous blockbuster album.

---

[3] **ESL** **puritan:** Adhering to a strict moral code.
[4] **libido:** Sex drive.

According to a source, her label is privately worried that she has been 33
tarting it up too much. For her part, Pink says artists are just using what
they've got.

"I don't think there's anything wrong with being sexy, but people use 34
what they have," she says. "If people have a great voice, then you use
your voice; if you have a great mind, then you speak a lot; if you have a
great body, then you take your clothes off."

That may work if you're 20-something, but Evanescence's Lee isn't 35
the only person who finds the trend disturbing among such established,
talented female artists as Toni Braxton, Liz Phair and LeAnn Rimes.

Gina Vivinetto, pop music critic for Florida's *St. Petersburg Times,* 36
noted in an article last summer that it's as if someone had issued a memo
to every woman in rock. "No matter how seriously she once took herself,
no matter how good her voice or her level of talent, she must start looking
like a tramp."[5]

EXERCISING VOCABULARY

1. Amy Lee uses a play on words in paragraph 13 when she describes female
   artists who depend on sex for record sales as "just stripping it all away." Explain the dual meaning of this expression as it is used here.

2. In paragraphs 10 and 11, the authors mention the nuances between various
   expressions of sexuality. How much difference does a nuance indicate? What
   is ironic about a nuance making a substantial difference in record sales?

PROBING CONTENT

1. According to psychologist Terry Pettijohn, how do social and economic conditions affect our preferences? What effect do these preferences have on music
   sales?

2. What kind of songs were popular when this article was published? To what
   do the authors attribute this?

3. Which pop music star "has played the sex card most often"? What effect has
   this had on sales of her music?

CONSIDERING CRAFT

1. Describe the authors' attitude toward female singers using sex to sell their
   music. Find several words or phrases that imply this attitude. In contrast,
   what language do the authors use to describe female vocalists who do not
   use sex as their primary marketing strategy? How do these language choices
   reveal the authors' attitudes?

[5] **ESL** tramp: A woman of questionable morals.

2. The authors quote a number of sources. Identify four or five of them and draw some conclusions about why their thoughts and ideas are included here. What effect does their inclusion have on the essay?

RESPONDING TO THE WRITER

Look again at the photograph that opened this chapter. Are female pop stars ignoring their talent in favor of too much emphasis on sexuality? Can the same be said about male pop stars? Why or why not?

For a quiz on this reading, go to bedfordstmartins.com/mirror.

The Digital Music Renaissance

ANDREW LEONARD

According to the January 17, 2005, issue of *Newsweek*, twenty million music tracks were legally downloaded in 2003. In 2004, that number was 140 million. That's fourteen million albums. How much time and money do you spend managing your music collection? For writer Andrew Leonard, whose essay "The Digital Music Renaissance" first appeared on *Salon.com* on July 1, 2004, there is no joy like a 120 gigabyte hard drive backed up with the 2,700 songs he has carefully collected. Leonard asserts that the world of digitized music has reenergized his appetite for music, made him a happier, better consumer—and even a bigger spender, despite the record industry's attempts to put the brakes on digital access. In Leonard's house, the future is already here.

Andrew Leonard is the editor of *Salon.com*'s technology and business department and also a contributing editor to *Newsweek*. He has been covering the Web since 1994, and his work has appeared in the *New York Times Book Review*, *The Nation*, *Wired*, and the *Far Eastern Economic Review*. He is also the author of *Bots: The Origin of New Species* (1997).

THINKING AHEAD

Do you download music to your computer? Do you own an iPod? How have these innovations changed the music industry, music listeners, and the ways they relate to each other?

INCREASING VOCABULARY

core (adj.) (1)

nefarious (adj.) (5)

irate (adj.) (6)

avid (adj.) (7)

conducive (adj.) (7)

rife (adj.) (8)

purveyors (n.) (8)

discerning (adj.) (9)

cloistered (adj.) (11)

surreptitiously (adv.) (14)

inept (adj.) (15)

I bought a 120 gigabyte external hard drive to back up my music collection on Sunday. It was a moment of relief. I now have about 13 gigs of music—around 2,700 songs—on my home computer, and the prospect of losing it all in a hard drive crash has been giving me the cold sweats. All those evenings spent ripping my own CDs, transferring the mixes friends had made for me, making sure all the identifying information was correct—I couldn't bear the thought of doing it all over again. For the rest of my life, backing up my entertainment files is going to be one of my core

1

missions. When I send my kids off to college, one of my parting words of wisdom will be, "Remember to back up your music files!"

Amid the relief, there was also satisfaction. Thanks to computers and the Internet, I am now a better, happier and more productive consumer of music than I have ever been. I am exposed to more new music, I listen to more old music, and I purchase more of all kinds of music. I've spent more money buying music this year than in any of the previous 10 years.

The music industry hates this. By their every indication, record executives appear to be unhappy that I am more engaged with popular music. They are busy cooking up half-baked copy protection schemes that will prevent me from ripping[1] my own newly purchased CDs. They are pushing legislation intended to criminalize all kinds of behavior and technology. Rather than make it easier for me to spend money, they would rather I return to the neolithic[2] times when if I heard a song on the radio I liked, I would have to trudge to the record store and spend $18 on bloated filler. Why am I not excited?

I'll return to their nuttiness in a minute. But first let me explain in more detail why I'm experiencing a musical renaissance in my own head.

Some people might wonder why a grown man would spend hours every night ripping CDs he already owns to a computer — unless his nefarious plan is to make them all available on peer-to-peer file-trading networks. After all, there *is* usually some decrease in sound quality when you compress a music file. Why voluntarily listen to lower quality sound?

Those people have yet to experience the joy of creating playlists from one's entire collection, or the surprise that comes from iTunes randomly playing some tune you'd forgotten you owned or never listened to that closely. Or maybe they don't appreciate how much easier making mixes for their friends is when one's whole collection is point-and-click accessible. I suppose there are still people who don't understand how much more fun it is to have all your music at your immediate command. (Or how frustrating it is when it isn't! My 9-year-old daughter became irate when I told her she could not burn a CD from iTunes on the family computer, because it was streaming iTunes over my wireless network from my work computer in the basement. To her, everything should be accessible, all the time. The Internet already seems to come through the air, why not all of popular music, too?)

Having my whole collection available on my hard drive combined with the opportunities presented by the rest of the online universe of music psychologically reengaged me with music. I'm not talking about peer-to-peer networks — I was never an avid file-trader (though I appreciate how the spread of such networks finally forced the industry to allow things like iTunes). I'm talking about the creation of a new world conducive to choice and experiment — and purchase — that is a direct result of music being more accessible than ever before.

[1] **ripping:** Copying.
[2] **neolithic:** From the Stone Age; outdated.

This includes things like Salon's own Wednesday Morning Download,   8
which provides a nifty little human filter pointing to free or cheap downloads of singles that I find irresistible. The Web is rife with people recommending music! This includes sites like Music from TV Commercials—so if I hear a snippet[3] of some cool tune on a Bud Light commercial, I can look it up on the Web and be watching a video of the band in seconds. This includes, of course, iTunes, and all the other commercial online purveyors of music. I was shocked, a week or two ago, that an indie-rock, alt-country loving friend of mine had never heard the album *Reckoning* by R.E.M. Minutes later, I had purchased it for him from iTunes and we were listening to it.

Ease of access enriches our lives. I am not just a happier consumer   9
now; I am a *better* consumer, more discerning, more informed, more confident to pull the trigger on a purchase. I read a review of an album on the day it comes out, and before night has fallen, I own it—something that rarely happened before. Previously, by the time I got to the record store, I had long forgotten the positive reviews I might have read. And listening to so much music feeds a virtuous cycle: The more I hear, the more I want to hear.

But the record industry still doesn't get it. A couple of nights ago, I   10
searched iTunes for the song "Days Go By" by Dirty Vegas. I found it, but was annoyed to learn that it had been designated as "album only." In other words, I could not purchase the song for 99 cents—I had to buy the whole album. So, naturally, I bought nothing at all. I don't like having my arm twisted. Again, I'm not a file-trader, but that kind of heavy-handed bait-and-switch treatment might very well encourage me to look for the song on Kazaa or to ask a friend to burn it for me. So now the studio, the artist, the song writer and the retail outlet are all out their percentage of my purchase.

This kind of behavior is a microcosm of everything that the industry   11
has been doing wrong for years. I won't buy CDs that I can't rip to my hard drive. If legislation is passed that outlaws my CD burner and prevents me from making mixes for my friends, I'll return to my cloistered past, unaware and unengaged with all the music being created in the world. And if I'm exposed to less music, I'll buy less music.

I can understand the fear that motivates record company executives.   12
As is blindingly obvious, the economics of recorded music have changed. Never mind Kazaa or even iTunes; as I've written before, the reality that the 13 gigs of music on my external hard drive can be picked up and plugged into my neighbor's computer is a chilling shot across the bow to every studio interested in profiting from its backlist of recorded music.

I don't want to get bogged down in questions of whether it would be   13
right or wrong to slurp up the record collections of my friends wholesale (I will concede, the prospect seems icky). The laws of supply and demand

---

[3] **snippet:** A small piece or part.

have a way of sidestepping morality. Like it or not, the day is coming—soon—when your neighborhood flea market will, for some laughable fee, sell you 50,000 songs on a portable hard drive the size of your wallet.

The only way to stop this would be to create a music industry Big   14
Brother[4] with the power to look into each and every one of our computers and scour it clean of anything we don't individually have a deed signed in blood for. This is, of course, exactly what the industry is trying to do. The CD *Contraband*, by Velvet Revolver, a band made up of former members of Guns N' Roses and the front man of the Stone Temple Pilots, comes equipped with copy protection software, that, like spyware, surreptitiously installs itself on your computer when you pop the CD into the drive, and then, theoretically, prevents you from ripping the CD.

Early reports indicate that *Contraband*'s copy protection is hopelessly   15
inept and easily circumvented. But what can't be done technologically may be achievable legislatively. The Inducing Infringement of Copyright Act, moving through Congress at alarming speed, could potentially outlaw, say its critics, everything from CD burners to iPods. Either way, there appears to be no sign that the industry has learned the obvious lessons of the last few years—that making it harder to listen to music can only backfire.

Instead of trying to prevent me from enjoying my own music, the   16
recording industry should be working as hard as it can to get *everything* online and available, cheaply. It should be making it easier for me to rip and burn to my heart's content. Because when I'm happy listening to music, it doesn't take much encouragement for me to spend more money. I've got about 90 gigs left on my hard drive to fill up!

EXERCISING VOCABULARY

1. In paragraph 10, Leonard expresses his dissatisfaction with having to buy an entire album to own one song. He accuses the record company of subjecting him to "bait-and-switch treatment." What does this expression mean in sales? What does Leonard's use of it here imply?

2. The author refers to the music industry's behavior as "a microcosm of everything that the industry has been doing wrong for years" (para. 11). Explain what a microcosm is and how the term applies here.

PROBING CONTENT

1. How has Andrew Leonard become "a better, happier, and more productive consumer of music" (para. 2)? Why has this happened?

2. Why is the behavior of consumers like Leonard alarming to record companies? To what extent does Leonard admit that their concerns are justified?

---

[4] **Big Brother:** The leader of the totalitarian government in George Orwell's 1949 dystopian novel *1984*; government surveillance.

3. If Congress should pass a bill like the Inducing Infringement of Copyright Act, what might result? How would this affect music consumers? How would it affect the music industry?

CONSIDERING CRAFT

1. Clearly Leonard is opposed to tighter music-industry controls on the way he listens to music. How might he have expanded this essay to offer a more balanced view of this topic? Would that make his essay more or less effective? Why?

2. In paragraph 3, Leonard begins to criticize the record industry, but in paragraph 4 he leaves that argument to explain why he personally feels so strongly about this topic. Then in paragraph 10 he returns to his criticism. What do you think the author hoped to accomplish by using this organizational strategy? How effective do you think this strategy is in this essay?

RESPONDING TO THE WRITER

Is Leonard's fear of "a music industry Big Brother" (para. 14) justified? How likely is it that CD burners and iPods will be outlawed? Support your opinion.

For a quiz on this reading, go to bedfordstmartins.com/mirror.

How Hip-Hop Holds Blacks Back

JOHN H. MCWHORTER

How has rap music changed the conversation about race in America? Are the harsh lyrics of some rap artists meant to shock, entertain, enlighten — or just sell records? In "How Hip-Hop Holds Blacks Back," which first appeared in *City Journal* in the summer of 2003, scholar and author John H. McWhorter says that this music has become a destructive force in the black community: "By reinforcing the stereotypes that long hindered blacks, and by teaching young blacks that a thuggish adversarial stance is the properly 'authentic' response to a presumptively racist society, rap retards black success." McWhorter traces the rise of hip-hop from its light-hearted beginnings to the "angry, oppositional" stance that he believes transformed rap into the multibillion dollar industry it is today.

John H. McWhorter writes extensively about linguistics, race, and cultural issues. Currently an associate professor of linguistics at the University of California at Berkeley, McWhorter has written articles for the *Wall Street Journal*, the *New York Times*, *The New Republic*, the *Washington Post*, the *Chronicle of Higher Education*, and the *National Review*. He does regular commentaries for *All Things Considered* and has appeared on the TV shows *Politically Incorrect* and *Good Morning, America*. His books include the best-selling *Losing the Race: Self-Sabotage in Black America* (2000), *The Power of Babel: A Natural History of Language* (2002), and *Authentically Black: Essays for the Black Silent Majority* (2003). His most recent book is *Defining Creole* (2005).

THINKING AHEAD

Is hip-hop music an accurate representation of black culture? Why does gangsta rap outsell all other hip-hop music? To what extent have your values, standards, and ideas been formed by the music you listen to?

INCREASING VOCABULARY

ambling (v.) (2)
exempt (adj.) (2)
mainstream (adj.) (2)
bellicose (adj.) (3)
retards (v.) (4)
suffuses (v.) (5)
insidious (adj.) (6)
ebullient (adj.) (8)
edgy (adj.) (9)
ominous (adj.) (9)

misogynistic (adj.) (16)
sinuous (adj.) (19)
nihilistic (adj.) (26)
extricate (v.) (30)
disseminating (v.) (32)
debilitating (adj.) (32)
decrying (v.) (36)
rampant (adj.) (36)
bigotry (n.) (36)

Not long ago, I was having lunch in a KFC[1] in Harlem, sitting near eight African-American boys, aged about 14. Since 1) it was 1:30 on a school day, 2) they were carrying book bags, and 3) they seemed to be in no hurry, I assumed they were skipping school. They were extremely loud and unruly, tossing food at one another and leaving it on the floor.

Black people ran the restaurant and made up the bulk of the customers, but it was hard to see much healthy "black community" here. After repeatedly warning the boys to stop throwing food and keep quiet, the manager finally told them to leave. The kids ignored her. Only after she called a male security guard did they start slowly making their way out, tauntingly circling the restaurant before ambling off. These teens clearly weren't monsters, but they seemed to consider themselves exempt from public norms of behavior—as if they had begun to check out of mainstream society.

What struck me most, though, was how fully the boys' music—hard-edged rap, preaching bone-deep dislike of authority—provided them with a continuing soundtrack to their antisocial behavior. So completely was rap ingrained in their consciousness that every so often, one or another of them would break into cocky, expletive-laden rap lyrics, accompanied by the angular, bellicose gestures typical of rap performance. A couple of his buddies would then join him. Rap was a running decoration in their conversation.

Many writers and thinkers see a kind of informed political engagement, even a revolutionary potential, in rap and hip-hop. They couldn't be more wrong. By reinforcing the stereotypes that long hindered blacks, and by teaching young blacks that a thuggish adversarial stance is the properly "authentic" response to a presumptively racist society, rap retards black success.

The venom that suffuses rap had little place in black popular culture—indeed, in black attitudes—before the 1960s. The hip-hop ethos can trace its genealogy to the emergence in that decade of a black ideology that equated black strength and authentic black identity with a militantly adversarial stance toward American society. In the angry new mood, captured by Malcolm X's upraised fist, many blacks (and many more white liberals) began to view black crime and violence as perfectly natural, even appropriate, responses to the supposed dehumanization and poverty inflicted by a racist society. Briefly, this militant spirit, embodied above all in the Black Panthers,[2] infused black popular culture, from the plays of LeRoi Jones to "blaxploitation" movies, like Melvin Van Peebles's *Sweet Sweetbacks' Baadasssss Song*, which celebrated the black criminal rebel as a hero.

But blaxploitation and similar genres burned out fast. The memory of whites blatantly stereotyping blacks was too recent for the typecasting

---

[1] **ESL** **KFC:** An acronym for Kentucky Fried Chicken, a fast-food restaurant.
[2] **Black Panthers:** Members of a militant group of African Americans who were active in the 1960s and 1970s.

in something like *Sweet Sweetbacks' Baadasssss Song* not to offend
many blacks. Observed black historian Lerone Bennett: "There is a certain grim white humor in the fact that the black marches and demon-
strations of the 1960s reached artistic fulfillment" with "provocative
and ultimately insidious reincarnations of all the Sapphires and Studds
of yesteryear."

Early rap mostly steered clear of the Sapphires and Studds, beginning   7
not as a growl from below but as happy party music. The first big rap hit,
the Sugar Hill Gang's 1978 "Rapper's Delight," featured a catchy bass
groove that drove the music forward, as the jolly rapper celebrated himself as a ladies' man and a great dancer. Soon, kids across America were
rapping along with the nonsense chorus:

> I said a hip, hop, the hippie, the hippie,
> to the hip-hip hop, ah you don't stop
> the rock it to the bang bang boogie, say
> up jump the boogie,
> to the rhythm of the boogie, the beat.

A string of ebullient raps ensued in the months ahead. At the time, I   8
assumed it was a harmless craze, certain to run out of steam soon.

But rap took a dark turn in the early 1980s, as this "bubble gum"   9
music gave way to a "gangsta" style that picked up where blaxploitation
left off. Now top rappers began to write edgy lyrics celebrating street warfare or drugs and promiscuity. Grandmaster Flash's ominous 1982 hit,
"The Message," with its chorus, "It's like a jungle sometimes, it makes me
wonder how I keep from going under," marked the change in sensibility.
It depicted ghetto life as profoundly desolate:

> You grow in the ghetto, living second rate
> And your eyes will sing a song of deep hate.
> The places you play and where you stay
> Looks like one great big alley way.
> You'll admire all the numberbook takers,
> Thugs, pimps and pushers, and the big money makers.

Music critics fell over themselves to praise "The Message," treating it   10
as the poetry of the streets — as the elite media has characterized hip-hop
ever since. The song's grim fatalism struck a chord; twice, I've heard
blacks in audiences for talks on race cite the chorus to underscore a point
about black victimhood. So did the warning it carried: "Don't push me,
'cause I'm close to the edge," menacingly raps Melle Mel. The ultimate
message of "The Message" — that ghetto life is so hopeless that an explosion of violence is both justified and imminent — would become a hip-hop
mantra in the years ahead.

The angry, oppositional stance that "The Message" reintroduced   11
into black popular culture transformed rap from a fad into a multibillion-dollar industry that sold more than 80 million records in the U.S.
in 2002 — nearly 13 percent of all recordings sold. To rap producers like

Russell Simmons, earlier black pop was just sissy music. He despised the "soft, unaggressive music (and non-threatening images)" of artists like Michael Jackson or Luther Vandross. "So the first chance I got," he says, "I did exactly the opposite."

In the two decades since "The Message," hip-hop performers have 12 churned out countless rap numbers that celebrate a ghetto life of unending violence and criminality. Schooly D's "PSK What Does It Mean?" is a case in point:

> Copped my pistols, jumped into the ride.
> Got at the bar, copped some flack,
> Copped some cheeba-cheeba, it wasn't wack.
> Got to the place, and who did I see?
> A sucka-ass nigga tryin to sound like me.
> Put my pistol up against his head—
> I said, "Sucka-ass nigga, I should shoot you dead."

The protagonist of a rhyme by KRS-One (a hip-hop star who would 13 later speak out against rap violence) actually pulls the trigger:

> Knew a drug dealer by the name of Peter—
> Had to buck him down with my 9 millimeter.

Police forces became marauding invaders in the gangsta-rap imagina- 14 tion. The late West Coast rapper Tupac Shakur expressed the attitude:

> Ya gotta know how to shake the snakes, nigga,
> 'Cause the police love to break a nigga,
> Send him upstate 'cause they straight up hate the nigga.

Shakur's anti-police tirade seems tame, however, compared with Ice- 15 T's infamous "Cop Killer":

> I got my black shirt on.
> I got my black gloves on.
> I got my ski mask on.
> This shit's been too long.
>
> I got my 12-gauge sawed-off.
> I got my headlights turned off.
> I'm 'bout to bust some shots off.
> I'm 'bout to dust some cops off. . . .
>
> I'm 'bout to kill me somethin'
> A pig stopped me for nuthin'!
> Cop killer, better you than me.
> Cop killer, fuck police brutality! . . .
>
> Die, die, die pig, die!
> Fuck the police! . . .
> Fuck the police yeah!

Rap also began to offer some of the most icily misogynistic music   16
human history has ever known. Here's Schooly D again:

Tell you now, brother, this ain't no joke,
She got me to the crib, she laid me on the bed,
I fucked her from my toes to the top of my head.
I finally realized the girl was a whore,
Gave her ten dollars, she asked me for some more.

Jay-Z's "Is That Yo Bitch?" mines similar themes: 17

I don't love 'em, I fuck 'em.
I don't chase 'em, I duck 'em.
I replace 'em with another one. . . .
She be all on my dick.

Or, as N.W.A. (an abbreviation of "Niggers with Attitude") tersely   18
sums up the hip-hop worldview: "Life ain't nothin' but bitches and
money."

Rap's musical accompaniment mirrors the brutality of rap lyrics in its   19
harshness and repetition. Simmons fashions his recordings in contempt for
euphony.[3] "What we used for melody was implied melody, and what
we used for music was sounds—beats, scratches, stuff played backward,
nothing pretty or sweet." The success of hip-hop has resulted in an ironic
reversal. In the seventies, screaming hard rock was in fashion among young
whites, while sweet, sinuous funk and soul ruled the black airwaves—a
difference I was proud of. But in the eighties, rock quieted down, and
black music became the assault on the ears and soul. Anyone who grew
up in urban America during the eighties won't soon forget the young men
strolling down streets, blaring this sonic weapon from their boom boxes,
with defiant glares daring anyone to ask them to turn it down.

Hip-hop exploded into popular consciousness at the same time as the   20
music video, and rappers were soon all over MTV, reinforcing in images
the ugly world portrayed in rap lyrics. Video after video features rap stars
flashing jewelry, driving souped-up[4] cars, sporting weapons, angrily ges-
ticulating at the camera, and cavorting with interchangeable, mindlessly
gyrating, scantily clad women.

Of course, not all hip-hop is belligerent or profane—entire CDs of   21
gang-bangin', police-baiting, woman-bashing invective would get old fast
to most listeners. But it's the nastiest rap that sells best, and the nastiest
cuts that make a career. As I write, the top ten best-selling hip-hop recordings are 50 Cent (currently with the second-best-selling record in the nation among all musical genres), Bone Crusher, Lil' Kim, Fabolous, Lil' Jon
and the East Side Boyz, Cam'ron Presents the Diplomats, Busta Rhymes,
Scarface, Mobb Deep, and Eminem. Every one of these groups or performers personifies willful, staged opposition to society—Lil' Jon and

[3] euphony: A pleasing combination of sounds.
[4] ESL souped-up: Modified for greater speed.

crew even regale us with a song called "Don't Give a Fuck"—and every one celebrates the ghetto as "where it's at." Thus, the occasional dutiful songs in which a rapper urges men to take responsibility for their kids or laments senseless violence are mere garnish. Keeping the thug front and center has become the quickest and most likely way to become a star.

No hip-hop luminary[5] has worked harder than Sean "P. Diddy"   22
Combs, the wildly successful rapper, producer, fashion mogul, and CEO of Bad Boy Records, to cultivate a gangsta image—so much so that he's blurred the line between playing the bad boy and really being one. Combs may have grown up middle-class in Mount Vernon, New York, and even have attended Howard University for a while, but he's proven he can gang-bang with the worst. Cops charged Combs with possession of a deadly weapon in 1995. In 1999, he faced charges for assaulting a rival record executive. Most notoriously, police charged him that year with firing a gun at a nightclub in response to an insult, injuring three bystanders, and with fleeing the scene with his entourage (including then-pal Jennifer "J. Lo" Lopez). Combs got off, but his young rapper protege Jamal "Shyne" Barrow went to prison for firing the gun.

Combs and his crew are far from alone among rappers in keeping up   23
the connection between "rap and rap sheet,"[6] as critic Kelefa Sanneh artfully puts it. Several prominent rappers, including superstar Tupac Shakur, have gone down in hails of bullets—with other rappers often suspected in the killings. Death Row Records producer Marion "Suge" Knight just finished a five-year prison sentence for assault and federal weapons violations. Current rage 50 Cent flaunts his bullet scars in photos; cops recently arrested him for hiding assault weapons in his car. Of the top ten hip-hop sellers mentioned above, five have had scrapes with the law. In 2000, at least five different fights broke out at the Source Hiphop Awards—intended to be the rap industry's Grammys. The final brawl, involving up to 100 people in the audience and spilling over onto the stage, shut the ceremony down—right after a video tribute to slain rappers. Small wonder a popular rap website goes by the name rapsheet.com.

Many fans, rappers, producers, and intellectuals defend hip-hop's vio   24
lence, both real and imagined, and its misogyny as a revolutionary cry of frustration from disempowered youth. For Simmons, gangsta raps "teach listeners something about the lives of the people who create them and remind them that these people exist." 50 Cent recently told *Vibe* magazine, "Mainstream America can look at me and say, 'That's the mentality of a young man from the 'hood.'" University of Pennsylvania black studies professor Michael Eric Dyson has written a book-length paean[7] to Shakur, praising him for "challenging narrow artistic visions of black identity" and for "artistically exploring the attractions and limits of black

---

[5] **luminary:** A celebrity.
[6] **ESL rap sheet:** A list of crimes that a criminal has committed.
[7] **paean:** A tribute.

moral and social subcultures"—just one of countless fawning treatises on rap published in recent years. The National Council of Teachers of English, recommending the use of hip-hop lyrics in urban public school classrooms (as already happens in schools in Oakland, Los Angeles, and other cities), enthuses that "hip-hop can be used as a bridge linking the seemingly vast span between the streets and the world of academics."

But we're sorely lacking in imagination if in 2003—long after the civil   25 rights revolution proved a success, at a time of vaulting opportunity for African Americans, when blacks find themselves at the top reaches of society and politics—we think that it signals progress when black kids rattle off violent, sexist, nihilistic lyrics, like Russians reciting Pushkin.[8] Some defended blaxploitation pictures as revolutionary, too, but the passage of time has exposed the silliness of such a contention. "The message of *Sweetback* is that if you can get it together and stand up to the Man, you can win," Van Peebles once told an interviewer. But win what? All Sweetback did, from what we see in the movie, was avoid jail—and it would be nice to have more useful counsel on overcoming than "kicking the Man's ass." Claims about rap's political potential will look equally gestural in the future. How is it progressive to describe life as nothing but "bitches and money"? Or to tell impressionable black kids, who'd find every door open to them if they just worked hard and learned, that blowing a rival's head off is "real"? How helpful is rap's sexism in a community plagued by rampant illegitimacy and an excruciatingly low marriage rate?

The idea that rap is an authentic cry against oppression is all the sillier   26 when you recall that black Americans had lots more to be frustrated about in the past but never produced or enjoyed music as nihilistic as 50 Cent or N.W.A. On the contrary, black popular music was almost always affirmative and hopeful. Nor do we discover music of such violence in places of great misery like Ethiopia or the Congo—unless it's imported American hip-hop.

Given the hip-hop world's reflexive alienation, it's no surprise that   27 its explicit political efforts, such as they are, are hardly progressive. Simmons has founded the "Hip-Hop Summit Action Network" to bring rap stars and fans together in order to forge a "bridge between hip-hop and politics." But HSAN's policy positions are mostly tired bromides.[9] Sticking with the long-discredited idea that urban schools fail because of inadequate funding from the stingy, racist white Establishment, for example, HSAN joined forces with the teachers' union to protest New York mayor Bloomberg's proposed education budget for its supposed lack of generosity. HSAN has also stuck it to President Bush for invading Iraq. And it has vociferously protested the affixing of advisory labels on rap CDs that warn parents about the obscene language inside. Fighting for rappers' rights to obscenity: that's some kind of revolution!

---

[8] **Pushkin:** Alexander Pushkin, a nineteenth-century Russian poet.
[9] **bromides:** Tired, commonplace ideas.

Okay, maybe rap isn't progressive in any meaningful sense, some ob-　28
servers will admit; but isn't it just a bunch of kids blowing off steam and
so nothing to worry about? I think that response is too easy. With music
videos, DVD players, Walkmans, the Internet, clothes, and magazines all
making hip-hop an accompaniment to a person's entire existence, we need
to take it more seriously. In fact, I would argue that it is seriously harmful
to the black community.

The rise of nihilistic rap has mirrored the breakdown of community　29
norms among inner-city youth over the last couple of decades. It was just
as gangsta rap hit its stride that neighborhood elders began really to notice that they'd lost control of young black men, who were frequently
drifting into lives of gang violence and drug dealing. Well into the seventies, the ghetto was a shabby part of town, where, despite unemployment
and rising illegitimacy, a healthy number of people were doing their best
to "keep their heads above water," as the theme song of the old black sitcom *Good Times* put it.

By the eighties, the ghetto had become a ruleless war zone, where　30
black people were their own worst enemies. It would be silly, of course, to
blame hip-hop for this sad downward spiral, but by glamorizing life in the
"war zone," it has made it harder for many of the kids stuck there to extricate themselves. Seeing a privileged star like Sean Combs behave like a
street thug tells those kids that there's nothing more authentic than ghetto
pathology, even when you've got wealth beyond imagining.

The attitude and style expressed in the hip-hop "identity" keeps blacks　31
down. Almost all hip-hop, gangsta or not, is delivered with a cocky, con-
frontational cadence that is fast becoming—as attested to by the rowdies
at KFC—a common speech style among young black males. Similarly, the
arm-slinging, hand-hurling gestures of rap performers have made their way
into many young blacks' casual gesticulations, becoming integral to their
self-expression. The problem with such speech and mannerisms is that they
make potential employers wary of young black men and can impede a
young black's ability to interact comfortably with co-workers and customers. The black community has gone through too much to sacrifice upward mobility to the passing kick of an adversarial hip-hop "identity."

On a deeper level, there is something truly unsettling and tragic　32
about the fact that blacks have become the main agents in disseminating
debilitating—dare I say racist—images of themselves. Rap guru Russell
Simmons claims that "the coolest stuff about American culture—be it
language, dress, or attitude—comes from the underclass. Always has and
always will." Yet back in the bad old days, blacks often complained—
with some justification—that the media too often depicted blacks simply
as uncivilized. Today, even as television and films depict blacks at all
levels of success, hip-hop sends the message that blacks are . . . uncivilized.
I find it striking that the cry-racism crowd doesn't condemn it.

For those who insist that even the invisible structures of society rein-　33
force racism, the burden of proof should rest with them to explain just

why hip-hop's bloody and sexist lyrics and videos and the criminal behavior of many rappers *wouldn't* have a powerfully negative effect upon whites' conception of black people.

Sadly, some black leaders just don't seem to care what lesson rap conveys. Consider Savannah's black high schools, which hosted the local rapper Camoflauge as a guest speaker several times before his murder earlier this year. Here's a representative lyric: 34

> Gimme the keys to tha car, I'm ready for war.
> When we ride on these niggas smoke that ass like a 'gar.
> Hit your block with a Glock, clear the set with a Tech. . . .
> You think I'm jokin, see if you laughing when tha pistol be smokin —
> Leave you head split wide open
> And you bones get broken. . . .

More than a few of the Concerned Black People inviting this "artist" to speak to the impressionable youth of Savannah would presumably be the first to cry out about "how whites portray blacks in the media."   35

Far from decrying the stereotypes rampant in rap's present-day blaxploitation, many hip-hop defenders pull the "whitey-does-it-too" trick. They point to the *Godfather* movies or *The Sopranos* as proof that violence and vulgarity are widespread in American popular culture, so that singling out hip-hop for condemnation is simply bigotry. Yet such a defense is pitifully weak. No one really looks for a way of life to emulate or a political project to adopt in *The Sopranos*. But for many of its advocates, hip-hop, with its fantasies of revolution and community and politics, is more than entertainment. It forms a bedrock[10] of young black identity.   36

Nor will it do to argue that hip-hop isn't "black" music, since most of its buyers are white, or because the "hip-hop revolution" is nominally open to people of all colors. That whites buy more hip-hop recordings than blacks do is hardly surprising, given that whites vastly outnumber blacks nationwide. More to the point, anyone who claims that rap isn't black music will need to reconcile that claim with the widespread wariness among blacks of white rappers like Eminem, accused of "stealing our music and giving it back to us."   37

At 2 a.m. on the New York subway not long ago, I saw another scene — more dispiriting than my KFC encounter with the rowdy rapping teens — that captures the essence of rap's destructiveness. A young black man entered the car and began to rap loudly — profanely, arrogantly — with the usual wild gestures. This went on for five irritating minutes. When no one paid attention, he moved on to another car, all the while spouting his doggerel.[11]   38

This was what this young black man presented as his message to the world — his oratory, if you will.   39

[10] **bedrock:** A foundation.
[11] **doggerel:** Poor-quality poetry.

Anyone who sees such behavior as a path to a better future—anyone, 40
like Professor Dyson, who insists that hip-hop is an urgent "critique of a
society that produces the need for the thug persona"—should step back
and ask himself just where, exactly, the civil rights–era blacks might have
gone wrong in lacking a hip-hop revolution. They created the world of
equality, striving, and success I live and thrive in.

Hip-hop creates nothing. 41

EXERCISING VOCABULARY

1. From what more familiar word is *blaxploitation* derived? What does the original
   word mean? What does this derivation of the word imply about its meaning?

2. In paragraph 6, the author talks about the "stereotyping" and "typecasting"
   of blacks by whites earlier in America's history. What is the connotative
   meaning of these words? What is their denotative implication? Who were the
   "Sapphires and Studds of yesteryear"? How did these figures illustrate stereotyping and typecasting?

3. In paragraph 10, McWhorter writes about an idea that became "a hip-hop
   mantra." What is a mantra? How and when is a mantra generally used? What
   exactly is this mantra for hip-hop?

PROBING CONTENT

1. How did rap music begin? When did its focus change? Who was responsible
   for this transformation?

2. Why does gangsta rap dominate the hip-hop music scene today? What often
   happens to other rap music? Why? Who clearly portrays the gangsta rapper
   image? How does he do this?

3. What is McWhorter's opinion of the idea that "rap is an authentic cry against
   oppression" (para. 26)? What evidence does he provide to support his viewpoint?

4. How do some black leaders excuse the excesses of rap music? Why does
   McWhorter discount these excuses?

CONSIDERING CRAFT

1. McWhorter's thesis is clearly stated early in his essay. Locate and write down
   the thesis statement. What are the advantages and disadvantages of placing
   the thesis where it is?

2. McWhorter includes some very graphic lyrics. Why are they included when
   some readers may find them offensive? What effect do they have on you as a
   reader?

3. This essay concludes with a single sentence. What effect does McWhorter achieve with this strategy? Why doesn't he use a single-sentence paragraph anywhere else in the essay?

RESPONDING TO THE WRITER

McWhorter sees no redeeming features in the hip-hop music he condemns here. Do you agree? Why or why not? If you don't agree, what merit do you see in this music? What messages do you think rap music sends?

For a quiz on this reading, go to bedfordstmartins.com/mirror.

To the Academy with Love, from a Hip-Hop Fan

JAMILAH EVELYN

Whatever your stance on hip-hop, you cannot deny that it is a part of the lives of many college students. Do professors therefore have a responsibility to better understand this music and the culture that has formed around it? Jamilah Evelyn thinks they do, and in "To the Academy with Love, from a Hip-Hop Fan," she encourages professors to see the positive side of hip-hop — "its poetic, solicitous and uplifting facets." What do you find positive about hip-hop?

Jamilah Evelyn was formerly the editor of *Black Issues in Higher Education*, where this essay first appeared on December 7, 2001. She has also served as editor of *Community College Week* and has written about minority issues for several other education publications. Evelyn is currently an assistant editor at the *Chronicle of Higher Education*, a weekly newspaper that covers important issues at colleges and universities across the country.

THINKING AHEAD

To what extent do you think college professors are obligated to be aware of the major influences on the lives of their students? What are those major cultural influences? What is their relevance to classroom discussions?

INCREASING VOCABULARY

empathetic (adj.) (2)
rapport (n.) (2)
devotees (n.) (2)
enhanced (v.) (2)
hue (n.) (4)
vulgarities (n.) (4)
misogyny (n.) (4)
incarnation (n.) (4)
sadism (n.) (6)
demoralizing (n.) (6)

facet (n.) (6)
confounds (v.) (7)
cadre (n.) (7)
inclusive (adj.) (8)
introspective (adj.) (8)
prolific (adj.) (8)
revelry (n.) (9)
sanctioning (n.) (11)
solicitous (adj.) (12)
disengaged (adj.) (13)

While putting together the cover story for this edition, a source asked me if I thought it was the academy's[1] responsibility to get to know and understand hip-hop—the music and its accompanying culture.

Pausing first, I replied: It may not be a professor's job to run out and buy the latest Jay-Z CD in order to better identify with her students. But the extent to which academe[2] can develop an empathetic rapport with the devotees of this cultural phenomenon is partly the extent to which academe's reach will be further enhanced. And yes, I do think it's the academy's responsibility to find new ways to extend its reach.

Too many potential students, potential dropouts and potential great black (and other) leaders are at stake.

For better or worse, hip-hop has molded several generations of college students—black, white, and every hue in between. With its vulgarities, its black political consciousness, its misogyny, and its soulful nourishment, this latest incarnation of black expression has quite simply taken the world by storm.

So love it or hate it. But do attempt to understand it.

As a member of the "hip-hop generation," and an admitted hip-hop fan, I too am distressed by any celebration of black sadism, ho-ism[3] and the effect such money-making demoralizing has on our youth. But the fact that violence sells is indicative more of American pop culture in general than of this one particular facet. The recipe for that disaster is easy to explain.

Perhaps what disappoints and confounds me more is seeing a cadre of scholars—often clever enough to be unmoved by the media's misplaced stereotypes—dismiss a whole genre of black music and its fans.

Where else besides higher education's forgiving, reflective and ideally inclusive sphere should we expect introspective exchanges on the music and the society that shapes it? Who else besides a professor, conscious of the thoughtful and intellectual side of kids otherwise cast as degenerates,[4] should we expect to give a ringing endorsement of hip-hop's prolific protégés?[5]

Hip-hop is so much more than the rump-shaking, "ice"-flossing,[6] gangster revelry that fuels the record industry's multibillion dollar sales every year.

That said, let us all keep in mind that even the dark and demoralized side of hip-hop is no more than a byproduct of the capitalist mindset that higher education often endorses.

---

[1] **the academy:** Colleges and universities.
[2] **academe:** The academic world.
[3] **ho-ism:** Prostitution.
[4] **degenerates:** People who act in ways that many others feel are immoral.
[5] **protégés:** People whose careers are furthered by a person of experience or influence.
[6] **"ice"-flossing:** Flaunting expensive jewelry (ice).

So before we collectively disregard what the student on this edition's cover dubbed "the soundtrack of our lives," it would perhaps be a better strategy to show some understanding. We can accept and reach out to our students — the b-boys,[7] the hoochie mamas[8] and the thugged out[9] among them — without sanctioning the more destructive ethos[10] that unfortunately defines so much of the music today.

Truth be told, I was pleasantly surprised at the number of scholars I talked to who see hip-hop's redemptive aspects. Many even encourage their students to draw on its poetic, solicitous and uplifting facets to prepare their papers, understand current events, indeed to change the world.

But I would encourage more of their colleagues to recognize that hip-hop's fruitage[11] includes the disengaged learner as well as the Rhodes Scholar.[12] It includes the kid who never even made it to college and the one who exceeded everyone's expectations.

It also includes the editor of a magazine devoted to making sure that higher education opens more doors, expands more minds and reaches out to ever more students who traditionally have been left out of the equation. Anyone committed to that mission has got to keep it real.

EXERCISING VOCABULARY

1. Evelyn expresses surprise that other professors "see hip-hop's redemptive aspects" (para. 12). What kinds of activities are usually referred to as redemptive? What aspects of hip-hop fit the definition of something redemptive? How do they fit?

2. The author insists that anyone who wants to keep education's doors open to a wide range of students "has got to keep it real" (para. 14). Keep what real? What does she mean by *real* here? How can this be accomplished?

PROBING CONTENT

1. According to Evelyn, what should a professor's obligation to hip-hop be? Why? What would this accomplish?

2. Why, in the author's opinion, is a university environment the ideal place to evaluate hip-hop? What should a professor be able to see in hip-hop's listeners that others might miss?

---

[7] **b-boys:** Gang of men or boys, originally a basketball term.
[8] **hoochie mamas:** Slang for sexy women.
[9] **thugged out:** Gangster-like.
[10] **ethos:** The distinguishing character or guiding belief of a person, group, or institution.
[11] **fruitage:** The product or result.
[12] **Rhodes Scholar:** A recipient of one of numerous scholarships founded by Cecil J. Rhodes to allow gifted students to study at Oxford University in England.

CONSIDERING CRAFT

1. This article was published in an academic journal called *Black Issues in Education*. Who is likely to read this journal? How are Evelyn's writing style and vocabulary indicative of her awareness of this reading audience? Use examples to discuss how this essay might be different if it had been written for a university student publication.

2. Evelyn admits in paragraph 6 that she is a hip-hop fan. How does having this information early in the article influence your reading of her essay? Why did the author feel that it was necessary to let her readers know her position?

RESPONDING TO THE WRITER

To what extent do you agree with Jamilah Evelyn that the university is a good environment in which to study hip-hop music? Explain what you think might be gained by such discussions. How receptive would most of your professors be to the inclusion of rap's positive and negative aspects in classroom discussions?

For a quiz on this reading, go to bedfordstmartins.com/mirror.

DRAWING CONNECTIONS

1. Jamilah Evelyn dismisses some of the negative aspects of hip-hop by stating, "But the fact that violence sells is indicative more of American pop culture in general than of this one particular facet" (para. 6). How would John H. McWhorter respond to her statement? Use specific evidence from McWhorter's essay "How Hip-Hop Holds Blacks Back" to support your response.

2. What arguments might Evelyn use to attempt to convince McWhorter that adults can reach out to young people through hip-hop without condoning the music's "more destructive ethos" (para. 11)? Would McWhorter be convinced? Why or why not?

Wrapping Up Chapter 8

REFLECTING ON THE WRITING

1. Choose a popular female or male vocalist and write an essay examining the role that sexuality plays in this artist's lyrics, live performances, music videos, and marketing.

2. Following Stephen Corey's model in "A Voice For the Lonely," choose a recently deceased musical artist and write an essay about the impact of his or her life and death on you. Be sure to identify songs that were special to you; you may wish to include some lyrics. Include details about when you first became aware of the artist's music, to what extent you became a fan, and how you first learned of the artist's death.

3. Using Andrew Leonard's essay, Stephen Levy's article "iPod Nation" in Chapter 9, and your own ideas and experiences, write an essay about the relationship between music and technology today and in the future.

4. Following Jamilah Evelyn's example in "To the Academy with Love," choose a style of music and write an essay in which you describe the benefits to our culture of that type of music. Be sure to defend the music you choose against the most obvious criticisms made against it and also to include specific references to artists and songs that illustrate your points.

CONNECTING TO THE CULTURE

1. Choose a genre of music with which you are not familiar. Do some research on the origins of the music, the prominent artists involved, and the popularity of the music. Listen to as much of this music as you can find on CDs and videos over a period of at least several days. Then write an essay in which you detail your experiences. Be sure to discuss how easy or difficult it was for you to spend time with this new music and describe its effects on you, both as you listened and as you reflect on the experience.

2. Select one style of music that you would not normally listen to and write an essay in which you explore its history, its current popularity, the way its artists are treated by the media, and your predictions for its future. Be sure to refer to specific artists and especially well-known songs that best represent the type of music you have chosen.

3. Write an essay in which you explore the role of music in movies, in television shows, or in commercials. Choose specific examples to illustrate the degree to which music influences, enhances, or detracts from your chosen medium.

4. In an essay, explore the idea that listening to each other's music may be able to bring people of various cultures to a better understanding of each other. How would this exchange take place? How willing would people be to undertake such an experiment? What factors might hinder the success of such a project? What changes in our world might result? How lasting would the effects be?

FOCUSING ON YESTERDAY, FOCUSING ON TODAY

Once upon a time, music came from a radio or phonograph that had to be plugged into an electric outlet, as seen in this photo from 1944. Listening selections were limited, and sound quality was poor by today's standards. Families gathered around large wooden radios to hear the latest episode of *The Lone Ranger* or the evening news. Listening was a shared activity. Now we live in an iPod world in which we listen to whatever we choose, whenever we wish, wherever we happen to be. Listening is often an individual activity. In fact, listening to an iPod allows us to screen others out, just as this pedestrian does as he walks past an iPod ad plastered on a wall in San Francisco in 2004.

How has the mobility of music changed things for the individual consumer? For the music industry? For society? How has technology altered the place of music in our lives? What will be the next big innovation in technology that affects music?

"Turn the Radio Up!"

CHAPTER 9

This Blog's 4 U

Pop Culture Powers Up

Here's the ultimate remote control. All of life is neatly reduced to a series of buttons. Everything is included: love and hate, pleasure and pain, past and future, war and peace, even life/death. This piece was designed by artist Nebojsa Seric-Soba and is titled "Just a Click Away: Remote Dreams of Complete Control."

- What is the significance of the title of this piece?
- What point do you think the artist was making about our post-9/11 culture?
- On a standard remote control, what is normally located on the top right? Why is this significant?
- Why does trust have an on/off button?
- Who do you think holds the remote control for your life?

Research this topic with TopLinks at bedfordstmartins.com/toplinks.

Isn't it miraculous what technology can do for us? We've got iPods, robots, self-service check-out, cell phones, computers, digital phone service, and remote controls for garage doors, car doors, CD players, and television sets. Did you know that if you buy your Thanksgiving turkey from the right company, you can go online with a certificate number to find out how old your main course was, what farm it lived on, and what it ate to become round enough to grace your table? Did you know that in 2003 Microsoft experimented with a portable toilet called an iLoo, which had, in addition to the standard equipment, "a built-in, high-speed Internet connection, wireless keyboard and height-adjustable plasma monitor"? Did you know that since 1999 a school district near Pittsburgh, Pennsylvania, has eliminated the "I forgot my lunch money" problem by using fingerprint scanning units in school cafeterias? And parents can get a record of what their money paid for—Cheetos and a Coke or spaghetti and milk? These startling technical tidbits came from the March 1, February 1, and April 1, 2005, issues of *CIO* (Chief Information Officer) magazine, respectively. Every month there is another new application of existing technology or an introduction to brand new technology. Well, that's progress. But what if you crave good old-fashioned interaction with another breathing human? You may be out of luck. Megan Santosus, whose Reality Bites column appears regularly in *CIO* magazine, makes a dire and ironic prediction: "Machines are cheaper, but people are sweeter. Someday, only the rich will be privileged enough to deal with human beings. The poor will be forced to use technology" (April 1, 2005).

Welcome to Your Second Life

Joe Stafford

Have you ever wanted to become the character you are manipulating in a video game? Do you use a version of your real name online, or do you create a completely different identity? To what extent are the lines between "anonymous" and "deceptive" sometimes blurred in online communication? In "Welcome to Your Second Life," which appeared in the January 23, 2005, edition of the *Austin American-Statesman*, reporter Joe Stafford goes where many people may wish to go: deep into an alternate reality called Second Life. It's an online community where people who log on become their cartoon alter egos, called *avatars*, to inhabit a city of 20,000 people on twelve virtual square miles. "Murder and stealing are not allowed in Second Life, but virtually everything else is," Stafford notes. So what do real people do in this virtual world? According to the author, "They fly airplanes, hold fashion shows, host poetry readings. They dance endlessly. They marry, cheat, divorce, remarry." Sounds a lot like real life, doesn't it?

Joe Stafford is a staff writer for the *Austin American-Statesman*. An artist with a lifelong interest in theater, Stafford cofounded, in 2002, the Austin, Texas, branch of Gag Reflex, a comedy improvisation group modeled after Chicago's Second City.

THINKING AHEAD

How much time do you invest in playing video games? Why are you and so many other people willing to take time away from real life to play them? What are your favorite games? Why are you or others attracted to these games? What are the advantages and disadvantages of playing video games?

INCREASING VOCABULARY

sashays (v.) (2)	viable (adj.) (42)
dabble (v.) (5)	intangible (n.) (50)
unfettered (adj.) (8)	recoil (v.) (54)
sprawl (n.) (13)	altruism (n.) (67)
mutates (v.) (13)	proliferation (n.) (67)
fledgling (adj.) (15)	sordid (adj.) (68)
amassing (v.) (17)	forays (n.) (68)
mandatory (adj.) (32)	unhampered (adj.) (71)
demographically (adv.) (37)	ambience (n.) (74)

On the edge of a shimmering lake, five men gather in the shadow of a rugged wooden cross to talk about their faith in Jesus. Drifting smoke renders the scene strikingly biblical, a snapshot from the days of the apostles. A creature—part woman, part red fox—sashays by.

"Nice cross," it says.

This make-believe place is Second Life, a virtual world where creatures talk and only two of the Ten Commandments have been handed down.

People from dozens of countries log on to dabble in this realm, picking who or what they want to be, how they want to look and how they choose to behave.

They appear as avatars—vivid, 3-D pixelated[1] presences—in a mad masquerade played out on the cutting edge of the technologically possible.

Second Life is a tiny Xanadu[2] existing only on the servers of a California company and in the minds and hard drives of its subscribers, a city of almost 20,000 souls on 12 square miles of virtual land.

Murder and stealing are not allowed in Second Life, but virtually everything else is. Nobody needs to eat; the laws of physics are optional. So what do Second-Lifers do when unfettered by such real-life concerns as gravity, hunger and mortality?

They worship and sin, acquire property and build on it, hold protest marches, raise money for worthy causes and buy and sell things, even though they have no material needs.

University students log on to study cyber-architecture. Subscribers with disabilities enter a world where physical limitations don't exist.

Here you can find virtual proselytizers[3] and prostitutes, virtual couples, virtual designers and artists and virtual gamblers. Soap opera-style drama abounds, fads rise and fall, people play games within the game. They fly airplanes, hold fashion shows, host poetry readings. They dance endlessly. They marry, cheat, divorce, remarry.

The virtual world has its own money and economy, but it's also possible to make real money—thousands of dollars, in some cases—buying and selling creations in Second Life.

The result is a willy-nilly[4] Wild West of sprawl badly in need of a few zoning regulations, a completely unpredictable place that mutates so quickly that it can never be fully explored.

Calling Second Life a computer game would be wrong. Games typically have a goal, and Second Life does not. At least, no more of a goal than real life, or RL, as it's called inside the world.

---

[1] **pixelated:** Composed of the smallest elements of an image in video display.
[2] **Xanadu:** The summer palace of Kubla Khan from the dreamlike poem "Kubla Khan" by Samuel Taylor Coleridge.
[3] **proselytizers:** People who attempt to convert others to their beliefs.
[4] **ESL willy-nilly:** Unorganized.

"The point is that Second Life evolves as a function of what people   15
like and dislike," says Philip Rosedale, head of Linden Lab, the company
that created the fledgling world.

Everything in Second Life is created by, and owned by, its subscribers.   16
Every aspect of the world — gender, personal appearance, construction of
buildings, animations that make avatars jump or act silly — can be modified by the people living there.

Second Life is not about armed conquest, explosions or amassing   17
point totals. It simply is about living in a different place, a place where
virtually nothing is impossible.

Having a new baby in real life sure can cut into your Second Life.   18

Take it from Lynne Randoll, also known as Kali Quartermass. In real   19
life, Randoll lives in Pflugerville with her husband, Dan Harris, known
online as Jher Quartermass. The two are married in both the real and virtual worlds.

In real life, he's a Unix administrator. She's a veterinarian. Now in   20
their late 30s, they met through an online chat group that gathered Thurs-
day nights at Austin's Dog & Duck Pub.

Randoll sometimes holds their 8-month-old daughter, Amelia, in one   21
arm while typing single-handedly at her computer. Dan sits at his own
keyboard nearby.

They are side by side in real life, spending time together in Second   22
Life, where they like to build things and buy and sell virtual real estate for
a profit.

The Quartermasses like to socialize, make friends and go on virtual   23
dates to oddball events such as Xwing's Giant Snail Race or the Discs of
Tron Arena, two of many games that have arisen within the world.

"We still go out together in real life," Kali says. "Just not every night."   24

It's not a world for everyone, they say, but appeals mostly to a   25
computer-literate and creative crowd.

"When I first played Second Life," Jher says, "I thought, 'This is what   26
cyberspace is supposed to be.'"

Another Austin-area Second Lifer is Loki Pico, an orange-skinned,   27
horned bull-man who likes to build roadside attractions such as madden-
ing mazes and an upside-down house. In real life, he's Wes Pryor. Currently between jobs, Pryor says he has cash reserves to live for a few
months, leaving him time to spend up to six hours online at a stretch.

"I've made lots of friends in Second Life," he says.   28

Philip Rosedale is the CEO of Linden Lab, the San Francisco company   29
he founded in 1999. It launched Second Life in 2003.

Rosedale agrees to be interviewed within Second Life, so he logs on as   30
Philip Linden and meets a reporter on a trolley car in virtual London,
where the two ride in circles and chat.

Rosedale says that ever since he was a young man, he dreamed of cre-   31
ating a place like this, where creative people could come together and
shape their world.

About five years ago, the mandatory ingredients—powerful comput-   32
ers linked by broadband connections—began to emerge. Rosedale predicts
explosive growth for Second Life as the technology becomes commonplace (more than half of Internet users nationwide now use broadband,
according to NetRatings, a company that tracks such figures). In a burst
of optimism, Rosedale predicts that Second Life will reach a million users
in three years.

After 18 months, with about 20,000 registered users and some 1,500   33
or so logged on at any one time, Second Life is a cult phenomenon within
a booming industry.

By comparison, last year's blockbuster City of Heroes, the superhero   34
role-playing game created by NCSoft in Austin, boasts almost 10 times
that many registered users.

"We're after those early adopters who will help create the world,"   35
Rosedale says. "We're not trying to create a consumer experience right from
the start."

The slow-growth approach is yielding about 20 percent monthly growth   36
in customers and revenue, Rosedale says.

Demographically, Second Life attracts a different audience from tradi-   37
tional online games. For starters, most online multiplayer games such as
Everquest or World of Warcraft draw about 25 percent of their audience
from teens under 18. Second Life tries to keep minors out, requiring a
credit card and a pledge that the user is an adult.

And, strikingly, Rosedale says, about 38 percent of Second Life's sub-   38
scribers are women, more than double the average for online games.
Women also play longer, accounting for about 50 percent of the time
spent online in the world.

Linden's business model is to make money from what amount to vir-   39
tual property taxes.

Players pay $9.95 to enter the world and need never pay another   40
penny if they choose. But if they want to build a house or open their own
shop, they need to buy space and pay fees.

On the lowest level of ownership, for instance, a user can purchase 512   41
square meters of virtual real estate for $9.95 monthly. Prices increase from
there, up to a $1,000 initial fee and $200 monthly rent for a 16-acre virtual
island.

The privately held company doesn't release financial details, and some   42
experts say its business model has yet to prove viable, including Julian
Dibbell, an expert on virtual worlds and author of the book *My Tiny Life*
which examines the phenomenon of online role-playing.

But Rosedale isn't alone in his optimism. In October, the company   43
announced receipt of $8 million in venture capital from Benchmark Cap-
ital and an undisclosed amount from Omidyar Network, led by Pierre
Omidyar, founder of the online auction site eBay Inc. All of that will be
used to add to the staff of 25 and to find ways to enhance the virtual
world.

Second Life is an inevitable step beyond the usual online games in two   44
important ways, Dibbell says.

It "actively encourages a real-world economy exchange rate," he says,   45
"and they gave all intellectual property rights to online content to the
users."

Who in their right mind would spend thousands of dollars on virtual   46
real estate?

"It is an expensive hobby to be involved with," admits Katykiwi   47
Moonflower. She owns an island, a kind of treasure-laden lovers' paradise
called Gypsy Moon.

In real life, Moonflower is a successful Washington lawyer, and she   48
says she takes an interest in the legal issues of virtual property and virtual
vice that arise in Second Life. She's married, 43, with no children, and her
husband, an engineer, travels often.

At least that's what she says during a conversation held within the   49
game. She won't reveal her real name, and as with much of what's said in
Second Life, there's really no way to confirm her statements.

Perhaps the most treasured possession in Second Life isn't money. It's   50
an intangible: anonymity.

Midwest Dayton, director of the Christian group building the   51
church by the lake, will reveal only limited real-life information about
himself. For the record, he says he's a 50-something married father of
three who teaches at a university in Oklahoma. "Temptation is temptation. Hearts are hearts. People call this a game, but there are real fingers
on those keyboards," he says, virtual Bible in hand, standing before the
small gathering of like-minded men whose stated goal is to spread the
word of God in Second Life. "These are real souls that can still be
reached."

Since their first meeting, the nondenominational virtual congregation   52
has grown to about 15 members and has bought land in Second Life and
built a large glass cathedral.

Anonymity serves a different purpose for the character known as   53
Wilde Cunningham, an avatar operated by nine people from Philadelphia
who have physical disabilities and use wheelchairs. Their real-life case-
worker, known as Lilone Sandgrain in Second Life, says she provided
them with an account and they raised enough donations in the online
world to buy a more powerful computer. They gather and make group decisions about where to go and what to say.

"In here, people don't see us and recoil because of our appearance,"   54
Cunningham says. "We don't have to repeat ourselves 100 times to be understood. In here, everyone is on equal footing."

Even in a virtual world, customer service is a pain in the backside.   55
Take it from Munchflower Zaius.

"I'm in customer service hell again," says the self-employed designer,   56
patiently explaining for the thousandth time via instant message to a new-
bie customer how to take a shirt out of a box.

Zaius, who also won't give her real name, designs a popular line of edgy skins—essentially full-body tattoos—and goth[5] clothes. She's a tattoo-emblazoned, much-pierced flamboyant, a magnet for admirers, friends and freaks, and among the most successful of Second Life's entrepreneurs. 57

In her real life, she says, she's a 27-year-old mother of two young kids from Oregon who works online from home. She has no tattoos. Making and selling stuff in Second Life is her real job. Zaius says she makes upwards of $175 a day selling to other users at a dozen shops around Second Life. 58

Linden Lab says its most savvy users do, indeed, earn up to $4,000 a month buying and selling in Second Life. During a speculative real estate boom last summer, some users cleared up to $6,000. 59

Most games discourage such profit-making. But Second Life embraces real-life market forces. Items are sold for the in-world currency, Lindens, abbreviated as $L, which have a cash equivalent at various online currency exchanges. For instance, a rocked-out, tattoo-covered sex god skin can sell for upwards of $L3000, or about $15 in U.S. currency. People can't buy them fast enough. 60

"Once a currency has currency anywhere, it's a real currency," Dibbell explains. "Linden dollars have an exchange rate with U.S. dollars, and it's no less legitimate than the exchange rate for the Turkish lyra or the Indian rupee or whatever." 61

Zaius has created a whole line of skins, from snow-white, red-lipped, rose-with-thorns goth skins, anatomically detailed, to elemental elf skins to sexy tattooed tan-lined skins and all shades between. More than half the people in Second Life are wearing skins Zaius designed. 62

"Don't ever make Second Life your real-life job," she warns, citing the stress and fast pace of her online life, "or else you'll have to find an escape from your escape." 63

Everyone in Second Life communicates through typed chat, and they almost universally resist the use of live-speech software, for the simple reason that a real voice breaks the fantasy. And Second Life is all about the fantasy. 64

Newcomers are warned that much of Second Life contains content termed "mature." Dibbell says he believes that an emphasis on sex in an online world is a symptom of something lacking with the gaming experience, but Rosedale says it isn't the place of Linden Lab to judge the content of Second Life. 65

"I think that sex has its place in the emerging medium," he says. "As a first form of exploration." Rosedale has an optimistic take on human nature: that extreme freedom will bring out the best in people. Because Second Life offers more choices than real life, he says, "In this environment, our behaviors and thinking are actually better." 66

[5] **ESL goth:** Relating to a contemporary Gothic style featuring black clothing with chains and studs and often accompanied by tattoos and body piercings.

Examples of altruism abound. Popular areas include a virtual AIDS   67
quilt, a virtual Vietnam Memorial and, recently, a proliferation of charity
events for Asian tsunami victims.

But perhaps because of its anonymity and freedom, Second Life has a   68
sordid side, with an abundance of gambling houses, displays of wanton
sexuality, occasional forays into overt racism and attempts to ruin the
game for others—known online as "grieving." In one example, a player was
banned for breaking the user agreement by creating a "virtual Berlin," which
vividly depicted a Holocaust complete with 3-D depictions of lynchings and
ovens and swastikas.

And though displays of racism are forbidden, one clear social division   69
is between people who travel the world as people and people who appear
as animals, called "furries." In what feels like tribal division, the furries
keep mainly to their own areas and tend not to associate with more
human-looking types.

Classes at several universities, including the University of Texas and   70
Trinity University in San Antonio, have dipped into Second Life to study,
among other things, online architecture, game design and the uses of digital space.

At UT, Anne Beamish teaches a class in the school of architecture   71
called Designing Digital Communities, in which students enter Second
Life to study the essence of public spaces in a world unhampered by real-
world physics.

Among her most interesting conclusions, Beamish says, is that in a   72
digital world in which gravity and other physical rules don't apply, people
still have an initial tendency to build ordinary suburban homes or fake
burger joints or malls. Things familiar.

"We fall back on what we know, on what we're comfortable with,"   73
she says. "People stick with the real-life rules even though they don't have
to. It's a world where you can do anything you want, and yet we duplicate
instead what we already have."

One of Beamish's students, Brockett Davidson, known as Brockett Far-   74
ber in Second Life, built a kind of virtual "sacred space" within Second
Life, which succeeded until sprawl took over and ruined the ambience.

"But my experience in Second Life has mostly been really wonderful,"   75
he says. "I started off as seeing it as a game and quickly came to see it as
something more. I really do understand how people form real intimacies
in there."

At Trinity University, Aaron Delwiche takes his class of 15 into the   76
world en masse, and they design games within the game. Last spring they
designed a virtual scavenger hunt that forced players to explore Second
Life and virtually photograph its many sights.

Inevitably, Delwiche says, some of his students get caught up in the   77
social scene and stay on after the class is done.

The social aspects of the world are, in fact, among its most powerful. Re-   78
lationships in Second Life develop with remarkable speed. "If your feelings

are real in real life, then they're real there, too," Dibbell says. "That's hard for people who've never spent time in these places to really grasp. It doesn't work to say, 'Oh, someone's bothering you; turn off the computer,' because people have a real emotional investment in it."

EXERCISING VOCABULARY

1. People who play Second Life appear online as avatars. What is an avatar? Why would a person wish to become an avatar?

2. In paragraph 12, Stafford calls Second Life a "virtual world." Then, in paragraph 17, he writes that Second Life is "a place where virtually nothing is impossible." What does the word *virtual* mean as used in paragraph 12? What does *virtually* mean in paragraph 17? Why is the author's play on the word *virtually* ironic?

PROBING CONTENT

1. What two things are not allowed in Second Life? What is unusual about life in this virtual world?

2. Why is it incorrect to call Second Life a game? Why can the Second Life environment never be fully explored?

3. How is Second Life different from most video games? Who plays Second Life? How do Second Life players compare with people who play more traditional video games online?

4. How does Linden Lab make a profit from Second Life? What are the company's business prospects?

CONSIDERING CRAFT

1. Stafford introduces us to many of the people who inhabit Second Life. Why does he include detailed information about many of the participants? What effect does he probably expect meeting these people will have on the reader?

2. What is the tone of this essay? To what extent can readers learn Stafford's attitude about Second Life from reading this article? Cite several portions of text that support your answer.

RESPONDING TO THE WRITER

If you were a Second Life subscriber, what would your avatar be like? Describe his or her appearance, personality, ambitions, job, education, and housing.

For a quiz on this reading, go to bedfordstmartins.com/mirror.

Text Messaging: Take Note

JENNIE BRISTOW

Strange things happen when a new kind of technology starts being used by young people and gradually flows into the mainstream. When a teenager types "How r u?," we accept it as teenage jargon. When a mature business professional types the same message, is it efficient, unprofessional, or just plain silly? Not too long ago, the guardians of the English language were re-nouncing e-mail as the murderer of grammar and letter writing. Now, in the January 22, 2001, edition of the *London Guardian*, Jennie Bristow takes on the newest threat to the English language.

Jennie Bristow is a London-based journalist who currently contributes to the online publication *spiked*. She has been a columnist for the *Daily Telegraph*, and her byline has appeared extensively in the United Kingdom's print and broadcast media. She is the author of *Maybe I Do? Marriage and Commitment in Singleton Society* (2002).

THINKING AHEAD

Do you use text messaging? How well do you read and understand all the abbreviations and altered words that are used? How did you learn what they meant? To what extent has text messaging affected your writing in other forms — like notes, letters written by hand, or papers written for classes? If you don't use text messaging, explain how you think this form of communication might be affecting the English language.

INCREASING VOCABULARY

misgivings (n.) (2)   succinctly (adv.) (9)
deficient (adj.) (8)   penchant (n.) (10)

---

f you're going to write a column about text messaging, I know it's the   1
done thing to use the lingo (as in the best-selling guidebook *WAN2TLK: ltl bk of txt msgs*). Sorry.

I am not one of the world's great text messagers. Until last week, I   2
had a mobile phone that was so big, basic, and ancient that people started asking, "Is that a WAP[1] phone?" (Answer: no, it's a crap[2] phone.) I am also, I suppose, too grammatically old-fashioned for my age. I like words; I like sentences; I like punctuation. Even as a teenager, I had misgivings about the Me 4 U graffiti, and suffered a nerd-like compulsion to correct it on school toilet walls.

---

[1] **WAP:** Wireless Access Protocol, an early cell-phone technology.
[2] **ESL** **crap:** Slang for of poor quality.

But I cannot get into this idea, promoted by Dr. Ken Lodge of the   3
University of East Anglia, that text messaging is destroying literacy. Dr.
Lodge claims that, by abbreviating the English language to the extreme
and by substituting numbers for letters, we can lose sight of what it means
to read and write properly.

"I think it's a weird way to communicate," said Dr. Lodge. "Inevitably   4
it'll affect the way people talk to each other." He points out that "there are
already problems with university students with their inability to write English. The more people use it, the less they'll be aware of different styles of
communicating."

There is a temptation here to point out that if Dr. Lodge's grasp of   5
grammar is anything to go by, students may be better off without it
(although maybe the issue is the way the reporter has paraphrased his
comments—which could support Dr. Lodge's argument). In either case,
the question is: what are we really talking about here? Is the technology
the problem—or something else?

That young people don't know no grammar is fairly obvious. My edu-   6
cation in English grammar stopped with nouns (being words), verbs (doing
words) and adjectives (describing words). What grammar I did learn came
through modern languages; and that only happened because frustrated
French language assistants could not believe our ignorance. Even now, I
can tell you what the pluperfect of a French verb is, but defining the pluperfect tense *itself*? Forget it.

But the grammar issue is about education. Teachers have not taught it—   7
with the consequence, as many commentators have remarked, that when
young teachers are forced to teach grammar through the U.K. National Literacy Scheme, they don't even know what they are supposed to be teaching.
Even if grammar is high on today's government's list of educational priorities, it is suffering from having been educationally unfashionable. Nothing to
do with mobile phones.

In any case, text messaging has very little to do with grammar. If   8
young people write a bad letter, you can tell they are grammatically deficient. Text messaging, by contrast, is just note writing. If I leave a note for
my husband reading "GONE 2 SAINSBRY J," I do not expect him to criticize the lack of paragraph breaks (or anything else—after all, who's
cooking?). It might not be poetry—but it gets the point across.

Brendan, my colleague on *spiked*, is trained as a proofreader. The re-   9
sult? He sends terrible text messages: all proper words, in sentences with
full stops, which take you forever (4eva?) to read. Just as I have bought
a slinky new mobile phone, which might encourage me to get into text
messaging, my colleague Helene (the original It[3] girl—she's had the
same model for months) tells me that the phone turns your text messages
into proper words. Regardless of how succinctly and numerically I write,

---

[3] **It girl:** A fashionable woman whose style others copy—a reference to Clara Bow, the star
of a 1927 film called *It*.

everybody receiving my messages will think I am doing a Brendan. Damn.

I do have to confess to a formality-fetish with email. I thought my   10
penchant for using a proper form of address, and always including a sign-off, made me infinitely superior to the people who reply to my carefully crafted emails with statements like "OK." But then somebody told me about a colleague of his, who maintains that anybody who writes emails as though they were letters obviously has too much time on his hands. Fair enough.

There is a problem with people's use of text messaging and email—   11
but this is about sloppiness, not grammar. Email might be more like memo-writing than letter-writing; but while it is good to be succinct, whatever you write has to be comprehensible. people who write an un-punctuated stream of consciousness with no capital letters excEpt for those in tHE WRong places and words spelt worngly should as far as im concerned be lined up against a wall and given a damn good talking to by their least favorite ex-schoolteacher.

Email is supposed to ease communication—not make the recipient   12
spend hours with a dictionary, wondering "What the hell is this supposed to say?" Be informal, if you like; be efficient, certainly. But if any of this is going to benefit us, in work or socially, other people need to understand what we are saying. Otherwise we'll all be climbing the walls of a modern-day Tower of Babel.

EXERCISING VOCABULARY

1. In the first paragraph, Bristow writes, "I know it's the done thing to use the lingo." What does she mean by the expression "the done thing"? What does the word *lingo* mean? Who would understand the lingo to which she is referring here?

2. Bristow confesses in paragraph 10 that she has "a formality-fetish with email." What is a fetish? What would a formality fetish cause a person to think or do?

PROBING CONTENT

1. What is the difference between what the British government thinks about grammar and what is actually happening in schools? Why is there a difference?

2. In paragraph 9, the author expresses her concern that her new phone may cause her friends to "think I am doing a Brendan." Who is Brendan? What does she mean by this expression? Why will what she fears happen?

3. According to Bristow, what is the real problem with text messaging and e-mail? In any kind of communication, where should the emphasis be placed? Why?

CONSIDERING CRAFT

1. Reread the first sentence of paragraph 6. What is unusual about this sentence? Now reread paragraph 11. What is unusual there? Why did Bristow choose to write these parts of her essay this way? What does doing so accomplish?

2. In the final sentence of this essay, Bristow laments that text messaging may have us all "climbing the walls of a modern-day Tower of Babel." When does a person feel like "climbing the walls"? What is he or she feeling? Where was the Tower of Babel? Why was it built? When? What happened as a result of its being built? How well does this allusion work to illustrate Bristow's point?

3. How does knowing that Bristow wrote this for a London-based newspaper influence your reading? Find several clues in the text that indicate that the original audience for this article was British. How do these references influence you as an American reader?

RESPONDING TO THE WRITER

How strong are your grammatical skills? Why? Have email and text messaging eroded your skills? Will the next generation have fewer English-language skills? Whom or what will be to blame if they do? To what extent do you think that Bristow's concern about the failure to communicate is a problem in our society?

For a quiz on this reading, go to bedfordstmartins.com/mirror.

iPod Nation

STEVEN LEVY

In the fall of 2004, Duke University provided iPods for its entire freshman class, all 1,650 new students, at a cost of over $500,000 for the iPods, research, and a computer specialist's salary. The iPods play tunes, but their primary purpose was to deliver preloaded information about things freshmen needed to know and future downloadable course material. In "iPod Nation," Stephen Levy explores the omnipresence of the stylish little digital music machine that put Apple CEO Steve Jobs back on top and led to the iTunes Music Store, a second blockbuster hit for his computer company. Levy contends that these two products are changing forever the way we listen to music. "People who use iPods wind up listening to more music, and with more passion," Levy asserts.

Steven Levy has been writing about digital technology and its effects on our society for over twenty years. Currently, he is a senior editor and an award-winning technology columnist for *Newsweek* magazine, where he has worked since 1995. He is the author of five books, including *Hackers* (1984), *Artificial Life* (1992), and *Crypto* (2001). His writing has appeared in *The New Yorker*, the *New York Times Magazine*, *Harper's*, *Premiere*, and *Wired*. "iPod Nation" first appeared as the cover story for the July 26, 2004, issue of *Newsweek*.

THINKING AHEAD

Do you own an iPod? Would you like to own one? Why? How do or would you use it? What is your opinion about how iPods influence the way we buy, listen to, and appreciate music?

INCREASING VOCABULARY

guru (n.) (1)

ubiquity (n.) (2)

implicit (adj.) (2)

capacious (adj.) (3)

impenetrable (adj.) (3)

incandescent (adj.) (3)

telltale (adj.) (4)

glitches (n.) (6)

revitalized (v.) (7)

solvent (adj.) (9)

synchronization (n.) (11)

austerity (n.) (12)

accolade (n.) (13)

savvy (adj.) (14)

felicitous (adj.) (14)

eschew (v.) (21)

lament (v.) (21)

S teve Jobs noticed something earlier this year in New York City. "I was on Madison," says Apple's CEO, "and it was, like, on every block, there was someone with white headphones, and I thought, 'Oh, my God, it's starting to happen.'" Jonathan Ive, the company's design guru, had a similar experience in London: "On the streets and coming out of the tubes, you'd see people fiddling with it." And Victor Katch, a 59-year-old professor of kinesiology[1] at the University of Michigan, saw it in Ann Arbor. "When you walk across campus, the ratio seems as high as 2 out of 3 people," he says.

They're talking about the sudden ubiquity of the iPod, the cigarette-box-size digital music player (and its colorful credit-card-size little sister, the Mini) that's smacked right into the sweet spot where a consumer product becomes something much, much more: an icon, a pet, a status indicator and an indispensable part of one's life. To 3 million-plus owners, iPods not only give constant access to their entire collection of songs and CDs, but membership into an implicit society that's transforming the way music will be consumed in the future. "When my students see me on campus with my iPod, they smile," says Professor Katch, whose unit stores everything from Mozart to Dean Martin. "It's sort of a bonding."

The glue for the bond is a tiny, limited-function computer with a capacious disk drive, decked in white plastic and loaded with something that until very recently was the province of ultrageeks and music pirates:[2] digital files that play back as songs. Apple wasn't the first company to come out with a player, but the earlier ones were either low-capacity toys that played the same few songs, or brick-size beasts with impenetrable controls. Apple's device is not only powerful and easy to use, but has an incandescent style that makes people go nuts about it. Or, in the case of 16-year-old Brittany Vendryes of Miami, to dub it "Bob the Music Machine." ("I wanted to keep it close to my heart and give it a name," she explains.)

Adding to the appeal is the cachet of A-list approbation. "I love it!" says songwriter Denise Rich. "I have my whole catalog on it and I take it everywhere." She is only one voice in a chorus of celebrity Podsters who sing the same praises voiced by ordinary iPod users, but add a dollop[3] of coolness to the device, as if it needed it. Will Smith has burbled[4] to Jay Leno and *Wired* magazine about his infatuation with "the gadget of the century." Gwyneth Paltrow confided her Pod-love to *Vogue* (her new baby is named Apple—coincidence?). It's been seen on innumerable TV shows, movies and music videos, so much so that Fox TV recently informed Josh Schwartz, producer of its hit series *The O.C.*, that future depictions of music players would have to forgo the telltale white ear buds. Schwartz, himself a 27-year-old who still hasn't recovered from the shock of having

---

[1] **kinesiology:** The study of how parts of the body move.
[2] **ESL music pirates:** People who download music illegally.
[3] **dollop:** A small amount.
[4] **burbled:** Talked excitedly.

his unit stolen from his BMW, was outraged. "It's what our audience uses and what our characters would use," he says.

People who actually create music are among the biggest fans: "The layout reminds the musician of music," says tunester John Mayer. And couture maven[5] Karl Lagerfeld's iPod collection is up to 60, coded in the back by laser etching so he can tell what's on them. "It's *the* way to store music," he says. Lagerfeld's tribute to the iPod is a $1,500 Fendi pink copper rectangular purse that holds 12 iPods. It is one of more than 200 third-party accessories ranging from external speakers, microphones and — fasten your seat belt — a special connector that lets you control your iPod from the steering wheel of a BMW.

Music hits people's emotions, and the purchase of something that opens up one's entire music collection — up to 10,000 songs in your pocket — makes for an intense relationship. When people buy iPods, they often obsess, talking incessantly about playlists and segues,[6] grumbling about glitches, fixating on battery life and panicking at the very thought of losing their new digital friend. "I'd be devastated if I lost it," says Krystyn Lynch, a Boston investment marketer.

Fans of the devices use it for more than music. "It's the limousine for the spoken word," says Audible CEO Don Katz, whose struggling digital audiobook company has been revitalized by having its products on Apple's iTunes store. (Podsters downloaded thousands of copies of Bill Clinton's autobiography within minutes of its 3 a.m. release last month.) And computer users have discovered that its vast storage space makes it a useful vault for huge digital files — the makers of the *Lord of the Rings* movies used iPods to shuttle dailies[7] from the set to the studio. Thousands of less-accomplished shutterbugs store digital photos on them.

iPods aren't conspicuous everywhere — their popularity seems centered on big cities and college towns — but sometimes it seems that way. "I notice that when I'm in the gym, as I look down the treadmills, that just about everybody in the row has one," says Scott Piro, a New York City book publicist. And the capper came earlier this year during the *Apple vs. Apple* case — wherein the Beatles' record company is suing the computer firm on a trademark issue. The judge wondered if he should recuse[8] himself — because he is an avid iPod user. (The litigants[9] had no objection to his staying on.)

In 1997, when Steve Jobs returned to the then struggling company he had cofounded, he says, there were no plans for a music initiative. In fact, he says, there wasn't a plan for anything. "Our goal was to revitalize and get organized, and if there were opportunities we'd see them," he says.

---

[5] **couture maven:** An expert or knowledgeable enthusiast in designer fashions.
[6] **segues:** Smooth transitions.
[7] **dailies:** Rough, unedited clips of film that are reviewed on the same day they are shot.
[8] **recuse:** To remove from participation because of bias.
[9] **litigants:** People involved in a lawsuit.

"We just had to be ready to catch the ball when it's thrown by life." After some painful pink-slipping[10] and some joyous innovating, the company was solvent.

But in the flurry, Jobs & Co. initially failed to notice the impending revolution in digital music. Once that omission was understood, Apple compensated by developing a slick "jukebox" application known as iTunes. It was then that Apple's brain trust noticed that digital music players weren't selling. Why not? "The products stank," says Apple VP Greg Joswiak. 10

Life had tossed Jobs a softball, and early in 2001 he ordered his engineers to catch it. That February, Apple's hardware czar,[11] Jon Rubinstein, picked a team leader from outside the company—an engineer named Tony Fadell. "I was on the ski slopes in Vail when I got the call," says Fadell, who was told that the idea was to create a ground-breaking music player—and have it on sale for Christmas season that year. The requirements: A very fast connection to one's computer (via Apple's high-speed Firewire standard) so songs could be quickly uploaded. A close synchronization with the iTunes software to make it easy to organize music. An interface that would be simple to use. And gorgeous. 11

Fadell was able to draw on all of Apple's talents from Jobs on down. VP Phil Schiller came up with the idea of a scroll wheel that made the menus accelerate as your finger spun on it. Meanwhile, Apple's industrial designer Ive embarked on a search for the obvious. "From early on we wanted a product that would seem so natural and so inevitable and so simple you almost wouldn't think of it as having been designed," he says. This austerity extended to the whiteness of the iPod, a double-crystal polymer Antarctica, a blankness that screams in brilliant colors across a crowded subway. "It's neutral, but it is a bold neutral, just shockingly neutral," says Ive. 12

Assessing the final product, Jobs bestows, for him, the ultimate accolade: "It's as Apple as anything Apple has ever done." 13

The October 2001 launch was barely a month after 9/11, with the country on edge and the tech industry in the toilet.[12] Skeptics scoffed at the $399 price and the fact that only Macintosh users, less than a twentieth of the marketplace, could use it. But savvy Mac-heads saw the value, and the iPod was a hit, if not yet a sensation. What pushed it to the next level was a number of Apple initiatives beginning with a quick upgrade cycle that increased the number of songs (while actually lowering the price). Then Apple released a version that would run on Windows and Mac, dramatically increasing the potential market. Finally, after intense negotiations with the record labels, Apple licensed hundreds of thousands of songs for its iTunes Music Store, which blended seamlessly with the iPod. As with the iPod itself, the legal-download store was not the first of its kind but was so felicitous and efficient that it leapt to a 70 percent market share. 14

---

[10] **ESL** **pink-slipping:** Firing from a job.
[11] **czar:** An absolute ruler; one with great authority and power to control.
[12] **ESL** **in the toilet:** In serious danger of failing.

Then sales began to spike. No one was surprised that Apple sold an   15
impressive 733,000 iPods during the Christmas season last year, but the
normally quiet quarter after that saw an increase to 807,000. And last
week Apple announced that sales in the just-completed third quarter, traditionally another dead one—hit 860,000, up from 249,000 a year ago.

That total would have been higher had Apple not had problems get-   16
ting parts for the latest iteration,[13] the iPod Mini. Though critics praised
its compactness and its panache[14]—a burnished metallic surface made it
look like a futuristic Zippo[15]—they sniffed at its relatively low capacity
(only 1,000 songs!). But apparently there were lots of people like Los Angeles chiropractor Pat Dengler, who saw the Mini as a must. "At first I
thought, I already have an iPod, I don't need it," she says. "But after I
played with it, I thought, I really dig it. Now I use them both." Dengler
was lucky, as many had to suffer through a month-long waiting list. To
the delight of Apple (and the chagrin of Sony), the no-brainer description
of the iPod is "the Walkman of the 21st century." And just as the Walkman changed the landscape of music and the soundscape of our lives, the
iPod and the iTunes store are making their mark on the way we handle
our music, and even the way we listen to it.

The store has proved that many people will pay for digital music (though   17
certainly many millions of gigabytes of iPod space are loaded with tunes
plucked from the dark side of the Internet). "The iPod and iTunes store
are a shining light at a very bleak time in the industry," says Cary Sher-
man, president of the Record Industry Association of America. Since just
about everybody feels that within a decade almost everybody will get their
music from such places, this is very big.

An equally big deal is the way the iPod is changing our listening style.   18
Michael Bull, a lecturer at the University of Sussex, has interviewed thousands of iPod users, finding that the ability to take your whole music collection with you changes everything. "People define their own narrative
through their music collection," says Bull.

The primary way to exploit this ability is the iPod's "shuffle" feature.   19
This takes your entire music collection, reorders it with the thoroughness
of a Las Vegas blackjack dealer and then plays back the crazy-quilt
mélange.[16] "Shuffle throws up almost anything—you don't know it's
coming but you know you like it," says Bull. "Because of this people often
say, 'It's almost as if my iPod understands me.'"

Shuffle winds up helping people make connections between different   20
genres of music. "People feel they're walking through musicology,"[17] says
rocker John Mayer. These abilities have a predictable effect: people who
use iPods wind up listening to more music, and with more passion.

---

[13] iteration: Version.
[14] panache: Style.
[15] ESL Zippo: A brand of cigarette lighter.
[16] crazy-quilt mélange: A mixture in random order.
[17] musicology: The scholarly study of music.

And since the iTunes store encourages customers to eschew buying entire CDs, instead buying the best song or two for a buck a pop, it's easy to see why some think that the era of the CD is playing its final tracks, a circumstance many will lament. "The one cool thing about a CD is really getting to know an album," says iPod fan Wil-Dog Abers, bassist for the hip-hop collective Ozomatli. "I don't know what we're gonna do about that."

In Silicon Valley, the question is what Apple can do to maintain its dominant position in the field. While Apple execs say that they are surprised at how lame[18] the competition has been to date, it's reasonable to think that rivals might eventually close the gap. Almost all the hounds chasing Apple use technology from its longtime rival Microsoft. And Sony, whose initial efforts in the field were constrained by the copy-protection demands of its music unit, is introducing a new line of digital players this summer. "We feel that the experience is as good as Apple's, and we have the Walkman brand, which has sold 200 million units. We're in the game," says Sony America's CEO Howard Stringer. Meanwhile, the ultimate competition may come from services that stream unlimited music for a monthly fee, like Real Networks' Rhapsody. "The fat lady isn't even on the stage yet," says Chris Gorog, CEO of Napster.

But at the moment, the iPod *is* the category. And everything points to a humongous Christmas season for the iPod. The introduction of the new iPods this week extends the company's technology lead. If Apple, as promised, manages to get enough drives to satisfy the demand, the Mini iPod may achieve the ubiquity of its wide-bodied companion. And later this summer, when computer giant HP begins selling a cobranded version of the iPod, consumers will be able to get iPods in thousands of additional retail stores.

All this is infinitely gratifying for Steve Jobs, the computer pioneer and studio CEO who turns 50 next February. "I have a very simple life," he says, without a trace of irony. "I have my family and I have Apple and Pixar. And I don't do much else." But the night before our interview, Jobs and his kids sat down for their first family screening of Pixar's 2004 release *The Incredibles*. After that, he tracked the countdown to the 100 millionth song sold on the iTunes store. Apple had promised a prize to the person who moved the odometer to 10 figures, and as the big number approached, fortune seekers snapped up files at a furious rate. At around 10:15, 20-year-old Kevin Britten of Hays, Kans., bought a song by the electronica band Zero 7, and Jobs himself got on the phone to tell him that he'd won. Then Jobs asked a potentially embarrassing question: "Do you have a Mac or PC?"

"I have a Macintosh . . . *duh*!" said Britten.

Jobs laughs while recounting this. Even though Macintosh sales have gone up recently, he knows that the odds are small of anyone's owning a

---

[18] **lame:** Ineffective, weak.

Mac as opposed to the competition. He doesn't want that to happen with his company's music player. "There are lots of examples where not the best product wins," he says. "Windows would be one of those, but there are examples where the best product wins. And the iPod is a great example of that." As anyone can see from all those white cords dangling from people's ears.

EXERCISING VOCABULARY

1. In Levy's original article, a line of text across the title reads "In just three years, Apple's adorable mini music player has gone from gizmo to life-changing cultural icon." What is a gizmo? What is a cultural icon? How are the two different?

2. The author states that iPods have "the cachet of A-list approbation" (para. 4). Define *cachet*. What does *approbation* mean? Who is on an A-list? What does having A-list approbation signify about iPods?

3. Karl Lagerfeld's pink copper rectangular purse is one of many third-party accessories for iPods. Explain what a third-party accessory is. Why are these being created? What does their prevalence say about iPods?

PROBING CONTENT

1. Why have iPods become so important to so many people? What do iPods represent? How do some people feel about their iPods?

2. How was the iPod developed? Why were the original iPods white?

3. What surprises occurred with the sales of iPods? What obstacles has Apple encountered?

4. How do musicians and others in the music industry feel about iPods? Why?

5. In what ways are iPods changing people's listening styles? What one iPod feature has been particularly important to these changes? How?

CONSIDERING CRAFT

1. Locate several sentences or phrases throughout this essay that indicate Levy's attitude about iPods. What is his attitude? How clearly is that attitude communicated here?

2. Although no other manufacturer has achieved Apple's level of success with the iPod, Chris Gorog of Napster says, "The fat lady isn't even on the stage yet" (para. 22). To what operatic expression is Gorog alluding? What does this expression mean? Why does Levy include this quotation when many readers may not know what Gorog is implying? What does the expression indicate about Gorog's attitude?

3. In paragraphs 2 and 11, Levy uses sports terminology to discuss the rise of the iPod. Pick out the baseball and softball language in these two paragraphs. Why does he use this language? How effective is it in advancing his point in the essay?

RESPONDING TO THE WRITER

How do the facts that celebrities own iPods and that we see them on television shows like *The O.C.* contribute to the iPod's success? Have iPods really changed our relationship with music? In what ways? Why?

For a quiz on this reading, go to bedfordstmartins.com/mirror.

Blog

WILLIAM SAFIRE

Blogging is big. In an article in the February 15, 2005, issue of *CIO* magazine, the Pew Internet and American Life Project reported a fifty-eight percent increase in the number of blog, or "Web-log," readers between February and November 2004. Their report also revealed that approximately fourteen million Internet users in the United States (one out of every ten Internet users) have made a comment on a blog. And *USA Today* reports that the number of blogs posted by American military members in Afghanistan and Iraq is skyrocketing (May 12, 2005). In this July 28, 2002, column written for the *New York Times*, William Safire explains what a blog is, where the word came from, and where the word and its concept may be going.

William Safire is a distinguished journalist, author, political commentator, historian, and lexicographer. He is also well known as one of President Richard Nixon's speechwriters. He has been a fixture at the *New York Times* since 1973, writing both political commentary and his weekly On Language column. He is the author of twenty-five fiction and nonfiction books, including the Civil War novel *Freedom* (1991); *Spread the Word* (1999), one of several collections of his *New York Times* commentaries; and *Lend Me Your Ears: Great Speeches in History, Updated and Expanded Edition* (2004). His most recent novel, about the beginning of freedom of the press in America, is titled *Scandalmonger* (2000).

THINKING AHEAD

Do you blog? What do you think of this form of communication? How personal is it? What effect does the popularity of blogging have on other forms of communication? Will the popularity of blogging last? Why?

INCREASING VOCABULARY

upbeat (adj.) (1)	coerce (v.) (4)
incurable (adj.) (1)	snide (adj.) (4)
entrepreneurs (n.) (2)	lexicon (n.) (5)
musings (n.) (3)	burgeoning (adj.) (7)
titillate (v.) (3)	

In an upbeat Independence Day column in the *Wall Street Journal*, 1
Peggy Noonan, the incurable optimist, wrote about all "the lights that didn't fail" America—from cops and firemen to peach-growing farmers and cancer-curing scientists, from local churches to TV comedians to *blogging.*

Blogging? She explained the word as "the 24/7 opinion sites that offer   2
free speech at its straightest, truest, wildest, most uncensored, most thoughtful, most strange. Thousands of independent information entrepreneurs are
informing, arguing, adding information."

Blog is a shortening of *Web log*. It is a Web site belonging to some   3
average but opinionated Joe or Josie who keeps what used to be called
a "commonplace book"—a collection of clippings, musings and other
things like journal entries that strike one's fancy or titillate one's curiosity.
What makes this online daybook different from the commonplace book is
that this form of personal noodling[1] or diary-writing is on the Internet,
with links that take the reader around the world in pursuit of more about
a topic.

To set one up (which I have not done because I don't want anyone to   4
know what I think), you log on to a free service like blogger.com or
xanga.com, fill out a form and let it create a Web site for you. Then you
follow the instructions about how to post your thoughts, photos and clippings, making you an instant publisher. You then persuade or coerce your
friends, family or colleagues to log on to you and write in their own loving or snide comments.

"Will the *blogs* kill old media?" asked *Newsweek*, an old-media pub-   5
lication, perhaps a little worried about this disintermediation leading to
an invasion of alien ad-snatchers. My answer is no; gossips like an old-
fashioned party line,[2] but most information seekers and opinion junkies
will go for reliable old media in zingy[3] new digital clothes. Be that as it
may (a phrase to avoid the voguism[4] *that said*), the noun *blog* is a useful
addition to the lexicon.

Forget its earliest sense, perhaps related to *grog*, reported in 1982 in   6
the *Toronto Globe and Mail* as "a lethal fanzine punch concocted more or
less at random out of any available alcoholic beverages." The first use I
can find of the root of *blog* in its current sense was the 1999 "Robot Wisdom Weblog," created by Jorn Barger of Chicago.

Then followed *bloggers*, for those who perform the act of *blogging*   7
and—to encompass the burgeoning world of Web logs—*blogistan* as
well as the coinage[5] of William Quick on the *blog* he calls *The Daily Pundit*, the *blogosphere*. Sure to come: the *blogiverse*.

EXERCISING VOCABULARY

1. In paragraph 5, Safire uses the word *disintermediation*. What do each of the
   component parts of this word mean (*dis-inter-mediation*)? When these components are combined, what does the new word mean?

---

[1] **noodling:** Experimenting creatively.
[2] **party line:** A telephone line shared by several households.
[3] **zingy:** Lively.
[4] **voguism:** A currently fashionable statement.
[5] **coinage:** An invented word or phrase.

2. In paragraph 6, the author notes that *blog* is "perhaps related to *grog*," once defined as "a lethal fanzine punch." What is grog? To whom is it generally available? What is a fanzine? What ingredients might make up a punch? When all these words are put together, what is Safire implying about blogging?

3. Why does Safire include all the new words derived from *blog* in paragraph 7? What does their formation indicate about blogging?

PROBING CONTENT

1. What is a "commonplace book"? In what ways is a blog similar to a commonplace book? How are the two different?

2. What steps are involved in setting up a blog site? How difficult and expensive is it to do so?

CONSIDERING CRAFT

1. In paragraph 5, Safire cites *Newsweek*'s concern about blogging "leading to an invasion of alien ad-snatchers." What are aliens usually accused of snatching? Why would *Newsweek* be concerned about ad snatchers? How does this expression sum up Safire's opinion about *Newsweek's* concerns?

2. Safire's newspaper column on blogging is a kind of writing known as extended definition. How does this kind of definition differ from the kind of definition that you find in a dictionary? What additional information does it include? How does the tone here differ from that of a brief dictionary definition?

3. This is a brief column. If Safire wanted to expand his thoughts, what other subtopics might he include? How would such inclusions strengthen or weaken his essay? Why?

RESPONDING TO THE WRITER

What influence or effect do you think the popularity of blogging will have on traditional media sources like television, magazines, and books? What segments of the population are most attracted to blogging? Explain your response.

For a quiz on this reading, go to bedfordstmartins.com/mirror.

Our Biotech Bodies, Ourselves

James Pethokoukis

Can we invent our way around aging and disease? Should we? How would society change if human beings could anticipate 150 productive years of life instead of 75? In "Our Biotech Bodies, Ourselves," which first appeared in the May 31, 2004, issue of *U.S. News & World Report*, James Pethokoukis explores the debate raging among ethicists and scientists who are negotiating thorny new ground with each carefully researched advance. One bioethicist points out that technology is already ahead of public policy in many areas. While some organizations work to close off controversial research avenues like human cloning, others rush to discover the therapeutic value of equally controversial areas like stem-cell research.

James Pethokoukis is a senior editor at *U.S. News & World Report*, where he also writes the Next News Science and Technology column for the magazine's Web site, usnews.com. His articles have also appeared on techcentralstation.com.

THINKING AHEAD

If you were given the opportunity to enhance some aspect of yourself physically or mentally, would you choose to do so? What would you elect to change? Why? Do you believe that human beings should be genetically designed? Do you support stem-cell research? Cloning? Where do you think the line should be drawn between what scientists can do and what they should do? Who should set the limits?

INCREASING VOCABULARY

prowess (n.) (1)	articulating (v.) (11)
fodder (n.) (2)	theoretical (adj.) (11)
disquiet (n.) (3)	tangible (adj.) (11)
nascent (adj.) (4)	therapeutic (adj.) (11)
profound (adj.) (6)	rhetoric (n.) (13)
tweaks (n.) (8)	spawn (v.) (13)
longevity (n.) (10)	catalyst (n.) (13)

What if, by taking a drug, you could possess an IQ of 250? Or by tinkering with your genes, have the athletic prowess of a decathlete?[1] Or by injecting yourself with stem cells, live to be 160? Would you do it? Would these enhancements make you less human? If everyone did this, would the world become a paradise full of

---

[1] **decathlete:** An athlete who competes in ten different track-and-field events.

self-actualized[2] superpeople? Or a dystopian[3] Stepford[4] society devoid of essential human values such as compassion for the less blessed?

What seems like fodder for a science fiction potboiler[5] has become a matter of deadly serious debate among scientists and ethicists. In a speech last year before a gathering of enhancement advocates, William Sims Bainbridge, a deputy director at the National Science Foundation who studies the societal impact of technology, warned that "scientists may be forced into rebellion in order to carry out research prohibited unnecessarily by powerful institutions."   2

A few months later, Leon Kass, chair of the President's Council on Bioethics, was expressing the advisory panel's profound "disquiet" with a biotech-enabled, post-human future that "cheapens rather than enriches America's most cherished ideals." The council's 325-page report, *Beyond Therapy: Biotechnology and the Pursuit of Happiness,* takes a decidedly dim view[6] of the impact of such issues as radical life extension, mood and intelligence-enhancing drugs, and genetic therapies.   3

At the core of the conflict lies a fundamental question: How far should homo sapiens be allowed to go? Nascent technologies like genetic engineering, stem-cell therapy, and neuropharmacology promise not only to cure our diseases but to enhance our bodies, even to turn us all into the Six Million Dollar Man[7] — better, stronger, and faster.   4

Clash

But not everyone thinks humans should be bioengineered. "Our increasing ability to alter our biology and open up the processes of life is now fueling a new cultural war," says Gregory Stock, director of the University of California–Los Angeles's Program on Medicine, Technology, and Society and author of the pro-enhancement book *Redesigning Humans.*   5

Yet isn't arguing about whether mankind should transform itself into a race of superhumans a little like arguing about whether the first Mars colony should have a bicameral or unicameral legislature? Kass doesn't think so. "These topics are not futuristic," he says. "Some of these issues are already here. Choosing the sex of your children is here. The use of stimulants on children to improve performance is here. Steroid use is here. Drugs that affect mood and temperament are here. . . . There is something profound going on here that will affect our identities and the society we live in."   6

Indeed, there are hints that genetic engineering might be able to alter mankind in some astounding ways. Researchers at the University of   7

---

[2] **self-actualized:** Having achieved one's full potential.
[3] **dystopian:** Marked by a poor quality of life.
[4] **Stepford:** Refers to Ira Levin's novel *The Stepford Wives,* in which all the women of an upper-middle-class town in Connecticut are robots.
[5] **potboiler:** A piece of inferior fiction produced for money.
[6] **ESL** **dim view:** A low opinion.
[7] *Six Million Dollar Man:* A 1970s television show about an astronaut who is badly hurt in a test flight and has his body rebuilt by scientists to be better and stronger.

Pennsylvania have boosted levels of a protein in mice that makes them more muscular throughout life. Southern Illinois University scientists extended one mouse's life span to nearly twice the normal length.

But governments around the world are already putting brakes on this type of research, especially as it applies to humans. President Bush famously banned the federal funding of research on new embryonic stem-cell lines in 2001. A year later, the South Korean government raided BioFusion Tech, a company backed by the Raelian religious sect, after the group announced that a Korean woman would give birth to a clone[8] — even though cloning isn't illegal there. And at least 17 countries have banned germ-line modification, which alters reproductive cells so that genetic tweaks will be passed down to future generations.

"How we respond to these threats to enhancement today will lay the groundwork for dealing with the ones that emerge in the future," says enhancement activist James Hughes, a lecturer in health policy at Trinity College in Hartford, Conn. Political scientist Francis Fukuyama agrees that policies need to be shaped before these technologies fully ripen — although Fukuyama, member of the bioethics council and author of *Our Posthuman Future*, counts himself a bioconservative. "If you don't shake people up now, then you will get these gradual changes that are going to end up leading us to a place that we're not going to be comfortable with," he says.

Side Effects

Why worry about human enhancement? After all, what's not to like about, say, doubling the average human life span? But the bioethics council wonders in its report whether we would achieve a "stretched rubber band" version of longevity in which our active, healthy years would be extended, but so would our years of decline and decay. "Having many long, productive years, with the knowledge of many more to come, would surely bring joy to many of us," says panel member William Hurlbut, a bioethicist at Stanford University. "But in the end, these techniques could also leave the individual somewhat unhinged from the life cycle. Do I want to live to be 100? Sure. But to 250 or some other dramatic extension? No."

Bioconservatives acknowledge, however, that human enhancement may be inevitable. Even Kass admits that the council's report focused on the problems of enhancement rather than its benefits because the advantages of longer lives and better brains are so obvious "they don't need articulating." It's easy to argue the "con" position, says UCLA's Stock, about issues like the use of embryonic stem cells as long as the benefits are merely theoretical. Once those benefits become tangible, though, "the debate will be over," says Stock. Indeed, the potential therapeutic value of stem-cell research has already prompted more than 200 House members and Nancy Reagan to urge Bush to alter his ban.

---

[8] **clone:** A person or thing that is an exact replica of the one from which it is derived.

With the proliferation of plastic surgery, for example, or the use of   12
Ritalin by achievement-crazed students hoping to score better on the SAT,
enhancement seems to be the wave of the future. Even Bush's Department
of Commerce appears to be buying into it. In a 2002 joint report with the
National Science Foundation (coauthored by Bainbridge among others),
the agency recommended a national research-and-development effort to
enhance humanity in order to create a world where human brains communicate directly with machines, and scientists "control the genetics of
humans" to make bodies "more durable, healthier . . . and more resistant
to many kinds of stress, biological threats, and aging processes." If successful, the effort will "create a golden age that would be a turning point
for human productivity and quality of life."

Or not. Science could render all this high-flying rhetoric just that.   13
Stem-cell and protein therapies, after all, have yet to spawn any successful
treatments for disease, much less provide the catalyst for launching a new
stage of human evolution. In 2000, researchers used gene therapy to cure
two French boys of an inherited immune-system disorder but in the process gave them leukemia. Who knows what other dangerous side effects
these new therapies will bring? It is, as they say, too early to tell—but
judging by the intensity of the debate, not any too early to fight.

EXERCISING VOCABULARY

1. The debate about human enhancement through technology often pits ethicists against scientists. What do ethicists study? What do they support?
   What is their position in this debate?

2. In paragraph 13, the author refers to the promise of human biological enhancement as "high-flying rhetoric." What is rhetoric? In what sense is this
   rhetoric high-flying? How does the use of this expression reveal the author's
   opinion about the promise of biological enhancement?

PROBING CONTENT

1. What is the position of the President's Council on Bioethics on the possibilities of biotechnology? Where has the Council expressed its views?

2. What are some of the biotechnical enhancements in practice today? How significant are these, according to Leon Kass, chair of the President's Council on
   Bioethics? Why?

3. To what types of biotechnical research have some governments already reacted unfavorably? Why? Cite specific examples from this essay.

CONSIDERING CRAFT

1. How would you describe the author's tone in paragraph 6 when he asks, "Yet
   isn't arguing about whether mankind should transform itself into a race of

superhumans a little like arguing about whether the first Mars colony should have a bicameral or a unicameral legislature"? What is the difference between a bicameral and a unicameral legislature? How relevant is that difference to this essay's topic? What point is he trying to make? What does this question imply about the author's viewpoint?

2. The author notes that the report of the President's Council on Bioethics seems to address the possible problems associated with human enhancement rather than its possible benefits. To what extent is this true of the whole essay? Why do you think the author chose this approach? What was his purpose in writing this piece?

RESPONDING TO THE WRITER

Do you think that Leon Kass and the President's Council on Bioethics are right to be concerned about the possible applications of biotechnical enhancements for humans? What could happen if the technology is allowed to progress as fast as science permits?

For a quiz on this reading, go to bedfordstmartins.com/mirror.

From Ivory Tower to Academic Sweatshop

ALEX WRIGHT

Should education be a business? Should the demands of the marketplace determine how and what students learn? How closely should corporate and educational institutions be allied? In "From Ivory Tower to Academic Sweatshop," Alex Wright explores the rise, fall, and rise again of online adult education, as well as its effects on teachers, students, curricula, and university economies. Both employers and students are demanding a more efficient university "product" with educational outcomes designed to satisfy not the curiosity of the mind but the requirements of the job.

Alex Wright is a writer and architect based in San Francisco. He has written on topics ranging from quantum physics to book preservation for publications including *Salon.com*, the *Utne Reader*, *New Architect*, *Think*, *Harvard Magazine*, *Design Times*, *Boston Business*, *Boxes and Arrows*, and *Library Journal*.

THINKING AHEAD

Have you ever taken a course online? Would you like to? Why? What did or would you like about that method of delivering course content? What did or would you dislike? What is gained and what is lost in distance education?

INCREASING VOCABULARY

keen (adj.) (2)	misconstrued (v.) (36)
booming (adj.) (2)	auspices (n.) (41)
swirling (v.) (2)	boon (n.) (43)
wrenching (adj.) (7)	savvy (n.) (46)
caricature (n.) (9)	ascendancy (n.) (47)
doling (v.) (9)	benign (adj.) (47)
dubious (adj.) (10)	charismatic (adj.) (48)
adjunct (n.) (15)	deployed (v.) (53)
replicating (v.) (22)	nascent (adj.) (57)
leverages (v.) (23)	porous (adj.) (60)
idiosyncratic (adj.) (23)	dire (adj.) (62)
mandate (n.) (28)	

As he walked into the gloomy, windowless auditorium inside Denver's Colorado Convention Center, Geoff Hunt remembers thinking, "God, there are a huge number of people here." 1

Hunt, a history professor at the nearby Community College of Aurora, had accepted a friend's invitation to attend the University of Phoenix 2 graduation ceremony for its Denver-area students. Hunt was keen to take a closer look at Phoenix, the for-profit juggernaut[1] whose booming distance-learning programs were changing the calculus of higher education at schools nationwide, including his own. Outside the Aurora faculty lounge, dark rumors were swirling of state bureaucrats talking up a troubling notion: the "professor-less classroom."

Hunt listened intently as the commencement speaker, a Phoenix professor who had recently been named Faculty of the Year, gave a speech describing how Phoenix had transformed her role as a professor. "She defined her job," he remembers, as "delivery of chapters."

That phrase, Hunt says, "just sent chills down my back."

Hunt isn't the only faculty member feeling the chill. As distance learning grows into a $5 billion a year market—up 38 percent in 2004 alone—virtual classrooms are no longer the sole province of dot-coms and for-profit schools like DeVry and Phoenix. Top universities such as Harvard, Stanford, and Duke now offer full credit for online courses. On campuses nationwide, distance learning is moving out of the pedagogical[2] fringe and into the institutional mainstream.

While faculty continue to debate the educational merits of online teaching (a recent national survey found their opinions roughly divided), most agree that distance learning is here to stay. To some optimists this is an unqualified good thing—a chance to increase access to educational opportunities and to break down the hierarchies of traditional university bureaucracies. For every worried Geoff Hunt, another teacher is happily working at home, content never to see the inside of a lecture hall. But others are more alarmed and are beginning to wonder whether their jobs will ever be the same.

Just as the Internet brought wrenching operational changes to many corporations, so online learning is triggering a seismic shift in the academic power structure. Those changes stretch far deeper than the visible presentation layer of courseware, online discussions and multimedia presentations. Distance learning is changing not only teaching methods but also the shape of the curriculum itself. As schools reach out to a market composed largely of professional, career-minded students, they face growing pressure to cater to employers' agendas; in some cases, even wiring themselves into the corporate information technology (IT) infrastructure.[3] If a company like Lucent underwrites online courses at a business school, it expects a direct return on its investment.

"Universities are not simply undergoing a technological transformation," writes York University professor David F. Noble, a vocal critic of distance learning. "Beneath that change, and camouflaged by it, lies another: the commercialization of higher education."

When a cat named Colby earned an M.B.A. online from Trinity Southern University in Plano, Texas, last year, distance-learning critics found

---

[1] juggernaut: A large, overpowering force.
[2] pedagogical: Associated with teaching.
[3] infrastructure: The inner composition.

a ready caricature for a popular stereotype: distance-learning schools as glorified diploma mills, doling out easy credentials to anyone with a Web browser and a credit card.

Indeed, plug the words "distance learning" into Google and you'll see   10
ads in the right-hand column of the Web page for dubious alma maters like Almeda University, promising your choice of associate's, bachelor's or master's degree with "No Books! No Courses! No Studying!" But if distance learning were so easily dismissed, one might expect a little less enthusiasm from the 97 percent of public universities that now offer online courses. Last year, an estimated 3 million students took at least one class online and 600,000 students completed all of their coursework online.

While many educators continue to insist on the irreplaceable quality   11
of in-person teaching, numerous studies show that under the right circumstances, and with certain subjects, online students achieve learning outcomes similar to those in physical classrooms.

Even critics acknowledge that distance learning opens doors for work-   12
ing professionals and residents of remote areas who would otherwise have limited access to higher education. But these students differ significantly from on-campus students, who often take years off to immerse themselves in a particular discipline. Distance learning students are typically older, mid-career, and careful about managing their time. They favor practical, skill-building courses like those in business, nursing, accounting, computer science and other marketable trades.

"Hitting the sweet spot[4] in online education today means going after   13
the working professional who wants to advance their career by taking courses," says Philip DiSalvio, program director of Seton Hall University's SetonWorldWide program.

While many schools also endeavor to offer "soft" subjects in the hu-   14
manities online, the market overwhelmingly favors professional education. "There is strong pressure to make education more technical, more like training," says Andrew Feenberg, research chair in philosophy of technology at Vancouver's Simon Fraser University. "That pressure comes both from the corporate world, and from students themselves, who are very career oriented." The result: a growing commoditization of the curriculum and a tendency for schools to market education as a "product."

At some schools, the boundaries between physical and virtual class-   15
rooms are dissolving into so-called blended learning environments that incorporate the Internet as an adjunct to the traditional lecture hall. Many faculty now routinely take advantage of courseware like Blackboard or WebCT to publish their lesson plans and lecture notes and to moderate online discussions as an extension of the classroom experience.

Noah Butter is working on his master's degree in library and information   16
science at San Jose State University, a blended program that incorporates

---

[4] **ESL** **hitting the sweet spot:** A baseball term for connecting a ball with the perfect spot on a bat; being exactly in the right place.

online and offline courses. Of the 11 classes he has taken so far, four have met exclusively online, including his two current semester classes in online searching and information technology. All of his courses involve some form of online component, some meeting in person as infrequently as twice a semester.

Butter has discovered that online courses are no cakewalk.[5] "Online courses are a lot more work," he says, pointing out that classes require students to participate actively in online discussions and to stay on top of a constant stream of e-mail. Indeed, Butter feels that he has gotten more for his money from online classes than from some of his in-person classes. "It depends on the teacher," he says. "When teachers don't use the technology, and you only meet a few times during the semester, you end up feeling a little ripped off." **17**

But while Butter knows he is acquiring the professional skills he needs to pursue his chosen career, he sometimes longs for a more traditional campus education. "I have missed having more student and teacher face-to-face interactions," he says. "In the courses where I have met students in class, I wished we could have spent more time together." **18**

Given the demonstrated effectiveness and broader outreach made possible by distance learning, only the most strident Luddite[6] would argue that distance learning has no place in the arsenal of modern instruction. But the larger effect of distance learning technology extends beyond student-teacher dialectics[7] and into the realm of institutional power relationships. **19**

In addition to external market pressures, corporate influence also manifests itself in the expanding role of commercial software vendors, administrators and information technology professionals, who not only wield a growing influence over teaching methods, but who also bring to bear corporate values like teamwork, accountability and an overarching emphasis on "the customer." **20**

Arlene Hiss is a former Indy race-car driver, now the owner of a commercial recording studio and an occasional washboard player in a bluegrass band. She lives in a geodesic dome[8] in Lake Elsinore, Calif., where she logs on each week to conduct an undergraduate class in critical thinking at the University of Phoenix Online. A Phoenix professor since 1991, Hiss loves teaching in the distance-learning program. "They give you everything: the syllabus, the textbook, weekly assignments," she says. "They put the lectures on the Web." By "lectures," she means the written documents furnished to her, and her students, by the Phoenix courseware servers. **21**

With a Ph.D., M.B.A., and 30 years of teaching experience, Hiss is perfectly qualified to create her own course materials. But Phoenix has built its business through economies of scale, developing a course once **22**

---

[5] **ESL cakewalk:** Derived from a children's game; not difficult.
[6] **Luddite:** One of a group of 1800s English workers who destroyed machinery that they feared would take over their jobs.
[7] **dialectics:** Discussions based on logical argument.
[8] **geodesic dome:** A lightweight structure shaped like half a sphere.

and then replicating it, so that many teachers can administer the same course to the school's vast 200,000-plus student body.

That model of replicable courseware is taking hold at other schools as well. When she's not teaching at Phoenix, Hiss leverages her Phoenix experience to develop courseware for the University of Liverpool, where she works as a so-called module manager, creating class syllabuses and assignments for online business classes. After she develops the course, Hiss then oversees a network of lower-paid instructors who teach the class using her materials. The other instructors are welcome to make suggestions, but as the module manager, Hiss has the final say, ensuring that teachers won't make idiosyncratic changes to the curriculum.   23

When she's not teaching at Phoenix or Liverpool, Hiss also finds time to teach online courses at Capella University, Southern New Hampshire University, and Upper Iowa University.   24

Hiss may have her hands full, but she's happy. "As long as my eyes work, as long as my fingers work, and as long as my computer works, I can't even imagine going back to the ground." Teaching at Phoenix gives her time to juggle other teaching jobs, manage her recording studio, play with her bluegrass band, and enjoy the freedoms of the contractor lifestyle. But personal freedom is one thing, academic freedom quite another. Like the other 8,000 faculty members who teach at Phoenix Online, Hiss will never have tenure.   25

Computer-based distance learning has been around in one form or another since the 1970s. But most of those efforts remained confined to academic computing labs until the Internet boom of the 1990s. The explosion of Web access, coupled with advances in educational software, set the stage for an expansion that quickly mushroomed into a dot-com-era boom.   26

Amid the contagious optimism of the IPO era, universities began investing aggressively in online learning initiatives. Starting around 1998, big schools like UCLA, NYU, Temple, Columbia, and Cornell all kicked off heavily funded virtual-campus initiatives. Other schools hedged their bets[9] by joining online consortia like UNext (funded by Larry Ellison and Michael Milken, among others) and the Western Governors' University.   27

In many cases, these dot-edu projects took shape as for-profit subsidiaries, owned by the parent institutions but operating with a clear mandate to generate profits. In some cases, universities launched their dot-edus as joint ventures with commercial software companies. In 2000, four companies—Kaplan Ventures, Knowledge Universe, Pearson, and Sylvan Ventures—invested $3.6 billion in online initiatives.   28

To the M.B.A.s and university administrators who led the charge, the dot-edu business looked like an unbeatable proposition: a proven product, new markets unbounded by geographic constraints, economies of scale in the form of "write-once, run-anywhere" courseware, and potentially higher operating margins than all those labor-intensive physical classrooms.   29

[9] **ESL** **hedged their bets:** Invested in both sides to ensure winning.

"The dream was to transform colleges into record companies, selling 30
CDs and 'colleges in a box' for $49.95," says Feenberg. "But the people
who made these predictions had never themselves used the technology for
education and knew almost nothing about it."

Amid a flurry of press releases and mostly breathless media coverage, 31
the dot-edus built their businesses in a hurry, only to find themselves staring down a stark reality: the students never showed up. "University presidents and administrators were talked into this by computer companies and
journalists," says Feenberg. But like many other would-be Internet entrepreneurs, the dot-edus discovered that building an Internet business turned
out to be considerably more complicated than buying a few million dollars'
worth of hardware and software, hiring pricey consultants, and waiting for
the money to pour in.

Worse, faculty members were getting restless. 32

The UCLA faculty threatened to walk out when the administration is- 33
sued a dictum[10] requiring the submission of lesson plans to the for-profit
subsidiary (without offering the faculty a dime in extra compensation).
More galling yet, the administration wanted to invite corporate sponsors
to paste their logos across the professors' syllabuses, in exchange for a
$10,000 "curriculum development" fee. Similar protests erupted at other
schools, as the faculty rose up to defend the curriculum against what they
perceived as shameless profiteering.

By 2001, the dot-edu bubble was bursting fast. NYUOnline closed its 34
doors after burning through $25 million of the school's money; Temple
shut down its dot-edu before it even opened; Wharton's online business
school—in no small irony—filed for bankruptcy; UNext laid off half its
staff; and Harcourt Higher Education, an ambitious online venture that
had launched with much fanfare and a plan to enroll 50,000 students by
2005, shut down in 2001 after enrolling a grand total of 32 students.

Other schools managed to keep their dot-edus afloat, but with drasti- 35
cally lowered expectations. "The overselling was so enormous that it was
self-defeating," says Feenberg. The result: a boom-and-bust cycle familiar
to anyone who bought Internet stocks in those days.

"E-learning was massively misconstrued early on," says Matthew Pit- 36
tinsky, the chairman and co-founder of Blackboard, "with predictions of
the transformation of higher education—where everyone would go to the
elite schools online—that just proved to be plain false."

With millions of dollars' worth of software and infrastructure sitting 37
on the shelf, however, administrators and university information technology departments weren't about to just pack up and admit defeat. After all,
distance learning was hardly a failed business model. DeVry and Phoenix
were flourishing; and the corporate education market was going like gang-
busters. The business was still out there; they had just gotten the formula
wrong.

---

[10] **dictum:** An announcement made with authority.

For many faculty members in the late 1990s, the dot-edu bubble may ³⁸ have seemed a distant rumble: an emblem of that era's speculative excesses and of the vainglory[11] of administrators and dubious Internet visionaries. Now, fast-forward to 2005. Just as many companies spun out their Web operations as dot-com subsidiaries in the late 1990s, only to bring them back into the fold after the IPO market evaporated, so have many of the dot-edu initiatives found new life back on campus.

SetonWorldWide launched in 1998, at the height of the dot-edu ³⁹ boom. Growing slowly and deliberately, Seton today enrolls about 300 online students. DiSalvio, the program's director, expects the online school to fold itself back into the university mother ship over the next few years. "We started out as an entrepreneurial unit, but as online education has become mainstream within the school, as it's become more prevalent and accepted, we see the logic of decentralizing the program and putting it into the respective schools and colleges, under the management of the deans."

Although many schools made the mistake of approaching distance ⁴⁰ learning as an entirely new product during the dot-edu boom, they are now beginning to recognize its potential as a new channel in the supply chain. And just as the Web has enabled many companies to reengineer their supply chains to integrate more closely with partners and customers, so some schools are beginning to integrate their distance-learning programs more deeply with corporate agendas.

At Arizona State University, students can now earn not only a fully ⁴¹ accredited MBA online from the W. P. Carey School of Business, but many of them do so under the auspices of the school's Corporate Program, in which local employers like Lucent and ChevronTexaco partner directly with the business school to create tailor-made M.B.A. programs for their employees.

When a Lucent employee enrolls in a managerial economics class on- ⁴² line, the course Web site comes pre-populated with a set of Lucent financial data, which provides the fodder[12] for most of the class exercises. To earn the M.B.A., the student must undertake an applied project that produces a measurable business outcome for the employer. "The goal is to realize a cost saving for the corporation," says Steve Salik, the manager of delivery systems and strategic development for the business school. "By having the students achieve that cost savings, [the corporation] can recoup[13] the entire cost of the program."

Corporations aren't the only customers looking for that kind of deep ⁴³ integration. In 1999, the U.S. Army launched eArmyU, a distance-learning network that ties together 29 accredited universities into an online learning consortium.[14] The network offers degree programs through a centralized

---

[11] **vainglory**: Excessive pride.
[12] **fodder**: Raw material.
[13] **recoup**: Regain.
[14] **consortium**: A group.

portal developed under contract by IBM. To date, 30,000 active-duty soldiers have enrolled in eArmyU; program administrators hope to have 80,000 student-soldiers enrolled by the end of 2005. The Army program has proved a great boon for schools like Excelsior College in Albany, where active military make up more than 25 percent of the student body.

While soldiers in Iraq and Afghanistan undoubtedly benefit from access   44
to educational opportunities, their academic freedom is hardly unbound. The Army will reimburse students only for classes taken within strict degree requirements, and it won't reimburse for elective classes that fall outside those requirements; you won't find Uncle Sam footing the bill for Renaissance poetry seminars. "The military wants courses that are relevant to what they're doing," says Susan Nash, the associate dean of liberal arts at Excelsior and a longtime distance-learning professor. Recently, she has worked with the Army to develop practical course offerings with titles like "Leadership in Difficult Times." "I can understand their reasoning, but I think it's bad for education," Nash says. "If we're not careful we're going to lose the ability to think spontaneously. We're being programmed."

As schools react to growing institutional pressures, faculty are discover-   45
ing that those influences extend beyond the contents of the course catalog. "Institutions have put in place a production process that hadn't existed before," Pittinsky says. Just as the Web transformed the role of the information technology staff in many corporations—bringing them out of the back office and into the front line of marketing and sales operations—so online learning technologies are changing the makeup of academic organizations.

The most dramatic change for most academic departments has been   46
the emergence of IT professionals from the administrative back office to the forefront of curriculum development. "Seven or eight years ago, the only systems administrators [on campus] would be managing things like e-mail systems, systems that really didn't touch teaching and learning at their core," Pittinsky says. "They were this kind of back-office priesthood. Now, you see an entire group of professionals who have the tech savvy to manage systems at a large scale, but they are also consultative to faculty on instructional design."

The ascendancy of information technology staff is changing the way   47
courses get produced and is introducing a corporate organizational model into the traditionally benign dictatorship of the lecture hall. For faculty brought up in the old school, amid the Byzantine[15] hierarchies of academic departments, the new model of integrated teamwork may take some getting used to.

"There are some faculty who get it, and some faculty who don't,"   48
DiSalvio says. "We have found there are some faculty who may be charismatic in person, but they are terrible online."

Those faculty who do participate in online-course development often   49
have to adjust to the unfamiliar dynamics of team-based course design. In

---

[15] **Byzantine:** Referring to an ancient empire; highly complicated.

many cases, that means faculty members work as part of interdisciplinary curriculum-development teams, alongside other skilled "knowledge workers" like instructional designers, systems administrators and media specialists.

"If you look at how a lot of [courseware] is really being produced, 50 they're sweatshops," Nash says. "You have these busy people creating these objects—like multiple-choice tests, or little games, or learning objects— these are people who are paid nothing, whereas other people are paid a lot for overseeing it, like factory owners."

"Our professors are content experts. That's all they are," says ASU's 51 Salik, voicing a not-uncommon administration view of the professor's role in online-course development. For institutions, the reduction of faculty to "content experts" does yield clear economies of scale. That sentiment also echoes an old dot-com ethos: separating content from delivery. Says Salik: "If the executive education director calls me up and says, 'This guy from Honeywell is here, and they want a one-day executive education seminar, but they want one piece from course A, one piece from course B, one piece from course C,' we can roll that together and send it out the door in about 20 minutes."

The reuse of online courseware will likely extend not just between 52 courses in a single school, but between institutions as well. "Once universities start learning how to cooperate with each other through productive associations," Nash says, "I think we'll see a lot more sharing of learning objects, a lot more sharing of strategies and even revenue."

The prospect of assembly-line course production and the repurposing 53 of courses between schools seems to confirm some of the critics' worst fears. "Faculty have much more in common with the historic plight of other skilled workers than they care to acknowledge," Noble writes. "As in other industries, the technology is being deployed by management primarily to discipline, de-skill and displace labor." And while breaking instruction into modules may yield tangible benefits to students and employers, faculty find themselves in an increasingly reactive posture to institutional pressures on the curriculum.

The trend, Feenberg says, leads toward "deprofessionalization," 54 which he describes as "taking highly respected and reasonably well-paid professionals and substituting them with part-time people who would have no regular employment, sub-contractors, and so forth."

Whether online learning spells a new age or a dark age for higher edu- 55 cation, even its most strident critics agree that distance learning will be part of the educational firmament for a long time to come.

But if the Internet has taught us anything, it is this: Open networks 56 have a way of undermining institutional agendas, and putting power back in the hands of individuals.

While corporate software vendors and university administrators 57 seem to be steering the distance-learning agenda today, there are signs of a nascent open-source movement on the horizon that just might upset the balance.

In 2002, MIT announced an ambitious initiative to publish all of its   58
course materials online—free of charge—through the MIT OpenCourse-
Ware projects. By 2007, the school hopes to have the full contents of all
2,000 of its courses available on the Web. By making its course materials
freely available, the school hopes to encourage academics at other institutions to do likewise and percolate a broad resource-sharing movement
among universities.

Already, many professors are contributing their materials to public   59
open-learning object repositories, freely available on the Web and easily
accessed through ad hoc[16] courseware using personal publishing tools like
blogs or HTML editors.

It's too early to say whether these experiments will ever pose a   60
threat to the corporate distance-learning economy, but they hold out at
least the possibility of a new model of courseware development. "I think
there's a strong force back to the individual," Nash says. "I think that
eventually stuff won't be so locked away. I think we'll see more porous
borders."

That kind of porousness might someday even call into question the   61
structure of educational institutions themselves. No less a futurist than
Peter Drucker has predicted that by 2020, "the universities of America, as
we have traditionally known them, will be barren wastelands."

Whether or not such a dire scenario comes to pass, a more open   62
model of distance learning does seem to hold out at least the possibility
that institutional pressures might give way to a renewal of personal bonds
between teachers and students. "There's an old saying that the ideal college is Mark Hopkins on one end of a log, and a student on the other,"
Pittinsky says. "When you break the classroom out of the limitations of
time and place, that becomes a lot more achievable."

But that Arcadian[17] ideal seems a long way away from the commer-   63
cial reality of today's distance-learning market. "The reduction of education to a kind of simplified training violates one of the most basic features
of all human societies: the personal transmission of culture," says Feenberg, who wonders just how far we have come from the deeper origins of
teaching, when an elder would gather children around the fire on some
ancient evening and say: " 'This is the story my father told me, and I'm
going to tell it to you, and you will tell it to your children.' And then he
tells them a story about plants and animals, and the gods."

EXERCISING VOCABULARY

1. "Online learning is triggering a seismic shift" in the way universities do business, the author asserts in paragraph 7. What kind of event usually involves a
seismic shift? How well does this metaphor fit distance learning? Why?

---

[16] **ad hoc:** Latin for "for this"; created to resolve a short-term problem.
[17] **Arcadian:** Simple and innocent, from a region in ancient Greece.

2. One of the factors influencing distance learning has been "a growing com-moditization of the curriculum" (para. 14). What does *commoditization* mean? What has changed as a result of this commoditization?

PROBING CONTENT

1. What phrase delivered by the speaker at the University of Phoenix's gradua-tion particularly upset Geoff Hunt? Why was he upset?

2. What are some advantages of distance learning mentioned in this essay? What are some disadvantages? How are distance-learning students often dif-ferent from on-campus students?

3. Why did the "dot-edu" or online education business look so attractive to the businesses and universities that launched it? What did their plan lack? What were the results?

4. Describe some of the ways that online education is changing colleges and universities. Cite specific examples from the article.

CONSIDERING CRAFT

1. In paragraph 2, Wright comments that "distance-learning programs were changing the calculus of higher education." Describing the failure of the first dot-edus, Wright states that "they had just gotten the formula wrong" (para. 37). Why does he use words like *calculus* and *formula*? Why is such word choice particularly well suited to his purpose in this essay? Would using more of this kind of language strengthen or weaken the essay? Explain your response.

2. Wright uses a number of quotations here. How does his choice of sources to quote indicate to the reader his opinions about distance learning? Select sev-eral specific quotations that support your answer.

RESPONDING TO THE WRITER

How would you respond to Peter Drucker's prediction that by 2020 "the universi-ties of America, as we have traditionally known them, will be barren wastelands" (para. 61)? Discuss the reasons for your response to Drucker. How would Wright respond?

For a quiz on this reading, go to bedfordstmartins.com/mirror.

Education in the Ether

Vicky Phillips

Suppose that you had attended a virtual high school and taken most or all of your courses online. How would your high school experience have been different? Since 1990, Vicky Phillips, author of this essay, has worked with over 7,000 online learners but has never met one of them. Content to be "the guide on the side" rather than the traditional "sage on the stage," Phillips says the distance-learning model works by putting education where Plato intended it to be — not on campus but "in the minds of the students."

Vicky Phillips is a pioneer in distance learning and adult education and has helped numerous colleges and corporations design online learning programs. Her articles about online education have appeared in *Salon.com*, *Nation's Business*, *HR Magazine*, and *Internet World*, and she is quoted widely in national news media. She is the author of *Never Too Late to Learn: The Adult Student's Guide to College* (2000), was the lead author for *Best Distance Learning Graduate Schools: Earn Your Degree without Leaving* (1998), and coauthored *Peterson's Writer's Guide to Internet Resources* (1998). "Education in the Ether" first appeared in *Salon.com* on January 26, 2005.

THINKING AHEAD

Who was your favorite teacher? Why? How would your life be different if you had never met any of your high school or college teachers personally? What are the advantages and disadvantages of knowing both your professors and your classmates at college instead of working independently from your dorm room?

INCREASING VOCABULARY

ether (n.) (3)
keen (adj.) (6)
convene (v.) (8)
sage (n.) (13)
edifying (adj.) (13)

entity (n.) (14)
harks (v.) (17)
eschew (v.) (18)
fling (v.) (18)

O n a recent business trip a man asked me what I did for a living. I replied that I wrote and taught college courses. 1

"Oh?" he said. "Where do you teach?" A peculiarly honest answer came out of my mouth before I could think: "Nowhere," I said. 2

It's true. Since 1990 I have taught and counseled for what a friend of mine calls "keyboard colleges" — distance-learning degree programs. Where I teach is inside that electrically charged ether that lies between my phone 3 jack and the home computers of a group of far-flung,[1] generally older-than-average college students.

In 1990, I designed America's first online counseling center for distance   4
learners. Since then I've worked with more than 7,000 learners online. I've
flunked a few of them. I've never personally met any of them.

For want of a clearer explanation of my career situation, I told the   5
man who inquired that I teach in cyberspace. "I'm a virtual professor," I
tried explaining. "Distance learning . . . online degree programs . . . virtual
universities."

The man's face remained as blank as a clear summer sky. I couldn't   6
tell whether he was silent out of respect or keen confusion. I imagined
both to be the case, so I settled in to explain what I have to explain frequently these days: the decline of the American college campus and the
rise of the American educational mind—as I see it.

Distance learning, or educational programs where pupil and professor   7
never meet face-to-face, are nothing new. Sir Isaac Pitman of Bath, England, hit upon the idea of having rural residents learn secretarial skills by
translating the Bible into shorthand, then mailing these translations back
to him for grading. He began doing this in 1840. And he made mounds of
money doing it.

I don't teach shorthand; I teach psychology and career development. I   8
write many of my own lessons, though, just as Sir Isaac had to do. My
penny post[2] is the World Wide Web. I post assignments to electronic bulletin boards and send graded papers across the international phone lines
in tariff-free e-mail packets. I convene classes and give lectures in online
chat rooms when need be.

Is this any way to dispense a bona fide[3] college education? Can   9
people learn without sitting in neat rows in a lecture room listening to
the professor—aka[4] the Sage on the Stage?

Yes, absolutely. Hell, why not? In fact, while many people find it hard   10
to imagine a college with no campus, I nowadays find it hard to imagine
teaching anywhere other than in the liberal freedom that is cyberspace.

In cyberspace, I listen, read, comment and reflect on what my students   11
have to say—each of them in turn. What they know, they must communicate to me in words. They cannot sit passively in the back row twiddling
their mental thumbs as the clock ticks away. They must think; and horrors of horrors, they must write. Thinking and writing: Aren't these the
hallmarks of a classically educated mind?

I know my students not by their faces or their seat position in a vast   12
lecture auditorium; I know them by the words and ideas they express in
their weekly assignments, which everyone reads online.

---

[1] **ESL far-flung:** Geographically distanced.
[2] **penny post:** Postal system in nineteenth-century England that charged one penny to send
    a letter.
[3] **bona fide:** Latin for good faith; genuine, real.
[4] **ESL aka:** Also known as.

I am not a Sage on the Stage—I am more a Guide on the Side. Often   13
what the students "say" or write to one another, or the way they incorporate their work and career ideas into their papers and debates with each
other, is more practically edifying than anything I could dish[5] their way.

My average college "kid" is 40 years old. More than a few are in their   14
50s or 60s. They are telecommuting to campus because they could not, or
would not, uproot their careers and kids or grandkids to move to a college
campus—an entity modeled after the learning monasteries of medieval times.

Many of them know what they are talking about. Even more so, they   15
know what they came back to college to learn. A cyber-education suits them
because it respects their abilities to define for themselves what knowledge
is and to go after it. It encourages them to argue their points and their perspectives without the censoring of a professor, who might be tempted to
step in to "calm down" or "refocus" an otherwise wonderfully enlighten-
ing classroom debate.

They are experiencing something very different from the traditional   16
factory model of American education, in which everyone on the assembly
line is delivered the same standardized units of information (lectures and
textbooks) and then must pass the same quality inspection (objective
exams). This factory model—where students sit in neat rows, holding up
their hands for permission to speak, clock-watching their way through
textbooks and lectures that are broken into discrete knowledge widgets—
has never been shown to be an effective way to learn. It has, however,
been proven to be a convenient way for colleges to record on transcripts
that a standard body of knowledge has been duly delivered.

Maybe teaching a liberal arts curriculum via a virtual environment   17
makes more sense to me because it harks back to what I learned to be a
true liberal arts education. Studying philosophy in Athens, Greece, I was
taught that to learn anything, one had to throw away textbooks and note-
books—mere memory tools—and instead rely on one's native ability to
think critically. (Really—my philosophy of Plato professor broke my pencil in two and raged at the idea of note-taking.)

I was taught what Plato defined to be the nature of a true liberal edu-   18
cation. It is independent of time and place. Real education does not occur
on a campus. It occurs in the minds of the students. Good students eschew
memory—a simple learning trick—in favor of developing their abilities
to debate and argue their way through an issue. In short, good students develop their abilities to fling words and ideas at each other with intellectual
accuracy.

Plato and his students wandered around Athens arguing their way to   19
understanding. While my cyber-students do have textbooks, the books are
learning aids; they are not the only pool of knowledge the students will
drink from. Instead, they will learn also from the collaborative efforts of
online debates, conferences and papers. They will think about what they

[5] **dish:** To deliver.

have to say, and they will come to class each week amazingly prepared to argue and type their way toward insight.

The virtual university: Oddly enough, it's just what a classical philoso-   20
pher like Plato would have practiced—had there been an Internet way back when. Me? I'm in favor of less learning taking place on a campus and more that happens in the minds of the participants.

EXERCISING VOCABULARY

1. What is and where is cyberspace? How does the term apply to Phillips's teaching?

2. In paragraph 16, Phillips writes that typical college lectures are "broken into discrete knowledge widgets." What does *discrete* mean here? What is a widget? What characteristics do widgets have? What kind of connotation does this expression have for education?

PROBING CONTENT

1. Who was the first person to offer distance learning? When did this occur? What were the course requirements?

2. What does Phillips teach? How does she interact with her students? Why is she so enthusiastic about her method of delivering instruction?

3. Describe most of Phillips's students. Why does online learning appeal to them?

CONSIDERING CRAFT

1. In paragraph 11, Phillips notes that, in cyberspace, students cannot just "sit passively in the back row twiddling their mental thumbs." What does it mean to twiddle your thumbs? When do people do so? What are they expressing? How can this be done mentally instead of physically?

2. The metaphor for traditional education that Phillips chooses in paragraph 16 clearly reveals her thoughts about this approach. What is her metaphor? What does it imply about traditional education? How does it do this?

3. In paragraph 17, Phillips discusses when she formed her philosophy about teaching. Why is it important that she include it here? How does it affect your reading of her essay to have this information about her own education?

RESPONDING TO THE WRITER

Would you like to take an online class from Vicky Phillips? What would be the benefits? What would be the risks? How well do you think you would do in such a course? Why?

For a quiz on this reading, go to bedfordstmartins.com/mirror.

DRAWING CONNECTIONS

1. How does the role of the faculty teaching online courses as described in Alex Wright's "From Ivory Tower to Academic Sweatshop" differ from the role Vicky Phillips assigns to herself in "Education in the Ether"? Which instructor mentioned by Wright would share Phillips's views about online instruction? Why?

2. Compare the focus of Wright's and Phillips's essays on online education. How does this difference in focus cause the two writers to develop their essays very differently?

3. Both authors reach back historically to showcase a model of teaching, but the models they choose are very different. Discuss the two historical examples and explain how each one reflects the point of view of the essay in which it is found.

FOCUSING ON YESTERDAY, FOCUSING ON TODAY

Is a family chess game your idea of excitement? At least playing chess would pull members of your family together, and some conversation would be required. In this image, former *Chicago Daily News* columnist Mike Royko and his wife Carol watch a chess game between their sons at home in November 1971. Today, technology seems to be steering us more and more toward isolation. We plug in our iPod earphones to shut out other people or retire to our bedrooms to watch our favorite television shows.

On the other hand, the little girl at her computer keeps up a running dialogue—with her cybercompanions but essentially with herself. It's too dangerous to play outside, so she resorts to the friends she can find across the ocean. It's eight at night, and she's still by herself, a latchkey child in an electronic world.

How has advanced technology affected the American family? What have been some of its negative effects on communication? Now describe some positive effects of advanced technology on communication among family members. Which have been more significant—the positives or the negatives? Why? How might we alleviate the negative effects?

Family Night, 1970s Style

Still Home Alone

The caption that originally appeared with this photo reads, "I'm alone most of the time. I've learned to keep busy. I don't like eating by myself, though. I message my friends a lot. I even have e-friends in Australia and France. My mom doesn't want me to play outside in the park anymore 'cause it might be dangerous. I went to my friend Alison's birthday party. We got to play outside in the woods all day. She's lucky 'cause she has two dogs. I'd love to have a dog. Wow, it's eight, mom should be home soon. Hold on, my friend Tracy just messaged me."

REFLECTING ON THE WRITING

1. Using James Pethokoukis's essay, "Our Biotech Bodies, Ourselves," select one biotechnical innovation that he mentions to research further and write an essay about. You might consider an aspect of genetic engineering such as cloning or stem-cell research. Be sure to include the progress of the research thus far, any applicable laws governing this research and use, and any political, ethical, religious, or moral implications.

2. Using Steven Levy's "iPod Nation" as a model, select one technological invention and develop an essay about it. You should include the history of the device, a description of its users, their feelings about it, what the future holds, and its impact on our culture.

CONNECTING TO THE CULTURE

1. Choose a blog site and participate in its online conversations for at least a week. Write an essay in which you describe your experiences, including who you met online, what the topics of discussions were, what rules and etiquette you had to follow, and what you learned about online communication.

2. Survey at least twenty-five fellow students to see whether they have ever taken a distance learning course. Take notes and describe the students' experiences in an essay. Be sure to include what they feel are the benefits and the drawbacks of learning in cyberspace.

3. Observe students on your campus to see how many of them use iPods. Ask them to describe their relationship with their iPod (including how often they listen, what they listen to, and where they listen) and the ways that ownership has affected their musical habits. Write an essay in which you discuss and analyze your findings.

4. Americans seem to be increasingly obsessed with technology. We spend hours every week playing video games, text messaging, chatting on cell phones, blogging, emailing, and listening to music through headphones. Choose one of these technologies to research. Then write an essay in which you discuss the emotional, moral, legal, and physical ramifications of Americans' passion for the technology you selected.

Evaluating and Documenting Sources

When you research topics of interest in popular culture, you are going to want to augment your own thoughts and ideas with credible sources that support your position. You may think that it will be difficult to locate such sources. On the contrary, for most topics, you'll find a wide array of potential material to incorporate into your work. You won't be able to use everything, so you will have to make some important choices so that you can focus on the most legitimate and persuasive evidence.

As you begin, remember two important things. First, because popular culture involves what's popular, it changes rapidly. Remember the Spice Girls? Old news, right? Consequently, the more recent your source, the more valuable that source is to your research. A *Rolling Stone* article on current music trends isn't current if it was written in 1997, although it may still be useful if you are seeking a historical perspective.

Second, all sources are not created equal. Some publications or Web sites are created specifically to further the writer's own views. Material on the Internet is often posted without being evaluated. Let the researcher beware. You will want to establish certain basic information about any source you plan to rely on for information—for example, its date of posting or publication or the person or organization that is responsible for the veracity of the site's or the magazine's content. Learning to recognize and evaluate the bias embedded in some potentially useful material may require a little detective work, but it is essential to the authenticity and credibility of your own research.

In Chapter 2, we suggested a list of questions to ask as you deconstruct media images. Let's start with a similar list of questions to help you learn to evaluate the usefulness of possible electronic and print sources:

1. Where is the source material located?
2. What is the date of the publication, posting, or update?
3. Who is the author?
4. When the material was written or posted, who was its intended audience?
5. Is the material a primary source or a secondary source?

Just as we do when deconstructing a visual image, let's take the most easily answered questions first.

Where Is the Source Material Located?

The first important question to ask about potential source material is "Where is it located?" If the article or advertisement is in print form, in which magazine, newspaper, or journal does it appear? What can you find out about this publication? How long has it been in circulation? Who publishes the book, newspaper, or magazine? Who sponsors this Web site? What's the purpose of the Web site or print source? Check the titles of other articles listed in the table of contents. What patterns or similarities do you see? Are different viewpoints represented?

Answers to most of these basic questions can usually be found on a page near the front of the publication. Journals, whose articles are generally closely scrutinized by editors and reviewers before they are published, are even more likely than magazines to provide such particulars. Remember that scholarly journals, unlike popular magazines, are published less frequently, are peer reviewed, and are often written for a select audience of professionals.

If your source is electronic, you may not find this information as readily. Some Internet sources are affiliated with journals, magazines, newspapers, or professional organizations. These sites are generally reliable and may include relevant dates, biographical information about the author, and general information about the site itself. However, remember that anyone can host a Web site and post whatever he or she chooses, whether or not it is accurate. Wouldn't it be embarrassing to find out that you've quoted a seventh grader's Lindsay Lohan site in a college paper? You'll want to reference only reliable Web sources that clearly reveal ownership and other factual documentation.

What Is the Date of the Publication, Posting, or Update?

How recently was this online information written and published? Magazines and journals usually print a date on the cover. Weekly publications give you more current information about popular culture topics than monthly ones do, and daily newspapers stay ahead of both. Some journals are published only once or twice a year, but they may still provide important background for your research.

Articles on the Internet may have the date of the site's creation or most recent update or may not have any date. You might have to use clues to judge how recently the information has been gathered. Check the information against other dated sources. Read carefully for dates and events mentioned within the article itself.

Who Is the Author?

Book authors' names are readily available, and sometimes a note on the book jacket will list important biographical data. Periodical authors who have established reputations will be identified by name either near the beginning or end of the article. A few lines about the author—other articles or books written, current position held, any literary recognition received, or other specific information that makes the author more credible than others on that subject—may also be included. Tiger Woods's writing about the best golf courses, for example, would automatically carry more clout than the average weekend golfer's. Journals generally offer a great deal of specific information about their authors' professional accomplishments and affiliations.

On the other hand, many magazine articles are written by staff writers who work full-time for the publication, providing material on whatever topic they are assigned. Still other articles are written by freelance writers who are hired by the publication or Web host to contribute one article on one particular topic at a time. Such authors may or may not be named. Whatever you can learn about authors, famous or not, will help you to read the articles more accurately and alert you to any particular bias or viewpoint. Clues about the author's angle and tone may also present themselves in the writing. An author who professes in the opening paragraph of a review to be a great fan of Julia Roberts is not likely to be truly impartial about one of her movies.

Internet sources should list at least the author's name. We suggest treating with caution any Internet article that lists no author at all. Be diligent in trying to find the author of an Internet source. You may need to go back to the home page if the author's name does not come just before or just after the essay.

As your research on a popular culture topic progresses, chances are good that a few authors' names will appear as references in several different sources. This is testimony to the author's credibility and an indication that this author's thoughts and opinions on this topic are generally sought after and respected.

When the Material Was Written or Posted, Who Was Its Intended Audience?

Do readers of the source belong to a particular age group, ethnicity, interest group, or occupational group? *Teen Magazine*, for example, is clearly marketed toward a certain age group, as is *Modern Maturity*, one of the publications of the American Association of Retired Persons. Perhaps the publication or site is intended for a special-interest group. Publications like *Dog World* fit this category. Some magazines, such as *Time*, *Newsweek*, *People*, and *Reader's Digest*, are written to appeal to a much wider audience.

Knowing the target audience for a publication will help you evaluate any common knowledge, vocabulary, values, and beliefs that writers expect most readers to share.

Journals tend to be directed to specific target audiences, which frequently consist of people in the same profession. Often in such publications the language and style used will be baffling to the outsider yet easily understood by members of the profession. The medical terminology used in the *American Journal of Nursing* may sound like unintelligible jargon to someone outside the field of medicine. Remember, if you don't understand what you are reading, that material may have little value to you as a source.

In some cases, if the specifics of a complicated journal article are important to your research, you may want to consult a specialized dictionary. These references will help you decipher language unique to one field of study—like law, psychology, or engineering.

Is the Material a Primary Source or a Secondary Source?

Determining whether material is a primary or secondary source may not be as easy as finding the date of publication or the author's name, but this distinction isn't difficult. When you see *Star Wars, Episode III: Revenge of the Sith* and then describe in a paper how George Lucas employs technology to develop the character of Yoda, you are using a primary source—the movie itself. When you read an article that compares George Lucas's use of technology in the *Star Wars* trilogy and in the prequels in *Entertainment* magazine and then quote the author of that article in your own work, you are using a secondary source—the article about the movies.

Let's take one more example. If you watch a television interview with Denzel Washington about the role of black actors in American films and refer to that interview in your research, that is a primary source. You saw the interview yourself. However, if you miss the television show and read a review of it in the next day's Life and Arts section of your local newspaper, then you'll be using a secondary source when you incorporate information from the review in your paper.

With primary sources, you are in direct contact with the music, film, novel, advertisement, or Web site. You develop your own interpretation and analysis. With secondary sources, someone else is acting as a filter between you and the CD, the play, the short story, or the painting.

Both types of sources are valuable. After all, not many of us saw the Beatles' last live concert in person. But with secondary sources you will want to be alert for any bias or viewpoint of the author's that could affect the credibility of the source material.

Practice in applying these five questions will help you to become confident about the value and validity of the sources you use to support your own ideas.

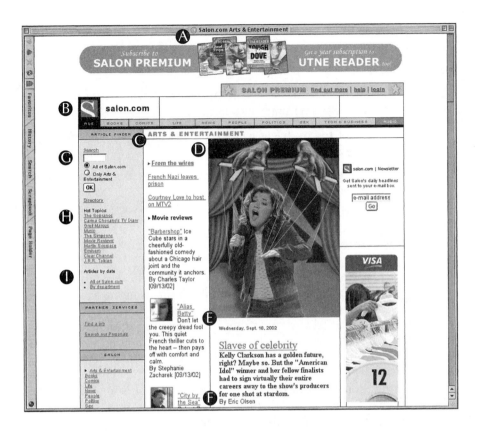

Here is an example of a Web page you might consult during your research into a popular culture topic:

- Item A identifies the group as a company (.com), not a school (.edu), an organization (.org), or a government agency (.gov).
- Item B offers a link to the Web site's home page.
- Item C provides a heading to let you know what part of the site you are viewing.
- Item D uses an engaging graphic image that is related to the subject matter of a general topic.
- Item E provides a date for the issue.
- Item F provides the name of the author below an article title.
- Item G allows for a search function.
- Item H provides links to other topics within the site that might be of interest.
- Item I provides links to additional articles.

EXERCISE

After closely examining the Web screen shot on p. 385, answer the following questions:

1. Who is the intended audience for this Web page? What aspects of this site provide clues to help you identify its audience?

2. What elements of this Web site indicate the reliability or unreliability of its information?

3. What aspects of this site let you know that this Web-based company wants its audience to return to the site often?

Documenting Electronic and Print Sources

Now we are ready to take those sources for which we have established relevance and the proper credentials and think about using them in a paper or other research project.

Attention, please! Always write out a complete citation for any piece of material that you are seriously considering as a source for your research. That way, days after you put the bound volume of periodicals back on the shelf, you won't have to go through all fifty volumes to locate one article that contains just the right quotation or statistic. Also, always print out a hard copy of anything from the Internet that you consider using. The fact that you knew the URL today doesn't mean you'll know it a week from now or that the same information will be posted again in exactly the same place.

Here are some examples of the correct ways to document your sources in the body of your paper. We also provide examples of the correct ways to document your sources in your Works Cited page at the end of your paper. This is a brief listing and isn't meant to be the only reference you should consult. If you need additional information on documenting sources, ask your professor to recommend a text or go to *Research and Documentation Online* at <dianahacker.com/resdoc>. All the citations here follow the Modern Language Association (MLA) format. Before writing any paper, check with your instructor to see which format is required.

MLA Format for In-Text Citations

You should provide an in-text citation every time you quote from, paraphrase, or summarize an outside source. Your citation should directly follow the sentence or sentences in your paper that refer to the source information. Consult the following models when you cite sources within your essay.

BOOKS OR PERIODICALS

When you use a quotation and do not name the author within your text, you must put both the author's name and the page number in parentheses at the end of the quotation. The complete citation that identifies the book's title, date, and place of publication will be found in the list of Works Cited:

"The fact is that much of advertising's power comes from this belief that advertising does not affect us. The most effective kind of propaganda is that which is not recognized as propaganda" (Kilbourne 27).

If a work has four or more authors, list all of their last names, or list the first author's name followed by *et al.*, which means "and others":

"In another scenario, where a woman gives birth to her own clone, would she be her child's mother or twin sister with a different age?" (Borem, Santos, and Bowen 83).

If you mention the author's name in your text, then only the page number needs to be in parentheses at the end of the quotation:

Kilbourne states that "much of advertising's power comes from this belief that advertising does not affect us" (27).

If an article or a Web page does not have an author, either use the complete title in the text or use a short form of the title within the parentheses before the page number. Use quotation marks around titles of essays and other short works.

Fashion companies hope that "by making an ordinary product 'exclusive' they can add a note of urgency to splurge spending" ("Putting a Limit on Labels" 12).

If you *paraphrase*, or express in your own words, an idea from a source, you must still include a citation:

Every day, the average American spends nearly an hour watching, listening to, or reading advertisements (Jacobson and Mazur 193).

Before Title IX's implementation in 1972, fewer than 300,000 high school girls played competitive sports. By 1997, that number had increased to 2.4 million (U.S. Department of Education).

MLA Format for Works Cited

At the end of your essay, you must provide a list of the sources from which you quoted, paraphrased, or summarized. Put the entire list in alphabetical order using the author's last name and the title as it appears on the title page of the source. If your source has no author, alphabetize it by the first main word of the title. Double-space your Works Cited page, and indent the second line of each entry five spaces. MLA prefers that the titles of books, movies, record albums, television programs, and so on be underlined to clearly distinguish the title from surrounding words, but italics are also acceptable.

BOOKS

One Author

Kilbourne, Jean. Can't Buy My Love: How Advertising Changes the Way We
    Think and Feel. New York: Touchstone, 1999.

Two or More Authors

Borem, Aluizio, Fabricio R. Santos, and David E. Bowen. Understanding
    Biotechnology. Upper Saddle River: Prentice Hall, 2003.

Jacobson, Michael F., and Laurie Ann Mazur. Marketing Madness: A Survival
    Guide for a Consumer Society. Boulder: Westview, 1995.

PERIODICALS

Signed Magazine Article

Will, George F. "Electronic Morphine." Newsweek 25 Nov. 2002: 92.

Unsigned Magazine Article

"Women's Dissatisfaction with Body Image Greater in More Affluent
    Neighborhoods." Women's Health Weekly 21 Mar. 2002: 12.

Signed Newspaper Article

Barnes, Steve. "In a World Where Sex Sells, One Group Isn't Buying."
    Austin American-Statesman 5 June 2005: K1, K9.

Unsigned Newspaper Article

"Putting a Limit on Labels." Wall Street Journal 14 June 2002: W12.

Signed Editorial

Cohen, Adam. "America's Favorite Television Fare? The Normals vs. the
    Stigmatized." Editorial. New York Times 2 June 2002: WK18.

Journal Article

Birmingham, Elizabeth. "Fearing the Freak: How Talk TV Articulates Women
     and Class." Journal of Popular Film and Television 28.3 (2000): 133–39.

ELECTRONIC SOURCES

Web Site

United States Department of Education. "Title IX: Twenty-Five Years of
     Progress." 9 July 1997. 29 July 2002 <http://www.ed.gov/pubs/
     TitleIX/>.

Online Magazine Article

Goldberg, Michelle. "Flag-Draped Voyeurism." Salon.com 9 July 2002. 1 Aug.
     2002 <http://www.salon.com/mwt/feature/2002/07/09/ground_zero/
     index.html>.

OTHER SOURCES

Published Interview

King, Stephen. "Ten Questions for Stephen King." Time 1 Apr. 2002: 13.

Broadcast Interview

Tarantino, Quentin. Interview. Charlie Rose. PBS. WGBH, Boston.
     26 Dec. 1997.

Personal Interview

Salomon, Willis. Personal interview. 14 Apr. 2001.

Print Advertisement

T Mobile BlackBerry. Advertisement. U.S. News & World Report
     23 May 2005: 23.

Television Advertisement

Nike. Advertisement. NBC. 7 June 2005.

Sound Recording

U2. How to Dismantle an Atomic Bomb. Universal, 2004.

Television Program

"Daddy Knows Best." Cold Case Files. Narr. Bill Kurtis. A&E. 6 Sept. 2004.

Radio Program

"Natural Santa Claus." All Things Considered. Host Robert Siegel. NPR. WGBH,
     Boston. 29 Nov. 2004.

Film

Star Wars, Episode III: Revenge of the Sith. Dir. George Lucas. Perf. Ewan
    McGregor, Natalie Portman, Hayden Christensen, Ian McDiarmid, Samuel
    L. Jackson, and Christopher Lee. Lucasfilm, 2005.

Speech or Lecture

Mahon, Maureen. "This Is Not White Boy Music: The Politics and Poetics of
    Black Rock." Stanford University, Stanford. 30 Jan. 2002.

ACKNOWLEDGMENTS (continued)

Julia Alvarez. "I Want to Be Miss America." From *Something to Declare* by Julia Alvarez. Copyright © 1998 by Julia Alvarez. Published in paperback by Plume in 1999 and originally in hardcover by Algonquin Books of Chapel Hill in 1998. Reprinted by permission of Susan Bergholz Literary Services, New York. All rights reserved.

Dan Barden. "My New Nose." Originally published in *Gentleman's Quarterly*, May 2002. Copyright © 2002. Reprinted with permission of Dan Barden. Dan@danbarden.com.

Jennie Bristow. "Text Messaging: Take Note." From *The Guardian*, January 22, 2001. Reprinted by permission of the author. www.spiked-online.com.

Dave Carr. "On Covers of Many Magazines, A Full Racial Palette Is Still Rare." From *The New York Times Business/Financial Desk*, November 18, 2002. Copyright © 2002 by The New York Times Company. Reprinted with permission.

Damien Cave. "The Tyranny of 'Abercrappie.'" This article first appeared in *Salon.com*, www.salon.com, March 3, 2000. An online version remains in the Salon archives. Reprinted with permission.

Jay Chiat. "Illusions Are Forever." From *Forbes ASAP*, October 2, 2000. Forbes, Inc. Reprinted by permission of *Forbes Magazine* © 2004 Forbes, Inc.

Delia Cleveland. "Champagne Taste, Beer Budget." Originally appeared in *Essence* magazine, March 2001. Adapted from an essay published in *Starting with "I"* (Persea Books, 1997). Reprinted by permission of the author, freelance writer and author of *Fallin' Out*.

Dan Cook. "Lunchbox Hegemony? Kids and the Marketplace, Then and Now." From *LiP magazine*, August 20, 2001. Reprinted with permission by the author.

Stephen Corey. "A Voice for the Lonely." Originally published in *In Short: A Collection of Brief Creative Nonfiction* edited by Judith Kitchen and Mary Palmer Jones. Published by W.W. Norton, 1996. Copyright © 1996 by Stephen Corey. Reprinted by permission of the author.

Douglas Cruickshank. "Crazy for Dysfunction." The article first appeared in *Salon.com*, www.salon.com. An online version remains in the Salon archives. Reprinted with permission.

H. D. "Dying to be Bigger." From *Seventeen* magazine, December 1991. Reprinted by permission of the author.

Emily Eakin. "Greeting Big Brother with Open Arms." From the *New York Times*, January 17, 2004. Copyright © 2004 by The New York Times Company. Reprinted with permission.

Jamilah Evelyn. "To the Academy with Love, from a Hip Hop Fan." From *Black Issues in Higher Education*, December 7, 2000, volume 17, issue 21, p. 6. Copyright © 2000 Cox, Matthews & Associates. Reprinted with permission from *Black Issues in Higher Education*.

John Follis. "Mad Ave." From *Adbusters* #20, Winter 1998. Copyright © 1998 by John Follis. Reprinted by permission of Adbusters Media Foundation.

Heather Havrilesky. "Three Cheers for Reality TV." This article first appeared in *Salon.com*, www.salon.com, October 14, 2004. An online version remains in the Salon archives. Reprinted with permission.

David Jacobson. "Pop Culture Studies Turns 25." This article first appeared in *Salon.com*, www.salon.com. An online version remains in the Salon archives. Reprinted with permission.

Hemal Jhaveri. "Searching for a Real Gay Man." As published on *Poppolitics* at www.poppolitics.com. October 22, 2003. Reprinted by permission of the author.

Jon Katz. "How Boys Become Men." Originally published in *Glamour* magazine, 1993. Copyright © 1993 by Jon Katz. Reprinted by permission of Sterling Lord Literistic, Inc.

Hayley Kaufman. "Belly-Baring." Originally titled, "Belly-Baring Fad Not Cute as a Button." From the *Boston Globe*, February 11, 2002. Copyright © 2002 by Globe Newspaper Company (MA). Reproduced with the permission of the Globe Newspaper Company (MA) in the format Textbook via Copyright Clearance Center.

Louise Kennedy. "Barrier Between Adults' and Children's Entertainment Is Breaking Down." From the *Boston Globe*, January 13, 2002. Copyright © 2002 by Globe Newspaper Company (MA). Reprinted with the permission of the Globe Newspaper Company (MA) in the format Textbook via Copyright Clearance Center.

Stephen King. "Why We Crave Horror Movies." Originally published in *Playboy* magazine, December 1982. © Stephen King. Reprinted with permission. All rights reserved.

Susan Brady Konig. "They've Got to Be Carefully Taught." From *National Review*, September 15, 1997, p. 46. © 1997 National Review, Inc., 215 Lexington Avenue, New York, NY 10016. Reprinted by permission.

Eric L. Wee. "Shlock Waves Felt across U.S. Campuses." From *The Dallas Morning News*, June 3, 1998. Copyright © 1998 The Washington Post. Reprinted with permission.

Gaby Wood. "Meet Marnie." From *The Observer*, July 18, 2004. Copyright © 2004 Guardian Newspapers Limited. Reprinted with permission of Guardian News Service.

Alex Wright. "From Ivory Tower to Academic Sweatshop." This article first appeared in *Salon.com*, www.salon.com, January 26, 2005. An online version remains in the Salon archives. Reprinted with permission.

J. Peder Zane. "Men Peek Out from the Cave." From the *Newsobserver.com*, August 19, 2003. Copyright © 2003 NewsObserver. Reprinted with permission from The News & Observer Publishing Company, Raleigh, North Carolina.

ART CREDITS

Chapter 2: To Have and To Hold. "Le Plus Beau Jour de la Vie," from *Doubletake* magazine, Fall 1997. Courtesy Jean-Christian Bourcart.

Mallard Fillmore cartoon by Bruce Tinsley, from the *Austin-American Statesman*, January 27, 2002. Reprinted with special permission from King Features Syndicate.

Diet Coke ad 30532020, The Advertising Archive.

Chapter 3: Mother and Daughter in India, © Joe McNally.

Beauty pageant, Getty Images.

"Freedom from Want," AAED001806. Printed by permission of the Norman Rockwell Family Agency. Copyright © 1943 The Norman Rockwell Family Entities/© Swim Ink/Corbis.

Modern-day TV family, Charlie Powell.

Chapter 4: American Gothic Plastic Surgery, Victor Juhasz.

Two images of nose fixed by plastic surgery, Dan Winters Photography.

Nude woman by Renoir. Kobal Collection, the Art Archive/Jean & Paul Guillaume collection/Dagli Orti (A).

Body Shop ad—Real-Life Barbie Doll, The Advertising Archive.

Chapter 5: D & G Men's Show, Italy, 7348446 (006IM). Antonio Calanni/AP/Wide World Photos.

"Body Rites" ad by Chris Kane. From the *Austin Chronicle*. Reprinted with permission.

Hathaway ad, 30503402, The Advertising Archive.

Skechers ad, 30532632, The Advertising Archive.

Chapter 6: Tommy Girl Perfume ad, The Advertising Archive.

Shirley and Son cartoon—Jerry Bittle. Shirley and Son © Reprinted with permission of United Feature Syndicate, Inc.

Aunt Jemima Pancake Flour ad, 30532708, The Advertising Archive.

Häagen Dazs ad with nude woman, 30527795, The Advertising Archive.

Chapter 7: "She Has Your Eyes," Shannon Mendes. www.adbusters.org/shannonmendes.

Psycho movie still, The Picture Desk/The Kobal Collection.

Scream movie still, The Picture Desk/The Kobal Collection.

Chapter 8: Britney Spears and Madonna kiss, 6911242, Julie Jacobson/AP/Wide World Photos.

Miss Venus Ramey in front of a radio, 498160, AP/World Wide Photos.

Ipod ad, 7515766, Jeff Chiu/AP/Wide World Photos.

Chapter 9: Remote control digital ED: ppmsca 02040, Library of Congress.

Family playing chess, 5701205 (000XH), Charles Knoblock/AP/Wide World Photos.

Girl with computer, Diane Bondareff/Polaris Images.

Index of Authors and Titles